SIAM IN TRANSITION

SIAM IN TRANSITION

A Brief Survey of Cultural Trends in the
Five Years since the Revolution of 1932

By

KENNETH PERRY LANDON

Assistant Professor of Philosophy
Earlham College, Richmond, Indiana

GREENWOOD PRESS, PUBLISHERS
WESTPORT, CONNECTICUT

The Library of Congress cataloged this book as follows:

Landon, Kenneth Perry, 1903–
    Siam in transition; a brief survey of cultural trends in the five years since the revolution of 1932. New York, Greenwood Press [1968]
        ix, 328 p. fold. map. 24 cm.
        Reprint of the 1939 ed.
        Bibliography: p. 237–247.

    1. Thailand.   I. Title.

DS584.L3 1968   915.93′03′4   68–57615
                                                                                             MARC

Library of Congress   [3]

Originally published in 1939 by University of Chicago Press

Reprinted from an original copy in the collections of the New York Public Library, Astor, Lenox, and Tilden Foundations

Reprinted in 1968 by Greenwood Press, Inc.,
51 Riverside Avenue, Westport, Conn. 06880

Library of Congress catalog card number 68-57615
ISBN 0-8371-0521-8

Printed in the United States of America

10 9 8 7 6 5 4 3 2

PREFACE

In a world of transient values and shifting ideals where modification and adjustment are manifest in every department of life, one factor that may be regarded as invariable is change.

Ways of transportation have changed from the ox-cart, the elephant, the horse, the footpath and the canoe, to the automobile, the electric train, the airplane and the ocean liner. Time that was formerly told by the sun, by the heavens, or by the appetite, is now told by the jewelled watch and other precision instruments. Homes that were built of leaves, rough-hewn planks and bamboo, are built of bricks, ferro-concrete and composition tiles. Light, when not provided by the sun and moon, was produced by the smoking torch, then by the candle, the oil lamp, and finally, crowning glory, by the electric bulb. Power that was formerly man or horse-power is now silently transmitted through shining cables, and has the ability to perform the modern miracles of a technological world.

Applied science has transformed the physical life of man and has made actually possible a manner of living, for the wealthy, that mankind a thousand or five hundred years ago would have considered heaven on earth, Utopia attained. The face of the world has been re-made. In the remaking man has had to discover new explanations for life. Old ways of living, old patterns of community life, have been revamped. Traditional securities have been shaken. The word "maladjustment" has come into popular use to describe economic, political, and moral difficulties that have arisen.

What applied science has done for the physical world, scientific ways of thought have done for ideologies inherited from the old social order. Man's moral, religious, and social thinking has shifted to suit a changing world so that he may be at home in the new environment.

The purpose of the present study is to describe modern trends in Siam in order to show what is happening to the Siamese way of life, and so to indicate how Siamese are adjusting themselves to a technological world.

It is an interesting fact that, while there are thousands of volumes on the Orient discussing in detail such subjects as Japanese gardens and Chinese windows, Siam's share in a library of these would be one medium-sized bookcase. And most of this slim sheaf of books would consist of traveller's reports of what they have seen. The books on any phase of Siamese life published in English since the revolution of 1932, which suddenly transformed the last absolute monarchy in Asia into something approaching a democracy, can be numbered on the fingers of one hand. Since none of them has been relative to the subject here discussed, the material for it has been drawn from Siamese sources, newspapers, pamphlets, interviews, and official government reports. It therefore represents the first furrow in a field yet to be ploughed. The temptation to write a book on each chapter was almost irresistible, and it is to be hoped that many books treating the subjects discussed in greater detail than has been possible here may soon be available.

This opportunity is taken to thank Prince Sakol Varavarn for information on crime and prostitution, Mr. David S. Green of the Statistical Department of the Siamese Government for figures on many phases of Siamese life, Dr. Harley Farnsworth MacNair for generous advice and guidance as to the organization of the material, and Dr. A. Eustace Haydon for the methodology.

K. P. L.

Chicago, Ill.,
February 1st, 1939.

TABLE OF CONTENTS

	Page
INTRODUCTION	1

CHAPTER

I. POLITICAL TRENDS 9
   1. The Revolution of June, 1932 9
   2. The Causes of the Revolution 18
   3. The Leaders of the Revolution 24
   4. The Results of the Revolution 27
   5. Luang Pradist's Economic Policy 29
   6. The Revolution of June, 1933 31
   7. The Royalist Rebellion 36
   8. The Abdication of King Prajadhipok 39

II. POLITICAL TRENDS (Continued) 44
   1. The Trend toward Decentralization in Government .. 44
   2. Personal Liberty under the Constitution 46
   3. The Decline of the Nobility 50
   4. The Rise of the Military 54
   5. Siam's International Relations 57

III. ECONOMIC TRENDS 61
   1. The New Economic Policy 61
   2. The Loss of Capital Funds 64
   3. The Means Employed to Regulate and Encourage Trade 68
   4. Tin, Rubber, Teak, and Rice 70
   5. Other Sources of Income 76
   6. Commerce and Trade 77

IV. ETHNIC TRENDS 82
   1. The Siamese 82
   2. The Malay 83
   3. The Chinese 86

V. EDUCATIONAL TRENDS 96
   1. The Present Organization of the School System .. 96
   2. Primary and Secondary Education 98
   3. Extra-curricular Activities 104
   4. Religious Influences in Education 106
   5. The Universities 109
   6. Siamese Students Abroad 111
   7. Libraries and Literature 112

Chapter

		Page
VI.	MEDICAL TRENDS	114
	1. Medical Beginnings	114
	2. The Development of the Medical School	117
	3. The Difficulties Impeding the Spread of Modern Medicine	120
	4. Public Health	131
	5. Hospitals	133
VII.	TRENDS IN METHODS OF COMMUNICATION	137
VIII.	TRENDS IN CHARACTER, CRIME, AND FAMILY LIFE	143
	1. Siamese Character	143
	2. Crime	151
	3. Woman's Place in Society	156
	4. Family Life	166
IX.	TRENDS IN RECREATIONS, ARTS, AND CRAFTS	171
	1. Recreation	171
	2. Arts and Crafts	176
X.	RELIGIOUS TRENDS	182
	1. Traditional Hinayana Buddhism in Older Siam	182
	2. Brahmanism in Siamese Buddhism	191
	3. Spiritism in Siamese Buddhism	195
	4. A Summary of the Older Siamese Religion	201
XI.	RELIGIOUS TRENDS (Continued)	206
	1. Modifying Influences	206
	2. Conservative versus Liberal	209
	3. The Rise of the Layman	217
	4. Buddhism for the Young	220
	5. The Absence of Missionary Zeal in Siamese Buddhism	224
	6. The Rise of Rationalism	226
	7. New Religious Goals	230
	8. A Summary of the Modern Siamese Religion	231
BIBLIOGRAPHY		237
APPENDIX I		249
	A. System of Transliteration	249
	B. Buddhist Calendar	249
APPENDIX II		250
	A. The Decree Proroguing the People's Assembly	250
	B. Government Communique Regarding the Proroguing of the People's Assembly	251
	C. Act Concerning Communism	251

		Page
D.	Government Communique on the Political Prisoner, January, 1934.	252
E.	Final Reunion of the Royal Family	253
F.	A Typical Confession of Fraud	253
G.	A Discussion of the Siamese Family	254
H.	King Prajadhipok's Abdication Announcement	257

APPENDIX III

A.	National Economic Policy of Luang Pradist Manudharm	260
B.	First Draft—Social Insurance Act	294
C.	First Draft—Economic Administration Act	298
D.	Minutes of a Meeting of a Committee to consider a National Economic Policy at Paruskavan Palace	303
E.	Report of the Commission on the alleged Communism of Luang Pradist Manudharm	319

INDEX 325

SIAM IN TRANSITION

INTRODUCTION

THE Siamese are a branch of the Thai people, who formerly lived north of the Yangtze River in the comparatively small area which today constitutes Szechwan Province in western China. Before the beginning of the Christian era they had started on a long and centuries-slow migration toward the rich farming lands of the tropical and sub-tropical south. The first step in this gradual shifting of a people brought them into what is now Yunnan Province. Here they organized themselves into communities, over each of which was a Pa-Lau, or Father of the Group. Several communities were banded together under the lordship of a Pa-Muang, or Father of the State. Tribes of Thai are still living in Yunnan, where they have intermarried with Chinese to such an extent that the modern Yunnanese are a Thai as well as a Chinese people.

Gradually the Thai flowed south down the three river valleys of the Irrawaddy, the Salwin, and the Mekhong, into Burma, Siam, and Indo-China. By the twelfth and thirteenth centuries of the Christian era they had settled in the northern areas of what is now Siam. They found their new home inhabited by the Semang, a negrito people, whom they displaced. Semang may still be found in the twentieth century, pushed back into the hills where land was too poor to attract the Thai. Other tribes whom the irresistible flood of the Thai slowly submerged were the Khmer, Yuan, Lawa, Mon, and Malay, as well as lesser unnamed and forgotten peoples. The Khmer were living in the area to the east of modern Siam, as were also the Yuan; the Lawa were in the valleys and plains of central Siam; and the Mon were in the west. The Malay, whom the Thai met farther south in the peninsula, were related to the Mon-Annam people. They were probably the descendants of the Mon-Annam who had intermarried with islanders from still farther south. Hard on the heels of the Thai came Chinese seeking trade and commerce.[1]

[1] W. A. Graham, *Siam* (London: Alexander Moring, Ltd., 1924), I, 102-177.

In the thirteenth century of the Christian era Siam was the melting pot for these various races. Siamese, as a written language, dates from this period. The alphabet was probably a Khmer one, which King Rama Khamheng adapted to the spoken dialect of the Thai. Some of the letters are of Sanskrit and Pali origin. If the new written language had been intended merely for the use of the Thai themselves no symbols to indicate tones would have been necessary. Thus, for instance, in writing English, it is not necessary to mark accents and inflections for the person who has spoken the language from childhood because he knows from practice the proper accent and inflection; and it is only when he hears a foreigner grossly mangle English by mistakenly accenting the wrong syllable or using an inflection or rhythm different from the accepted one that he realizes that a problem of pronunciation exists. When the Thai language was written, not only were symbols chosen to indicate sound, but in addition a small number of symbols were devised to be written above the syllables to indicate the proper tone. The mechanical exactness of the system suggests that it was superimposed on the language for the benefit of non-Thai speaking peoples who were to be included in the Thai family.

In the early centuries of the Christian era what is now Siamese territory was under the political influence of three different powers. The eastern Menam basin was a province of the Khmer Empire; the western Menam basin was under the Mon; the Malay peninsula was under the Kingdom of Palembang in Sumatra. The whole area into which the Thai migrated comprises modern Burma, Siam, Indo-China, and Malaya.

Present-day Siam extends from the fifth to the twenty-first degree of north latitude, and from the ninety-seventh to the one hundred and sixth degree of east longitude. From this it may be seen that the country is long and narrow. It is shaped like a kite with an over-all length, including the tail, of 1,020 miles. The body of the kite-shaped area is almost square, being about 480 miles from east to west, and approximately the same from north to south. The tail-like area is about a hundred miles wide and has about 1,300 miles of coastline.

The Menam River rises in the mountains to the north and empties into the Gulf of Siam. It is navigable by small boats, in flood season, all the way up to Chiengmai. The life of the people quite naturally formed itself around the river which offered transportation facilities, and enriched the rice lands.

The mountainous region in the north extends as far as modern Lampang and then gives place to a low monotonous plain, ideal for rice cultivation. There are no mountains of note from Lampang south to the peninsula proper, at which point a range of mountains swings over from Burma to form the backbone of the peninsula.

The Thai have always been agriculturists. This fact explains the tenacity with which they fastened themselves upon the land as they drifted south. The formation of the country into which they moved favoured their natural inclinations. They grew rice, vegetables, and fruits. The extensive waterways and the sea provided occupation in fishing.

The climate, which is believed to have varied very little since the Thai first came, is tropical with a high humidity which tends to loosen the fibre of determination and to encourage lassitude. There are local variations of temperature and climate. The central plain area, for instance, during the hot and rainy seasons from March to October, seldom has temperatures above ninety-eight degrees or below seventy-nine degrees Fahrenheit. The cool season from October to February has a maximum temperature of about ninety-two degrees and a minimum of about fifty-seven degrees Fahrenheit. Northern Siam, which is cut off from sea breezes, is slightly hotter during the day, and, because of altitude, is often cooler at night. The maximum is not more than three degrees higher and the minimum not more than four degrees lower than the figures for the central plain. Eastern Siam is not only a low land, but is cut off from cooling breezes by surrounding hills. During the hot season the land is burned with the heat and a maximum temperature several degrees higher than the temperature of the northern area is reached. The temperature variation during the day is also greater than the variation in the north because of excessive radiation. The mildest climate and the lowest range of temperatures are found in southern, or peninsular, Siam which has the sea on both east and west. There the temperature is seldom above ninety-five degrees or below sixty-eight degrees Fahrenheit.

The temperatures mentioned are related to the rainfall and humidity. Southern Siam has as much as one hundred inches of rain in a year while northern Siam has about sixty inches, and the central plain fifty inches or less. Eastern Siam falls short of even the central plain average.

The tropical condition of the country makes Siam a land of natural plenty in which the people can scarcely starve. Bananas and other fruits grow everywhere in abundance. Rice comes up in rich opulence with a mere scratching of the land and with a minimum of effort on the part of the cultivator.

The first historical Siamese dynasty was established by Rama Khamheng at Sukhodaya in A.D. 1257. Rama Khamheng was not only a great military leader but was also the founder of Siamese cultural life in the sense that in his reign the Siamese language was given a form of written expression, rock inscriptions were made, and important racial and cultural expressions were recorded for posterity.

Sukhodaya was the capital of Siam for a century until A.D. 1350, when invaders of the same racial stock came in and overthrew the reigning king. Out of a period of uncertainty a new dynasty emerged at Ayudhia. Phra Chao U Thong was the genius who began a new line of kings. From A.D. 1350 to 1767 Siam's kings reigned at Ayudhia.

The Portuguese first came to Siam about 1518 to carry on trade.[1] They identified themselves with Siam to the extent that there were Portuguese volunteers in the Siamese army during the Burmese-Siamese wars of the latter part of the sixteenth century. Three Portuguese ships, taking part in the defence of Ayudhia in 1548, were destroyed.

The Dutch came to Siam about 1598, to be followed by the English in 1612. English and Dutch influence waxed as Portuguese influence waned. The Dutch blocked the mouth of the Menam River to force a favourable treaty from reluctant Siam. In 1664 the treaty was signed with the Dutch East India Company, the first formal treaty signed with any European power. The truculent disposition of the Dutch merchants offended the Siamese, and Dutch-Siamese trade lapsed after 1706.

In the latter half of the seventeenth century King Phra Narai was himself the principal Siamese merchant in his kingdom. His agent in all foreign relations was a Greek named Constantine Phaulkon, whom he made his confidential minister. Ayudhia, the capital,

[1] Dates are in the Christian era unless otherwise stated.

had a mixed population of Siamese, Malays, Annamese, Cambodians, Burmese, Indians, Japanese, and Europeans. The Japanese had come for trade as early as 1620. Many among them were religious refugees who fled Japan at the time of the persecution of the Christians. Ayudhia was regarded as one of the most important trading centres of the Far East. It was a clearing house for the products of China, Japan, Sumatra, and India. Those of the foreign residents who had not come to Ayudhia for trade were for the most part prisoners of war brought there by victorious armies, or the descendants of such prisoners.

The French came in 1662. A Roman Catholic mission was sent to Ayudhia to convert the Far East. The missionaries hoped to touch the lives of Japanese, Indians, Chinese, Malays, and Cambodians, who would then return to their own countries as missionaries to their own people. The mission from France had the official support of Louis XIV, who sent envoys and letters to Siam and in return received the first Siamese ambassadors ever sent to Europe.

Constantine Phaulkon was pro-French and discouraged the Dutch and English trade. As a consequence, the Dutch, from their stronghold in Malacca, interfered with Siamese trade. The English went so far as to declare that they had, without cause, suffered severe financial losses and demanded indemnity. They seized a Siamese trading vessel as part payment. War seemed imminent.

To protect Siam from the Dutch and English, the French, in 1687, sent six warships and 1,400 soldiers to act as mercenaries in the service of Siam. French troops were stationed at Bangkok, Mergui, and Ayudhia. At the latter place, the capital, the French formed the king's private guard. At that crucial moment, in 1688, Roman Catholic priests pressed their religious mission and sought the conversion of the king. Phra Narai was not inclined to become a Christian. Siamese nobles fearing for the safety of their country plotted against the French and their own king. They killed Phaulkon and three possible successors to the throne. The king, being on his death-bed, was allowed to die naturally. French troops withdrew and Siam closed its doors to Europeans for a time. Although individual Europeans continued to reside in Siam, diplomatic relations with European nations were not reopened until the early part of the nineteenth century.[1]

[1] Luang Chun Kasikan *et al., Prawat Sat Syam* (3rd ed.; Bangkok: Sri Heng Press, 1935), pp. 172-174.

War with Burma broke out in 1759 and continued, between monsoon seasons, until 1767, when Ayudhia fell to the Burmese. The city was burned and the written records of Siamese history were lost.

Siam was in a completely disorganized condition with various aspirants for power attempting to gain the ascendancy. Phra Chao Krung Dhonburi, popularly known as Phya Tak, began to emerge as the most powerful among them. Within five years of the sacking of Ayudhia he re-established the independence of Siam and transferred the capital to Dhonburi, now a section of Bangkok. Phya Tak did not found a dynasty but prepared the way for the Chakri dynasty. The Chakri kings governed as absolute monarchs from 1782 until 1932, when they accepted a constitutional form of government.

The Chakri dynasty, for the first three reigns, was handed down from father to son. The second of the three kings, Phra Buddha Loes Fa Nobhalai, who reigned from 1809 to 1824, should in natural course have been followed by his son, Mongkut. However, a younger half-brother secured the throne and Mongkut went into the Buddhist priesthood until after his brother's death in 1851. During the quarter of a century of retirement Mongkut obtained a scholarly education in the Pali language and in the wisdom of Buddhism. He became a friend of newly arrived American missionaries and from them learned English, Latin, and the scientific lore of Europe and America.

Under the title of Phra Chom Klao, Mongkut ruled from 1851 to 1868. In his reign, relations with foreign countries were regulated by treaties, commerce was encouraged, and approval was given Western educational ideas by allowing the ladies of the American Mission to visit and teach the ladies of the palace. King Mongkut went so far as to engage Mrs. Anna Leonowens, an English woman who was living in Singapore at the time, to come and live in the palace as tutor to his heir, Chulalongkorn, and other of his children.

King Chulalongkorn ruled from 1868 to 1910 under the title Phra Chula Chom Klao. He is recognized by Siamese as one of their greatest historical figures. Under his rule progressive steps were taken to adjust Siam to a new way of life. The old feudal system was gradually abandoned and a civil service was organized for the administration of the nation. Slavery was abolished, the judicial system was revised, the salaries of officials were adjusted, the farming out of taxes was abandoned, and the system of taxation was improved. By 1885 a postal system had been organized. A railroad was begun in 1892. Public gambling was controlled. The consumption of opium was lessened.

Siamese and French clashed for the second time in 1893, when the colonial expansion of the latter brought pressure upon the Siamese borders. The French blockaded Bangkok, demanding large concessions, and it was not until 1905 that the last of their troops left. The treaty of 1907 with France, and of 1909 with Great Britain, modified the system of extraterritoriality. Siam continued to be an independent country, but with about half the territory that she had had before the French blockaded Bangkok.

King Chulalongkorn was the first Siamese monarch to go far abroad. He visited the Straits Settlements, Java, India, and Europe; the latter twice. He was so impressed with Western knowledge that certain selected sons were educated abroad. All of Siam's kings since his day have received part of their education in Europe.[1]

King Chulalongkorn was succeeded by his son, Phra Mongkut Klao, popularly known as King Vajiravudh, who reigned from 1910 to 1925. He was a brilliant man with a great love for art and the theatre. He wrote, or translated, many plays in such beautiful Siamese that some of his writings have become required reading in the schools. He established the Boy Scout movement. Special commissions were appointed to study the economic situation. A national savings system was begun. Other notable acts were the introduction of surnames, the reform of the calendar, the establishment of a national system of education, the limiting of compulsory labour, the abolition of public gambling houses and of the Lottery Farm, and compulsory vaccination.

Train service to Penang was opened in 1922 with a weekly train making the trip in thirty-four hours. This service linked Siam much more closely with Malaya and Europe.

In 1925 King Vajiravudh died. He was succeeded by his younger brother, Prajadhipok, who reigned from 1925 until his abdication in 1935. The reigning sovereign is his nephew, Ananda Mahidol, who is, in 1938, a school boy in Switzerland.

[1] *The Directory for Bangkok and Siam* (Bangkok: The Bangkok Times Press, 1937-38), pp. 3-4.

King Prajadhipok's first act upon ascending the throne was to appoint a Supreme Council of State to act as an advisory body. The Committee of the Privy Council was created in 1927. High points of the reign were the establishment of wireless service, the balancing of the budget in 1926-27 by an extensive reduction in the numbers of government officials, the making of new treaties which gave Siam full fiscal autonomy in 1927, the preparation of Don Muang airport for international air service, the coming of the taxicab, the celebration of the Centenary of Protestant Missions in 1928, and the economic survey of the kingdom made by Dr. Carle Zimmerman of Harvard University in 1930.[1] As far as its government and leading citizens were concerned, Siam was taking its place in a technological world. For the nation at large, the pace of modernization and adjustment was still very slow. The revolution in 1932 accelerated that pace by inaugurating a definite ten year period in which the whole nation culturally and economically was to be advanced along modern lines.

[1] *Ibid.*, pp. 4-10.

CHAPTER I

POLITICAL TRENDS

1. THE REVOLUTION OF JUNE, 1932

IN 1932, Siam was enjoying such political peace and quiet that it seemed hardly possible for a revolution to come. St. Clair McKelway remarked:

> When His Majesty King Prajadhipok of Siam was in the United States last year, he told his interviewers that all movements and improvements in his country came from above. At the time I thought it was one of the wisest and most profound remarks I had ever heard about Siam.[1]

But, at five o'clock on the morning of June 24th, 1932, the revolution had begun. Machine guns, tanks, and other military equipment raced through the streets to various palaces. H.R.H. the Prince of Nagor Svarga was the first to be visited. A half-brother to the king, he was also Minister of the Interior. By one o'clock in the afternoon about forty important persons were held prisoners in the Throne Hall. The following ultimatum was sent to the king:

> The People's Party consisting of civil and military officials have now taken over the administration of the country and have taken members of the Royal Family such as H.R.H. the Prince of Nagor Svarga as hostages. If members of the People's Party have received any injuries the Princes held in pawn will suffer in consequence. The People's Party have no desire to make a seizure of the Royal possessions in any way. Their principal aim is to have a constitutional monarchy. We therefore enjoin Your Majesty to return to the Capital to reign again as king under the constitutional monarchy as established by the People's Party. If Your Majesty refuses to accept the offer or refrains from replying within one hour after the receipt of this message the People's Party will proclaim the

---

[1] St. Clair McKelway, "Siam Tries a People's Party," *Asia*, Vol. XXXII (November, 1932), p. 555.

Constitutional monarchial government by appointing another Prince whom they consider to be efficient to act as King.

Signed,
Col. Phya Bahol Balabayuha
Col. Phya Song Suratej
Col. Phya Riddhi Aganey[1]

King Prajadhipok was at his summer palace at Hua Hin when he received the ultimatum. His answer, in an unofficial translation, was as follows:

June 25th, 1932.

To the Military in Defence of Bangkok:
I have received the letter in which you invite me to return to Bangkok as a constitutional monarch. For the sake of peace; and in order to save useless bloodshed; to avoid confusion and loss to the country; and, more, because I have already considered making this change myself, I am willing to co-operate in the establishment of a constitution under which I am willing to serve.

Furthermore, there is a possibility that, if I decline to continue in my office as king, the foreign powers will not recognize the new government. This might entail considerable difficulty for the government.

Physically I am not strong. I have no children to succeed me. My life-expectancy is not long, at least if I continue in this office. I have no desire for position or for personal aggrandisement. My ability to advance the progress of the race alone constrains me.

Accept this sincere expression of my feelings.

Prajadhipok

Political difficulty of some sort had been expected by many people before it came. Some expected it definitely for April 6th, 1932, when the Memorial Bridge, in commemoration of one hundred and fifty years of the Chakri dynasty, was to be formally opened by the king. There was a legend that the dynasty would last only one hundred and fifty years. Rumours of the wildest nature were abroad. Some people said they had seen a nun, in white clothes, scurrying across the bridge at night. Others said that they had seen Chao Tak, the military leader who had re-established order after the sack of Ayudhia, cross the bridge at night. All agreed that blood would be shed. On the day of the ceremony extra guards were called out. As the king passed they suddenly wheeled, turning their backs toward the king and their faces toward the people. Nothing happened.

[1] *Bangkok Times*, June 24th, 1932.

A few hours after the *coup d'etat* a printed leaflet was scattered throughout Bangkok announcing what had been done and the reasons for doing it. The purpose of the leaflet was to inflame the people and so to guarantee the success of the revolution. Within two days the leaflet was recalled. By the first of July the People's Party announced that King Prajadhipok was favourable to their venture and inflammatory publications and statements were decreased. The primary announcement to the people was as follows:

When the present king came to the throne the people hoped that he would give an equitable administration. Their hopes were unfulfilled. The king was above the law even as his predecessors had been. His relatives and friends, even when without ability, were given the highest government positions. The king allowed government officials to be dishonest. They took personal graft in governmental building projects, in buying supplies, and in the exchange of government money. The king elevated the royal class and permitted them to oppress the common people. The king ruled unwisely and allowed the country to fall into decay, as the present depression proves. The government of the king, who is above all law, is unable to right these wrongs.

The government cannot right the above wrongs because it does not rule for the good of the people as do the governments of other countries. The government regards the people as servants, as slaves, even as animals, not as men. Instead of helping the people, the government oppresses them. The taxes collected are used personally by the king. In a year he receives many millions of the people's money. As for the people, for them to earn even a little money requires them verily to sweat blood. If the people cannot pay taxes their property is seized or they are forced to labour without pay. Royalty sleeps, eats, and is happy. No other nation gives its royal class so much. Perhaps only the Czar and the Kaiser have been so favoured.

The king's government rules dishonestly with guile. It claims to help business and trade but does not actually do it. It despises the common people. Those who pay taxes hear it said of themselves that they cannot have a voice in the government because they are too stupid. But if the people are stupid then royalty is stupid too, for both are of the same race. Actually the people lack opportunity for education. It is the royalty that withholds educational opportunity. It is feared that when the people are educated they will be unwilling to allow royalty to oppress them.

Let us have a clear understanding. This country belongs to the people. Where does the money come from that royalty uses? It comes from the people. The country is poor because of this custom of draining off the wealth of the people. Farmers must abandon their fields because they receive inadequate profit. Students graduate from school and find no employment. Soldiers are dismissed from service and must starve. This is the work of a government above the law. It oppresses the lower civil officials and dismisses them with no pension. Money collected by taxation should be used on behalf of the nation and not for the enrichment of royalty. The savings of royalty are sent abroad to foreign banks to await the day when a bankrupt nation is abandoned by its rulers who go to live abroad. This is evil work.

For these reasons the people, civil officials, the army, and the navy, have formed a People's Party and have seized the powers of government. The People's Party feels that the way to alleviate conditions is to establish an assembly which can include the best thinking of many minds. This is better than the thinking of one man. As to the chairman or president of the nation, the People's Party does not wish to seize royal prerogative and so has invited King Prajadhipok to continue to be king under a constitution. He will not be able to act without the agreement of the assembly. The People's Party has announced this intention to the king. If he refuses, or if he does not answer within the time set, he will be regarded as a rebel against his race. It will then be necessary to have a democratic form of government. That is, the president will be a commoner elected by the assembly for a limited period of time. By this system of government the people may hope to prosper and have work. The country is naturally rich. When the taxes are used for the good of the nation then the nation must prosper. The new government will rule with intelligence, not blindly as the old government did. The People's Party has established the following platform:

1. The freedom and equality of the people in politics, in the law courts, and in business, must be maintained.
2. Peace and quiet, with no harm to anyone, must be assured.
3. A national economic policy must be drawn up to guarantee remunerative work to everyone.
4. Equal privilege for everyone must be guaranteed. No one group shall enjoy special privilege at the expense of others.
5. The people shall have freedom and liberty except in those cases where freedom and liberty disagree with the above four points.
6. The people must be given the most complete education possible.

People! Help the People's Party accomplish these aims. The People's Party requests everyone who had no share in seizing the power of government, to remain quietly at home, pursuing their usual activities in a peaceful way. Do not interfere with the activities of the People's Party. By helping the People's Party you help the nation, the people, and yourself. The nation will be independent, the people will be safe from danger, everyone will have work, everyone will have equal privilege and none will be servants or slaves. It is past the time when royalty can oppress the people. Everyone wants peace and prosperity. The People's Party will accomplish these things.

The rabid expressions of the People's Party softened a little within the first day when it became apparent that the party actually wielded the powers of government. Although in the above announcement the leaders declared that if the king were unwilling to comply with their request they would establish a republic, with a commoner elected to act as president for a limited term, in the letter to the king they merely said that they would select another prince to be their monarch under a constitution.

On the afternoon of June 24th, 1932, H.R.H. Prince Nagor Svarga was persuaded to sign a statement which read:

> Since the People's Party has seized the power of government in order to make Siam a constitutional monarchy, I request the soldiers, civil officials, and the people, to help keep the peace (to obey the orders of the leaders of the People's Party for the sake of race and nation). Do not shed the blood of our own Siamese people unless it is absolutely necessary.
>
> PARIBATRA
>
> June 24th, 1932.

The words in parentheses were in the original document offered to the prince for his signature. He crossed them out and substituted the final sentence.

On the evening of the 24th of June there was a radio broadcast to the nation at large. The leaflet, which had been distributed on the streets during the day, was read twice. The minutes of a meeting of the People's Party were also read. The various ministers and their chief assistants had attended this meeting by special invitation. Luang Pradist Manudharm addressed the assembly and described the plans and purposes of the People's Party. He announced that the primary intention of the party was to give the country a constitution. The king had been requested to return to Bangkok as a constitutional monarch. Temporary military rule had been set up to be maintained until a constitution was actually in force. The constitution would be presented to the People's Party by a committee delegated to draft it, as soon as possible. Later the assembly in which final authority was to be lodged would be selected by the people. For the present that was impossible. A temporary assembly would be appointed from among the leaders of the People's Party.

Luang Pradist admitted that the members of the Party lacked experience in governmental routine. Accordingly, the Party was inviting capable and experienced civil officials to accept membership in the first People's Assembly. When the country should become quiet and orderly again, a second period of the Assembly would be begun in which the people were to be allowed to select one half of the membership. The People's Party would select the other half. The third period of the Assembly would begin when over one half of the voting population had obtained the equivalent of a primary education. After ten years of the first and second periods of the assembly, if the educational goal was still unreached, the third period of the assembly would start automatically. In the third period the people were to elect all of the membership of the People's Assembly.

Luang Pradist announced that the plan, as above outlined, would be submitted for consideration to the Assembly of the first period. He then requested the Minister of Foreign Affairs to announce to the representatives of the powers the change of government. He believed this would prevent intervention. He then asked the People's Party and their guests the Ministers whether they would request the powers to accept the new form of government. H.H. Devawongs Varodaya, advised the People's Party to await the answer of the king. If the king should comply with their request, the relations of the government with other nations would not be affected. It was agreed to wait, but the Minister of Foreign Affairs was advised to inform the representatives of other nations that the People's Party had formed a new government. The various ministries were told to carry on their duties as usual. Any business over and beyond ordinary governmental routine was to be referred to Phya Bahol, who was in charge of the Bangkok military forces and responsible for martial law. The various ministers accepted these orders with the exception of the Minister of Foreign Affairs and the Minister of the Palace. Chao Phya Varapangas, the First Grand Councillor of the Palace, ordered Phya Rajaval Bhanusisatha to maintain peace and quiet in the Royal Household and not to oppose the People's Party. The Police Department was transferred from Phya Adhikarana to Phya Puresa Bamrungkica. The vessel Sukhodaya was ordered to Hua Hin to bring the king to Bangkok. The assembly closed the meeting that night with the singing of the Maharoek Mahachai, a new nationalist song which had been prepared in advance. The music was written by the director of the Royal Orchestra. It replaced the usual Khawaraphuthacao, which is the Siamese "God Save the King."

On the morning of the 25th of June it was reported that Prince Purachatra, who was in charge of the Royal State Railway, had fled in a locomotive to Hua Hin to confer with the king. Several times he was reported shot or captured, but he made the trip safely. He and several other high officials held a conference with the king. If they had chosen to do so, they could have fled on south to Malaya. On the afternoon of the same day they decided to return to Bangkok by a special train, declining to use the Sukhodaya which the People's Party had sent, and arrived about midnight.

The first official act of the king was to grant pardon to all of the revolutionists. The statement was issued on June 26th. In the evening Khawaraphuthacao was played over the radio instead of the new nationalist song Maharoek Mahachai. The pardon was worded as follows:

> His Majesty the King is pleased to proclaim that there is now in existence a People's Party who have a strong desire to effect certain changes in order to remedy some defects existing in the government of Siam and the Siamese Nation in the same way as has been done in other countries. Hence the Party have acquired the power to control the State, with the aim to bring about a constitutional administration, and have requested us to accept the Kingship of Siam as heretofor under the new constitution of the country. In other countries such a change has never been brought about without strife and bloodshed, this being the first time in the history of the world that such a change has been effected without the use of force.
>
> Although some members of the Royal Family and some officials have been brought to the Throne Hall and detained, this is merely a measure of precaution for the safety of the Party concerned, and also that the change may be carried out smoothly. In no wise could such action be considered as assault or rough usage. What has been done is merely for the maintenance of order, and with due regard to the high rank of the persons concerned in every respect.
>
> As a matter of fact we have long contemplated the institution of this constitutional monarchy and what the People's Party have done is quite right and received our appreciation. In view of the good intention toward the country and the whole people, it cannot be considered that such action was based on evil intention in the least.
>
> Therefore we issue this statement after applying our autograph thereto and we decree that any action of any individual of the People's Party, if it should happen to be contrary to any existing law, is not to be considered to be in fact against the law.
>
> Enacted this 26th of June, B.E. 2475
(M.R.) PRAJADHIPOK[1]

[1] *Bangkok Times,* June 27th, 1932.

Some doubt exists as to the authorship of this letter. It has been suggested that it was composed in whole or in part by the leaders of the People's Party and presented to the king for his signature immediately upon his return to the capital. It has even been suggested that considerable pressure was brought to bear to secure the signature. Probably it represents a compromise. It apparently confirms the rumour that the king had intended to grant a constitution after his return from America on October 12th, 1931. The subject had been discussed in the Supreme Council of State. Unfortunately the Council had been unable to agree as to the form of the constitution and as to the right moment for its promulgation.

On June 27th, 1932, Prince Damrong and Prince Narisra were returned to their palaces with strong guard "for their protection". A fellow prisoner in the Throne Hall, Prince Nagor Svarga, was not allowed to return to his palace until July 3rd, 1932. He was then allowed only time enough to adjust his personal affairs before leaving the country as an exile. It was feared that if he stayed there would be bloodshed. He was regarded as one of the most powerful leaders of the old regime and the chief obstacle in the way of a constitutional form of government. He left with his family for Sumatra where he has since made his home.

On the 27th of June, King Prajadhipok announced his acceptance of a provisional constitution. It provided that the country should be governed by a king, an assembly, a state council, and the law courts. The assembly was to have three periods of life, two of which were temporary. The first period was to last six months from the date of the revolution. The assembly was to have seventy members appointed by the Military Council of Bangkok, which was responsible for martial law during the first period. During the second period the assembly was to have members of two categories. One category of membership was to be appointed, the other was to be elected by the people. The appointed membership was to equal the elected membership numerically. The third period of the assembly was to begin when over one-half of the voting citizens should have acquired a primary education or its equivalent. If the educational goal was not attained within ten years of the date of acceptance of the temporary constitution, the third period of the assembly was to begin anyway. In the third period all members of the assembly were to be elected by the people.

The first meeting of the People's Assembly was held on June 28th, 1932. Phya Manopakorn, a member of the old civil service, was appointed Chairman of the Executive Committee. Chao Phya Dharmasakti was elected Chairman of the People's Assembly. Phya Manopkorn selected fourteen members for his first state council as follows:

Phya Bahol Balabayuha	Phya Song Suratej
Phya Riddhi Aganey	Phya Prija Jolayudh
Phya Srivisar Vacha	Phya Pramuan Vijjapul
Phya Prasasana Biddyayudh	Luang Pradist Manudharm
Luang Pibul Songgram	Luang Dej Sahakorn
Luang Sinddhu Songgramjai	Nai Prayun Pamon Montri
Nai Tua Labanukrom	Nai Nab Baholyodhin

It is interesting to note that all of the members of the state council were of the commoner or Khun Nang class.

The new state council accepted as its platform the six-point statement of the People's Party in its original announcement:

1. The freedom and equality of the people in politics, in the law courts, and in business, must be maintained.
2. Peace and quiet, with no harm to anyone, must be assured.
3. A national economic policy must be drawn up to provide remunerative work for everyone.
4. Equal privilege for everyone must be guaranteed. No one group shall enjoy special privilege at the expense of others.
5. The people shall have freedom and liberty except in those cases where freedom and liberty disagree with the above four points.
6. The people must be given the most complete education possible.

A committee was appointed to draw up a permanent constitution for acceptance by the king. The members of the committee were Phya Manopakorn, Phya Deb Vidura, Phya Nitisastr Baisal, Phya Prida Naroebesr, Luang Pradist Manudharm, and Luang Sinad Yodharaks.

Forty-one army officers were dismissed from the service; four were raised to the rank of Lieutenant-Colonel; ten were raised to the position of Major; twenty-two were raised to the rank of Colonel. Five navy men were raised to the rank of Captain.

The new government discontinued the field tax, the salary tax, and other assessments, and levied an income tax instead.

On December 7th, 1932, the leaders of the People's Party had an audience with King Prajadhipok, the purpose of which was to ask his pardon formally for any lack of respect accorded him during the excitement of the revolutionary period. Commonly seen in the daily attitude of pupil to teacher, this sense of respect is raised to a supreme degree when the person of the king is involved. The revolution displayed the Siamese love of personal liberty while the act of asking pardon of the king showed their sense of respect, their good manners. Thus the Siamese carried courtesy even into their revolution. The act of seeking pardon did not, however, mean that they would not oppose the king again. The king was, in fact, opposed until he abdicated.

From June 28th until December 10th, 1932, the constitution was in process of preparation. On the latter date King Prajadhipok accepted the permanent constitution in a ceremony at the Throne Hall. Representatives of foreign nations, the state council, and the members of the assembly attended.

The constitution provided for administrative, legislative, and judicial departments of government. The supreme state council was to be composed of twenty members called *rathamontri,* or state councillors, some of whom were to be in charge of the various ministries. Other members were to be without portfolio.

2. THE CAUSES OF THE REVOLUTION

When one compares the bloodless revolution in Siam to the bloody, life—and property—destroying revolutions in France, Russia, or Spain, one realizes that Siam had done something new and different. The question naturally arises as to why Siam had a revolution at all. A young newspaper man who had spent several years in France and who later became Director-General of the Department of Fine Arts, Luang Vichitr Vadhakarn, suggests four reasons for the overthrow of the absolute monarchy.[1] He is a close friend of the leaders of the revolution, although he did not join the movement officially until after the *coup d'etat.*

He says that the extensive changes in government positions made by King Prajadhipok when he ascended the throne was the first reason for dissatisfaction. In the reign of King Vajiravudh the more important government positions had been in the hands of commoners of the Khun Nang class who had risen to high rank

[1] Luang Vichitr Vadhakarn, *Kan Mu'ang Kan Pok Khrong Khong Krung Syam* (Bangkok: Thai Mai Press, 1932), pp. 85-117.

by their own ability. Siam has but two distinct classes of people—commoners and royalty. The Khun Nang were commoners of high rank. As long as the Khun Nang were in positions of influence the common people felt that they had a share in governing the land.

In King Vajiravudh's reign, eight of the twelve ministries had been administered by Khun Nang. King Prajadhipok, however, had shifted the balance of power until only four of the ministries were controlled by Khun Nang. This shift of power made many commoners feel that they were being ruled without adequate representation.

A commoner, no matter how high his rank, was subject to the laws of the land and might be tried in the law courts. A royal prince, no matter what he did, was regarded as above the law. He could not be brought to trial without the specific consent of the king. Royalty were as gods of the land, the heaven born, in the eyes of the common people. They were a class apart, responsible only to themselves and the king. One class of people thus had power to rule another class which was without legal means of redress even when grievously wronged.

A second reason for the change in government, as cited by Luang Vichitr, was the secretive methods employed by the administration. The rulers took care not to let the public know what they were doing. The people felt that what was secret must be bad. Occasional public statements of policy or plans were made, but they were not of great value to the people since they were usually issued in English and then translated into Siamese which followed the English idiom and was often unintelligible to the people. Misunderstanding arose between the people and the government. For instance, when the depression reached Siam, H.R.H. Prince Purachatra was sent to Indo-China, China, Malaya, and India to study market conditions. Large sums of public money were spent on the trip. When the Prince returned to Siam the public was not informed concerning anything of value that he had learned. The only statement made was that other countries were in a more serious condition than Siam. To make matters worse, the Prince showed movies of his trip and unfortunately only pleasure trips, banquets, and sports were pictured. The actual values of the trip to the nation were never revealed to the public.

A third cause for change in government, as suggested by Luang Vichitr, was an outgrowth of the second one. The government did not take the newspapers into its confidence and did not pass on to them official news. The reporters picked up as much news as they could from gossip and printed as much as they dared. Enmity between the newspapers and the government was the inevitable result. Censorship was established over newspapers and radio. Dissatisfaction spread through the papers to the people, subtly incorporated in apparently innocent articles and editorials.

A fourth cause for the change in government was twofold; it included the dismissal from government service of many officials and the levying of a new salary tax. The officials released were in the lower salary ranks. They became disgruntled when they failed to find new employment. The salary tax struck at the government officials more than at any other group. Explanations were asked, but the government remained silent. Many came to feel that there was no tax on income, or on principal funds, because such taxes would have to be paid by royalty and nobility, few of whom were caught in the net of the salary tax.

A second discussion of the rationale of the revolution was prepared by four men who were teachers at Suan Kularb school, one of the largest government schools in Bangkok. Their opinions have a semi-official flavour because the title page of their booklet records the formal permission of the Ministry of Education for its use in Siamese schools.[1] They point out that at the end of the reign of King Vajiravudh expenditures of government exceeded income. The primary problem of King Prajadhipok had been to balance the budget. Unwilling to borrow from a foreign power, he also did not wish to increase the taxes of the people. He decided, therefore, to economize by dismissing unnecessary government employees and by closing whole departments not vitally concerned with the process of government. The king began with himself and cut his own income from nine hundred thousand to six hundred thousand *baht*[2] per annum. This gave temporary relief until 1931, then disbursements were again exceeding income. Again officials in government service were dismissed as from 1932. The Ministry

[1] Luang Chun Kasikan *et al.*, *Prawat Sat Syam* (3rd ed.; Bangkok: Sri Heng Press, 1935), pp. 355-358.
[2] A *baht*, formerly called a *tical*, is the unit of Siamese coinage. It is usually worth about forty-five cents (U. S. Currency).

of War objected more strenuously than any other ministry when this later reduction in salaries and personnel became known. On February 5th, preceding the outbreak of the revolution in June, King Prajadhipok explained the reductions. One important paragraph of his explanation is as follows:

> I feel that I am born to a time of curtailment and enforced economies. I have imposed one reduction in salaries already and now must impose a second. And I am not sure of the future. It seems to be my fate that this burden should fall upon me. I have tried in every way to avoid further curtailment, but without success. It makes me feel more heavy-hearted than it did on the previous occasion. Formerly there were more employees than were needed so that it was proper to dismiss some, and, at that time, outside employment could be found for those dismissed. I accordingly was not unduly distressed when it became necessary to dismiss employees and to decrease salaries. But this second reduction will mean a reduction in the amount of work done. I know that the army, in particular, is not too fully staffed. This present cut will tend to destroy the efficiency of the department. But every ministry is in the same condition.

The budget was balanced, but a class of people was produced who felt injured and who were ripe for revolutionary propaganda.

In a private interview with the writer, a member of the royal family explained the revolution as follows:

A group of Bangkok students had learned that their nation was an absolute monarchy. They studied books to find out what that had meant in other nations in the past. They read about the evils of an absolute monarchy and jumped to the conclusion that their own country was suffering from the same evils. They felt that a change of government was called for from a theoretical or intellectual point of view. Other nations had changed, therefore Siam should change.

A second group of Siamese students in France and Germany approached the subject from another angle. They had become acquainted with the European point of view in politics and interpreted the condition of Siam in terms of the abuses discovered in European monarchies. They were in Europe during a period of king head-hunting. They learned the European methods of plot and intrigue. This group began to draw together as early as 1915-1920.

A third group, consisting of young military men and government officials, were spurred toward some radical act by personal debts.

These young men had learned from foreigners a system of spending more than they earned. The old economy was thrown over and a new spendthrift era came in. It was the fashion to borrow heavily. In debt, dissatisfied, ambitious, they were the seed-bed of revolutionary propaganda. The revolution provided an opportunity to start a new life on an even higher scale.

Friendly to all of these dissatisfied groups was Luang Pradist Manudharm, who constituted the catalytic agent which fused their purposes and urged them to boil over in revolution.

Certain it is that the revolution was not a mass movement of the people. The peasants were not demanding revolution. The average citizen was unaware of the need for a change in government. The existence of the People's Party was known only to people in Bangkok and to a few politically minded Siamese in the provinces. The idea that the nation would actually become a democracy, or even a constitutional monarchy, seemed absurd to the average citizen. The millions of people living in field, jungle, or village, or in the small towns, can be left out of account. They had no part in the actual changes that took place, and at first had little interest.

To say that economic depression and royal oppression caused the people to rise up in a popular movement, is inaccurate. Other nations have had an economic depression far more terrible than that of Siam. Other countries have had not just a few unemployed but thousands and tens of thousands of people starving on the streets. Other countries have had heavy, unfair taxes, so heavy that the taxes in Siam, in 1932, were light in comparison. As to the freedom of the press, one need but look at Germany, or Italy, or Russia, to realize that the press in Siam was not badly treated. Change in government was demanded by vigorous young men who had ability and keen minds.

Early in the reign of King Vajiravudh an attempt had been made at revolution similar to the one just described. At that time a party of army and navy men, civil officials, and private citizens had attempted to take over the powers of government. That attempt had not been a popular movement either. It had failed, not because it was not a popular movement but because the plans for revolution were known to the government. The leaders were arrested in time to prevent the overthrow of government.

The successful revolution was a duplicate of the one that had failed—with the one exception that it was better planned. There had been no Luang Pradist Manudharm in the earlier effort; even so the later attempt almost went the way of the earlier one. It is reported, on good authority, that Prince Nagor Svarga had been aware of the movement and had watched it develop. When he saw that it had become dangerous he called police and military leaders into conference with the intention of arresting the leaders of the revolutionary movement. However, he was a few hours too late.

The *Bangkok Times* summarizes the revolution as follows:

There is no evidence that the masses took any part in the recent Demonstration. The discontent of the salaried classes, and especially of the officers of the Army and Navy clearly counted for most in the movement. At the same time a contributory cause is to be found in the extension of education in Siam. Since the middle of the nineteenth century, when King Mongkut introduced Western methods and technique, increasing numbers of Siamese students have been trained in Europe. An educated class of officials, administrators, and officers, having once been formed, it was only a question of time and opportunity before they demanded a share in the government of the country.

Recently it has been necessary to make extensive salary cuts and to introduce taxation which for the first time touches the personal incomes of large numbers of the people. Also every young Siamese looks to government service for a livelihood and the service is no longer able to absorb the large numbers who pass through the schools. Siam has created an educated class without having been equally successful in providing suitable openings for employment of the new abilities. This is probably the reason for revolt for it is a natural turn from hope of government employ to politics.[1]

A later statement as to the revolution was:

The success of the revolution is explained by its character. There was no explosion from below but there was merely a readjustment. Capable men simply stepped into the shoes of the Princes and the thing was done. They called themselves the People's Party but the general public were spectators only. The King acceded quietly and the President of the new Senate complimented his party on having the King on their side. They recognize that the sovereign retains the love of the masses. There have been no persecutions of less appreciated members of the Royal family. Outwardly the new regime is democratic, but in practice so far it is a one party government of mildly Fascist complexion.[2]

[1] *Bangkok Times*, July 8th, 1932.
[2] *Ibid.*, August 13th, 1932.

A further paragraph rounds out the picture as follows:

The democratic idea had attained considerable growth. In some cases it was an innocent seed carried with simple education on Western lines; in other cases it was a growth assiduously cultivated for years by a small group of civil service and army men educated mostly in France and Germany. The People's Party which they founded has spread through all departments of government. When the signal was given these turned over allegiance from King to Party without question.[1]

Twenty-six of the seventy members of the first People's Assembly were men who had studied in Europe, many of them at the expense of the government or of the royal family. Eleven of the fourteen members of the first State Council had been students abroad.

3. THE LEADERS OF THE REVOLUTION

Luang Pradist Manudharm is usually regarded as the brains of the revolution. His name was originally Nai Pridi Panomayong. The average citizen under the old regime received a name from his parents and used it the rest of his life. However, if he entered government service and won a position for himself he was given a title and a new name to match the title. The titles usually granted were Khun, Luang, Phra, and Phya, in that order of importance. With the change of title there was often a change of name. The original or boyhood name was forgotten and the man was known by his title. Under the constitutional monarchy the granting of titles has been discontinued. However, those who received titles under the old regime continue to use them.

Luang Pradist was born of a typical Siamese family of considerable means and influence. He went through the regular Siamese schools and finally studied law at Chulalongkorn University, where he received the degree of Barrister-at-Law. He then went on to France where he studied until he received the degree of Doctor of Law. He also studied Economics and received a high degree in that department. When he returned to Siam he became a professor of law at Chulalongkorn University. He was appointed to the position of Secretary of the Department of Legislative Redaction. He also became Secretary of the Bar Association. After the revolution he was a member of the first State Council. In 1938 he was

---

[1] *Ibid.*, August 29th, 1932.

the Minister of Foreign Affairs, later in the year becoming Minister of Finance.

At the time of the revolution Luang Pradist was about thirty years old. In appearance he is a typical Siamese, slim, strong, with heavy black hair cropped close in the German style. His face is unremarkable except for his very healthy looking skin and unusually brilliant eyes, which are partly veiled under heavy lids. He is direct and friendly in his personality and has a manner that wins men. He is tremendously active mentally and physically, and the author of numerous books. His mind is extraordinarily brilliant. He has been the leader of the democratic and civilian group within the revolutionary party.

Another outstanding leader, who supplied the force to carry out the well-drawn plans of Luang Pradist, was Phya Bahol Balabayuha. His original name was Nai Pacan Baholyodhin. In his youth he was an army cadet. His ability earned him a study period in Germany, where he improved his knowledge of army methods. He was appointed a Lieutenant in the German Army. His first work in Siam was in the General Staff Department. He was transferred to the Artillery Section and later was installed as a professor in Army Intelligence in the Educational Section. He was returned to the leadership of the Artillery Section. Shortly before the revolution he was second in rank in charge of the Siamese Army. This was a very important post and placed him in a strategic position for his future work. He, with two other Colonels, led the troops in the revolution and signed the ultimatum to the king. In 1933 he became President of the State Council, Premier, and Siam's leading citizen.

A third leader whose name featured frequently in the news was Phya Song Suratej. His original name was Nai Thep Panadhuma. He studied in the army and became a Lieutenant. He was sent to Germany for further study and became a Lieutenant in the German Army. Upon returning to Siam he worked in the Engineers Section. He was later transferred to a professorship in the Educational Section. While in this department he was sent on a grand tour to inspect army work in America, Japan, and Europe. He was one of the three signers of the ultimatum to the king. He became a member of the People's Assembly and of the State Council. Feeling dissatisfied with some phases of the revolutionary movement he withdrew from politics and went to Chiengmai to take charge of the Military Training School.

The third signer of the ultimatum to the king was Phya Riddhi Aganey, whose original name was Nai Sla Emisiri. He studied in the Military Training School and became a Lieutenant of Artillery. Later he was put in charge of the artillery at Nagor Rajasima. He was again transferred to have charge of the King's Artillery. After the revolution he became a member of the State Council and served as Minister of Agriculture.

Luang Pibul Songgram, although he was one of the original planners of the 1932 revolution, took no prominent part in that affair. His personal name was Nai Blaek Srianong. He had won academic distinction as a young man in the cadet school in Bangkok and had been sent abroad to France for military study. At the time of the revolution he was a Major in the regular army and Equerry to H.R.H. Prince Narisa. After the revolution, along with sixty or more others of the revolutionary group, he became a member of the People's Assembly. He also became State Councillor without portfolio.

In 1933, he won public distinction by co-operating with Phya Bahol in the overthrow of the Phya Manopakorn Government. The second *coup d'etat* had as its purpose the re-convening of the People's Assembly. Luang Pibul clinched his position of political prominence later in the same year by suppressing the royalist rebellion, which was led by Prince Bavoradej.

On September 25th, 1934, Luang Pibul became Minister of Defence at the age of thirty-seven. By that time he was also a Colonel in the Army and Deputy Commander-in-Chief of the Army, second only to Premier Phya Bahol. He has been the leader of the militarist nationalist group within the revolutionary party. Three known attempts have been made on his life by assassins since 1934. He is unusually handsome, with a crest of thick black hair, and bold clear eyes. He is agile physically, and quick in his thinking, a man of action. On December 15th, 1938, he assumed the highest political position possible to a Siamese, and became Premier.

Another leader was Phra Prasasana Pidayayudara, whose original name was Nai Wan Juthina. He too studied in the Military Training School before doing graduate work in Germany. He also went to Switzerland where he completed his scholastic work. He served in Siam's expeditionary forces during the World War. On returning to his own land he became a professor in the Educational Section. He was later appointed to the General Staff, and finally became head of the Military Training School.

Chao Phya Dharmasakti, the first Chairman of the People's Assembly, had been Minister of Public Instruction from 1917 to 1926. He had also been on the Privy Council and on the Council of the Royal Institute.

Two other interesting characters were Phya Manopakorn, who became the Premier and who had formerly been Chief Judge of the Appeal Court, and Nai Charoen, a talented lawyer, who had spent twelve years in prison for his share in the abortive revolution in the days of King Vajiravudh. Nai Charoen became a member of the People's Assembly.

Every revolution needs an occasion or an incident of some sort. The occasion for the revolution of June 24th, 1932, was found in the purchase of thirteen expensive diesel locomotives. H.R.H. Prince Purachatra bought them for use on the Siamese State Railway. The large expenditure of money for locomotives in a time of financial depression gave the revolutionists an excuse to act.

4. THE RESULTS OF THE REVOLUTION

With the revolution an accomplished fact the question arises as to the status of the average citizen as compared to the status under the old regime. The privileges and duties of a citizen under the absolute monarchy, according to Luang Vichitr Vadhakarn were:

1. A citizen is born free and may not be bought or sold.
2. A citizen may make his living as he chooses. No one can force him into any one particular trade.
3. A citizen may be imprisoned only according to law.
4. A citizen may be punished only when he has broken a law that is in effect at the time. Punishment and fine must be according to law.
5. A citizen's home is inviolable. No one may enter by force. The police may search a citizen's home only as provided by law.
6. A citizen has rights over his own property and wealth, and no one may deprive him of them except by due process of law.

7. A citizen has a right to express his honest opinion in order to establish his own innocence. In so doing he may either praise or blame others, but he may not speak in such a way as to slander them.

8. A citizen has the protection of the law. He may appeal to the courts to try his case.

9. A citizen has the privilege of becoming a soldier.

10. A citizen has the privilege of privacy in his personal affairs.

11. A citizen has the privilege of disobeying the orders of his superiors, if those orders are contrary to law.

12. A citizen has the right to follow the religion of his choice.

The duties of a citizen under the old regime were covered under five points as follows:

1. A citizen must pay taxes as required by the government.

2. Every citizen, except the king, must pay a head tax.

3. A citizen must have some sort of employment, otherwise he will be reckoned as a homeless person.

4. Every male citizen, within the required age limits, is liable to military conscription.

5. Everyone must receive a primary education.

The constitutional monarchy added the following privileges:

1. The privilege of having an assembly or committee of the people exercise power over the nation, said assembly to receive power to act from the will of the people.

2. The privilege of choosing representatives to make the laws.

3. The privilege of demanding to know what the government is doing and what it is planning to do in the future.

4. The privilege of demanding that their representatives pass some certain acts.

5. The privilege of living in the country. The government has no right to expatriate anyone. It has the right to confine troublesome individuals within certain restricted areas in the country. This also means that the government has the responsibility of providing everyone with a place in which to live and work.[1]

Section One of the Constitution says: "Supreme power of the country is in the hands of the citizens." However, all privileges

---

[1] Luang Vichitr Vadhakarn, *Kan Mu'ang Kan Pok Khrong Khong Krung Syam* (Bangkok: Thai Mai Press, 1932), pp. 151 ff.

have not been exercised as yet. The date upon which the people may assume their full privileges depends on their progress in matters political and educational. After six years of the new regime a mild sort of Fascist government is still in effect. Many Siamese believe that it will continue indefinitely and that the time will never come when the People's Assembly will be made up of an elected membership as postulated for the third period of the assembly. At any rate, the people have become more vocal than ever before. They are not slow to express opinions on the work of government officials, and frequently have been able to have abuses corrected. The needs of a community for roads, schools, a water system, or a new market, are often stated plainly in the assembly forum.

5. LUANG PRADIST'S ECONOMIC POLICY

The new constitutional monarchy experienced no great difficulty until March, 1933, when Luang Pradist Manudharm presented his economic plan for consideration.[1] It was discussed in both the People's Assembly and the State Council. The plan included a number of radical changes for the nation. One of the most important changes was the purchase of farming land by the government. The plan was to issue bonds for the value of the land. The farmers would then become government employees in the sense that they would labour for the government, and in return would receive salary and pension. The government would be in charge of the main business of the nation, the raising and selling of rice. The plan would automatically eliminate the middleman, the rice buyer and wholesaler, who is usually a Chinese. Not much money need be exchanged, according to the plan, for the workers would be required to buy from government stores. Here again the profit system would be eliminated. A fair wage and pension would be made available.

On March 12th, 1933, a special committee of fourteen met to consider the economic plan of Luang Pradist. The names of some of the leading men of the country were on the roll call, among them Phya Manopakorn, Luang Pradist, Prince Sakol Varavarn, and Phya Song. In thirteen pages of minutes taken at the meeting the burden of opinion favoured a trial of the economic plan. Some

[1] See Appendix.

favoured putting the plan into operation gradually. Others favoured the immediate adoption of the whole scheme. Phya Mano led the opposition by suggesting that the government should attempt to better the economic situation in a more conservative way. He suggested that the co-operative society idea be encouraged by making more capital available to the peasants. His suggestions were: to enlarge the credit stores where the peasants could buy their supplies at cost; to establish granaries at local points and to buy up rice for shipment to Bangkok in order to eliminate the middle-man; to establish co-operative rice mills for the sale of rice direct to foreign countries; and finally to establish a settlement scheme for those people who have no lands. These societies would form public corporations and would keep the profits in the country.

The Committee agreed to render both a majority and minority report to the State Council. The plan of Phya Mano was, in effect, to continue along the lines laid out by the old regime in assisting the people as there was opportunity without any elaborate scheme which would alter the economic basis of the nation. The plan of Luang Pradist was to make a new start economically along entirely different lines, as outlined above. It was decided that if the government agreed with Phya Mano, Luang Pradist should be permitted to publish his plan on his own responsibility in an effort to make it appeal to the public.

On April 1st, 1933, Phya Manopakorn issued a statement to the public. He said that the State Council had fallen into two groups which could not co-operate. One group agreed with him in feeling that the economic plan of Luang Pradist was communistic. In the People's Assembly, where the matter was discussed, many members felt that the plan was communistic. Differences of opinion became bitter, without hope of reconciliation. As a consequence, Phya Mano prorogued the assembly. The disagreement between the assembly, which had the responsibility for making laws, and the State Council, which had the work of putting them into effect, was a very serious thing.

The public was not allowed to know the details of the economic plan of Luang Pradist. The *Krungdep Warasap* announced that it would discuss the policy, but the Minister of the Interior forbad all discussion. Other newspapers had long editorials on the subject. While admitting complete ignorance as to the nature of the policy, the newspapers generally agreed that some definite economic plans should be drawn up. Luang Pradist had been to see the king and had explained his plan in detail. When it was certain that the plan would not be accepted, Luang Pradist resigned his government post. On April 12th, 1933, he and his wife sailed for Europe.

A special gazette was issued by the government in which new State Councillors were appointed by royal decree. The People's Assembly was dissolved as was the old State Council. A new State Council was appointed and King Prajadhipok was to exercise the powers usually held by the Assembly until another Assembly should be elected.[1]

A government communique was issued to explain the drastic action of the above decree. The reasons given were that the assembly and council had been divided over the question of the plan of Luang Pradist until it was virtually impossible to transact normal business, and that the safety of the community was endangered.[2]

The government had lasted just 281 days, from June 24th, 1932, to March 31st, 1933.

An "Act Concerning Communism" was passed to safeguard the nation from that doctrine. It was definitely aimed against the nationalization of land, industry, capital, and labour.[3]

A further amendment to the Civil and Commercial Code was enacted which provided for the cancellation of any association "if it appears that the object or activities of the association have become a danger to the public peace, or are likely to cause unrest in the country."

6. THE REVOLUTION OF JUNE, 1933

On June 14th, 1933, Phya Manopakorn, Phya Rajawangsan, Phya Srivisar, Luang Pibul, and Nai Prayun, had a secret rendezvous in an open field at Bang Kabi. They went to the meeting by ones and twos to avoid notice. A number of soldiers stayed at the edge of the field to keep people away. They consulted over the latest political development which was the resignation of Phya Bahol, Phya Song, Phya Riddhi, and Phra Prasasana from both

[1] Appendix.
[2] Ibid.
[3] Ibid.

their government and army posts. The three men had said in their resignations that they were indisposed and wished to retire on pension.[1]

A large delegation of tramway men waited upon Phya Bahol to express their sorrow at his resignation, which was to take place as from June 24th, 1933. Expressions of goodwill were extended to him from all over the country. Later developments showed that his resignation was intended as a way of feeling out the sentiment of the country.

On June 20th, 1933, history repeated itself. Early in the morning, Phya Bahol and his military men arrested Phya Mano and other conservative leaders. Once again military equipment, machine guns, and tanks rolled through the streets while martial law was declared. The government was forced to resign and a telegram was sent to King Prajadhipok which read:

> To H. S. H. Prince Vipulya Svastivongse, His Majesty's Private Secretary;
> Now that it is necessary for the Army and Navy to seize the control of the Government with the intention merely to convene the Assembly of the People's Representatives, please therefore convey this information to His Majesty, and also inform His Majesty that the Army and Navy are as always filled with respect and have faith in His Majesty.
>
> COLONEL PHYA BAHOL BALABAYUHA
> LT.-COLONEL LUANG PIBUL SONGGRAM
> COMMANDER LUANG SUBHA JALASAYA[2]

This second revolutionary stroke was in many ways a duplicate of the earlier one a year before. With a few important exceptions it put the same men in power again. The year had seen the rise of Luang Pibul and the withdrawal of Phya Song, signer of the first manifesto. From this time forward Luang Pibul, Phya Bahol, and Luang Pradist have continued as the strong men in the government. Luang Pibul is the personification of the military, and, at the opposite end of the teeter-board, Luang Pradist is the civilian. Phya Bahol is the fulcrum.

The second *coup d'etat* might have been unnecessary if the People's Party had not been so willing to allow experienced civil officials to hold strategic positions while they themselves withdrew.

[1] *Thai Mai*, June 14th, 1933.
[2] *Daily Mail*, June 20th, 1933.

It was an unusual thing to see victorious revolutionaries humbly allowing older and more experienced men to assume positions of power and influence. Luang Pradist in his speech to the group which assembled on the evening of that first 24th of June had said frankly that the revolutionary group lacked political experience. As a consequence they had employed the older officials whom they found in office, or who had previously served under the absolute monarchy. From this time forward men from the previous regime in the higher positions were gradually dismissed and replaced by the revolutionaries themselves. Many if not most of the replacements were made from the Army and Navy. Thus the Minister of the Interior was chosen from the Navy, and the Minister of Public Instruction from the Army.

On the whole, however, the retention of the older civil officials was evidence not only of the paucity of experienced men in the ranks of the revolutionaries, but also of their good intentions, their genuine desire to help their race. The old civil servants not unnaturally retained a great loyalty to the king and to the old ways. The revolutionary group felt that the Phya Mano government had tried and almost succeeded in nullifying the gains of the revolution. When Phya Mano prorogued the assembly, he entrusted all the powers of the assembly to the king until such time as the assembly should be re-convened. Phya Bahol and his group were certain that the assembly would not be voluntarily re-convened. Therefore, they once again used the weapon which had so effectively served their purpose the previous year: force. The Phya Mano government had lasted eighty-one days, from April 1st, 1933, to June 20th, 1933.

The new leaders held a conference with the bankers and gave them assurances. A messenger, who was sent to interview King Prajadhipok at Hua Hin, brought back a reply in which the king expressed his willingness to re-convene the People's Assembly. A special meeting of the assembly was called, but only twenty-six members appeared. Most of the other members had gone home to the various provinces. Those who did come to the meeting were armed with revolvers, which they were required to check at the door. A few experts were invited to attend for consultation on political matters. They were H.S.R. Prince Varnvaidyakara Voravarn, Dean of the Faculty of Law at Chulalongkorn University,

Phya Komarakul Montri, former Minister of Finance, Phya Suriyanuvatr, H.S.H. Prince Sakol Voravarn, and Phya Nitisastr Baisal, a judge. As a result of the meeting a programme was outlined and a new government established, with Phya Bahol Balabayuha acting as Premier. He announced that he would serve only fifteen days until a political expert could be selected. He claimed to be a military man and unfitted for politics. When the time set expired he handed in his resignation, but the king urged him to continue and declined to accept his resignation. Phya Bahol controlled the military forces and more than any of the other revolutionary leaders had the confidence of the people.

One of Phya Bahol's first public statements was: "No element of communism shall ever creep into Siam as long as I possess any influence in the government. I will devote my life to protect the Constitution under our Most Gracious Majesty." He later added to that thought the following words:

I fully understand the position of our country and the necessity for guarding it against communistic tendencies, directly or indirectly. The Government of Siam shall never follow communistic ideals as long as I am in it.[1]

Phya Pramuan Vijjapul advocated the appointment of a commission to investigate the activities of the previous government. His idea was that the leaders of that government should be punished. After much discussion a committee of nine members was appointed. The committee accomplished little because public opinion was against political persecution. On July 27th, 1933, the assembly passed a vote of approval on practically all enactments which had been promulgated by the State Council of the Phya Manopakorn government. Thus, curiously enough, the ideas of Phya Mano triumphed in spite of his personal defeat. The economic plan of Luang Pradist was never again seriously considered. Phya Mano, shrewd and experienced politician that he was, knew that a peasant's dearest possession is his land. In many districts it is considered shameful to sell a section of rice land; since that land, in peasant thought, is the rightful inheritance of the children, whose very bread and butter it is. Government ownership of rice lands cut across the very fibre of the people's thinking. It could hardly have done anything else than pauperize the country.

[1] *Daily Mail*, June 21st, 1933.

With Phya Bahol, the friend of Luang Pradist Manudharm, back in power, the newspapers began to ask when Luang Pradist would return to Siam. Some newspapers wanted him to return immediately, some were indifferent as to whether he returned or did not return, others felt he should wait until after the December elections. On September 29th, 1933, Luang Pradist arrived in Bangkok as quietly as possible.

On March 12th, 1934, the government took an important step designed to make it possible for Luang Pradist to serve in some important public office. A commission was appointed to investigate the status of Luang Pradist with respect to communism. Two foreign experts were engaged to define communism and to render a report containing their opinion. Luang Pradist persuaded the commission that his economic plan, which was definitely communistic, was irrelevant to any discussion of his political position. Once that point was granted, Luang Pradist was of course cleared of suspicion.

If the investigation, resulting in a detailed report,[1] had no other value, it made the nation critically aware of the teachings of communism. The opinions of the two experts were recorded in the newspapers in full. There are probably few newspaper readers in Siam who are unfamiliar with the general doctrine of communism.

Since Siam was to have a partially elected People's Assembly, it was necessary to have a general election. The representatives to the assembly were not elected directly by the people but were elected by Tambol or District representatives. Consequently the first elections were of the Tambol representatives. Following is a brief comment on the system of election:

> Barring unconstitutional seizure of power, the Government party is assured of a majority in the Assembly for ten years. First of all, we have the temporary provisions of the Constitution under which half the members of the Assembly will be appointed by His Majesty the King, who will not depart from the recommendations of His Ministers. Then we have the Election Law, the working of which will be found to lend itself very readily to a managed election. Under its provisions no private candidate can make his appeal direct to the electors because they do not directly elect him. The people may want to have some particular man as their representative in the Assembly, but they will have no means of carrying out their will. Under this system nobody has any chance except the Government's candidate. If

[1] Appendix.

the next Assembly, therefore, has more than ten members sitting on the opposition bench, it will be a miracle.[1]

How well the actual elections developed may be seen in the following description:

Democratic government in Siam has begun to experience one of the checks that observers have expected as from day to day now, they watch the returns from the polling booths as the people of Bangkok vote for their Tambol representatives. The "check" is the general apathy on the part of the people toward the whole matter of who holds office or what the candidate stands for in policy.

It is certainly not a surprising development to people familiar with the mass of people on whom this right of franchise has suddenly been thrust. One of the things that the Government has to remember continually is that the people who, for the most part, cannot read or write, such as more than 95 per cent of the electorate in Siam, are not likely to go to the polls to vote, either now or for many years to come. Only education, which brings with it a consciousness of national and, in the long run, international affairs, will awaken the majority of the people in Siam to their duties at the polls.[2]

In Tambol Nagor Jaisri only 834 out of a possible 5,092 votes were cast for 22 candidates. In Tambol Talat Plu only 42 votes out of a possible 4,000 were cast for two candidates. In Tambol Ban Kaek 106 votes of a possible 1,366 were cast for three candidates. Some people voted simply for the novelty of it, dropping their votes into the first box available without knowing for whom they were voting. Many of the Tambols had no candidate at all and so had no voice in the actual election of representatives to the assembly.

7. THE ROYALIST REBELLION

Siam had hardly had an opportunity to feel at peace after the Phya Manopakorn affair when it was startled by letters sent out by two military officers, who had signed the second manifesto to the king, to such prominent men as H.H. Prince Devawongs, one time Minister of Foreign Affairs, H.H. Prince Dossiriwongs, H.S.H. Prince Sobhon, H.S.H. Prince Kaisaeng, H.S.H. Prince Chatra Mongol, Phya Sarabhaya, and Nai Prayun, former Secretary of the State Council. The recipients forwarded the letters to the newspapers which published them. The letters read as follows:

[1] *Daily Mail*, July 29th, 1933.
[2] *Ibid.*, October 4th, 1933.

July 16th, 1933.
Sir:
Both times that the People's Party seized the power of government they acted in an orderly fashion for the sake of the peace of the country and the freedom of the people. It appears from our investigations that you are planning to destroy the peace of the country by attempting to overthrow the present government. Such a move would interfere with the orderly progress of the nation.

In our position of responsibility as guardians of the peace we advise you to desist. If you insist upon causing trouble, our group will use strong measures to assure the peace of the country. This is not a threat designed to intimidate you, but is advice hopefully given.

With high respect,

LUANG PIBUL SONGGRAM
LUANG SUBHA JALASAYA

Newspaper editorials took the writers to task for sending out such letters to men of high position. The two officers claimed they had acted as private citizens. Several of the newspapers pointed out that as private citizens they were not in a position to use "strong measures" in case of disobedience.

Nothing happened until October 11th, 1933, when it became known that H.H. Prince Bavoradej, former Minister of Defence and close personal friend of King Prajadhipok, was indisposed and was staying at the home of Lieutenant-Colonel Phya Vijayendr at Korat. It also became known that great numbers of army officers and government officials visited him daily to inquire after his health.

On October 12th, 1933, martial law was proclaimed as rebellious troops, led by Prince Bavoradej, marched from Korat and Ayudhia against Bangkok. The grim realities of civil war had come to Siam. Feverish activity soon turned Bangkok into an armed camp bristling with artillery, machine guns, and soldiers.

The group led by Prince Bavoradej claimed that the Phya Bahol government had assimilated all authority and that the people had no voice in the government; and that, therefore, Phya Bahol and his group had violated the spirit in which the revolution had been conceived. Siam, so they claimed, was an oligarchy ruled by Phya Bahol and his associates and not a democracy at all. The newspapers gave special notice to King Prajadhipok's statement that he regretted the rebellion.

The same day, October 12th, 1933, a telegram was sent to His Majesty by Phya Bahol stating the problem involved and briefly outlining the plan of action. The telegram was as follows:

> May it please Your Majesty:
> Yesterday evening the Ayuthia engineering troops marched to Bang Khen and the Nakorn Rajasima (Korat) Army reached Don Muang.
> At about 2 p.m. today, Phra Saeng Siddhikarn conveyed a letter from Phya Sri Siddhi Songgram to me (Phya Bahol). The letter stated that the present Government has encouraged the people to disgrace and despise Your Majesty and that it recalled Luang Pradist Manudharm with the intention of launching a communistic economic scheme in this country; the letter demanded that the Government tender its resignation within one hour and stated that force will be used to seize control of the Government temporarily until a new State Council, which will not include any military officer, is appointed by Your Majesty.
> These two allegations are untrue, the present Government having taken immediate action against any person despising Your Majesty, and having given assurances that Luang Pradist will co-operate with the Government in its announced economic policy. The State Council will always continue to protect Your Majesty and safeguard peace and order. For these purposes, I, in the capacity of Commander-in-Chief of the Army, deem it expedient to proclaim martial law by virtue of the provisions of the Martial Law Act, B. E. 2457. The proclamation came into force at 2.45 p.m. today.
> The Government will deal with the situation so as to maintain peace and order in the Kingdom.
> COLONEL PHYA BAHOL BALABAYUHA.

A reward of 10,000 *baht* was offered for H.H. Prince Bavoradej, dead or alive. Similar rewards of 5,000 *baht* were offered for Phya Sri Siddhi Songgram and Phya Deb Songgram.

The rebellion had a very short life. By October 16th, the rebels had been driven away from the Bangkok area. The next day the airdrome at Don Muang was recaptured. On October 18th, the Petchaburi revolt was suppressed and Ayudhya was retaken. On October 24th, Phya Sri Siddhi Songgram was killed in action.

By the end of October the rebellious group were without hope. Prince Bavoradej fled by airplane to Indo-China to become an exile from Siam. It is to the credit of the government and to the spirit of the Siamese people that none of the captured rebels were badly treated. Some were imprisoned for a short time, some were tried by a special court and were condemned to life imprisonment or to execution. However, leniency was shown even to those condemned, in that their sentences were commuted to life imprisonment; other sentences were mitigated. The government issued a detailed statement as to the treatment of the political prisoner, showing that he was given adequate consideration.[1]

The first general election of the people's representatives to the assembly was held in December. The people elected seventy-eight representatives and an equal number was appointed by the government in the name of the king. Phya Bahol continued as Premier and Chao Phya Dharmasakti became President of the Assembly. The government thus constituted was to continue for a four year period.

8. THE ABDICATION OF KING PRAJADHIPOK

After the opening of the assembly, King Prajadhipok announced that he would have to undergo another eye operation in America. Both the State Council and the People's Assembly opposed the trip and begged His Majesty to invite the best surgeons to come to Bangkok. The king insisted on going. Before he sailed he remarked:

> I am obliged to make this journey for reasons of health. . . . I have full confidence in the present government with Colonel Phya Bahol as President of the State Council. . . . I have all along been in favour of a constitutional form of government.

On January 19th, 1934, Their Majesties arrived at Belawan and were received in state in Sumatra. They went not only to visit Prince Paribatra of Nagor Svarga, who had been exiled, but also to have a general family reunion,[2] by that time possible only outside of Siam.

Many of the important members of the royal family, most of whom were in exile, came to wait upon King Prajadhipok. Prince Nagor Svarga had been educated in Germany and other European countries. He had been a very active force in the political life of Siam until he was exiled to Sumatra. Prince Kambaeng Bejra was without doubt the best business man of the family, and one of the most efficient men in Siam. The Royal State Railway was his handiwork. He was the leading Rotary Club member in Siam.

[1] Appendix.
[2] *Ibid.*

After the 1932 revolution he went to live in Singapore, where he died in 1936. Prince Damrong, Siam's elder statesman and adviser to at least two kings, was a scholarly man who had developed the museum and library in Bangkok, and held many high government positions. After the revolution he went to live in Penang, S.S., and has occupied his time preparing his memoirs with the assistance of his two daughters, Princesses Poon and Pilai. He was denied a passport for the trip to Sumatra by the resident Siamese Consul in Penang, but was accommodated by the Dutch government. Phya Manopakorn, although not a member of the Royal Family, was an ardent royalist who had attempted to return the powers of government to the king and the State Council. In the military reaction that followed, his life was spared and he went to live in Penang, S.S.

It had been announced that Their Majesties would return to Siam in October. However, three Acts were promulgated during his absence which displeased the king, and caused him to delay his return. One Act amended the Penal Code, another, Penal Procedure, and the third, the Penal Code of the Army. It began to be rumoured that His Majesty might abdicate.

A mission of three men, Chao Phya Sridharma Dhibes, Chairman of the Assembly, Luang Damrong Navasvasti, Secretary-General of the State Council, and Nai Direk Jayanam, Secretary to the Minister of Foreign Affairs, was sent to interview the king, who was residing in England. Only Chao Phya Sridharma was of sufficient political stature and reputation to be in a position in any way to influence the king. The other two were young unknowns who had come into power with the People's Party.

The mission was unsuccessful and on March 2nd, 1935, King Prajadhipok signed a letter of abdication.[1] This letter took the form of a public statement setting forth at length his reasons for abdicating.

A book of five hundred pages was sold throughout Siam containing the discussions between the king and the government.[2] The impartial reader finds the king's demands moderate. Little that he asked had been granted. The assembly, in considering the issues between the king and the government which had precipitated the

[1] Appendix.
[2] Ibid.

abdication, did not take up at all the question of the right or wrong of the king's requests. The record of the assembly's discussions reveals the strange fact that they were entirely concerned with a question irrelevant to the issues involved. The assembly took the view that the king had accused the government of acting illegally in limiting his prerogatives. The legality of the government's acts was the only question which the assembly considered. Thus the whole main issue was side-tracked, perhaps intentionally. The assembly found the government "not guilty". In this confused atmosphere the abdication was accepted.

The real issue, where it did not concern the king's personal prerogatives like the right to grant pardons, was party-control of government. The country at large was ignorant of the ways of democracy. Illiteracy was high. If all the rights and privileges of democracy were granted an ignorant people suddenly, the results, to say the least, might prove unfortunate. On this point the leaders of the party were in complete agreement with the princes, whom they had supplanted. As one of our early American presidents said:

> A popular government without popular information or the means of acquiring it, is but a prologue to a farce or a tragedy, or perhaps both . . . The best service that can be rendered to a country next to giving it liberty, is in diffusing the mental improvement equally essential to the preservation and enjoyment of that liberty.[1]

Most of Siam did not have popular information nor the means of acquiring it. Most of the people could not read and were completely indifferent to politics, knowing only personal loyalties. Accordingly, the People's Party laid out a programme that assured them power for at least ten years, during which they hoped to accomplish the education of the nation.

Siam was not, then, a democracy, since it did not have a government which derived its power from "the consent of the governed". The king was correct when he said that the government was "government-by-a-party" rather than "government-by-a-people." It was government by commoners who had seized power, as opposed to government by princes who had inherited power. As the king had been to the left of the princes in his desire for a democracy which lodged more and more of the authority in the people, so he

---

[1] James Monroe, *Textbook on the History of Education* (New York: The Macmillan Co., 1905), p. 714.

found himself to the left of the Party, which was almost as conservative as the princes in the delegation of authority. Close study of the early documents of the People's Party reveal the patent fact that the leaders had never intended to turn over full power to the people at once. Many persons, however, had been misled into expecting this from the campaign oratory and enthusiastic newspaper publicity which followed the revolution.

But while it is correct to say that democracy had not arrived in Siam, the hope of democracy had. Soldiers, students, intelligentsia, had drunk deep of the strong wine of desire for *"Liberté, égalité, fraternité."* There was not the slightest chance that they would give up the hope of eventual democracy. To this hope, logically or not, they sacrificed the king.

Behind the discussion between king and government there was distrust. The king had been through the fire of revolution. He had had his prerogatives taken from him. He had seen his friends and relatives imprisoned and held as hostages, and, so far as he could see, to no avail. Democracy was not as yet a fact, nor did there seem any chance of its becoming so. On the other hand the government had had two strenuous affairs, one with Phya Manopakorn, and one with Prince Bavoradej, both of which were regarded by them as efforts to return the old powers of rule to the king. The king was probably afraid to trust himself to the government lest he become a hostage to fortune. The government was afraid to trust the king too far for fear he might destroy their platform, which assured them power for another ten years. The wisest remark in the whole discussion was made by the king when he said that a new king under the new government would have a better chance for success than he. He further advised that the new king be young enough so that he could not interfere with the new plans of government for several years.

Few kings have come through political revolution as unscathed, and with such dignity as King Prajadhipok. Few revolutionary governments have been able to establish themselves as quietly and with as little bloodshed as the Phya Bahol government.

The following telegram to His Majesty ended a period in the political history of Siam:

March 7th, 1935.

Siam Consulate
London

Please convey the following to His Majesty King Prajadhipok:

The Government has received the King's letter of abdication with regret. The Government presented the letter to the Assembly on March 6th and they also received it with sorrow.

The Assembly agreed to invite Prince Ananda Mahidol to become the King according to Section nine of the Constitution. Since the Prince is still quite young, the Assembly, according to Section ten of the Constitution agreed to set up a regency consisting of H. H. Prince Adityaib-ābhā, H. H. Prince Anuvatna Caturanta, and Chao Phya Yomaraj.

The Government begs to offer its blessing upon His Majesty, King Prajadhipok, and upon Queen Rambaibarni; may you both have peace and happiness in the future.

COLONEL PHYA BAHOL BALABAYUHA

CHAPTER II

POLITICAL TRENDS (Continued)

1. THE TREND TOWARD DECENTRALIZATION IN GOVERNMENT

ANANDA MAHIDOL was a ten-year-old schoolboy in Switzerland, living with his mother and brother, when he ascended the throne. He did not return to Siam for a visit or for a coronation ceremony until he landed in Siam on November 15th, 1938. He was hailed with enthusiasm. On January 13th, 1939, when he left Siam to resume his studies in Switzerland, more than 300,000 people lined the banks of the River Chao Phya to see him off. A regency of three acted for the young king in formal matters. The actual process of government was vested in the State Council, the People's Assembly, and the Courts of Law.

The general trend has been to allow the administration of government to become more and more a local matter. Formerly the country was divided into Circles or Montons, over each of which was a Lord Lieutenant or Tetsa. The Monton is comparable to the Province in China, or to the State in the United States. Each Circle or Monton was divided into Cangwats, comparable to the American county. Each Cangwat had a Governor. The Cangwat was again divided into Amphoes which were in turn divided into Tambols. These last two divisions were lesser divisions of the area into districts. Finally each Tambol was divided into villages. For example, Monton Bhuket had five Cangwats. One of these was Cangwat Trang which had five Amphoes. One of these Amphoes was Amphoe Tap Tiang which had about ten Tambols. The average Tambol had about ten villages. The only officials elected by the people were the village chief and the Nai Kamnan who was in charge of the Tambol. All Amphoe, Cangwat, and Monton officials were appointed from Bangkok. The officials sent out from Bangkok were frequently moved so that their administration might be impartial. The people had little to say in matters of government.

Until June, 1932, the government was an absolute monarchy. Executive power was exercised by the king who was advised by the Supreme Council of State and a Cabinet of eleven Ministers. A Legislative Council was created in 1895 but it seldom met. The Supreme Council of State was brought into being by King Prajadhipok immediately after his accession to the throne. It acted as an advisory body to the sovereign. The Supreme Council of State and the Cabinet Council met regularly and took the place of the Legislative Council. In 1927 a Committee of the Privy Council was appointed to deliberate and express opinion on matters of government. After the *coup d'etat*, June 24th, 1932, the government became a constitutional monarchy. According to the constitution, authority was vested in the Monarch, the People's Assembly, the Executive State Council, and the Courts of Law.

The country was at one time divided into eighteen Montons. In 1926 this number was reduced to fourteen. In 1932 a further reduction was made to ten. A radical change was made in 1933 when the Monton system was abandoned and the Kingdom was divided into seventy Cangwats. At the head of each Cangwat was a provincial commissioner. Two high commissioners were stationed in Bangkok. Inspecting commissioners were attached to the Central Administration.

On January 11th, 1934, a further move toward additional local autonomy was made by the passing of laws for municipal and local governments. Constitutional government was gradually being established from the top down, beginning with the People's Assembly and the State Council. The next step was designed to set up township local government according to Chapter II of the Local Government Act. Wherever there was a population of three thousand or more in a delimited area, and an average density of population in that area was not less than a thousand inhabitants per square kilometre, then the area could have Township Local Government. If the population did not meet the above specifications, an area could have a Commune or Tambol Local Government, and if the population in a stated area was thirty thousand or more, with an average density of not less than a thousand inhabitants to the square kilometre, then that area could have City Local Government.

In every case the pattern of government was the same as that of the national government. That is, the government was formulated in terms of an assembly and a council. The development of the assembly was to be carried through three stages to complete democracy. In the first period the membership was appointive. In the second period half of the members were elected by the people and the other half appointed. In the third period all of the members were to be elected by the people. Appointments in the first and second periods of the local assemblies were to be made by the council of civil service employees who comprised the local administrative government, and who were themselves appointed from Bangkok.

The various local governments were not to engage in national politics, but were to confine themselves to definite local functions. Thus the Tambol Local Government could promote public health work, provide drinking water, provide and maintain roads and paths, improve the people's means of livelihood, assist elementary education, and take measures for the public safety, peace, and morals. In addition it could maintain market places, cattle-sheds, slaughter-houses, provide a credit society, a pleasure park, or an electricity company. The Township Local Government could participate in almost all of the above activities and in addition might maintain a fire-fighting department, an innovation almost unheard of in Siam. The City Local Government had duties along more urban lines such as providing health centres, hospitals, poor relief, child welfare centres, and public lavatories.

2. PERSONAL LIBERTY UNDER THE CONSTITUTION

The common people are for the first time becoming vocal in governmental matters that concern themselves. They now have a medium of expression such as they have never had before.

This new-found sense of personal liberty has led some to experiment, to test the extent of their freedom. Is there freedom of religious expression? Is there freedom of the Press? Is there freedom of radio broadcast? Is there freedom of assembly? Is there freedom of speech? Is there the right to discuss any question whether political or not? Is there freedom to be a communist or a socialist?

First as to religious liberty: freedom to believe and practice any religion is definitely given to everyone but the king. The king must be a Buddhist. Buddhism is the State Religion. Siamese in general have every incentive to uphold Buddhism, which they have known and practiced for centuries. However, if one chooses another religion he need not fear persecution. Young men in government service usually say that they have better chance for advancement if they are Buddhists. But men of ability have won high positions in the civil service even though they followed a religion other than Buddhism.

South Siam has a large Malay population in Satul, Pattani, and other neighbouring towns. It might be said that the officials in that area are Siamese, the tradesmen Chinese, and the population Mohammedan Malay. The Mohammedans have freedom of religious expression without any fear of persecution.

The Christians in Siam are not localized but are in every part of the country. Numerically speaking, Christianity has not made much of an impression on Siam. The Protestant element, many of whom are Chinese or Laos, scarcely number ten thousand out of a population of more than fourteen million. The Roman Catholic group reports a greater number than the Protestants. All Christian denominations together are numerically but a slight percentage of the total population. Although the majority of the people continue to worship along traditional Buddhist lines there is freedom of religious worship.

Many of the civil officials feel that a young man seeking employment should have some religion, whether that religion be Buddhism or not. One may teach and write freely on religious subjects without fear of persecution from either people or government. The general tone of the nation, religiously, is one of tolerance. Religious assembly may be held at any and every time and place. One need but make his purpose clear and he may meet with others for religious purposes undisturbed.

Assembly for other than religious purposes is not easily accomplished. Permission must be asked of the local civil official, and the reasons for assembly set forth. Discussion of such a subject as communism is strictly forbidden. Assemblies of Chinese are suspect by the government. Attempts to set up athletic clubs are closely watched and often call forth adverse newspaper comment. An example of this was an attempt of Chinese at Tung Song to open an athletic club in 1936. They succeeded, but only after eighteen months or more of effort.

A reward was offered in 1932 for the capture and conviction of communists. At that time communistic leaflets were being distributed throughout Bangkok. The Police Department offered five hundred *baht* reward for information that would lead to the arrest and conviction of communists.[1]

Even a prominent leader of the 1932 revolution like Luang Pradist was not allowed to propagate a communistic plan. In order to discourage communism, the Phya Manopakorn Government passed a law against it. The law was an expression of disapproval not only of communism in general but of the economic plan of Luang Pradist Manudharm in particular. When Phya Bahol returned the original People's Party to power again in June, 1933, his first act was to assure the people of Siam that communism would not be permitted. It may be concluded that there is no freedom for communism in Siam.

The newspapers were first officially noticed during the reign of King Vajiravudh, when a law was passed to allow the government to censor the comments of the press on political subjects. King Prajadhipok, during the early years of his reign, ignored the newspapers. After his return from America in October, 1931, he called a press conference and allowed his secretary to describe his trip in America and to outline some future policies for Siam. When the Phya Manopakorn Government closed the People's Assembly a special press conference was held to justify the move to the public.

The Press Act of 1933, which came into effect on May 1st, 1934, was passed to make the newspapers harmless to the government. Section 18, (a) and (c), forbids the press to publish articles which may be detrimental to public order and good morals, or which are aimed against foreign powers which have treaty relations with Siam. Section 26 adds that in time of war, or when there is danger of internal disorder, the government may require all newspapers to submit material for publication to the official censor for his examination. Section 39 says that the Press Officer is empowered to cause to be published in the *Government Gazette* an order prohibiting to be imported or otherwise brought into Siam any printed

[1] *Thai Mai*, December 26th, 1932.

matter or newspaper specified by name in such order. Appropriate fines and punishments are listed to fit the case.

From June 2nd to November 29th, 1932, there were ten occasions on which a newspaper was closed either temporarily or permanently. Two papers were closed for three days, one for ten days, four for twenty days, and three for an indefinite period. Only one of the three was allowed to re-open. One was closed because it printed an article attempting to arouse Chinese hatred for the Japanese. Another was closed because it was unfriendly to Siam.

From May, 1933, to April, 1934, there were seventeen occasions on which the government found it necessary to close a newspaper. Four were closed for three days, one for seven days, and the rest were either closed absolutely or for an indefinite period of time. Three were closed because they were considered unfriendly, destructive of the peace of the country; three because of minor infractions; one for insolence and an unsatisfactory attitude toward the government; one for criticizing the military; one for failing to submit its subject matter for censorship; one for printing censored material; one for failing to submit the original copy for inspection; one for not submitting pictures for censorship; one for a story about the flight of rebels from Hua Hin; one for being in the trio of Siam Free Press papers that aroused the displeasure of the government; and another because its attitude was unsatisfactory. From that time on there were fewer newspapers in trouble with the censor. This was either because they had learned the part of wisdom or because the government had become more lenient. It is generally agreed that the former was the case.

The question of censorship was brought up again in November, 1936, by the *Nation*. It suggested that since the country was quiet and the government well established, there was no longer need for strict supervision of the newspapers. It was suggested that the news reporters be allowed to garner news from outside sources as well as from the Bureau of Censorship. The government refused to allow this.

It may be concluded, then, that Siam has very strict censorship of the Press. There is no freedom of the Press in Siam in the sense that there is freedom of the Press in the United States. All important news is sifted through the government Press Bureau. Not only is it heavily censored, it is often quite late reaching the public.

What is true of the Press is also true of the radio. All speeches over the radio are subject to censorship. Not every speech, however, is actually censored. For instance, a young military officer, Major Prayoon Ehamorn Montri, gave a radio talk on March 24th, 1937, that stirred the nation and caused the government considerable embarrassment. In his speech he made derogatory remarks about the elected membership of the People's Assembly. Nai Thong Indra, an elected member of the assembly, urgently demanded an explanation from the government, but he received no satisfaction.

An interesting subsequent development was that two days later, on March 26th, 1937, Nai Thong Indra and his friends applied for permission to register a political party. This was the first attempt, since the opening days of the constitutional monarchy in 1932, to start a political party. At that earlier date application was made to register a National Party, and permission was refused. Not only so, but the then existing People's Party was required to dissolve as a party and become merely a social club. This was done, it was said, because King Prajadhipok expressed the opinion that the nation was not ready for political parties.

Nai Thong Indra's party was to be called the People's Political Party. Headquarters were to be in Bangkok, with branches throughout the country. His application stirred hopes in other minority groups who wanted political representation upon a definite platform. If Nai Thong Indra's application was granted, then other applications would be sent in at once. By April 9th, 1937, a Labour Party had filed petition to be allowed to organize.

On May 20th, 1937, the Council of Ministers announced that the time was not yet ripe for party politics.[1] The Council thus endorsed the opinions of the Director-General of Police and of the Minister of the Interior.

The conclusion is that Siam does not yet allow free political expression either through the newspapers, the radio, or through political parties.

3. THE DECLINE OF THE NOBILITY

Another development under the constitutional monarchy is the decline of the nobility. Looking back over the history of Siam one

[1] *Siam Chronicle*, May 20th, 1937.

notes the gradual rise and glorification of the noble class. When the Siamese or Thai were still in southern China, in Yunnan Province, the leaders of the people were merely called "Pa Mu" or "Pa Lao", meaning the "father of the group". After they came south into the land that is called Siam today, the Brahman influence began to be felt. Exalted Sanskrit and Pali terms came into vogue. The national leader was called Maharaja or supreme king. Other titles were given royalty, and elegant ceremonies were instituted which elevated the royal family above all the common laws of mankind. In some official documents the name and titles of the king take up the whole first paragraph. Under the Chakri dynasty Siamese royalty reached its highest point. Kingship became divine and was hedged about with taboo. The king acted at times as a priest, at times as a magician, at times as the protector of religion, and always as the divine ruler. H. Quaritch Wales says:

> In Siam today we find the only certain relic of the cult of the Royal God in the symbolism of the Coronation Ceremony by which the Brahman priests call down the spirits of Visnu and Siva to animate the new king; but possibly also in the role played by the king as Siva now or formerly in the Tonsure, Ploughing, and Swinging Ceremonies, and in the Meru and Kailasa mountains used on certain ceremonial occasions. . . . No Buddhist King would have been flattered to have been told that he was the incarnation of a Hindu deity—and nothing more. The conception of the king under Hinayānism is obviously that he is a Bodhisattva or incipient Buddha, or else a Cakravartin (Universal Emperor), and this belief, which is still held by all orthodox Siamese Buddhists, is derived proximately from imitations of the great Sinhalese kings and is strengthened in the minds of the people by the evidences of the popular Indian Jātaka stories.[1]

Taboos around the person of the king show the point to which he has been exalted. His person was taboo, more especially the hair and head. On board the royal barges there were bundles of coco-nuts to be thrown to the king or any member of the royal family who fell into the water either accidentally or if the barge foundered. It was forbidden on pain of death for any person to lay hands on royalty even with the laudable object of saving them from drowning. A well known instance of the operation of this taboo is the death of King Rama V's first Queen, who was drowned in full view of numerous bystanders who dared not save her or her three children.

[1] H. Quaritch Wales, *Siamese State Ceremonies* (London: Stephen Austin & Sons, Ltd., 1931), pp. 31 ff.

It was taboo to look upon the face of the king. Until the days of King Rama IV (Mongkut), it was not permitted to watch a royal procession. People had to take side streets or stay in their houses when royalty was abroad. Anyone meeting a royal procession had to turn his back and fall prostrate upon the ground.

The king was not supposed to touch the ground. He was to be carried through space—even as the sun.

It was taboo to inquire after his health because the people were supposed to be kept in ignorance of such matters.

A practical taboo had to do with the royal food which was touched by no one but a confidential officer who sealed the plates, brought them to the king, and then tasted the food in the royal presence.

It was taboo to spill royal blood. This led to the custom, whenever a member of royalty was to be executed at the King's command, of tying the person in a velvet bag and beating him to death with sandal-wood clubs.

The personal name of the king was taboo. For this reason the king and people of dignity were referred to by titles.

It was not permitted to speak of or to the king with the common language. A high language was evolved to suit the special situation.

Since the establishment of a constitutional monarchy there has been a decline of royal prerogatives, divine kingship, and of the right to exercise any will but the will of the people. The leading members of the royal family were seized or put to flight at the time of the June 1932 Revolution. The king was given an ultimatum. Either he must accept a constitutional form of government, or another monarch would be chosen to replace him. After long drawn-out political disagreement with the government the king did abdicate, and a boy was selected as king. The kingship has become less important to Siam. A monarch is not even required politically as a figurehead, for there is no empire to be held together by sentiment.

The power and prestige of the nobility has waned rapidly. A nobleman was formerly above the law and was responsible only to the king. Thus a nobleman once struck and publicly humiliated a commoner in the railroad station in Bangkok, and the commoner could not retaliate in any way. Today that could not happen. In 1931 Wales wrote:

I think that it has been made quite clear that most of the Siamese State Ceremonies still retain very considerable importance in connection with the maintenance of the social integrity of the State. The chief function now performed by State Ceremonial is the preservation of the popular respect for ancient tradition, particularly with reference to the Absolute Monarchy. The Siamese are as yet quite unsuited to any other form of government, and, were the abolition of the kingship to come about in the near future, the whole social fabric of Siam would undoubtedly collapse like a house of cards. . . . Any attempt to curtail the traditional glamour surrounding the divine kingship is bound to react unfavourably on the established form of government.[1]

It may be seen in the light of what has taken place that Wales' fears were groundless. The people have calmly accepted the new order of things and will probably continue to accept them as long as the rice pots are filled, health is good, desires for pleasure satisfied, and religion is uncensored.

The decline of the nobility has meant a serious loss to Siam in valuable man-power. Many of the most brilliant and best-educated men of the nation are in the noble class. There seems no way to use their abilities under present conditions, since the Constitution expressly forbids their employment in any civil or military position except that of adviser.

Curiously enough, the nobility brought about their own downfall by a generous policy of educating likely youths abroad. These young men studied education, medicine, law, engineering, military techniques, forestry, and other modern subjects. It is these men who were educated by the nobles who now control the country, sit in the seats of government, and gather in the People's Assembly. The new nobility is a class of young intellectuals prepared by the traditional noble class.

Palaces and royal rest houses are no longer reserved for the use of the royal family in many places. Thus in Trang a summer house built for the very occasional use of the king has been turned over to the local municipality for its offices. In Petchaburi a handsome palace, that was lived in but a week and then allowed to stand idle for years, has been turned into an agricultural school. What Siam has she is determined to use. The Phya Thai palace in Bangkok is an army hospital. A school has been opened in the palace grounds at Bang Pa In.

[1] H. Quaritch Wales, *Siamese State Ceremonies* (London: Stephen Austin & Sons, Ltd., 1931), pp. 317, 318.

On March 4th, 1937, the Trang Municipal Assembly held its first meeting of the second period. At the first period there had been but eleven members to sit with the civil officials. This time there were eleven members elected by the people and eleven appointed by the local government. No civil servants sat in the meeting officially. This assembly will continue for four years and then all members will be elective and none appointed. The rights and powers of the people are increasing, while those of the noble class are coming down to meet them on a common level.

4. THE RISE OF THE MILITARY

Another trend, with a political significance, is the increased stress given the military of Siam. The power of the Army and Navy has never been excessive in proportion to the size and population of the country. Siam has been a buffer state between English and French colonies and so has depended on diplomacy rather than force to maintain its independence. The Army and Navy have been an "at large" police force to supplement the efforts of the regular police department. When the People's Party was ready to establish a constitutional monarchy in Siam it had to have the assistance of the military. Since then there has been a determined move to improve the military machine.[1]

The budget from April, 1933, through March, 1934, for the Ministry of Defence, was *baht* 15,051,278. This was an increase over the previous year of about *baht* 3,500,000. The budget from April, 1936, through March, 1937, for the same department, was *baht* 22,300,000. This sum was further supplemented by *baht* 1,000,000 for naval armaments. The budget from April, 1937, through March, 1938, allowed the military *baht* 26,000,000 with an additional million for naval armaments. In four years the military budget had almost doubled.

This military emphasis has met with considerable opposition. The elected representatives of the People's Assembly seemed generally to prefer a heavier expenditure for roads, education, and economic improvements. It was the government that insisted upon enlarging the military budget.

[1] *The Nation*, November 4th, 1938, quotes Luang Pibul, Minister of Defence, as saying that Siam now has over a million soldiers available.

In rate of increase, however, the educational budget has grown more than the military. Thus the educational budget from April, 1933, through March, 1934, was *baht* 3,731,494, which was an increase over the previous year of *baht* 245,088. The same department for the year April, 1936, through March, 1937, was *baht* 11,181,402. The appropriation had been more than trebled in three years. Almost another million *baht* was added to the budget for April, 1937, through March, 1938. Thus in four years the budget of 1934 was quadrupled. Even so, the educational funds are still less than half the amount of the military funds.

Discussion in the People's Assembly brought out the fact that the government considers armaments as of first importance, internal peace second, education third, and economics fourth.

The military emphasis seems out of character. The national character is peaceful and quiet. Many Siamese admit frankly that they are too soft-hearted for war, for the destruction of human life. To many it seems a step backward. However, new times have come to Siam. The country has been placarded with the picture of a soldier shaking his fist in the air. It bears the announcement that the kingdom is home, and the military is the fence about the home.

Seven new torpedo boats and two mine-layers were purchased from Italy and arrived in Siam in 1937. Other ships were being built in Japan to be ready in 1938, about ten in number.

On June 28th, 1934, Luang Pibul Songgram made a radio speech to explain the new stress on things military. He said it was done in order to preserve the independence of the nation. The constitutional monarchy was not inactive, as the absolute monarchy had been, in matters of armament. Later in his speech he assured the nation that the military forces were not the tools of one party or one group, but were the forces of the people of Siam. In answer to the question as to whom the military were going to fight, he said that they were preparing to prevent other countries from bullying or oppressing Siam. If need be, Siam would and could retaliate.

L'Impartial, a French newspaper in Saigon, reviewed the military developments of Siam. It asked the dramatic question:

Is the new Constitutional Government of Siam dreaming the dreams of her ancient kings? To reconstruct her large kingdom of the past ages by annexing the Laos country and part of Cambodia? The giving back to Cambodia of the three provinces of Battambang, Siemreap, and Sisophon in 1907 was a great wound to Siamese self-love.[1]

The government of Siam is in the hands of military men. The Premier from 1933-38 was Phya Bahol Balabayuha, Commander-in-Chief of the Army and idol of the people. Luang Pibul Songgram, Deputy Commander-in-Chief of the Army as well as Minister of Defence, became Premier, succeeding Phya Bahol, on December 15th, 1938. In 1937, the State Council had eleven out of twenty-two members who were military men. In 1938, there were eleven out of twenty-one who were of the military. In 1934, the People's Assembly had fifty-two out of seventy-eight members who were military men or of the police. In 1937, when there were two categories of membership in the Assembly, fifty-three out of the seventy-eight appointed members were military men, while only eight of the seventy-eight elected members were of the military or of the police. It would not be unfair to say that the government has a military emphasis.

After the Prince Bavoradej rebellion, important weapons of war with large stores of ammunition were called in from the provinces to the Bangkok depot. Another major rebellion against the government is virtually impossible. A nation once ruled by a royal family has become a nation ruled by a strong military minority. The change has been radical and yet the people have remained quiet under the change.

According to the Military Service Act every able-bodied man is liable to serve two years with the colours. Generally the young men are made available to either army, navy, or police, according to the need. If it happens, in any given year, that the ranks are already filled, then the annual conscription is not carried out. Before 1932, young men attempted to avoid conscription. Military service held no allure for them. But since then the prestige of the military has risen remarkably. Now that military men have entered politics and have assumed unusual authority, military life has gained new lustre in the eyes of young men.

Conscription, in some cases, has doubtless been detrimental, since it broke in on the educational period and took young men out of school. In general the experience has been helpful. Those who

[1] *L'Impartial*, February 8th, 1937.

have lived in small villages learn for the first time about drill, authority, discipline, care of the body, boiled food, and boiled water.
In a speech over the radio Phya Bahol said:

> We are imparting to the general public the knowledge of military work: for instance, the establishment of the Yuvajon movement, and the various talks given by Military Officers over the radio broadcast weekly.[1]

The Yuvajon is a new youth movement along military lines. It was founded by Luang Pibul Songgram, the Minister of Defence. It had its beginnings in 1935, and by the end of 1937 was known all over Siam.[2] Its object is to train youth in physical culture, military discipline, and organized co-operation. The youths are supplied with uniforms, drill as soldiers, and have occasional reviews by military officers. Its purpose is to instil a military spirit in the young men.

The Yuvajon are of three grades. The first, or practice stage, is for boys above fifteen years of age whose parents are willing to have them trained. The boys must be recommended by their school teachers. The second, or fully trained stage, is for boys in the secondary grades at school. The boys must be at least 145 centimeters tall and have a doctor's certificate for physical fitness. The third, or officers grade, is for students at Chulalongkorn University. Students who leave school may continue in the Yuvajon movement if they desire.

The traditional Buddhist, Siamese spirit is one of peace and quiet. The modern trend is to replace that gentle spirit with military zeal.

5. SIAM'S INTERNATIONAL RELATIONS

Another political trend is seen in Siam's international relations. At the time of the revolution, June 24th, 1932, Siam's chief anxiety was that France or England might send military forces to protect their nationals. Great care was taken not to inconvenience foreigners any more than was absolutely necessary. Guards were thrown around Legations, and in some cases were posted inconspicuously near private houses.

---

[1] Phya Bahol Balabayuha, "Siam's Progress Under the Constitution," *Siam Today,* January, 1937, p. 4.
[2] *The Nation,* November 9th, 1938, reports over ten thousand members in Bangkok and vicinity alone.

After the constitutional monarchy was well established, it began to renew a friendship with Japan. Japanese-Siamese relations had been moderately close in the days of King Phra Narai in the seventeenth century. When Japan withdrew from contact with the world, Japanese-Siamese friendship lapsed for two-and-a-half centuries, but in 1887 Prince Devawongs Varapakorn, then Minister of Foreign Affairs, went to Japan to negotiate a treaty along modern lines. Until after 1932 the friendship had been unobtrusive. The Siamese have ever been excellent politicians, as witnessed by the following paragraph:

> In the Government archives there are memoranda, notes, and other correspondence, showing how the late King Chulalongkorn was able to maintain the independence of the Kingdom in the seventies and eighties of the last century when annexation of territories in Asia and Africa was considered quite legitimate without having reference to equity and justice. Surely these people are not foolish enough to imagine that the present Siamese Government will not take advantage of this information when dealing with foreign powers.[1]

The question is amplified by Baron De Lapomarede:

> Can the Western Powers remain indifferent to the political upheaval of an Eastern State which, with a confidence rare in these distant countries, has unceasingly looked to them for advice? Great Britain, by the quantity and quality of her advisers, by the importance of her school and college students, and by the irresistible attraction which her monarchy holds for the Royal Family and aristocracy of Bangkok, was largely responsible for the intellectual formation of contemporary Siam. . . . America had taken over the medical faculty, France jurisprudence, Germany military science and technique. . . . The Western Powers invested capital in the country, creating banking houses, acquiring real estate. Here also Great Britain holds first place, with two-thirds of the foreign trade. . . . What attitude will New Siam adopt towards the aspiration of the nationalist movement which is becoming general in these sections of the Far East and tending to abolish even the semblance of a European supervision?[2]

The Siamese newspapers began to publish general articles on Japan and its way of life. Thus a Siamese newspaper student, who had gone to Japan to learn the trade, started a series of descriptive articles in the *Nation* for October 6th, 1936. The *Siam Chronicle* for April 4th, 1937, published a special "Siam and Japan Cultural

---

[1] *Bangkok Times*, April 4th, 1934.
[2] Baron De Lapomarede to the *Contemporary Review*, in the *Bangkok Times*, April 4th, 1934.

Mission" number. It described Japanese cultural life, business life, political life, recalled Siam and Japan's historic friendship, and expressed hope for more intimate relations in the future. Such articles have been general in scope but have been powerful in informing the average Siamese as to the position of Japan in the Orient.

In 1933, Siamese dancers and musicians were sent to visit Japan as a gesture of friendship. In March, 1936, Japan answered with an Economic Mission which not only carried on economic discussions but supplied Japanese plays and entertainments of a high order for prominent Siamese families. Boy Scout missions from Japan to Siam and from Siam to Japan were exchanged. The Siam Scouts took an elephant with them as a goodwill gift to the Japanese Scouts.

Trade relations with Japan have grown more important. Thus in 1925 Siam bought five million *baht* worth of goods from Japan. In 1935 Siam spent twenty-seven million *baht* in Japan. In ten years Japan's per cent of the total Siamese imports had gone from 3.41 per cent to 25.56 per cent. But this was not all. Goods consigned from Hongkong and included in imports from there, but whose origin was Japan, amounted to *baht* 1,317,612. Goods consigned from Singapore and included in imports from there, but whose origin was Japan, amounted to *baht* 2,556,473. Combining these figures with the exact figure of direct trade with Japan for the same period of *baht* 27,792,745 yields a grand total of *baht* 31,666,830 of trade with Japan. This gives Japan 29 per cent of the total import trade with all nations of *baht* 108,754,047. The following year from April, 1936, through March, 1937, maintained the high average of giving Japan 28 per cent of the total Siamese import trade. Figures for the year from April, 1937, through March, 1938, are not yet available. A decline in imports from Japan is expected, however, because of the war in China.

To show the shift of Siam's trade to Japan it is worth noticing that before the World War, Great Britain supplied Siam with 93 per cent of the grey shirtings imported. In the year from April, 1935, to May, 1936, no grey shirtings were listed as from the United Kingdom, but Japan shipped grey shirtings to the value of *baht* 1,169,524, or 95 per cent of the total grey shirtings trade, which amounted to *baht* 1,228,252.

Luang Pradist Manudharm, the Minister of Foreign Affairs, remarked on this subject:

> During the past years there has been a marked growth in the industrial connections between Siam and Japan. This progress in industrial and commercial intercourse between the two countries, it must be stressed once more, does not contain the least semblance of a background of political alliance, nor is it capable of having any repercussion whatever on the relations of Siam with other foreign nations.[1]

In 1936, Siam's treaties with foreign powers were allowed to expire, and the Minister of Foreign Affairs proceeded to negotiate new treaties. Most of the treaties, by 1937, had been operative for ten years. Siam felt that certain provisions restricted her jurisdictional and fiscal autonomy and so sought revised treaties. In November and December of 1937, treaties with England, France, Germany, Italy, and America were signed which granted Siam full and equal rights as an independent nation. France and England both relinquished all special privileges.

Kimpei Sheba, commenting on Siam's treaty with Japan which was signed in March, 1938, says that it grants Japanese subjects full liberty to reside in Siam in all respects on the same footing as native subjects. They are permitted, on the same footing as Siamese, to engage in religious, educational, and charitable work, and are permitted to own, lease, and occupy houses, factories, warehouses and shops, and to lease land for residential, commercial, industrial, religious, and other lawful purposes in the same manner as natives.[2]

Siam's friendship with Japan was shown in 1933, when she did not vote in the League of Nations to condemn Japan for the "Manchurian incident".

For several generations Siam has shown itself capable in political affairs. It knows how to balance powers. The new drift toward Japan merely means that there is a new imperialistically-minded power in the Orient which needs to be considered in order to maintain Siamese independence.

---

[1] Luang Pradist Manudharm, "Siam's Foreign Policy," *Siam Today*, July, 1936, p. 11.
[2] *Chicago Tribune*, March 10th, 1938.

CHAPTER III

ECONOMIC TRENDS

1. THE NEW ECOMOMIC POLICY

IN THE orginal platform of the People's Party, a platform that was affirmed and re-affirmed by the People's Assembly, was the statement that "a national economic policy must be drawn up to guarantee remunerative work to everyone." Luang Pradist Manudharm is generally believed to have been the one who formulated the purposes of the People's Party and drew up the original platform. By March, 1933, he had presented a plan which was intended to incorporate the economic principle expressed above. The government interpreted his plan to nationalize land, industry, capital and labour, as communistic in intent, and consequently rejected it.

Luang Pradist regarded his plan as a practical method of social insurance. He felt that the government should guarantee the welfare of every citizen. Thus far he expressed the sentiment of the constitutional government which followed the modern economic trend of making the government responsible for the well-being of the people. Luang Pradist and the government disagreed on the methods to be used. According to Luang Pradist the government was to be landlord of all productive lands. It was to be the banker for financing the projects of the peasants.

The government, after rejecting Luang Pradist's plan, formulated a plan of its own which was presented tentatively to the public in May, 1933. At that time the establishment of the new Ministry of Economic Affairs was announced. The Phya Manopakorn government which was in power was dissolved by military action the following month. However, on July 27th, 1933, the People's Assembly passed a vote of approval on the major acts of the Manopakorn government, and on September 20th, 1933, the Ministry of Economic Affairs outlined its programme for the welfare of the people as follows:

1. To lay down a financial policy which will enable the government to secure funds necessary for the general economic development of the country.

2. To consider the expediency of establishing an independent Currency Board whose function would be to manage the currency of the country.

3. To improve communications, i.e.
    a. To accelerate the work in connection with railways, posts, telegraphs, and telephones according to the programme as already laid down by the Ministry concerned.
    b. To construct a system of roads whereby eventually no part of the country will remain isolated from lack of communications, and which will ensure access to markets for economic products of the country.
    c. To make a survey of the internal waterways of the Kingdom and to plan a policy for their development. This policy will include the maintenance in good condition of canals at present navigable, the rendering navigable of canals now out of use where this is considered economically desirable, and will probably also entail the cutting of new canals.
    d. To develop air transport.

4. To substitute a more efficient system for the present uneconomical handling of imports and exports.

5. To carry out a survey of the natural resources of the country, agricultural, mineral, aquatic, etc., with a view to their exploitation and conservation.

6. To extend scientific researches in order to encourage the production of various kinds of goods.

7. To consider ways and means of increasing and improving facilities offered by the Savings Bank System and in addition to discover any other means whereby a habit of thrift may be encouraged among the people and a convenient safe custody provided for their surplus income.

8. To provide opportunities for those interested in commerce and industry to study and obtain practical experience in the subject in which they are interested: in other words to encourage apprenticeship.

9. To encourage the formation of a Siamese Chamber of Commerce.

Assistance should be given to agriculture as follows:

1. To consider ways and means of providing agricultural credit and in particular to extend the system of Co-operative Credit Societies, to establish silos for the storage of paddy, to make advances on the paddy so stored, and finally to establish a Central Agricultural Credit Institution.

2. To consider ways and means whereby agriculturalists who do not own land may acquire possession of land, and in particular to consider whether the attainment of this end may be facilitated by the establishment of Co-operative Land Purchasing Societies.

3. To extend agricultural experimental stations in order:
    a. To discover means of lowering the costs of production.
    b. To improve the quality of agricultural produce.

c. To disseminate among technical primary schools knowledge gained from such experiments.
   d. To encourage the cultivation of other crops after the rice-planting season, so as to provide employment for the farmers throughout the year.
4. To extend the irrigation system to assist agriculture.
5. To assist those who desire to take up agriculture but find themselves handicapped by the lack of lands or knowledge by
   a. Engaging experts to make a survey of vacant lands with a view to advising the government of the suitability of the different soils for crop-raising.
   b. Considering on the basis of the foregoing survey, the expediency of undertaking schemes of colonization.
   c. Giving any necessary advice.
6. To encourage the cultivation of other crops besides rice.

There are as yet only a few industries in Siam. Any persons desiring to set up an industry will be assisted as follows:

1. An adequate protection in respect of patents, trademarks, designs, samples, models, copyrights, and similar matters.
2. Any industry which the government desires to create, but which is too big an undertaking for private persons, shall be started by the government in the form of a public corporation, having private individuals as shareholders and conducted semi-officially.
3. To promulgate a law on the employment of labour with reference to the hours of work, health, and safety of employees. In drafting such a law due regard will be paid to the mutual interests of both the employers and the employees.

For commerce it is proposed:

1. To establish silos for the storage of paddy, and other agricultural produce, and to consider ways and means of arriving at a better organization of the trade in these commodities.
2. To find markets abroad for Siamese goods.
3. To appoint trade-agents in the interior of Siam and in foreign countries where it appears that such agents can further Siamese trade, to take measures for the prevention of the adulteration of Siamese products and for the advertising of Siam and Siamese trade.
4. To encourage the formation of Siamese export, import, transport, and insurance companies.[1]

It was agreed that the above programme should be carried out gradually. The following projects were selected from the plan to be begun at once:
   1. Extension of the Co-operative Credit Movement.

[1] *Daily Mail*, September 20th, 1933.

2. Investigations into the possibilities of forming Co-operative Land-Purchasing Societies.

3. Extension and co-ordination of means of transport.

4. Establishment of silos, and of means for the transportation of paddy.

5. Investigation of the possibilities of establishing silos for other agricultural produce.

6. Encouragement of savings.

7. Survey of foreign markets for Siamese goods, with appointment of trade-agents in selected centres.

8. Investigation of ways and means of forming a Central Agricultural Credit Institution.

9. Extension of agricultural experimental stations.

10. Investigations tending toward the drawing up of a programme of irrigation works in agricultural areas outside the present irrigation system, and the devising of a scheme for the greater utilization of the present irrigation works by building field-bunds in certain districts.

11. Engagement of an expert to make a survey of undeveloped areas, which are abundant, with a view to advising the government as to the suitability of the soil for various crops.

These projects were considered fundamental to the economic welfare of the majority of the people. The stress, as can be seen at once, was upon agriculture, which is the most important occupation of the nation.

2. THE LOSS OF CAPITAL FUNDS

One of the primary objectives of the plan was to provide for a means of saving for the people generally. The prosperity of a nation depends not so much on the amount of money on hand as on the speed of turnover. When large capital funds are sent abroad, the local turnover of money is decelerated. And again when large sums are hoarded the result is the same. Both things had happened in Siam. The upper classes had sent money abroad. The lower classes had buried it in the ground and converted it into jewelry.

Before the 1932 revolution, wealthy princes who realized that there was to be political trouble, prepared themselves for it by locating adequate funds in foreign countries. Common gossip gives the foreign deposits at many millions of pounds sterling. Several of the leading families are living abroad. They seem to be well provided with money. A few of the many known to have investments abroad are King Ananda, whose father was a wealthy man well known for his charities; Prince Nagor Svarga, who is now residing in Sumatra; Prince Purachatra, who, until his death recently, lived in Singapore; Prince Damrong in Penang; and Prince Chula, who has long lived in England. The extent of the investments abroad of King Prajadhipok, who is now living in England, is unknown to the public, but it must be considerable if one may judge from his generosity to relatives to whom he sends monthly aid. The draining away of such capital funds must of necessity have affected the active wealth of the nation.

Another loss of capital funds is caused by the hoarding of money, which the poorer people bury in the ground or convert into jewelry. The country has lacked a proper banking and savings account system. People who saved money had no place of security in which to store it. Many changed their money into silver ticals and buried them in tight cans. When the depression reached Siam some of these wished to cash in on their savings. There was heavy loss, however, because the authorities who inspected the money refused many of the ticals which had been badly corroded or disfigured. Out of a hundred ticals sometimes only ten or twenty were acceptable. Not more than one in three of the buried ticals was spendable in the market places.

Even though the government has allowed the Post Office Department in certain selected centres to accept money for deposit, the burying and hiding of money continues. There is widespread ignorance about the savings system even in the limited areas where it applies. How much money the average family hides away may be shown by the following example.

A rubber planter reported a robbery to the police. The family was apparently poor, certainly no more wealthy than any of the neighbours. Total income was derived from about two thousand rubber trees, only six hundred of which were being cut. It was reported that a thousand ticals worth of gold and silver had been stolen from a place in the roof where it had been hidden. A few days later the planter approached the owner of a large steel safe and asked permission to store two thousand ticals in bills there.

He was afraid that they would be stolen too. The privilege was granted for a short time, but the planter was advised to deposit his money with the Postal Savings Department. The deposit was made. It was the first deposit that had ever been made from that village and, as such, aroused considerable interest. A year passed by and the depositor received interest on the money. The idea of receiving interest delighted and amused the planter, who had expected to be required to pay for the service. It was a novel thought to him that the government would not only guard his money for him but would pay him for the privilege. When he was assured that after a year his first deposit was safe and that he was drawing interest on it, he announced that he had more buried money for deposit. This case is typical of hundreds of thousands of others who have hidden and hoarded their savings.

It is usual for a family to invest several hundred ticals in gold rings, buttons, chains, bracelets, and belts. A fairly well dressed woman in south Siam may be assayed at a couple of hundred ticals in jewelry. Women who prefer the modern ornaments frequently turn to diamonds and other precious or semi-precious stones for investment. In any case such a procedure means a frozen credit that brings interest neither to the nation nor to the individual. The government is making a serious effort to draw frozen assets back into circulation. When more money is in circulation the turnover will be more rapid, more business can be done, and more people will be economically secure. In passing, it should be said that the export of capital funds to China by Chinese immigrants living and working in Siam is another factor in the draining away of Siam's monetary resources. The Financial Adviser's report on the Budget for 1936-37 clearly indicates that these funds are far from negligible. He says:

An eminent Chinese banker congratulated his countrymen in 1932 on the fact that all through the depression Chinese immigrants into Siam had not diminished the scale of their remittances home, which he placed at an aggregate of $50 million per annum, a sum equal at the then rate of exchange to no less than *baht* 37 million. It is possible that this was an overestimation, and there are no means available in Siam of checking the calculation: but the statement is probably not far short of the truth. It is no secret that the Siamese himself does not take kindly to commerce, and most of the internal, and practically all of the external trade is in foreign hands. The trouble lies in the fact that nearly all the profits of internal trade are remitted and not retained in the country. They form part of the invisible imports. Siam has a favourable balance of indebtedness on paper and, in so far as this is not liquidated by the acquisition of foreign credit balances on national account, it is cleared by other invisible imports such as remittances of profits earned by entities carrying on business in Siam, payments for freight and insurance, and private remittances, these last mainly for account of Chinese immigrants to their families in China.

A reference to the table on page 12 will show that, if remittances to China were no more than *baht* 30 millions per annum, the surplus left available for the satisfaction of the other invisible imports amounted to only *baht* 8½ millions in B.E. 2476, while last year the balance was definitely negative. It was only in B.E. 2477, when the surplus after allowing for remittances to China was some 27 millions, that there was any room for hoping that some acquisition of foreign credit balances on national account had taken place, and reference to the former Financial Adviser's reports will show that B.E. 2475 was the only year of the preceding five years when the balance was not in reality a negative one. These facts show how little the national wealth can be growing and, as most of the country's commerce is in foreign hands, a larger favourable trade balance in practice simply means larger remittances abroad: little of the increased wealth stays at the country's disposal.

A point of considerable importance is the rise last year in the total payment abroad on the Government's account, which was mainly due to purchases of naval and military armament.

Siam's equilibrium is delicately poised and sight should never be lost of the Chinese remittance factor. It is therefore all the more essential to move very circumspectly in such matters as armament programmes, machinery orders, etc., etc., which can only be satisfied by payments out of the country; i.e. by putting an extra strain on the balance of indebtedness. A poor rice harvest, it is well known by experience, is quite sufficient to have a very detrimental effect on the balance of trade and on the State revenues: if this effect be intensified by imprudent previous Government commitments for foreign purchases, the country may find itself involved in serious financial difficulties with far-reaching and embarrassing consequences.

Careful attention should be devoted to any measure or series of measures the object of which is the retention of a larger share of the country's earnings; for attainment of this object would result in the building up of those resources of development which are today so strikingly non-existent.

Under existing legislation it is impossible for the government to stop the movement of money abroad. It has attempted to limit collections among Chinese for war purposes. To some extent investments abroad by Siamese are balanced by foreign investments in Siam. Accurate figures, however, are not available.

The high price paid for gold in the United States has resulted in the conversion of much jewelry into cash. Since the government has recalled all silver ticals and replaced them with paper bills, which, if buried, are quickly consumed by termites, the need for adequate savings facilities is acute. The need, coupled with the educational activities of the Postal Savings Department, it is to be hoped, will result in heavy deposits, and thus release much frozen capital.

3. THE MEANS EMPLOYED TO REGULATE AND ENCOURAGE TRADE

Along with the government's attempt to release capital funds is its interest in the encouragement of trade, the protection of trade, and intelligent planning for the future. Private organizations are also active in the field of trade stimulation. The Bangkok International Chamber of Commerce is one of these. It represents the interests of the European and American firms that do business in Siam. The Chinese tradesmen are represented by the Chinese Chamber of Commerce. The Chinese are the petty tradesmen of the nation. The wealth of the country passes through their hands in the everyday purchases of necessities and luxuries. The Chinese are also the middlemen between the European firms and the Siamese, thus enhancing their position in trade.

In July, 1934, the Siamese Chamber of Commerce had its first formal meeting and was opened by the State Councillor in charge of the Ministry of Economic Affairs. Previously the Siamese had no need for a Chamber of Commerce because the Siamese were not in trade. They were either agriculturists or government employees and officials. Only within the last decade have Siamese made a serious effort to enter commerce and trade. They are learning business methods, typing, shorthand, book-keeping, carpentry, black-smithy, automobile repair, and other similar activities.

The government has encouraged trade and has attempted to protect it from sharp practices. Weights and measures are regulated by law. There is also legislation guaranteeing protection of copyright. Hair tonics, cigarettes and other articles of trade which have been misrepresented have been forced to be withdrawn from the market. The companies that have perpetrated the fraud have been required to make up all financial losses suffered by other

ECONOMIC TRENDS 69

firms as a result of the fraud and to make newspaper confession of the misrepresentation.[1]

In order to establish a basis for intelligent social and economic planning, a census of the nation was taken on March 27th, 1937. It was planned to secure figures showing the birth rate, the death rate, the financial status of the family, the numbers of foreign nationals in the country, the numbers of adherents of the various religions, the extent of education, the numbers of persons employed in the different trades and their places of employment, the extent of unemployment, and the numbers of the physically incapable such as the deaf, dumb, or blind. These figures are to form a basis for future planning for the welfare of the people.

Certain significant figures are already available. H.S.H. Prince Vivadhana Jaya, Director-General of the Department of Customs, gives the following figures to show the progress of Siam financially:[2]

YEAR	GOVERNMENT REVENUE baht	GOVERNMENT EXPENDITURE baht
1929-30	107,117,934	107,102,488
1930-31	96,322,219	96,304,915
1931-32	78,948,233	87,482,123
1932-33	79,651,369	70,232,969
1933-34	83,694,195	72,680,757
1934-35	92,801,280	75,487,886
1935-36	94,147,491	84,585,008

For the year 1936-37, the estimated income was *baht* 101,042,035. During the year business improved and the total income was finally estimated at *baht* 107.2 millions as over against an estimated expenditure of *baht* 111.8 millions. The deficit was covered by an existing balance. In the year 1937-38 the newly established municipalities had to be provided for, but even so the estimated income was *baht* 104.8 millions for national expense.

It is significant that when Siam made a change to a constitutional form of government its finances were at a low ebb. Fortunately the new government began its life at the moment when national revenue started to increase. This made the new government look very successful to the people.

[1] Appendix.
[2] Vivadhana Jaya, "Siam's National Finances," *Siam Today*, July 1936, p. 17.

There are no authoritative figures available for the value of internal trade, so that it is necessary to use government revenue and the value of exports and imports as some sort of an approximate index of business conditions. Siam is fortunate in that its exports maintain a safe balance over imports as shown by the following figures:[1]

YEAR	IMPORTS baht	EXPORTS baht
1932-33	89,497,423	152,522,494
1933-34	92,963,000	144,079,000
1934-35	101,726,721	172,594,870
1935-36	108,754,047	158,218,323
1936-37	110,043,648	184,361,153

4. TIN, RUBBER, TEAK, AND RICE

In considering the specific products which constitute Siam's internal sources of wealth as well as the large body of her exports, one must include rice, tin, rubber, teak, vegetables, and fish. Her imports, broadly speaking, are manufactured goods. One of the important exports is tin ore. *The Directory for Bangkok and Siam* offers the following information:

> The mineral resources of Siam are extensive and varied, and embrace Cassterite (tin ore), Wolfram, Scheelite (Tungsten ores), Antimony, Copper, Coal, Gold, Iron, Silver, Lead, Molybdenum, Manganese, Zinc, Rubies, Sapphires, and Zircons.
>
> Of these minerals, however, only Tin, Wolfram, and Scheelite have to date been mined on a commercial basis, but gold is now also being profitably produced in the Pattani province. . . . Today there are about 38 dredges operating in Siam, and several more areas ready for equipment when permission is granted. . . .
>
> As no smelting works at present exist in Siam, all Tin ore won in the country is exported in the form of ore concentrates and is shipped to Penang or Singapore. . . .
>
> There are some 44 foreign tin mining companies registered in Siam, but these represent only about ten per cent of the mining community of the country. Most of the holdings consist of small areas poorly equipped from lack of capital and worked without much thought of technicalities.[2]

---

[1] *Annual Statement of the Foreign Trade and Navigation of the Kingdom of Siam* (Bangkok: Department of His Majesty's Customs), 1932-1937.

[2] *The Directory for Bangkok and Siam* (Bangkok: The Bangkok Times Press, Ltd., 1936-1937), pp. 221-225.

Tin mining affects the prosperity of south Siam more than any other region. Mines are found from Renong to the Malay border on the west coast, and from Chumpon to the Malay border on the east coast. The government limits tin production according to the quota allowed by international agreement. The present quota of 18,500 tons has been granted for five years from January 1st, 1937. Siam did very well for herself by obtaining so large an allowance. Her previous quota was only 9,800 tons.

The government taxes the tin industry for revenue. Taxes are laid not only on the tin exported but on the machinery that is brought in to dig the tin.

The value of the tin exported has risen steadily from *baht* 14.3 millions in 1932-33 to *baht* 29.8 millions in 1936-37. The industry is in a secure position financially.

The mining centres transform sleepy village life. A mine uses the labour of hundreds of men who, as a result, have money to spend. Retail shops are opened, houses are built, roads are constructed, automobiles are bought, and bus lines are started wherever a tin mine begins operations.

It is generally agreed that tin mining is bad for agriculture since it destroys the top soil. Many of the mines have had to reimburse peasants who claimed that their lands were ruined by tailings from the dredges. That mining to some extent destroys fields cannot be denied. However, an experiment was made by one miner who set out a small field of rice directly on the mine tailings. Without any addition of special fertilizer he grew a satisfactory crop of rice. This would seem to indicate that something could be done to reclaim land destroyed by dredges if the need for land became acute, at present a very remote possibility.

Some Siamese have opposed tin mining because most of the miners are European, Chinese, Malay, or Indian. The feeling is that the industry should be in the hands of Siamese labour. However that may be, the miners live in Siam, spend their money in Siam, and pay taxes in Siam. They supply the money, energy, and technical ability for an important industry. Tin is second only to rice in its importance as an export. It has proved to be a boon not only because of the income it provides the government in taxes, but because of the wealth it creates in the local communities. The Premier, Phya Bahol Balabayuha, on a trip through the southern provinces in 1936, remarked that the mining districts were economically secure, and further that the government need feel no anxiety for their continued prosperity.

Another valuable export is rubber. It is a comparatively recent source of wealth in Siam. Twenty-five years ago Trang Province was noted for its pepper gardens. Now, scarcely a pepper garden can be found. The pepper has all been dug out and rubber planted. Rubber became popular during the World War when prices soared. After the war the price decreased from over *baht* two per pound to a few *stangs* per pound. Communities that had been enriched by rubber had difficulty in making an ordinary living. Children were withdrawn from school. Medical care was sought only in dire extremity. More people turned to thievery and prostitution.

Rubber struck its lowest point in the year 1932-33 when the total value of rubber exported was only *baht* 396,692. The price was so low that few people cared to cut rubber at all. The price began gradually to rise so that the following year of 1933-34 saw the export of rubber to the value of *baht* 2,359,923. The total value trebled itself in 1934-35. In 1935-36 it rose another 50 per cent. The latest available figures giving the total for 1936-37 show a value of *baht* 23,536,347 for the rubber crop. Prosperity has returned to the rubber planting districts of Siam. These are all in south Siam and are coincident with the tin mining districts.

There are only a few large rubber plantations. The business is in the hands of the small planter who cuts two or three thousand trees and has an income, in good times, of from *baht* three to six per day during the cutting season. Some few rubber estates cut ten thousand or more trees, but they are the exceptions.

One important aspect of the rubber business has been its attraction for immigrant Chinese, who come into the country by the thousands for the express purpose of planting rubber. In many instances they homestead jungle areas, which they clear and plant. The Siamese are rarely found on rubber estates. Thus along the road from Kuan Niang to Satul there are many small estates owned and operated by Chinese who have come from Sitiawan and other Malayan cities. The Chinese have also settled along the railroad from Haad Yie to Bandon and have turned the country side into a forest of rubber trees. New towns have come to life, schools have been opened, stores and shops built, and medical centres have been made available.

The Chinese have also done some rubber planting in the Pattani area. However, the rubber cutter and the small estate owner is usually the Malay in that district.

James M. Andrews says of rubber:

> The farmer seems to produce very little rubber even though experience has shown that rubber plantations can be made decidedly profitable in south Siam. We need not be surprised that the people of the South derive little income from rubber if we remember that the great majority of them are not at all disposed to engage in energetic work. It is likely that a very large number of rubber trees in south Siam are untapped. . . . The world market has been glutted with rubber in the past few years and we may doubt if it will ever again pay as much for rubber as it has in the past. In addition to this is the fact that isoprene derivatives and other synthetic substitutes for rubber can now be produced almost as cheaply as natural rubber can be bought in the countries which make most use of this commodity. For many purposes the substitutes are better than the real thing, and there is every reason to believe that they will in future come into much wider use. If this be so there is little use in attempting to increase the rubber production of Siam.[1]

Mr. Andrews' comment was made during a period of financial depression in the light of the general agricultural income of the average Siamese. The rubber business is largely in the hands of the Chinese and the Malay. Rubber is of vital importance to the economic welfare of the nation and to the progressive modernizing of rural south Siam, for rubber is exceeded only by tin and rice in its value as an export.

Teak wood is a product of north Siam and may be regarded as a staple export, being fourth in export value. For the five years preceding the year 1935-36 the average value of teak exported was *baht* 4,435,541. The following year the export value advanced to the high mark of *baht* 8,651,730. The general upward trend of prices has included teak.

Andrews, in his economic survey, ignored teak, not only because it was outside of his particular interest in agriculture but because he probably decided that it had little influence on the income of the average Siamese. But teak contributes regularly to the national budget. Furthermore, the *baht* eight million or so that is derived from the sale of teak is largely spent in Siam and must be regarded as a stimulant to trade and commerce. Most of the large teak

[1] James M. Andrews, *Siam, Second Economic Survey* (Bangkok: The Bangkok Times Press, Ltd., 1935), pp. 28, 45.

companies have been owned and operated by Europeans. However, the present trend is away from foreign controlled companies. The government is not renewing the forest leases of the European companies. This policy will result in throwing the teak trade into Siamese hands. Probably the government itself will control and operate the logging enterprises of the future.

Rice is the principal product of Siam because it is the staple food as well as the most valuable export. For the five year period ending with 1935-36 the average export value of rice was *baht* 88,788,273. The value for 1936-37 was *baht* 95,944,444. It exceeded the export value of tin, which was second, by more than three hundred per cent.

Siamese rice leads the world in quality. In 1933 the announcement was made:

> Siam wins eleven of twenty prizes for rice at World Grain Exhibit in Canada. Following the receipt of news here that Siamese rice won the first, second, and third prizes as well as eight other awards. . . .[1]

Siam has a product of which it may well be proud. Unfortunately Siamese rice has been discredited by dealers who mix it with inferior varieties and sell it as Siamese rice. Consequently it has sometimes failed to bring the price that it deserves.

James M. Andrews says:

> Over 80 per cent of the population of Siam, and probably an even greater percentage of the utilized land of the nation, are engaged in agricultural productivity. Not all of the crops raised are sold, but farming and its allied activities form the direct source of most of the people's income and the ultimate source of most of the nation's revenue.[2]

On later pages he shows that the greatest benefit which the farmer derives from the soil is the food with which to feed his family and himself. In most parts of Siam little more is raised than is needed for home consumption. The only definite figures available to show the value of the crop are those which refer to cash or commodities which the farmer obtained by selling a part of his produce. The value of crops consumed is often higher than the value of crops sold.

[1] *Daily Mail*, August 4th, 1933.
[2] James M. Andrews, *Siam, Second Economic Survey* (Bangkok: The Bangkok Times Press, Ltd., 1935), p. 1, ff.

Andrews recommended that the farmers be instructed in modern farming methods. He also urged that the port of Bangkok be dredged so that large ships can enter. A rice exchange would thus be possible and the distribution of Siamese rice could be undertaken by Siamese. He also recommended that the Co-operative Society be encouraged.

The Co-operative Society was an answer to the need of the peasant for money to finance the growing of rice. In a self-contained economy where rice is grown for home consumption only, there is no need for a large working capital. But, since Siam was opened to foreign trade after the middle of the nineteenth century, rice has been grown for export as well. The export trade developed until there was an annual shipment of about a million tons of rice. Most of the rice for export is grown in the central area of Siam.

For a time the rice growers turned to private money-lenders for the needed capital. The results were disastrous for the peasant, who frequently lost his land or went heavily into debt. In 1916 the government made an arrangement by which the Siam Commercial Bank advanced credit up to the amount of *baht* 300,000 to the rice growers' organizations. The money was to be used to pay off debts, buy land, and purchase efficient implements. The members of each society were made mutually responsible for one another. Requirements of the society were that all of the members of a society live in the same village, know one another well, be persons of good reputation, and have some members who were able to read and write.

By 1933 the working capital of the societies had been increased to *baht* 1,500,000. At the beginning of the year 1935, the working capital had increased to *baht* 2,900,000. At that time there were 440 societies with a membership of 6,398. The movement has been encouraged more each year as its value was proved. Thus, for the Siamese year 1936-37 there were 208 new societies started with 2,916 members. The average loan per member was *baht* 386.

The practical educational value of the co-operative society idea cannot be overestimated. The farmers themselves are taught to keep accounts correctly. They acquire a practical knowledge of economic transactions and learn the value of united and co-operative action.

5. OTHER SOURCES OF INCOME

After the rice harvest is over the farmers often turn to vegetable gardening. A vegetable crop requires much hard labour, for it must be watered daily. Pests must be fought. Spraying apparatus is employed where the farmer is educated to its use and value. Vegetables are the second chief source of income for the average Siamese, who feeds his family from the garden and sells the excess.

The third chief source of income of the farmer is fruit. Bananas, sugar cane, mangoes, maprangs, and rambutans sell well. Other important products are the jackfruit, papaya, sera leaf, coco-nut, betel-nut and lamut. Tobacco, cotton and silk are raised, but have not yet become important money producers.

Fishing provides an important part of the income for the average Siamese, not in terms of cash received, but of food provided. At certain times of the year great crowds of people appear with fish baskets or traps at the edge of small ponds. If the pond is not too deep they line up and march across it, driving and catching the fish as they go. Small streams are closed at intervals with fish traps. The larger streams have traps along the shore at likely places.

Much fishing is done in the rice fields where the water is only four or five inches deep. It is difficult to see how the fish get into the fields, but they are there in great numbers. If the fields happen to be flooded while the rice is growing, the fish do much damage to the growing rice, which they eat.

More important efforts are made at fishing in the sea. A motor-boat trip along the coast is impressive because of the miles of fish traps that are set up parallel to the shore.

Siamese eat fish every day and from it derive the main protein element of their diet, which consists largely of rice, fish, and curry. The people would suffer if deprived of fish.

A farmer's wealth is shown by the number of his work animals. The more fields one has the more cattle one needs for work. When financial depression comes the animals are usually the first things sold to balance the family budget. In the south, the bullock is raised to be a fighting animal. Weekly bullfights produce income for the local government through a tax on spectators, which is collected as an admission charge. The cows are seldom if ever used for dairy purposes. Nor is the milk of the buffalo used. The average cow's udder is too small for the volume production of milk. Occasionally some progressive Siamese has attempted to start a dairy farm with imported cattle. There has been very little success.

Cattle are used either as work animals or are slaughtered for local consumption. The export of live buffalo and bullocks seldom exceeds a value of *baht* 100,000 a year.

Tobacco is a crop of growing importance in a number of districts in north Siam. The large tobacco importers are encouraging the production of native tobacco for the cheaper brands of cigarettes. They are making a gift of good seeds and plants to prospective growers, while at the same time offering to buy the crop produced. In 1937, the Department of Agriculture and Fisheries announced that tobacco growing on a large scale would be promoted and that an experimental station would be set up immediately. At the same time it was announced that cotton growing and poultry raising also would be encouraged.

6. COMMERCE AND TRADE

Turning now to commerce, it is interesting to discover that it is a field which the Siamese are only beginning to invade, although the government is doing much to induce Siamese labour and capital to enter new types of employment. Foreign trade, the most important business of the nation, is not in the hands of Siamese at all. The firms which handle the business are Chinese, European, Indian, and Japanese.

The small amount of trade that is done by Siamese is handled almost entirely by the women. Women of the rural areas go to market several times a week. They take such things as rice, fish, fruits, and vegetables, and they bring home those supplies which the household cannot produce. Only rarely do Siamese open stores for retail trade. The last decade has seen more Siamese enter into retail trade than entered it in the previous century. The Siamese is traditionally a rice grower or a government official. Although many well-educated Siamese have studied the theory of business and trade, or have studied the intricacies of some particular business, they lack practical experience.

The government is anxious to draw more Siamese into trade.

This trend is shown by the encouragement given vocational schools or vocational departments in regular schools. In an attempt to use the talent trained in the vocational schools the government itself is going into business. The railroad system shows the possibilities of a government conducted project. It has been a financial asset and has used a great deal of Siamese labour.

For the year 1937-38 the government plans to spend *baht* 1.2 millions for the development of the sugar industry. On April 12th, 1937, the corner stone of a new sugar factory was laid. The factory is located at Lampang in north Siam. At present, Siam imports annually from four to six million *baht* worth of sugar. An experimental farm has been started in conjunction with the factory in order to improve the sugar crop. The factory running at capacity can produce only about 25 per cent of the amount of sugar needed. The plan calls for the use of Siamese labour and the encouragement of investment of private capital in the sugar industry.

For the same year the government plans to spend about *baht* 800,000 in the development of the paper industry. A factory at Kanchanaburi was nearing completion in May, 1937. This factory is expected to produce ten tons of paper daily. Here, too, the Siamese will be encouraged to enter trade.

Other government projects are the development of home industries, of silk-worm culture, and of the cotton industry. Considering the cotton industry statistically, government encouragement is seen to be of substantial value. In the Siamese year 1933-34 raw cotton was exported to the value of *baht* 9,039. In 1934-35 the value rose to *baht* 15,157. In 1935-36 it rose to the unexpected height of *baht* 152,139. In 1936-37 it almost doubled again, and amounted to the sum of *baht* 242,450. If this rate of growth is maintained for a few years, cotton may become an important industry, not only for the national income, but for the peasant grower and for the Siamese business men that will be required. The Siamese realize the need for their participation in the commercial life of the nation.

To facilitate internal trade the government has drawn up a roads programme which, when finished, will equip Siam with a net-work of highways. The time needed to complete the system is from fifteen to twenty years. At present, large sections of the country are remote simply because communications are exceedingly poor.

To facilitate international trade and to make it possible for

ECONOMIC TRENDS

Siamese to have charge of the export of rice, a programme has been accepted for the eventual construction of a modern port at Bangkok. At present only small ships can cross the bar. Consequently large shipments of rice are made to Singapore and Hongkong, where Chinese middlemen prepare the rice for foreign shipment. In April, 1937, the newspapers reported that port construction would begin with the erection of wharves, warehouses, and other necessary port equipment. It was planned to dredge the bar later.

The various aspects of the government's planning for commerce and trade, as discussed above, have in view a common purpose, the economic betterment of the masses of the people whose financial status is poorer than the condition of the country seems to warrant. In order to show the financial standing of the average Siamese peasant and of the civil official who represents the favoured minority, two sample budgets are shown.

INCOME

	Baht
Salary per month	120.00
Saved from previous month	20.00
Total	140.00

EXPENDITURE

	Baht
Servants	8.00
Food	30.00
Rice and charcoal	8.00
Water	3.00
Electricity	4.00
Miscellaneous for house	10.00
Clothing (for two children)	4.50
Clothing	10.00
Theatre once a week	8.00
Total	85.50

The above budget was presented by a Siamese daily newspaper as the budget of an average Bangkok Siamese family.[1] Following is the annual budget of an average farmer in central Siam as worked out by James M. Andrews:[2]

[1] *Nation*, November 22nd, 1936.
[2] James M. Andrews, *Siam, Second Economic Survey* (Bangkok: The Bangkok Times Press, Ltd., 1935), p. 13.

Income

	Baht	Baht
Annual income (earnings) received from		
Crops	105.47	
Fishing	2.55	
Animals	1.85	
Land rentals	8.99	
Building rentals	2.44	
Handicrafts	34.09	
Labour	8.42	
Trading	11.97	
Professions	1.26	
Government pay	2.59	
Interest on loans	4.93	
All other	0.00	
Total	184.56	184.56
Capital income (liquidation) from sale of		
Land	14.20	
Buildings	1.41	
Animals	9.51	
Gold and silver	10.53	
Other capital goods	10.06	
Total	45.71	45.71
Loan reduction (repayments on loans)		19.42
Debt increase (money borrowed)		37.72
Extraordinary income (gifts, gambling gains)		4.88
Total Income		292.29

Expenditure

	Baht	Baht
Annual expenditure (costs of operation)		
Farming costs	33.76	
Fishing costs	1.65	
Animal costs	2.89	
Land rent paid	19.56	
Building rent paid	.30	
Food costs	49.80	
Clothing costs	12.65	
Household supplies	10.18	
Business costs	4.05	
Interest paid on debts	12.80	
All other costs (civil, transport, education, etc.)	29.82	
Total	177.46	177.46

EXPENDITURE—*Continued*

Brought forward	177.46
Capital expenditure (investment in capital goods)	
Land bought 16.99	
Buildings bought 8.94	
Farm equipment .. .. .43	
Fishing equipment .. .. .66	
Animals bought 6.43	
Gold and silver bought 1.80	
All other 1.65	
Total 36.90	36.90
Debt reduction (repayments on debts)	35.36
Loan increase (money loaned to others)	4.40
Medical costs	5.45
Ecclesiastical costs	21.12
Social costs	2.58
Extraordinary civil costs	2.22
Gambling losses and others	1.19
Total Expenditure	286.68

The Bangkok budget was for one month, while that of the farmer was for a year. Even so the Bangkok man received as much in a month as the farmer did in half-a-year.

The economic division between the peasant and the educated civil official or professional man is wide. One present trend is to attempt to bridge the gap by creating a Siamese middle class in commerce and trade.

The Siamese government is financially sound. All debts outstanding are liberally covered. The Financial Adviser, Mr. W. M. A. Doll, in an informal interview in 1937, remarked that the Siamese government could pay all debts and loans with cash and still have a slight balance.

The Siamese people are economically secure. Although the annual income of the majority of the people, if reckoned in terms of money, is very slight, few need to worry about food or shelter or clothing. The average community is self-sustaining.

The government's new economic policy is not being formulated in the face of such a depression as has faced many countries during the past ten years. It is a far-seeing plan for the progressive development of the national resources, and for the economic advancement of the citizens of the country.

CHAPTER IV

ETHNIC TRENDS

1. THE SIAMESE

SIAM has a polyglot population which uses several languages in the daily process of living. Siamese and Chinese are the two most frequently heard. Railroad station signs carry the name of the station in Siamese, Chinese, and English. English is for the convenience of Europeans, Malayans, Indians, and others who cannot read Siamese or Chinese.

The Siamese language is spoken in three main dialects, representing north, central, and south Siam. The dominant and official dialect is the Bangkok dialect, which is taught in all the schools throughout the kingdom. A Bangkok Siamese going north or south for the first time experiences considerable difficulty in understanding the language of the natives of those sections; at least he does for two or three weeks until his ear adjusts itself to the variation of tone. Bangkok Siamese live for years in the provinces and seldom learn to speak the dialects. It is amusing to hear a conversation between a Bangkok man and a southern Siamese. The two dialects flow along side by side in perfect amity and without confusion. Neither will yield to the other's dialect unless the southern Siamese has had school education in the Bangkok dialect, in which case he will give way and speak the Bangkok dialect, which is the official language of Siam.

The southern Siamese have maintained their individuality of speech even in these modern times. However, in other respects they have so identified themselves with the national interests that they are scarcely distinguishable from their Siamese cousins of the north. Siamese in the south generally feel that they are related in some direct way with the Thai in the Shan states. Some even go so far as to say that they are descended from the Thai Lu. They say that the Thai Lu speak with much the same accent as the southern Siamese. It is certain that the southern people are a distinct branch of the Thai and that they are gradually being absorbed into the Siamese race as a whole. The southern Siamese have been under the influence of the central government, first at Ayudhia and later at Bangkok, for centuries because communications by sea were easy.

A more unassimilated element of Thai people, in these modern times, is the Laos in north Siam. Some call them the Thai that have not yet come south. Their skin is lighter, they are taller, and they are more energetic than the Thai farther south. They have a different dialect and a different script. The central language has been affected by the Khmer, while the Laos has been affected more by the Mon.

The Laos people remain a distinct Thai group simply because until the last quarter-century communications were too poor for the way of life of the central plain people to affect them. Until a century ago the Laos Kingdom retained its independence. Bangkok administrators then replaced the old princes, who retained their titles and honours, but relinquished actual authority. When the railroad was constructed through to Chiengmai in 1922, a great stride was made toward unifying the nation. The Bangkok customs, language, and administration moved in rapidly. The content of national thinking and planning is supplied from Bangkok. The young Laos people when educated are almost indistinguishable from the Bangkok Siamese.

2. THE MALAY

The Malay in Siam is accepted rather than assimilated. The Malays live in the far south near the Malayan borderline and are centred around Satul, Pattani, Bangnara, and Yala. They adhere to the Mohammedan religion. They are cut off from their Siamese and Chinese neighbours by a difference in diet required by their religion. Their speech is different in that it is not only another language but that it is not tonal, as Siamese and Chinese are. It uses an Arabic alphabet with flowing script. In the thickly populated Malay area almost the only Siamese are those in official government positions. So ignorant have the Malay people been of the Siamese language that the officials to administer the southernmost provinces have frequently been chosen for their ability to speak Malay and to understand Malay customs.

Although the Siamese governed the Malay element, no serious effort was made to draw it into the Siamese family until the railroad was built through to Pattani in 1922. At that time Siam was linked with British Malaya by an international express service.

Since religious liberty is granted to all people, no effort is made to convert the Malay to Siamese Buddhism. However, some of the older Malay communities have members who speak both Malay and Siamese and who follow their religion only to the point of refraining from eating pork and wearing the tarboosh. A few have forgotten how to speak Malay.

Pattani was originally settled by Malay and Siamese people who held to the Buddhist religion. After the Arab influence became strong, the Malays turned to Mohammedanism. Not many Siamese accepted Mohammedanism, but those who did, at Satul and Saiburi, are known to the Malays as "Samsam".[1]

Ever since the founding of the Sukhothai dynasty, Pattani has attempted at various times to become an independent state. When the Burmese seized Ayudhia in 1767, Pattani and Saiburi declared their independence and remained independent until Bangkok was well established as the new seat of government. At the close of the reign of Rama I, Pattani revolted again, but was subdued and divided into seven districts called "mu'ang". The seven districts were governed from the city of Singora. In the reign of Rama V the seven "mu'ang" were united to form a "monthon" or circle. In the Siamese year of 1932-33 Monthon Pattani was absorbed by Monthon Sritammarat. The following year all monthons were abolished, each "mu'ang" was made self-governing and was called a "cangwat". Pattani is now one of the seventy "cangwat" of Siam.

Siamese Buddhist monks, as early as the opening of the twentieth century, attempted to provide primary educational facilities in the Pattani area. At that time the Malay people objected to Siamese education because they felt it was the prelude to a plot to get their children into the Siamese army. The language of commerce and of religion, in that area, was Malay. The Malays failed to see the value of a Siamese education.

Since the constitutional monarchy has been established, the authorities are determined that Siam shall be unified. They are unwilling that any part of the nation continue without modern

[1] Sophapalabut, "Cangwat Pattani," *Pattanisan,* 1936, p. 105.

educational facilities. They intend to provide free and compulsory education so that all of the people, whatever their origin, shall be equally prepared to meet the standards of a civilized world.

In thirteen years of compulsory education in the Pattani area but slight progress has been made. The children who went to school came out with a parrot-like knowledge of Siamese. Scarcely two per cent of the pupils used what they had learned. The average school on an average day could muster not more than forty per cent of the children enrolled. Pupils studied three or four years and then, within a year, forgot what they had learned. Many could read Siamese printing fluently, but without any understanding of the text. Few Malays in Siam can read or write any language, even their own. Malays involved in legal cases usually have to use finger prints instead of signatures on documents.

An inspector of schools summarizes the situation thus:

1. Malay adults object to purely Siamese education for their children because Siamese is not their language.
2. They object because their children have no opportunity to study Mohammedanism if Siamese is their language. They fear their children will be won over to Buddhism.
3. They object to having their children study for three years and still not know either Siamese or Malay well.

It is consequently suggested:

1. If the government intends to enforce the educational laws, those laws should be strictly enforced in order to guarantee the Malay people a basic Siamese education. Malay education should be allowed after the pupils have a Siamese foundation.
2. If an attitude of tolerance is to be shown, then it would be better to encourage a Malay education, using Siamese script for the Malay words.
3. After becoming familiar with Siamese script, the Malays could easily learn Siamese.[1]

In 1937, Cangwat Pattani had 83 schools, 177 teachers, and 8,326 pupils. Of this number, 5,958 were of the compulsory education age. Other children not in school, of the same age limits, who, according to the school law should have been in school, numbered 21,841. There was an average of two teachers to a school, and the average school had about 100 pupils.[2]

[1] Khun Canya Withan, "Kham Prarop Nai Ru'ang Kan Su'ksa Khong Chon Thai Islam," *Pattanisan*, 1937, pp. 74-79.
[2] Nai Pracha, "Kha Fak Panha Tu'n Tan Nu'ng Kha," *Pattanisan*, 1937, pp. 117-120.

The religious knowledge of the Malay people in south Siam is of an unprogressive type, far inferior to Mohammedanism in Malaya or Bangkok.

Fishing, farming, and petty trade provide most of these people with a livelihood. Fishing is an exhausting occupation. The income is very slight, seldom exceeding fifty *stangs* or one *baht* per day for a family. Those who are employed by others receive as little as twenty-five *stangs* per day as their hire. Here again the Chinese is the middleman who supplies the boat and the nets, and takes the fish for his business needs.

The farmer makes enough for the daily requirements of his family. The rice that is planted is of the poorest variety. The men leave the heavy work to the women, while they indulge in cock, bull, and goat fights. Indolence is a serious problem here.

As for merchandising, the trade is of the pettiest sort. Cakes, fish, and certain small articles needed for the simple daily life are about all that is sold. Here again the women do the work. Some few ambitious families open shops and sell cloth and household furnishings.

The Malay people in Siam form a large, undigested lump. The Malay problem is not as acute as the Chinese, for there are a million-and-a-half Chinese while there are only five hundred thousand Malays. To woo them into the Siamese family the government is stressing primary education.

3. THE CHINESE

For centuries there has been a Chinese problem wherever the Siamese have lived. It has followed them like their own shadow. It is as much a part of the national life as the growing of rice. The problem dates back beyond Siamese written history. When the Siamese, or Thai, were still in southern China, the contest had begun. The Thai fought the Chinese alone, fought them with the assistance of Tibet, and then tried taking them in as friends. The end was always the same. The Thai, in order to maintain independence, abandoned home and field and fled south. This experience was repeated again and again until the Siamese settled in their present home. During the Siamese-Burmese wars the Chinese of Siam assisted the Siamese in a number of battles. Their struggle in behalf of Ayudhia has been memorialized in a play by Luang Vichitr.

‹ The tendency of the Chinese is to smother the people around them with their commerce and customs. They are good citizens, but they remain Chinese. Fifty years ago the problem was not acute, for Siam was an empty land and could welcome great hosts of immigrants. It was the custom for Chinese men to come to Siam and settle down with Siamese wives. The children of these unions were brought up as Siamese. The problem of assimilation, thus, was not a difficult one. New blood and energy were pouring into the Siamese life stream. The race was kept fresh and vigorous. For example, a certain Chinese came to Siam with little money and plenty of ambition. He worked hard as a merchant, married a Siamese girl, and, when he died, left a large estate. His son was fluent in both Siamese and Chinese and likewise established a Siamese household. He combined the energy of the Chinese with the political acumen of the Siamese and rose to a high political position in the Bhuket area. In title he was a Lord Lieutenant; in reality he ruled as a sort of sub-potentate under the Siamese king in Bangkok. His Chinese name was Sim Bee and his Siamese title was Phya Ratsda. His brothers and descendants have had an important and integral part in the Siamese life along the western peninsular coast of Siam. The children of the Sino-Siamese marriages are good citizens. They form the backbone of the present constitutional government. They have energy, drive, and intelligence. They get things done.

Within the last two decades the Chinese problem has become acute because Chinese no longer come to Siam in great numbers without their wives and children. The trend has been to bring Chinese wives from China. The consequence is a close-knit Chinese community which places much emphasis on Chinese cultural life. Many Chinese in Siam scorn to marry their sons or daughters to any but pure-blooded Chinese.

Reginald Le May tells a tale of two Chinese from Swatow, named Nguan Heng and Hah Yong. They entered Siam with no other possessions than the clothes on their backs. Before separating to seek their fortunes they promised each other not to indulge in the luxury of pork, duck, or chicken, until each had saved a considerable sum. Nguan Heng kept his promise and soon made his fortune.

But Hah Yong was destroyed by his own appetite and ended up a poor man. The moral was drawn by Nguan Heng one day. He allowed Hah Yong to boil tamarind leaves from a small tree in his yard for food. The leaves on the small tree were soon exhausted. Hah Yong was then appointed to a large tree which was of such a size that he never was able to strip it of its leaves no matter how much he ate. His friend told him that when a poor man eats his income as rapidly as it comes in, he will be forever poor. If he waits until his savings are large before he eats, he can never exhaust the store. Le May makes the following comment:

> This story is perhaps the most significant and pregnant with meaning for Siam and the Siamese people today. . . . Nguan Heng may well be considered as the prototype of the modern Chinese, and Hah Yong as that of the modern Siamese. . . . The rice grower has always remained Siamese, and the Chinese have not as yet made any attempt to oust him from that basic position. But the rice dealer is Chinese. So is the rice-miller and all his coolies. So is the boat builder, an important handicraft in a country where rivers and canals form the highroads. So is the pawnbroker, the tailor, the boot-maker, the dyer of cloth, the furniture-maker, the iron-smith, the market gardener, the fish-dealer, the old tin can collector, and the hawker. One could go on adding to the list, almost *ad infinitum,* but I have no wish to weary the reader with a recitation of almost every craft known to man. Suffice it to say that, in practically every form of manual labour, the Chinese hold the field, and the Siamese sit by, watching all the requisite services of life being performed by the uniformly impersonal, very vociferous, but intensely industrious celestial. . . . Twenty years ago you could, figuratively speaking, count the number of Chinese women you saw in Bangkok on the fingers of your two hands. They were, indeed, one of the rarest sights. Today it is a very different story. . . . It means that all or most of the Chinese in Siam from henceforward will remain Chinese in thought and spirit. Their children will be taught in Chinese schools, which are springing up all over the country, their wives will talk to them always in Chinese, they will care less and less even to learn Siamese themselves. . . . Thus in the course of time the Chinese in Siam, of whom there must be at least a million, will assuredly become as much foreigners as any European race in the country, and those million foreigners will have practically the entire trade of the country in their hands.[1]

Le May's opinion is important not only because of his long residence in the country but because his official position as Adviser to the Ministry of Commerce and Communications has given him

[1] Reginald Le May, *Siamese Tales Old and New* (London: Noel Douglas, 1930), pp. 71, 165.

ETHNIC TRENDS 89

unusual opportunity to appraise the national scene. Since Le May wrote, the Chinese has begun to oust the Siamese from his position of rice grower. Rice growing has been attempted as a Chinese community project between Patalung and Haad Yie. Chinese families have banded together to work several thousands of acres of rice land. They have worked it with modern machinery and tractors. In each area worked the community has built its own rice mill.

James M. Andrews notes the fair attitude of the Chinese toward the Siamese in the matter of debt. His data indicates that, although the Chinese are a dominant factor in the economic life, they are not an unfair nor an unfriendly factor. He feels that the evil agency of Chinese money-lenders has been grossly exaggerated by public opinion. He shows that Chinese demand slightly lower average interest rates than do the Siamese, and that they are as often willing to demand no interest as are the Siamese.[1]

The goodwill of the Chinese community was demonstrated at the first half-year anniversary celebrations of the new form of constitutional government in December, 1932. The parade included the leading merchants of Bangkok, the leaders of the Chinese Chamber of Commerce, the leaders of various Chinese clubs, and the children and teachers from several Chinese schools. They marched for five hours through the streets bearing standards inscribed in Chinese characters which told of their goodwill toward Siam in general and the new constitutional government in particular. The parade ended at the club-house of the People's Party where it massed to hear speeches by some of the leading government officials. The Chinese community then offered a programme of entertainment, and made a financial donation to the Siamese cause.

A mechanical move to make Chinese stores appear more Siamese was instituted in October, 1936, when every storekeeper was required by law to place the Siamese as well as the Chinese name of his shop on his signboard. All merchants were listed with the government according to their type of trade. Each shop-owner had to report his name, his trade name, the type of business, his place of business, his headquarters and branches, the length of time he had been in business, and other similar details. When the listing was accepted,

---

[1] James M. Andrews, *Siam, Second Economic Survey* (Bangkok: The Bangkok Times Press, Ltd., 1935), pp. 311-314.

he received a license which was to be posted in a prominent place. The law set the fine for recalcitrant merchants who failed to comply with the provisions of the law in the allotted time at *baht* 500.

Until recently the Chinese have been a transient population that ebbed and flowed with trade. Within the last decade the Chinese have been moving on to the land in order to grow rubber and rice. One large area where Chinese have bought up the land is from Kantang to Huey Yot in the south. Most of this is planted in rubber. Going north from Tung Song along the railroad, Chinese communities have sprung up that have likewise settled on the land. Some of the settlements are so new that they have no railroad station to grace the town. The train stops where the houses are most numerous. South of Patalung the Chinese have taken up thousands of acres for the communal growing of rice.

Chinese who settle on the land and invest their time, strength, and effort in one locality, are loth to leave. A definite trend on the part of Chinese is to become a more stable element in the community with less shifting of residence from town to town in search of trade.

There are a number of Chinese newspapers printed in Siam and sold throughout the nation. Every small village, where Chinese congregate, has its Chinese reading room. And every small town is visited periodically by the Chinese bookseller, who spreads his hundreds of volumes out on the street for all to see. His kerosene lamps burn far into the night as prospective buyers chose between the famous "San Kuo" or the Mandarin language love story of some movie queen.

There is a Chinese Chamber of Commerce in Bangkok which attempts to assist the Chinese in Siam in a business way. Siam has no Chinese Minister to represent the Chinese politically, because Siam has no diplomatic relations with China. If there were such a representative, he would be a very powerful man. He would have the wealth of the nation behind him. Chinese in Siam are under Siamese rule. Their passports read: "Chinese race, Siamese Sovereignty."

Aside from a closer control of Chinese trade and commerce, the government is trying along two lines to solve its Chinese problem, which, if not dealt with properly, might well swamp the nation. The first part of the programme is to deter immigration in order not to increase the magnitude of the problem. The second part of the programme is educational. It aims at teaching Chinese enough of the language and customs of their new homeland to make them good Siamese citizens.

The first attempt to retard immigration put a tax of *baht* 30 on every person entering the country. Even people who had lived in Siam ten, twenty, or more years, and who happened to be caught outside of the Siamese boundaries when the law went into effect, had to pay the required sum to get back home. When it is remembered how poor the Chinese peasants are, it is easy to understand how such a tax would keep many people out of the country.

War and famine conditions in China continued to make life in that country almost unendurable for many. Whole families already in Siam saved frantically to bring relatives and friends to the peaceful haven which they had found.

When it was found that immigration was not materially retarded, the entry fee was raised to *baht* 100 per person. Thus, if a Chinese man brought his wife and one child over fourteen into Siam, he had to pay *baht* 300 in tax. At the same time the officials required those who 'entered Siam to have some means of support, and a minimum amount of money on which to begin life so that they would not become public charges.

To everyone's surprise immigration continued at a high level. In the Siamese year 1932-33, the excess of arrivals over departures was 17,448. The following year showed no decrease. The year 1934-35 showed the desired decrease. There was an excess of only 4,030 arrivals over departures. This indicated that Chinese immigration had come to a pause. The following year of 1935-36 brought excess immigration over emigration to the number of 9,939. So official figures show that Chinese immigration is still considerable, although the annual average from 1934 to 1936 is only a third of what it was in the period from 1928 to 1930.

A law forbidding or limiting the use of a commodity often produces an illicit trade in that commodity. Back-door immigration became a serious problem almost as soon as the law went into effect. Why pay a tax of *baht* 100 when much less would hire a guide to conduct a party of immigrants over the border? The newspapers in the early months of 1937 suggested that Chinese were entering Siam in as large numbers as ever, but through underground channels. One group of illicit immigrants were caught near Chumpon. There were about four hundred who had landed from Chinese junks on a quiet beach in the peninsula. Only a few hundreds of such newcomers have ever been caught, and the number of those who have not been caught can only be imagined. Some Chinese regard it as a good sporting proposition to see how many friends they can help across the border. A Registration of Aliens Act was enacted as the answer. It was to become effective in August, 1937. Every foreigner is now required to carry on his person a Certificate of Registration. This Act offers a practical technique for checking on aliens. Chinese who have come into Siam without paying the tax can now be caught more easily than before.

The larger problem is how to assimilate the present Chinese population. Since the Chinese home has become a factor in the situation, Chinese parents desire more and better schools in which to educate their children in the national language and culture of China. The policy of the government, in answer to the Chinese schools with their narrow racial emphasis, is to enforce the educational law which requires that all children within the compulsory age limits, regardless of race, study in the Siamese language for a prescribed number of hours per week. Chinese, like English or French, was regarded as a foreign language to be studied but a few hours per week.

The Chinese objected loudly to this restriction as soon as it went into effect. In practice, it meant that their children could study Chinese only until they were seven years old, at which point the children had to begin their primary education in Siamese. A child who had completed his primary study in Siamese, or who was more than fourteen years old, could again study Chinese. The result was, at least where the law was strictly enforced, that every young Chinese acquired a thorough knowledge of reading, writing, and speaking in Siamese, usually before he began his Chinese education. The government counted on the natural human weakness to follow the easier path. Siamese is an easier language than Chinese. When one has a language that is ready for use, that is easy to read and write, it requires considerable energy to turn to the difficult language of the ideograph.

For a time Chinese opposition to the government educational

policy softened, since it was discovered that the schools could accept the government schedule and then ignore it except on days when an inspector came to perform his duties. On such days Siamese books were much in evidence. However, in time, enforcement became rigid and many recalcitrant schools were closed.

One immediate result of the closing of Chinese schools was that Chinese parents began to send their children to China or Malaya for study. This was only possible for the wealthy, but it was amazing to see how many hundreds of children left Siam. In a few cases the pupils went in a body with their own teachers and started schools again outside of Siam.

The Chinese made a formal protest under the auspices of prominent individuals, against the educational law, and asked to be allowed to continue as in the past. There were 6,137 names of individuals and 332 names of shops signed to the request. The list bore the names of leading Chinese from all over Siam. The petition recalled to the government the centuries of friendship between China and Siam, pointed out the important Chinese contribution to commerce and trade, expressed the wish that the children from Chinese homes be allowed to grow up with a knowledge of the Chinese language and customs, and appealed for the privilege of continuing the Chinese schools.[1]

The government's answer shifted the issue from the particular to a more general field of discussion by saying that the law applied to all foreign residents in Siam, and that the Chinese ought not to ask special privileges. On May 22nd, 1933, the government reaffirmed its enforcement policy. Discussion and accusation continued in lively fashion through 1937.

The schools that had been closed began to open again as they fell into line. However, since it was recognized that it would be a handicap for a Chinese merchant not to know Chinese, the government granted a more liberal allowance of time for the desired study than had been contemplated at first. The average Chinese school teaches Chinese three hours a day to children under the compulsory school age, one hour a day to children of the compulsory school age, and three hours a day to children beyond the compulsory school age limits. It provides the children with a knowledge of both Siamese and Chinese.

[1] *Thai Mai,* March 28th, 1933.

The *Nation,* the paper that is usually regarded as expressing the opinions of H.S.H. Prince Varnvaidyakara Voravarn, who is an adviser to the present government, summarized the Sino-Siamese relationship in Siam by using the metaphor of a householder and his guest.[1] The writer pointed out that the Chinese and Siamese have politics, friendship, commerce, and even blood relationships in common. However, since the Chinese nationalistic spirit has increased, the Chinese in Siam have shown discontent with the local government, particularly in educational matters. Many articles have been written for newspapers in China by Chinese resident in Siam, claiming that the Siamese government was unfair to Chinese, but when the Chinese Trade Mission came from China, led by Dr. Lin Pin, its report showed that the Chinese in Siam were better treated than Chinese in other foreign countries. The editorial claimed that Siam is the home of the Siamese and that the Chinese are guests. The house-owner must have the right to govern his home for his own good. The supervision of education, the imposition of an immigration tax, and the control of the spread of alien habits and customs are lawful enterprises of government. They are necessary to guarantee the position of the Siamese in the Siamese national home.

The writer of the editorial recalled two interesting bits of history in order to show the improved status of the Chinese in Siam. The first reference was to the "Ang Yee" trouble that swept Siam about thirty years before. The government was not strict at that time and the Chinese organized in clans and started "Ang Yee" wars. If one group captured a member of another group, he was killed without regard to the laws of the land. A group called "Plong Liam" had more influence than any other clan. It administered two kinds of death to its victims. The hot death was accomplished by burying the victim in hot coals. The cold death was carried out by tying the victim in a bag and dumping him into the river. "Ang Yee" warfare spread all over Siam. The government and the Siamese people were distressed, so were the Chinese; but the government was powerless to control the lawless elements among the Chinese.

The second reference was to the collection of the head tax. The Siamese for twenty years paid *baht* seven per year, while the Chinese

[1] *Nation,* November 27th, 1937.

paid only *baht* one and fifty *stangs*. The government revised this so that both Siamese and Chinese paid *baht* six. The Chinese were angered, disorders arose, shops closed their doors as a protest against the allegedly unfair treatment meted out to the Chinese by the government. The Chinese refused to see that their rights and privileges remained as usual and that the government was merely asking them to pay as much as the Siamese had been paying for years. And now again in modern times, when the government insists on controlling the Chinese education within its borders as well as Siamese, the Chinese object. The article closed with the opinion that the intelligent Chinese realized that they were being fairly treated.

This opinion was corroborated by Mr. Ong Thye Chee, Manager of the Oversea-Chinese Banking Corporation, Limited, and President of the Chinese Bankers' Association of Siam. He said:

> Siam welcomes the foreign immigrant and affords him equal treatment and equal privileges, so much so that the intelligent foreigner in the country usually identifies himself with the Siamese in national thought and aspiration. . . . It cannot for a moment be denied that the economic and general status of the Chinese in Siam is enviable, even tending to eclipse the Siamese themselves. With the possible exception of British Malaya, Siam has afforded the Chinese immigrants the cleanest, widest, and most independent home. . . . No immigrant with a tinge of love for this land of his adoption will have any cause to resent the reasonable measure adopted by the government.

The leading Chinese have come to realize that there is no use struggling against the inevitable, and, more, that what the government is asking is only fair. It will be interesting to watch the progress made, to see if, by limiting immigration and by giving Chinese youth a Siamese education, the large unassimilated mass of Chinese can be absorbed into the Siamese nation.

CHAPTER V

EDUCATIONAL TRENDS

1. THE PRESENT ORGANIZATION OF THE SCHOOL SYSTEM

THE personal example of King Mongkut was of unusual propaganda value for modern education in Siam. The king, who lived in the middle of the nineteenth century, not only obtained a scholarly knowledge of Pali and Buddhism, but also studied English, Latin, History, Mathematics, Astronomy, and acquired a fair knowledge of the world's geography. Furthermore he engaged a tutor for his children who taught them according to European standards.

The beginning of government-sponsored public education was officially made by King Mongkut's son, King Chulalongkorn, who in the year 1891-92 organized the first Ministry of Education. The government chose the English system of education as adaptable to Siamese needs. In 1921-22 a law was passed requiring children between the ages of seven and fourteen to attend school. A revision was made in 1933 which changed the compulsory age limits to "from eight to fifteen" years. Every child was required to attend school, if able to do so, and if there was a school to attend. Actually the law was not enforced because there were few schools and few teachers. As recently as 1932, only about 88 per cent of the local districts actually attempted to enforce the primary education law. In 1937 the Ministry of Public Instruction announced that every part of the kingdom had some sort of school available for primary grade children.

Education for the masses has not yet reached a high standard. Only within the last decade have the educational requirements for a head teacher of a school been raised to matyome six, which is two years less than the graduate standards of an American high school. As recently as 1910, an American missionary, Dr. E. P. Dunlap, was appointed "Special Commissioner of Public Schools and Lecturer to all the Schools of Trang Province." His work was to organize public schools, inspect existing schools, advise the teachers and school boards, assemble the people in the villages and lecture them on the values of education, and suggest means by which they might support such schools as were organized. The schools were free, suported by moderate taxation. At that time there were but two primary grades in Trang. Some districts in Siam were far ahead of Trang in educational progress, and others lagged behind. It is enough to realize that the general push for education is recent. A widespread craving for educational benefits has come to the small towns only in these past five years.

There are four types of schools listed by the government. They are, according to official designation, government schools, local schools, private schools, and municipal schools. The "government" school is one wholly maintained and controlled by the Ministry of Public Instruction. Government schools are intended to be models for progressive education. They are supposed to be the show window of education. Their organization and methods are to be adopted as far as possible by other schools. To date they come far short of the ideal.

A "local" school is created by a village or a commune under the inspection of the government. The District Officer may set up such a school if he feels it is needed. Most of these schools are located in temple grounds. Local schools provide only primary education. Secondary education is given in the government schools, many of which give no primary education.

A "private" school may be a school run by a qualified individual for profit, or it may be one run by a community. Most of those now in operation are evening schools offering primary education or stressing special subjects such as English. Some of the finest schools of Siam are private schools. Among them are Assumption College, of the Roman Catholics; Bangkok Christian College, Wattana Wittaya Academy, Prince Royals College, and Dara Wittaya Academy, of the American Presbyterian Mission; Vajiravudh College, founded by His Majesty Rama VI; and Rajini School, which was founded by the Queen Mother Sri Bajrindra.

Another very popular private school is the Amnuy Sin School, Bangkok. It is particularly interesting because it was established recently by a Siamese Board made up largely of young Siamese who had been engaged themselves in educational work. It is devoted to the development of a high scholastic standard and to the preservation and propagation of the best from the true Siamese tradition. The school has attained such a reputation that the government has more than once tentatively expressed a willingness to take it over, but so far the governing board of the school has preferred to keep the school a private institution.

In areas under municipal organization, elementary schools have been organized and maintained by the municipal governments. Such schools are called "municipal" schools. Generally speaking, they are primary schools.

When the constitutional government was first established, the government decided that education would be the best preparation for full democracy. In the year 1933-34 the appropriation for education was *baht* 3,731,494. In three years the appropriation was trebled until it amounted to almost *baht* twelve millions. The ambitious goal of the new government was to give at least a primary education to fifty per cent of the voters of Siam within ten years. Toward the end of 1937 one district officer estimated that about ten per cent of the population eligible for education had attained the minimum goal of a primary education. On the other hand a Bangkok official of high standing considers that the one third mark has been passed. The truth probably lies somewhere between the two.

2. PRIMARY AND SECONDARY EDUCATION

Primary education includes the first four years of study. These four grades are called the pratome grades. Secondary education has until recently included the following eight years of study, which are called the matyome grades. These eight grades have been divided into two stages of four grades each. The higher four grades have been divided into two sections with either a linguistic or scientific major. Examinations have been conducted by a special board appointed by the Ministry of Public Instruction. One who passed the eighth matyome was allowed to apply for university study or civil service examination.

A revision of the secondary grades has now been instituted. The number of grades has been reduced to six. The six grades are divided into two stages of three grades each. The instruction usually given in the seventh and eighth standards is regarded as college preparatory work and must be taken at the university preparatory school in Bangkok. This centralizes all college study and allows the government to spend less money on the students of the higher two grades.[1] Since there are no private colleges in Siam, the term "college" found in the names of some of the private schools listed above is a misnomer.

The educational programme as revised is arranged in a number of levels to suit various grades of intelligence. The lowest level is a primary grade education of four years, followed by two years of vocational training to prepare pupils for a life work. The next level carries the students through the third standard of the secondary grades, likewise followed by two years of vocational training. The third level takes the pupils through the sixth standard of the secondary grades and is followed by two or more years of vocational training suited to that degree of education. Those choosing to go to the university continue college preparations through the seventh and eighth standards of the secondary grades and then study law, medicine, or other university studies. Entrance into the college preparatory school is by competitive examination. There will doubtless be changes and variations made in the scheme as it is adjusted to actual experience.

The programme intends that everyone shall be prepared for some definite life work to suit his ability. A useless educated class is not desired.

In the Siamese year 1933-34, a survey of pupils was made in those sections where the primary education law was in force. There were 1,562,574 children that should have been in school. Since there were not enough schools to receive them, and not enough teachers to teach them, the compulsory-study age was made elastic to fit the size of the schools and the number of teachers. Some districts enforced the law for children aged eight to fourteen, some from nine to fourteen, and some from ten to fourteen. In the following year of 1935 the survey showed 1,756,233 children that should be in school. Those actually in school numbered 1,026,547.

In 1934-35 it was reported that over 100,000 children could not

[1] *Nation*, March 22nd, 1937.

get to school because of poor communications, or because of the difficulty of traversing dangerous paths. In many districts life is still primitive and children are cut off from school by thick jungle.

Six thousand more children are unable to get an education because they are blind, deaf, dumb, or abnormal in some other way. As yet there are no schools for abnormal children.

Annually new schools are being erected. In 1931-32 there were 219 new schools opened, in 1932-33 another 757 schools were added, in 1933-34 another 425 schools were completed. Most of them are modest frame buildings reminiscent of the little red schoolhouse of former days in the United States.

In 1934-35 Siam had a total number of 9,001 schools. There were 244 government schools, 1,055 private schools, and 7,702 local schools. It may thus be seen that the local schools are the medium for educating the masses of the people. In actual numbers the government schools registered 53,474 pupils, the private schools had 62,513 pupils, and the local schools had 988,208 pupils.[1]

The education of girls lags behind that of the boys. In 1934-35 the government schools were teaching 36,986 boys and only 16,488 girls. Private schools were teaching 37,542 boys and 24,971 girls. The local schools were teaching 582,466 boys and 405,742 girls. Altogether 656,994 boys, but only 447,201 girls were going to school. The education of girls has come in modern times. The first important girls' school was begun in the Wang Lang district of Bangkok by a brilliant American woman named Harriet Pettit House about sixty years ago. It proved to be a success and focused much attention upon this type of education. The woman who brought this school to a place of prominence and leadership in the field of education for girls, and gained public acknowledgement for her achievement from King Prajadhipok, was Miss Edna S. Cole, who is living in retirement in the United States. Since the primary education law was passed in 1921-22, the increase of pupils, whether boys or girls, has been about the same.

With compulsory education and a paucity of school buildings, it was natural that some sort of co-education should develop. Co-education is common in the primary grades but less common in the secondary grades where the boys and girls usually attend

[1] Educational statistics have been drawn from the report of the Ministry of Education for 1934-35.

separate schools. In 1934-35, schools featuring co-education numbered 8,506. Less than 500 schools in Siam had no co-education. Pupils in co-educational schools numbered 1,066,917. On the surface it would appear that co-education is entirely acceptable in Siam. In the primary grades this is so, but when the children reach secondary school the general belief has been that they do better if separated into boys' and girls' schools. Most parents insist upon separate schools for girls of secondary school age. Co-education as it is understood in the United States is not in favour in Siam except in the primary grades and in the university where women have gone to seek a higher education.

In 1934-35, the distribution of pupils as to educational standing shows the importance of primary education. There were 1,050,211 pupils in primary grades, 44,784 in secondary grades, and 5,058 in vocational training grades. Only four per cent of the pupils were in secondary grades. Well over 90 per cent of all educational work in Siam is done in primary grades. In those primary grades it may be shown that 76 per cent of the children were in grades one and two. The number of pupils in those grades was 801,571. When over 90 per cent of the children in school are in primary grades, and of them 76 per cent are in the first two grades, it can be realized how much work there is to do before there can be an educated citizenry capable of understanding national and international affairs. A ten-year educational programme stressing primary education is only a beginning. But it is a beginning.

The quality of study in the primary grades is indicated to some extent by the ages of pupils trying to learn the simple rudiments of reading and writing. In 1933-34 there were 39,302 children above fourteen years of age still in the primary grades. Modern methods of teaching children to read and write have not reached the majority of the schools. The teachers themselves are poorly prepared to teach, and cannot be blamed for not doing what they are unable to do. The teachers frequently have little more than a primary education themselves. As the teacher training programmes develop there should be improvement.

Vocational training, in theory, is supposed to be available to all students to fit them for their life work. The private schools offer foreign languages, shorthand, typing, cloth weaving, the study of ancient Siamese medicine suitable for use in the villages, handwork, and teachers training courses. The government schools offer a wider range of study. They have teacher training courses for primary and secondary grades, for agriculture, and for trade schools. Then there are courses in agriculture, carpentry, building, sewing, silversmithy; there are secretarial courses, courses for printers, for tailors, for housewives; and courses in the Chinese language—which is the commercial language of the country—for ambitious young Siamese who have a mind to contest the monopoly which the Chinese have had in commerce. The local schools offer carpentry, hat-making, agriculture, and handwork.

The newspapers regularly carry notices of some special vocational study. A full page advertisement invites young men to study carpentry and building. Another full page advertisement tells of a school that teaches languages for business purposes and claims to impart the most modern information on business methods. A secretarial school advertises courses in shorthand, typing, and bookkeeping. A full page advertisement tells of courses in sewing, dressmaking, and tailoring which are to prepare the student for practical work within sixty days. The vocational school is coming more to the fore and is perhaps a partial answer to the need of Siamese young people.

Another factor to be considered in the modern education of Siam is the influence of non-Siamese teachers upon Siamese and non-Siamese children. In 1934-35 there were 410 foreign teachers in private schools. Of these, 291 were Chinese, 3 Japanese, 31 Indian, 11 from other Asiatic countries, 11 English, 20 French, 1 German, 12 from other parts of Europe, and 30 Americans. The government engages a few European or American teachers for special positions. The amount of influence of the European and American teachers can scarcely be measured by their numbers, but must be measured by the things they accomplish. They are usually equipped with college or university degrees; many of them have done graduate work. They have all had experience as teachers in modern schools elsewhere and have usually had some special preparatory work in education. They are in Siam to establish model departments and schools. A model primary class is set up by one, a good physics class by another, a kindergarten by another. Some of them engage in the training of teachers. If all they succeed in doing is to produce some discontent with the ordinary type of education and stimulate a desire for a better school system, their work may be considered well done.

The majority of European and American teachers have as a complementary aim the teaching of their religion. The government does not object because it holds to the principle that children require some sort of religious instruction. The actual number of converts from Buddhism to some other religion, in the schools, may be regarded as almost negligible, but the influence of the European and American teachers cannot be measured by the reported numbers of converts. Probably their chief gifts to their pupils are new ways of thought, new character principles, and an increased readiness to question the existing scheme of things with a hope of bettering them.

The proportion of pupils to teachers is another important consideration. The government schools average twenty-two pupils to one teacher. In the primary grades the average is thirty pupils to a teacher, and in the secondary grades twenty to a teacher. In the vocational training classes the average is sixteen to a teacher. The distribution is not bad except in the primary grades.

The private schools have a better proportion of pupils to teachers: in the primary grades there are twenty-one to a teacher, and in vocational training classes ten to a teacher. The average is only nineteen to a teacher.

The local schools are in a seriously crowded condition, with about fifty pupils to a teacher. Frequently one teacher has more than one grade to teach. To obtain salutary results is a superhuman task. Only the most primary of primary educations can be expected.

One reason for this condition in the local schools is the poor wages paid the teachers. There is little incentive to be a skilled teacher when the salary paid scarcely exceeds the income of a peasant.

The government statistics for 1934-35 show that a government school pupil cost *baht* 26.71 per month, while a local school pupil cost only *baht* 3.40 per month. The difference is accounted for, in part, by the salaries paid the teachers. A government school teacher receives an average of *baht* 48.71 per month, while a local school teacher receives an average of *baht* 14.09 per month. At the rate of exchange of .45 the government school teacher receives $22.41 and the local school teacher receives $6.34 per month. According to the standards of living current in Siam a government school teacher can live comfortably if he does not have a large family, buys few books, and spends little on amusements. The teachers above that average can and do live well. A local school teacher cannot hope to support a family on his income. If he marries, he must look to his lands or his wife for financial assistance. As a consequence the teachers are often young people, just out of school, who have not yet found remunerative employment; or teachers who combine some other activity such as farming with their teaching. Such a system penalizes the masses of the people.

The question may be asked as to why there is such a discrepancy between the government and local school expenditure per teacher. The answer is to be found in the emphasis on the policy of making the government school a model institution after which the local schools are to pattern themselves. The teachers are better trained in the government schools. Many of them have received the best education possible in Siam, and some have been sent abroad for study.

A new project connected with the schools, that has made a beginning, is health work for school children. In some few schools the children are given physical examinations at stated intervals. The school doctors do all they are equipped to do, and beyond that advise the parents as to the care of the health of the children. This is a move in the right direction and should help to improve the new generation physically.

3. EXTRA-CURRICULAR ACTIVITIES

The Boy Scout movement has had an important place in the education of boys. King Rama VI founded the organization in 1911-12, so it is not a new movement. It is called "The Tiger Cubs Association", and is an official organization controlled by the Ministry of Public Instruction. The aim in general is to promote a high standard of citizenship as in other countries. In particular the movement tries to strengthen national ideals and foster a national spirit. The organization is popular. Every town and village has some interest in the Cubs. The Cub Leader is generally a school teacher, while the members are usually pupils in school. At times of national celebration they appear in great companies, in uniform, to parade the streets and sing inspiring songs. They have not engaged in camping activities to any great extent because of the wild nature of the jungle districts and the difficulties with mosquitoes. However, it is not uncommon to find a company of the boys camping out in temple grounds for a night or two. The organization has about 90,000 members. They try to be helpful according to the traditions of the movement. They help repair roads, dig wells for public use, assist the authorities to maintain order, and administer first aid to the sick or wounded.

The Junior Red Cross is another movement that influences the thinking of young Siam. It started in 1922-23 with the purpose of training young people to become effective adult members of the regular Red Cross Society. The members are taught to be merciful toward their fellowmen and to assist those in difficulty. They prepare supplies for health centres, give plays at the annual celebrations of the society, and establish first aid centres with medicine chests in needy places. There are about 100,000 members. The work of the society is valuable in inculcating helpful and unselfish ideals in the young people.

Sports are receiving a new emphasis in the schools, since it has been realized that they supply both physical and character values. Group exercises done in rhythm are popular everywhere. Football, basketball, net ball, and other games are in vogue. Some of the larger schools have shown themselves well able to develop good teams. Siam has welcomed competitive sports.

A Siamese private school published a pamphlet in 1937, telling of the methods and principles of education for that school. Education was defined as the preparation of children to be good and orderly citizens, and fitting them for their future place in life. In particular, so the pamphlet continued, the child must be prepared to think, to obey, and to have good manners. In the classroom the most modern educational methods are used, is the claim. In addition pupils are lectured on the glories of old Siam. They are taken on escorted tours of temples, palaces, public buildings, and other structures of note. Instruction is given to show the implication of these objects in national life. The theory is that if children are trained to an appreciation of the good and beautiful they will naturally desire the good and the beautiful. The pamphlet claimed that children involved in crime are usually poorly educated. The school attempts to bring to the children a realization of national importance. It also seeks to create a sympathetic feeling for the national religion of Buddhism. The swing away from the traditional religion is lamented. The school inculcates a sense of respect for the king, the leader of the nation. Lastly, an appreciation and understanding of the constitution is taught so that the new generation can properly evaluate the constitutional monarchy. This private school, in its methods and principles, is an innovation for Siam, but it clearly indicates a trend in education.

4. RELIGIOUS INFLUENCES IN EDUCATION

Education in Siam has always been linked with the religion of the people. In 1934-35 there were 6,519 schools out of a total of 9,001 that were located in temple grounds. Over 76 per cent of all education is under the influence of the Buddhist faith. Not all of these schools were established directly by monks. In modern times the clergy establish primary schools in those places where there is no school and no money to provide a school. In 1933-34 there were 1,219 schools that had been opened and sponsored by the clergy. The Ministry of Education made the comment that such schools would become regular local schools as soon as funds could be secured to manage them. It can be concluded that schools established by monks are but temporary solutions of the problem of an expanding educational programme. Most of the schools that meet in temple grounds have been established by regular educational agencies.

Schools established by monks probably offer more religious education than other schools in temple grounds. However, all of the schools have regular periods for religious instruction and character training. Over 89 per cent of the local schools, 42.3 per cent of the government schools, and 7.3 per cent of the private schools are located in temple grounds. Most of the children in Siam are being educated in close physical contact with the historical and accepted religion of the nation.

Several school inspectors have expressed the opinion that schools established by monks are all too often poor scholastically. The intention of the government seems to be to replace them with local schools. Religious influence upon pupils in schools established in temple grounds is not always strong. The influence of Buddhism depends upon the amount of respect accorded the monks in any particular temple by pupils and teachers. If the monks are poorly educated and have little knowledge, as is sometimes the case, the influence of Buddhism is slight.

A middle-aged Siamese gentleman contrasts the old and new in Siamese education, and in particular notes the waning of the influence of monks. He writes to urge a closer intimacy between education and religion. Forty years ago (about 1895), when he was a boy, were the good old days. On his way to school, if asked where he studied, he would answer politely that he studied at the temple. All schools were in the temple and the teachers were all monks. When he got to school the first thing he had to do was to serve his teacher. He must empty his cuspidor, bring him fresh drinking water and tea, and prepare his meal for him. When the monks had eaten the boys ate. School started at nine o'clock. There were no benches or chairs. Everyone sat cross-legged on the floor. The only studies were arithmetic and Siamese. Before noon the boys prepared and served tiffin to the monks and then took a nap. The educational day concluded at four o'clock. Before and after study the boys prostrated themselves before the monks and took part in religious ceremonies, and before they started for home they went to the monks to say good-bye. This was the equivalent of asking permission to leave. The pupils all had the highest reverence for the monks and were on intimate terms with them. The monks knew the parents of their pupils and the details of their home life. If anyone was sick in the home, the monks either sent medicine or went to visit and heal. If a boy was sick, the monks kept him at the temple and cared for him. After the pupils were grown, they still showed respect to even the littlest novice in the Buddhist Order because of what he represented. Most of the pupils became novices for a short time. If anyone showed disrespect for the temple by walking into the temple with shoes on, or by playing ball, or by forgetting to show respect to novices or monks, he was much criticized. The displeasure of his neighbours was visited upon him in matters of law and business. Even when graduated from temple schools the old contacts remained. The monk was the one who healed. In times of difficult decision the monk was consulted. When a new law was passed the monk gave the information on worship day. In matters of marriage, parents always consulted the monk. At long last the body of the devout old man, who so long before had been a pupil in the temple school, was cremated at the temple. The temple was the centre of the community in matters of health, education, assembly, sport, and religion. When the temple needed money the people were always ready to make contributions, for it had won their confidence. If any attempt were made to divide temple from home, monk from householder, philanthropy from work, the attempt was doomed to be a failure. Monk and temple were as close to the people and their homes as perfume to the powder in which it has been absorbed.

The writer of the articles then turns to modern education and traced the professional teacher's growing power over young Siam. Monks whose education was faulty have been dropped from teaching positions, until very few monks are found in the educational system. He laments the swing away from the temple influence which formed the character and culture of the present Siamese nation. He admits that the monk is no longer an important factor in education. In the modern temple school the children scarcely know the monks at all. They play ball and pitch pennies in the temple grounds. Even though the school is in the temple grounds the monks have no part in the instruction given. The writer closes his articles with a plea for the training of monks in the teaching profession, especially for the primary grades, so as to assure the continuity of the Siamese character in its traditional pattern within the sphere of the national religion.[1]

The place of the monk in education has been given official consideration, as is shown by a speech made by the Premier, Phya Bahol Balabayuha, at Korat. The Premier addressed an assembly of monks at the opening of a training school in primary education for monks. He said:

> The bond between religion and country and that between the temple and the home will be rendered more intimate by depending on education as the proper medium.
> The teaching of good behaviour to the children of the land, along with

[1] *Thai Mai,* February 13th, 14th, 15th, 1933.

physical, verbal, and mental training, should constitute the fundamental aim of education. The Dharma of the Great Teacher constitutes the best method for education in this direction. The monk is acknowledged to be learned and conducts himself according to Dharma and hence it is that there is none more worthy than he to impart such a training to children. . . . The idea of giving a normal training to monks so that they may assist the education of the children of the land henceforth is indeed a most excellent one in these difficult days.[1]

However, the use of monks in the educational system is a stopgap method used chiefly in times of financial stress. The trend is definitely toward a purely professional educational system.

5. THE UNIVERSITIES

Chulalongkorn University is the centre of higher learning in Siam. It seeks to produce a trained leadership. It was created in 1917 by amalgamating the Royal Medical College with the Civil Service College. The enrolment by departments for 1936-37 was:

Faculty of Medicine	106
Faculty of Arts and Sciences	473
Faculty of Engineering	94
Faculty of Pharmacy	1
Faculty of Architecture	32
Faculty of Nursing and Midwifery	166
Total [2]	872

A nation of fourteen-and-a-half million people thus has less than a thousand university students. At first glance this might not seem encouraging, but one must remember that only within the last five years has there been any popular demand for a university education. Fifteen years ago the average family was very well pleased if some of the children acquired a fourth matyome secondary education. Only within the last decade has there been a popular demand for sixth and eighth matyome secondary school education. Few parents even considered the university for their children. Now the educational vision has broadened, and more families are seeking a higher education for their sons and daughters. The movement is more sweeping among the families of civil officials and of those engaged

[1] *Bangkok Times,* March 16th, 1934.
[2] *The Directory for Bangkok and Siam* (Bangkok: The Bangkok Times Press, Ltd., 1937-38), p. 250.

in highly remunerative work than in other classes. For the first time there is not room enough in Chulalongkorn University for all who would study. It is frequently remarked that other universities are needed. The government, however, does not desire too large a white collar class. It is afraid that the nation cannot use the abilities of a large number of university graduates. This seems somewhat absurd when it is considered that there are only 500 or so doctors in all of Siam, to mention but one department.

In 1937, the University of Moral and Political Science was created out of the old law school. Its development and purpose are well described as follows:

> It is doubtless that the University of Moral and Political Science in Bangkok plays an important role in the educational advancement of Siam, and its activities should be worthy of special mention in the progressive march of this country along the lines of the present constitutional regime. The smooth and efficient functioning of a parliamentary regime requires not only enlightened voters but also an intelligentsia capable of taking part in the direction of public affairs, and to whom the voters may grant their confidence for the administration of the country. One of the main problems of the Constitutional government has been to carry out a comprehensive educational policy, fulfilling both the requirements, and while the compulsory primary education scheme was enforced and other progressive measures initiated in regard to public enlightenment, the new University of Moral and Political Science was created to promote the knowledge of legal and political sciences among the growing population.[1]

Besides many resident students there was a large correspondence department. The students of this department were scattered all over Siam. They were in residence for a short period only, usually about fifteen days at the completion of their correspondence course. The period of residence training was given over to teaching the students how to live under all circumstances. The course included lectures, sports, amusements, and inspection trips. In 1936-37 there were 77 graduates of the correspondence department who lived together for the fifteen-day period. The day started at six o'clock with exercises and military drill. They were taught how to fight and how to protect themselves from attack. There was at least one speech a day by a prominent man on the subject of how to win success in life. Hero worship resulted because the men who spoke were the leaders of the nation, men of brilliant and compelling

[1] *Siam Chronicle,* June 10th, 1937.

personality. This reacted very favourably for the new government. In the afternoons the students were shown the glories of Bangkok, ancient and modern, in order to encourage national pride.

6. SIAMESE STUDENTS ABROAD

The Siamese student who has spent several years abroad is a vital factor in modern Siam. Ever since the days of King Chulalongkorn there have been Siamese studying in foreign lands. Many Siamese studied in England, and as a result, the English school system was made the basis on which the Siamese system was planned. For thirty years the system was developed by English headmasters, until on the eve of the revolution there were primary, secondary, and university schools. Now that fewer students are being sent abroad to England some people fear for the continuity of the school system. This fear seems groundless, since although fewer students are being sent, those sent have been selected by competitive examination and are of high calibre. All too often family influence determined who was to be sent forty years ago.

The appropriation for Siamese students abroad for 1937-38 was reported to be *baht* 482,800. The dispersion of students was as follows: England had 32 students, France had 10, Germany 2, Japan 12, America 11, Philippines 11, India 1, and Indo-China 1. Twenty new students were to be sent during the year to Europe and to oriental countries for study.[1] Including privately sent students the totals are approximately as follows: America 50, England 100, Japan 200, Germany 20, France 50, and the Philippines 200.

The above figures fail to give a full picture of the Siamese foreign students. Mr. K. Noguchi, speaking for Japan, remarks that there are over 200 private and government students from Siam in schools there.[2] Most of the private students are interested in commercial and economics courses; some study medicine or dentistry; only a few are interested in fishery or agriculture. In order to make foreign study easier, Mr. Noguchi suggests the preparation of a Siamese-Japanese dictionary, the creation of a library of Japanese books in Siam, and the teaching of Japanese as a foreign language in the secondary schools.[3]

[1] *Nation*, June 18th, 1937.
[2] The Siamese Consulate in Japan reports altogether about 100 students.
[3] *Nation*, October 19th, 1937.

The students who have gone abroad have returned to benefit the nation. They are to be found in every department which requires highly trained men. The former generation of students were nominated for foreign study from favoured families, sometimes without adequate regard for ability. In spite of this, many of them have rendered fine service. The present generation of foreign students, since the beginning of King Prajadhipok's reign, have been chosen on a scholastic basis. The highly competitive nature of the examinations tends to eliminate all but students of exceptional ability, and so it may be expected that foreign students in the future will be of even greater value to Siam. Genius is occasionally found in these students. Thus a sixteen-year-old boy, Nai Prasert Nanagara, a former Suan Kularb student, who went to study in the Philippines, was hailed, in 1937, as a mathematical genius.

7. LIBRARIES AND LITERATURE

The public library, an important educational factor, has not been popularized in Siam as yet. The only important libraries are in Bangkok. One or two large provincial towns have made a small beginning. The idea is still a novel one in the provinces. In 1937, a certain private school in the south opened a school library. This was enough of an innovation to call forth several hundred of the leading citizens of the town. The library consisted of but three small cases of books in Siamese and English.

The Siamese as a race are just beginning to want quantities of reading material. It is not uncommon to hear Europeans say that they do not care to learn to read Siamese because there is nothing to read. The actual difficulty is not that there is nothing to read, but that it is not easily available. The National Library in Bangkok has a wealth of Siamese literature, but it must be read on the premises and is not available to any but residents of Bangkok with time to go to the library.

An increase in the quantity of Siamese printed matter must certainly affect the education of the nation. More newspapers, love stories, and cheap novels are sold than ever before. Where these gain a wide reading public there is bound to follow a circulation of good literature. Regular bookstores have been opened in the large population centres, which sell books on law, medicine, education, agriculture, politics, foreign nations, and other subjects. Many of the better books are translations from English or French and are the product of men trained abroad. Thus one fluent writer who spent several years in France and is at present in charge of the Royal Institute, Luang Vichitr Vadhakar, has many admirable books to his credit, and has done much to get the people into the habit of buying good books. The writing profession is just opening up in Siam and the Siamese are producing favourite novelists and serious writers as never before. The greatest single lack, which it is to be hoped will be remedied, to some extent at least, in the next five years, is in the field of children's books. At present the lack is so appalling that, outside of their school books, children have nothing to read except books, newspapers, and magazines intended for adults.

Phra Sarasasana Brapan, one time Minister of Education, attempted to develop a philosophy of education for Siam in a series of newspaper articles that appeared daily in the *Nation* over a period of several weeks. He recalled the popular phrase that was posted everywhere: "The kingdom is home, the military is the fence." He agreed that the people should support the military programme but contended that their best protection was universal education. He rather optimistically felt that education insures internal and international peace and security. Education sustains the abundant life of every individual and so of the nation. Education not only teaches people how to do things but why to do them. Life is thus given a reasonable dynamic and the people are enabled to make adjustments to changing ways of life.

CHAPTER VI

MEDICAL TRENDS

1. MEDICAL BEGINNINGS

PLAGUE, cholera, dysentery, malaria, hookworm, and other diseases, if their history could be written, would be shown to have had more influence on the Siamese character, religion, and economic position than is usually realized.

Prince Sakol Varavarn said:

> Disease has played an important part in shaping the course of Siamese history. Even before the Thai people penetrated the Khmer Empire, which in the first century of the Christian era extended throughout the Indo-Chinese peninsula, outbreaks of pestilence among their enemies had in A.D. 750 and 754 materially assisted them in repelling the Chinese invaders from Nan Chao, their original country, thus retarding their own entry into Siam for almost a hundred years. . . . . In 1350, the foundation of Ayudhya, which for over four centuries remained the capital of Siam, was directly due to an epidemic which caused the abandonment of U-Thong, a previous metropolis. . . . During the final siege of Ayudhya by the Burmese, the resistance of the inhabitants against their enemies, both human and microscopical, was so reduced by starvation that they became an easy prey to an epidemic.[1]

Following upon this the city was destroyed and Bangkok became the capital city of Siam. Thus disease was a contributing cause in the establishment of Bangkok.

The old-style Siamese doctor is still, in 1939, the one to whom the masses of the people in the country districts turn in time of sickness. Dr. Morden Carthew, in an address before the Bangkok Rotary Club, described a prominent Siamese healer:

> The first healer that I will try to describe is the late Phya Pitsanoo, a very celebrated physician who practiced in Bangkok in the reign of King Chulalongkorn and died some twenty years ago.
> He came from a family that had been healers for several generations, and his elder brother followed the same profession and had been given the title

[1] H.S.H. Prince Sakol Varavarn, *Public Health and Medical Service in Siam* (Bangkok: Public Health Department, 1930), pp. 1-3.

of Luang. . . . He was a thin spare little man and very active for his age, with a bright intelligent face full of humour, and with those perfect manners so often seen in Siamese. . . . On my first visit the hospital surprised, me, for it was cleaner, tidier, and better furnished than any other Siamese hospital in Bangkok, and that did not say very much. It was full of patients and there was a large proportion of women amongst them, another point which made it peculiar, for in those days it was very difficult to get a woman to go to the hospital. . . .

What specially struck me, however, was his manner to his patients; it was the perfect bedside manner, personifying kindness, sympathy, confidence in himself, firmness, and knowledge.[1]

Dr. Carthew related an incident in Phya Pitsanoo's medical practice in which he saved the life of a woman of eighty who was slowly dying of starvation. Other doctors had tried to persuade her to drink tinned milk. She refused. The doctor reminded her that she was very old, so old she was in her second childhood. He reminded her that in her first childhood she had had a wet nurse. In the end the eighty-year-old woman took her milk from a wet nurse and then swallowed two large white marbles of medicine which proved to be Mellins food. She lived for several years. Although the old man had no medical qualifications, Dr. Carthew regarded him as an excellent healer of the old school. In the medical history of Siam there have been many men like this, who inspired confidence and helped the people to the limit of their ability.

The empirical methods of India and China, modified by local usage, have been the basis for Siamese medical practice. The theory upon which they are founded is that the body is made up of certain elements such as wind, fire, earth, and water. If one element is out of balance a person becomes ill. The common expression for illness is "it is the wind". That is, the wind has thrown the body elements out of balance. Treatment, where it was not by medicines, was often by magic formula or incantation. Some doctors of the old school never resorted to this, however. Medicines were prepared from bark, roots, beans, and herbs. There was doubtless real medical value in many of the prescriptions. The pestle, the wheel for grinding, and the teapot for boiling were the instruments used to resolve the sticks, barks, twigs, or beans into medicine.

[1] *Bangkok Daily Mail,* May 8th, 1933.

Prince Sakol says that cholera was first mentioned in Siamese history in 1357. Smallpox, in 1534, was reported to have caused the death of Paromaraja IV. Plague was introduced from India in 1904. To meet these modern diseases European medical men came to Siam as early as 1676. At that time Jesuit missionaries opened a small hospital for King Phra Narai.[1]

Dr. Dan Beach Bradley was one of the founders of western medicine in Siam. In 1835 he established a public dispensary and surgery. In 1838 he introduced inoculation and vaccination. In 1839 he introduced the western method of obstetrics. In 1843 he established the first private hospital, and in 1851 began the practice of Homeopathic medicine. Vaccination against smallpox had but recently been recognized. Chloroform was just coming into use. Ether had not yet been discovered. Pasteur, one of the founders of bacteriology, was but a boy of twelve. Lister, who made antiseptic surgery possible was but a lad of seven. Dr. Oliver Wendell Holmes' paper on puerperal sepsis, which was to affect midwifery, had not yet been written. The hypodermic syringe was not yet known and the clinical thermometer was exceedingly crude. When we speak of the coming of modern medicine to Siam we need to remember that Siam was receiving it almost as soon as the rest of the world. Modern medicine and surgery have but recently come to the western as well as the eastern world. The point of interest is that the doctors were there on the field in Siam ready to act as transmitting agents for the new knowledge. American missionaries performed this great service for Siam. One cannot scorn the old type of medical practitioner of the orient without scorning the old type of practitioner of Europe. The methods and theories of both have been made obsolete by the new knowledge.

Surgery was something radically new to Siam. Previously there had been no knowledge of anatomy. Consequently, when surgery first began to be practiced by the new style of Siamese doctor, it was not always with complete success. Dr. Morden Carthew relates the horrible story of a woman with a large abdominal swelling who was operated on for an ovarian tumor. When the incision was made the surgeons were startled to have a large red thing the size of a baby's head stick up at them. Not knowing what else to

---

[1] H.S.H. Prince Sakol Varavarn, *Public Health and Medical Service in Siam* (Bangkok: Public Health Department, 1930), pp. 4-5.

do they tied it up with strong thread and cut it off. The patient died instantly. It was an enlarged spleen.[1]

2. THE DEVELOPMENT OF THE MEDICAL SCHOOL

The medical school in Bangkok dates back to 1880-81 when King Chulalongkorn was the reigning monarch. A terrible cholera epidemic struck Bangkok, taking about 30,000 lives. Temporary hospitals were put up in 48 districts. When the rainy season came the disease abated, and the hospitals were abandoned. His Majesty expressed a desire to establish a permanent hospital. Five of the leading men of the country were appointed a committee to consider the erection of a hospital. One of the five was H.R.H. Prince Damrong Rajanubhap. Civil officials and foreigners were invited to subscribe to the hospital project.

In 1886-87 the cremation ceremony of Chao Phya Jaya Siriraja was held. It was customary for the king to give liberally to such a cremation. On this occasion he determined to make the gift something of permanent value. He ordered that all the temporary houses required for the cremation ceremony be made of good timber. When the ceremony was over, the buildings were re-erected in the form of a hospital on a selected site. This was the beginning of the modern Siriraja Hospital. After a year of experiment the new Department of Hospitals was put under the Ministry of Education, which was administered by Prince Damrong.

At that time Siriraja Hospital consisted of:

1. Two wooden buildings with attap roofs, each with beds for ten people.
2. Two wooden buildings with attap roofs, each with beds for eight people.
3. A two-storey home for the resident physician.
4. An out-patient ward for storing medicine and treating out-patients.
5. Four wooden buildings for in-patients.
6. Two well-built buildings for patients of high rank.

The staff consisted of one doctor and his assistant, three dispensary men, and five coolies.[2]

[1] *Bangkok Daily Mail*, May 8th, 1933.
[2] *Year Book of 1930-31*, published by medical graduates of Chulalongkorn University; summarizes Siamese medical history.

The Medical School began simple instruction in 1888. Modern medicine was not yet acceptable to the people, and there was some doubt as to whether a doctor could make a living by the practice of the new medicine. It was difficult to find either teachers or pupils. At the beginning, the old and new methods of medicine were taught side by side. Mom Chao Ciak was the teacher of Siamese Medicine. Dr. George B. McFarland was the Professor of Surgery and Modern Medicine. The course of study was three years, combining both kinds of medicine. The first class was graduated in 1891.

In 1896, living quarters and a class-room building were erected for the resident students. A library and classrooms were provided in the school building. In 1899 the school was formally opened by the king and queen, and named "The Government Medical School". From that time on training was more regular and strict. In 1901 the course of study was expanded to four years. In 1905 a new ministry was established to oversee all the hospitals in the kingdom with the exception of Siriraja Hospital, which was reserved as a place of interneship for medical students. The Medical School and hospital have been continued under the Ministry of Education.

The new kind of doctors gradually won their way. Little by little the public began to switch their patronage from the old to the new. The teaching of Siamese medicine was gradually dropped from the curriculum. In 1910, the course was extended to five years of study; in 1914 it was increased to six years. The first four years, taken at the school for training civil officials, was a college course including the necessary science. In 1913, a department of pharmacy was begun which required three years of study.

On March 26th, 1916, King Vajiravudh decided to improve the university course for the training of civil officials and as a result Chulalongkorn University was organized. The Medical School was made a department of the university.

In 1921 the Rockefeller Institute was invited by the government to undertake the reorganization of the school on strictly modern lines. As a consequence, a new class room building was erected, six qualified doctors were sent to take charge of instruction in various departments, and scholarships for further study in America were given the most promising students. At least two students from each department were sent abroad.

After secondary school, medical students had two years of science and four years of medicine. The degree of Bachelor of Medicine was then given. The first class to receive the degree of Bachelor of Medicine was the class of 1928-29. This class and the class of 1929-30 were given their degrees together with the class of 1930-31, which was the first year that degrees were formally granted. The three classes together comprised 48 members.

In March, 1937, the following ceremony was held:

> The presentation of certificates to the graduates of the Chulalongkorn University took place on Saturday last by H.H. Prince Aditya, before a very large and distinguished gathering. The big hall of the University building was crowded to its fullest capacity by the friends of the students, the graduating students themselves, and the graduates of other universities, whose robes and the varied colours of their hoods made quite a picturesque appearance. The dais at the end of the room was filled by a chapter of five priests, whose chanting throughout the ceremony put the rite of solemnity upon the proceedings. Amongst those present we noted H. E. the Premier, Phya Bahol, and various other Ministers of State. His Highness, the President of the Council of Regency was met by the Minister of Public Instruction, the Rector of the University. . . . Having arrived in the big hall, H.H. Prince Aditya lighted the Candles of Worship, and listened to a report on the University. Thirty graduates, including two ladies, received their M.B.[1]

The other graduates, about 70 in number, were also granted their degrees at that time. Of this number 26 received certificates in nursing, and one a certificate in pharmacy.

The school of nursing and midwifery had its start in 1896 when the queen granted a sum of money for the purpose. After a three-year course the first graduating class of ten members completed their work in 1900. The school moved frequently and failed to progress. A new beginning was made in 1906 with courses for male nurses as well as for women.

The medical class of 1930-31 was the first to have more applicants than the school could accept. Only 25 could be received, so competitive examinations were held for the first time in the history of medicine in Siam. The same year the nursing school had 15 graduates.

The total number of graduates with the degree of Bachelor of Medicine is only 142. Including all of those graduated before the degree was granted there are hardly 500 doctors in Siam who have

[1] *Siam Chronicle*, March 29th, 1937.

had some training in modern medicine. The population is about fourteen-and-a-half millions. This means that there is a great need for more doctors. To make the need more urgent, most of the qualified doctors are located in the large population centres. The great mass of the Siamese who live outside of the cities are hardly touched by modern medicine.

Outside of Bangkok, practically all of the qualified Siamese doctors are in government employ, that is to say, they are health officers. Few of them are surgeons, and almost none of them are equipped with surgeries in which to operate even when qualified to do so. They have no X-ray machines, almost no instruments; and, in fact, encounter so many difficulties in their work that they are reduced to being little more than dispensers and dressers. They are comparatively well paid, receiving generally about *baht* 150 a month, as compared to an average of *baht* 45 for teachers in government schools. Their salaries are probably more than they could make in private practice in the provincial centres. They are, therefore, content to work for the government, which guarantees them a pension after fifteen years of service. If they are not discouraged by their inadequate equipment and their circumscribed opportunities for service, they are likely to be sometimes disheartened by lawsuits brought against them by their patients. These law suits are so very common as to be a further deterrent to private practice. The government doctor need not fear that his practice will be ruined by them, for, at worst, he will receive nothing more than a change of location, while the private practitioner may find himself without a profession.

3. THE DIFFICULTIES IMPEDING THE SPREAD OF MODERN MEDICINE

Western medicine has had to win its way slowly. A casual visitor to Siam can hardly appreciate the effort that has been expended to popularize medical theories and practices full of innovations that cut across the thinking of the race. Especially is this true of innovations that have to do with birth, health, and death. Surgery has never been a part of Siamese medicine. The very idea of making an incision in the skin is objectionable.

Dr. George B. McFarland, the first professor of modern medicine in Siriraja Hospital, relates some of the difficulties he met in winning public approval. Siamese medicine had to be taken in large quantities and people distrusted small pills. One day a lot of quinine was missing from the dispensary. Dr. McFarland asked the clerk who had bought it. He reported that a doctor of Siamese medicine had taken the quinine to mix with Siamese medicine for fever. The doctor had discovered that quinine was a remarkable aid. Respect for the new medicines was often won in such a roundabout way as this.

Dr. McFarland says that great difficulty was experienced in the collecting of samples of blood for inspection. Patients refused to have incisions or cuts made, on the grounds that their wind would come out and their blood would flow without ceasing, if they did. He tells how one day some lead and opium pills were put out in the sun to dry. A little girl, who was playing around, got some of them and swallowed them. She was in a serious condition when the doctor found her and revived her. It was an opportunity to teach the medical students the treatment for opium poisoning. That incident also succeeded in teaching them that even small pills have great powers.

Again, when plague first came to Bangkok the doctors were unfamiliar with it. Men in the prisons died rapidly. A Siamese doctor took a corpse for examination. During the process the back of his hand was slightly wounded and became infected. The doctor paid no attention to it and in a day or two was dead. This incident demonstrated to the medical students that disease could spread from person to person by infection.

And again, a number of stone operations had been performed and the stones kept for the students to examine. One day three stones disappeared. They had been taken by a doctor of Siamese medicine who ground them up and made a medicine for the removal of stones from the bladder. He did this on the basis of a Siamese proverb that parallels the one about the hair of the dog being good for his bite.[1]

Dr. A. G. Ellis, former Dean of Siriraja Hospital, spent about fourteen years creating a modern plant. Excavators, masons, carpenters, and plumbers, were busy throughout his period of leadership. The medical centre is now complete, in his opinion, except

[1] *Year Book of 1935-36*, published by medical graduates of Chulalongkorn University in Siamese; summarizes modern medical progress.

for a few exterior decorations. The future medical men of Siam will pass through this modern training school.

Dr. Boon Itt of Shellman Hospital, Pitsanuloke, is one of the outstanding graduates. In the *Year Book* of Siriraja Hospital for 1935-36, he advises the young doctors. His first advice is that at this juncture in Siamese medical history young doctors should not be specialists, but should be able to do as much as possible in both medicine and surgery. There are no general practitioners, let alone specialists in the country districts. If one tries to be a specialist, he can be of little value to the villagers; for if the doctor once admits that he cannot treat this or that, the people lose confidence in him.

He went on to say that his experiences at Pitsanuloke had taught him that people came to him only after the doctor of Siamese medicine and the spirit doctor had been consulted. The progress of modern medicine is naturally retarded when the people come to the doctor in extremity only. For instance, a woman was brought into the hospital who had been in labour for three days and nights. Several local doctors of Siamese medicine had worked on her without success. They had sat on her, exerted unusual pressure on her, even walked on her abdomen without being able to deliver the child. In the end they decided to try the doctor of foreign medicine. The woman was breathing but unconscious. Her eyes were yellow and her strength gone. The child was dead and decayed. Dr. Boon Itt removed the child, gave injections and treatment, but the woman died. The doctor was exhausted with his efforts. The parents of the woman took her away with disparaging remarks to the effect that they had brought her to the doctor of foreign medicine and she had died after all; therefore, the doctor of foreign medicine wasn't so much use after all.

The doctor seldom is given the opportunity of treating a case from the beginning. Modern medicine has not yet won the confidence of the people in the country districts. The average person's knowledge of modern medicine is derived from the quack who travels here and there giving injections for all diseases. The quack has only one idea, to give injections and collect a lot of money. Foreign medicine is blamed for the ensuing failures, and confidence is lost.

Dr. Boon Itt tells of a fever patient who came to see him. Three men had the same fever but only one came for treatment. In one week Dr. Boon Itt's patient recovered and went home. He immediately brought the other two men back with him for treatment. They explained that they had agreed to have one man go first to try out the foreign medicine, even though doctors of Siamese medicine claimed that foreign medicine was no good for fever.

The spread of modern medicine is hindered by lack of communications. A village only ten miles from the hospital is remote during the rainy season. In the dry season a sick person can walk the distance in three or four hours. In one case a man was shot in the leg and could not walk or ride. The water was deep in the fields and he could not be carried. Three days were required to bring him by boat to the hospital, a distance of ten miles.

Competition between the old and new system of medicine creates difficulties. The doctors of Siamese medicine live in the villages and are close to the lives of the people. What usually happens is that a patient tries first this doctor, and then that, and the modern doctor last of all. Lives are lost and bodies ruined. For instance, when an arm is broken the people prefer to apply oils rather than a stiff bandage, with the not unnatural result that broken arms seldom heal so as to be usable again. Even if they are treated in a hospital where the arm is properly bandaged, the patient will probably remove the bandage to use the arm. The old style of doctor has no professional objections to admitting that he can heal any and all diseases. Modern doctors cannot honestly claim to heal all diseases, but the people expect and demand a doctor who can heal everything, seemingly making little distinction between claim and performance. When a new-style doctor tells a patient that he cannot heal a disease, the patient thinks one of two things, either the doctor is not proficient, or the remuneration offered has not been large enough to tempt him. A man came to the hospital and asked for an injection for a certain disease which a quack had agreed to heal with one injection. The hospital doctor knew that one injection would give a good reaction but would not be a cure. A course of treatment was indicated. The patient went away, took the single injection from the quack, and when he had a good reaction, spread the news that the hospital doctor did not know very much about healing.

In another instance a woman was brought into the hospital after she had been in labour for three days. The village doctors had already done their work. The hospital doctor removed the dead child with instruments. Early the next morning the relatives came insisting that they be allowed to take the woman home so that she might be roasted by the fire as is the custom in Siamese medicine. The woman was very weak and could hardly stand the strenuous fire treatment. No argument would prevail and she was taken away. Small wonder that the maternal mortality is appalling. One realizes how modern doctors must struggle to win the village people, how extremely difficult their position is! Small wonder, then, that sometimes both their skill and their enthusiasm becomes blunted. The only answer to the problem is a regular presentation of the powers of modern medicine. It is essential that qualified doctors be thoroughly equipped with instruments, medicines, and hospitals. The present custom of supplying qualified doctors with small dispensaries and health centres, where injections and minor dressings can be given, is inadequate.

The modern quack is described accurately by a physician of wide experience as follows:

> The writer can state without hesitation or exaggeration that large numbers of simple ignorant villagers are not only made to part with their money under false pretences, but are also disabled, mutilated or maimed, and sometimes poisoned and killed by the injudicious use of potent drugs and improper irresponsible administration of injections by quacks. . . . The writer visited some Chinese mining camps and came across one of these medicine pedlars. This gentleman was dressed in full European costume with stiff collar, necktie, riding breeches and leggings. He was wearing gold rimmed spectacles and had a stethoscope displayed in one of his pockets. The writer had a unique opportunity of observing the gentleman in action who was holding forth the most wonderful tales of surgical feats he could perform, such as that of removing the brain, cleaning it and putting it back. He was also prepared to give a written guarantee to cure leprosy, consumption, sterility and impotency in men, and barrenness in women, by a single injection and a bottle of medicine, the value of which, however, would have to be paid half in advance and half after the cure. He also explained to the simple folk gathered there that he had an injection which when given would perfume the body so that when one sweats, a most exquisite odour would emanate from the body.
>
> In the course of his practice the writer has come across cases of Chronic Bronchitis, Asthma, Tuberculosis, Heart Disease, Kidney Disease, Hernia, Hydrocele, etc., who give a definite history of having received four or five intravenous injections, which from the description of the packing is without

doubt Neo Salvarsan, the use of which drug is much abused in Siam. The writer has personally seen numbers of people who are unable to bend the elbow due to inflammation caused by the unskillful intravenous injection of Neo Salvarsan where the major part of the solution escaped into the subcutaneous tissue.[1]

The first step in regulating the medical situation was the enforced registration of all doctors and nurses professing to be of the modern school of medicine. These were divided into first and second class doctors and first and second class nurses. The first class doctors are allowed to practice every phase of medicine and surgery. The second class doctors are limited to minor surgery, the sale of accredited medicines, and muscular injections. Intravenous injections and major surgery are forbidden them. The doctors of Siamese medicine who deal in roots and herbs are not registered.

The purpose of this action was to eliminate quack doctors who posed as qualified medical men. The value of registration is problematical, since it in no way hinders the practice of medicine by the old style doctors and midwives, among whom are many more instances of malpractice than among the inadequately trained doctors who lay some claim to being modern. There is a suspicion, not entirely groundless, that registration is being used as a discriminatory weapon. Thus all graduates of government medical schools are registered without difficulty, while graduates of some superior non-government schools can get nothing but the poorer rating. A graduate of the Yale Nursing School in the United States, for instance, was denied registration as first class because of a technicality. A graduate of Peking Medical Centre had great difficulty in getting his degree recognized. One member of the People's Assembly went so far as to suggest that only graduates of the Siamese Government Hospital be considered qualified to practice in Siam. Fortunately, in view of the appalling lack of doctors in every place in the kingdom but Bangkok, his colleagues did not agree with him.

Medical propaganda is regularly carried on through the newspapers. Glancing through the *Nation* for 1937, one finds articles on the need for keeping the body healthy, general health instruction, the evils of alcoholic drink, approved birth control methods, the value of birth control, why and how to have white teeth rather

[1] *Bangkok Times,* July 25th, 1933.

than the betel blackened ones of tradition, the cause and cure of tuberculosis, normal and abnormal menstruation, and other topics of interest. Even such subjects as birth control are not considered embarrassing and are discussed in public and in the newspapers. Thus a high ranking civil official while waiting in a railroad station, in a mixed group, pleasantly remarked that although he had four children he was not having any more. He had the matter under control and carefully explained the technique used.

One of the more dramatic aspects of the new medical work was seen at the time of a recent cholera epidemic. The nation mobilized as for war. The epidemic broke out early in 1937, a bad year for cholera. The front pages of the newspapers carried the week to week death toll with advice as to what to do about food, drink, and sewage. Headlines cried out: "Cholera spreads: Take care of what you eat and drink: Director-General of Public Health outlines simple measures to prevent epidemic."[1] In an average week there were 440 cases with 292 deaths. In an unusual week 844 cases and 594 deaths were recorded, of which 112 were in Bangkok alone. And this in the face of all that could be done by the medical forces of the kingdom. The programme was one of instruction and injection. A law was passed which required everyone to be injected. It was reported that a fine of *baht* 50 would have to be paid by delinquents. The government health centres injected people by the thousands. Everyone, from babes to ancients, gathered around to be injected. Names were noted in a book, and certificates were given them if desired. Many of the railroad stations had temporary injection stalls erected. All passengers coming from infected areas had to produce certificates or be injected. Some doubt was cast on the efficacy of the injections by the unwillingness of British health officials in Malaya to recognize Siamese certificates of injection. Passengers coming to Malayan states from Siam were required to be injected in Malaya by the local health authorities even when they were able to produce proof of a previous injection in Siam. In spite of all this strenuous effort, the epidemic was brought to a close only by the rainy season which purged the country, washed out stagnant and infected canals, and left Bangkok reasonably clean for another year.

Smallpox is seldom considered today as an epidemic problem.

[1] *Siam Chronicle*, April 6th, 1937.

MEDICAL TRENDS

In former years the smallpox-scarred face was the common one. An eleven year programme of national vaccination was planned and carried out by the Department of Public Health. It aimed at an annual increase of vaccinations up to a maximum of two million. By 1930 there was very little smallpox.

An anti-hookworm campaign was carried on for years and about two million treatments were given. The extent of the ailment is shown by the fact that 65.18 per cent of over 700,000 stools analyzed showed the presence of hookworm. Although treatment has been widespread, hookworm is as common as ever because the people continue to go barefooted.

Since 1904, plague has broken out occasionally in some parts of Siam. Korat began to have almost annual outbreaks. In 1912 about 800 people died there of plague. In 1917 another 7,000 lives were lost. A technique of control was evolved which keeps the country almost free of plague. Thus, on one occasion a dead rat was found in a kitchen just after a man had died suddenly in a house across the street. The Department of Health was notified. In a few minutes a truck-load of rat traps appeared. Traps were set up in every available corner of the house and grounds. Over a hundred rats were caught the first night and were dropped neatly into cans of disinfecting liquid. The rats were transported to a laboratory and examined. The report was negative.

Malaria is another very common disease. There are large sections of Siam where the disease is endemic. Some of the northern provinces are so infected with the disease that the majority of the population seem to have enlarged spleens, pale lips, and be subject to fevers. Hospitals in these areas for years derived much of their income from the sale of quinine. The value of quinine as a specific for the disease became quickly known. It was readily accepted and today is on sale very cheaply in every government dispensary or health centre, and in every medicine shop. Ignorance and lack of doctors still prevent much of the population from having the medical care needed. During some seasons it is not unusual to see a fever stricken village with one or two people sick in every home. Funeral processions are frequent. Malaria is a scourge that dissipates the physical abilities of thousands of people annually. The government has popularized a picture that compares the malarial mosquito to a tiger and purports to demonstrate that the mosquito is the more dangerous of the two. Almost everyone in Siam is familiar with the picture and yet not many houses outside of the larger population centres use mosquito nets.

An important article of trade of the average medicine shop is Neo-Salvarsan, and other medicines for the treatment of venereal diseases. Carle C. Zimmerman wrote:

> Outside of the market places there is practically no venereal disease in the country. Either the people have never had any such disease, or the germ strains have worn themselves out, or have been conquered by natural selection, or by native medicines. In this case exceptions must be made for the large market places and the port cities. These places with commercialized prostitution and their mobile populations ignorant of the first laws of hygiene, are probably about as much infected as the rural districts are free from this disease.[1]

Mr. Zimmerman, in 1931, reached a number of conclusions on the health of Siam. One was that the country was underpopulated because of the high death rate. After careful observation of all parts of the country he concluded that the death rate was unchecked by medical means. The majority of the people lived and died without material benefit from medicine. Mr. Zimmerman suggested the "junior" doctor plan, whereby a partially trained worker would be located in every part of Siam to maintain contact with and give instruction to the villagers. The government has developed this plan and the junior doctor is to serve for a temporary period until there are qualified medical men in all parts of the kingdom. In Siamese he is called "one who helps the doctor". It is proposed to train 410 of them, one for every Amphoe in Siam. The junior doctor studies only six months. His duties are:

1. To sell government medicines.
2. To administer first aid and to take serious cases to the nearest doctor.
3. To deal with epidemic diseases such as cholera, smallpox, plague, dysentery, and malaria.
4. To deliver public health lectures at intervals on the subjects of sewage, water supply, and cooked food.

In December, 1936, there were 150 junior doctors ready for service. Another group totalling 136 in number were being trained.

[1] Carle C. Zimmerman, *Siam, Rural Economic Survey* (Bangkok: The Bangkok Times Press, Ltd., 1931), p. 230.

The average salary was to be between *baht* 35 and 50 per month. The plan of training junior doctors has met with strenuous objections from the Siriraja Hospital group under the leadership of Dr. Ellis. They fear that its benefits will not compensate for the dangers involved if comparatively untrained persons are allowed to practice even in a limited way. However, support for the plan has come from many leaders in the National Assembly who are themselves from outlying districts and who realize the terrible need of their constituencies for even such elementary care as the junior doctors could give. These men have prevailed. The trend is to make modern medicine available in some measure to every part of Siam.

From the standpoint of the nation, leprosy is a minor but dramatic disease. It is not yet under control. Of the three leper homes in Siam, two are under the auspices of the American Presbyterian Mission, one at Chiengmai and the other at Nakon Sritammarat. Both of these homes receive grants-in-aid from the government, but are not fully subsidized. The third leper home is run by the government near Bangkok. It is estimated that there are 20,000 lepers in Siam and that instances of the disease are slowly increasing. Probably not more than 1,000 lepers are receiving treatment. The rest are quietly living their lives wherever they happen to be. There are no restrictions to keep them from mingling with uninfected people. Lepers in the later stages of the disease are recognized and are frequently shunned, but not always so. For instance, one leper in a large market town has continued to live with his wife and children and to run a bicycle shop which brings him into contact with many people daily. Although he has lived across the street from a government health centre for years, nothing has been done to isolate or instruct him. He has been repeatedly urged to go to a nearby leper home, but prefers his own way of life. In the early stages of his disease a Chinese doctor guaranteed to treat and cure him for *baht* 200. The "cure" left him worse than before. In Singora, a group of lepers, almost all vendors of food, wrote to Nakon Sritammarat to the leper asylum there to ask that treatment be sent to them, since they could not afford to abandon their business! They said that there were about thirty of them in the markets of that town.

No law isolating lepers can be effective until there is some place in which to house them. It is obvious that if 20,000 people are to be housed and fed by the government, it will cost a tremendous sum annually. A recent proposal has been made to isolate lepers by villages, and allow them to be self-supporting within their own community. It has been suggested that the clean children be separated from the leper communities and housed in orphanages. It was thought by the proponent of the plan that in a few generations leprosy would probably vanish, since it is not an inherited disease. Another proposal is to sterilize male lepers and segregate the, at present, clean children and so end the problem.

The leper problem has not yet been seriously dealt with simply because nobody knows just what to do with 20,000 lepers.

Men like Dr. Edwin C. Cort of McCormick Hospital, Chiengmai, and Mr. Hugh McKean of the Chiengmai Leper Asylum, both of whom have had long experience with the leper problem, do not believe that the solution is to be found in hospitalization. They believe that this solution is impossible in low-income lands. What they recommend out of their experience is: (1) the continuation of existing hospitals for lepers who voluntarily apply for hospitalization; (2) the extension of out-patient clinics with a well planned educational programme as well as a medical programme; (3) voluntary isolation of lepers into leper villages wherever the educational programme has made the lepers willing to do this; (4) aid of such villages by land-grants and local community support; (5) possible separation of "clean" children from leper parents.

The emphasis on voluntary separation is necessary at this step in public health work in Siam inasmuch as there is as yet no means to enforce registration of the disease, or isolation for the diseased person when discovered.

The latest research in leprosy suggests that leprosy, or more particularly the tendency to contract leprosy, may bear a direct relation to diet. If this is proved to be so, it may alter the existing means employed to try to prevent the spread of the disease.

Dr. J. Martin Oberdorfer, twenty-eight-year-old German doctor, is conducting research experiments in leprosy at Chiengmai. He is following up the discovery that he made in Africa that a certain root predisposes to leprosy. In Africa, Dr. Oberdorfer found that among tribes living on one side of the Niger River and eating the root, which the Siamese call *puawk* and the Hawaiians *taro*, five per cent had leprosy; while tribes on the other side of the river with whom the root was taboo were almost free of it, only one-fourth of one per cent of them having it. This root contains sapotoxin which seems to decrease the adrenal secretions and lower the vitality. Sapotoxin is found in some other plants as well. Dr. Oberdorfer is also experimenting with certain other theories relative to the therapeutic treatment of sufferers from the disease in the belief that the deformation which generally accompanies it may be lessened. Once it is established that sapotoxin predisposes to the disease, measures to prevent the spread of leprosy can probably be taken with a considerable success. The Siamese government has already in certain instances been able to materially decrease the use of certain vegetable products known to be harmful. Such instances have been local, but nevertheless do form a precedent on which to act.

4. PUBLIC HEALTH

The hotels that abound in every market centre are a definite menace to health. They are run by Chinese and are usually unscrubbed, smelly from sewage, urine, and pigs, and over-run with prostitutes. The average room is equipped with a double bed, having a thin mattress on a wooden bottom, a pillow, a bolster, a mosquito net that was bought and hung when the bed was new. There is a table, a chair, a spittoon, a wash basin, and—crowning glory of all—a guest toothbrush firmly chained to the window frame. The guest walks around in wooden shoes to keep off the floor, avoids shaking the bed when crawling in so that not too much dust will settle on the face, and cringes as he waits for the "zing" that proves that the local mosquitoes know where the cracks are between bed and netting. The nets are seldom long enough to tuck in under the mattress, but are draped around the edge of the bed. Their chief office is to hinder the paying guest from getting in and out of bed too easily, and to conserve all tuberculosis germs from the guests of former years.

The bath is a barrel of water in a little wooden shed where one may strip and pour water sparingly over the shrinking form. This shed is all too often the urinal as well as the bathroom. The toilet is a bucket affair or a shed at the rear, in which case the pigs are frequently the sewage disposal plant. For this service, and the privilege of driving the resident prostitute out of one's room, one pays a *baht* per day.

This is not just a foreigner's point of view. The same description of Chinese hotels is made by Chinese who must travel and live in them.

In many of the towns the government-controlled railroad has attempted to provide suitable rest-houses. Adequate quarters have been built and farmed out by the year, usually to Chinese who have had experience in the hotel business. In some cases very good service has been maintained. Little more could be desired than the hotel at Hua Hin. The general tendency has been for the rest-houses to decline toward the level of the Chinese hotels in the market. This has been the case in Haad Yie, Singora, and Tungsong. Rest-houses in all these are uniformly filthy.

In 1937, a clean-up campaign began to make itself felt in some of the hotels. A definite improvement has been noted in a few establishments. Mosquito nets have been washed, floors scrubbed, and bedding changed.

Although the Siamese as a race are clean people, soap is a modern importation. The country has always had the ingredients of soap at hand but little has been done with them. Soap with the bath is an innovation. Ten to fifteen years ago the average shop had one or two kinds for sale. Today the same shop has as many as 20 varieties.

Toothpaste has come in with soap and there are often as many as fifteen brands in a shop. Young Siam wants white teeth instead of the black fangs of the betel chewer.

The use of soap and a clean towel for dishes is not considered important by the lower classes of the people. The idea seems to be that water is clean and can scarcely be dirty. Water is sloshed over plates and glasses which are then dried with any old rag that happens to be hanging around. The writer will never forget the shock he felt when he discovered his Siamese cook wiping dishes with the bathing cloth which the cook used for everything from his nose to his feet. He could not see the enormity of his offence and assured the writer that the cloth was perfectly clean, for it was washed every day—on him—when he bathed.

The educated Siamese are as clean as the better class of any nation, perhaps cleaner. A class of Siamese boys were shocked when they read in an American book on hygiene that at least one bath a week was needed. They took two a day, showers, of course.

Lice and bed-bugs are as prevalent as the people. It is not unusual to see little girls sitting one behind the other, each picking lice from the head of the one in front. Boarding schools have to have a lice and bed-bug clean-up at regular intervals.

The disposal of market filth, which has been an unsolved problem, is now being made a responsibility of the new municipalities. The usual custom is simply to dump refuse in a convenient open space and let the flies breed as they may. Theoretically dumps are burned, but actually the burning is a mere formality and flies are terrible. A sewage disposal system has been developed by the Department of Public Health, but it is expensive. The dangers of cholera and dysentery are heightened by the flies from such dumps. The new local governments are responsible for the handling of refuse, urine, manure, and filthy water. They must control the placing of outhouses, safeguard the streams, and protect the wells. The people are being asked to join hands with the government to work out their own health salvation. Some efforts are crude, such as the new water system for a certain market centre. A scaffolding was erected and ten galvanized iron tanks, each holding about 100 gallons, were linked up into a system to supply water. The water was pumped from a well located under the tanks. The system is not beautiful nor very efficacious, but it is a beginning in the right direction.

5. HOSPITALS

Siam is still poor in its hospital equipment. Bangkok has the Bangkok Nursing Home, which is a British project; the St. Louis General Hospital, which is French; Takeda Hospital, which is Japanese; Chulalongkorn Hospital, which is a Siamese government hospital; and Siriraja Hospital, which is the training school for Siam's doctors. Besides these, there are a number of health centres and the Maternity Home of the American Presbyterian Mission. North of Bangkok there are hospitals at Pitsanuloke, Lampang, Nan, Chiengmai, Chiengrai, and Prae, all of which are under the auspices of the American Presbyterian Mission. South of Bangkok the same missionary organization has hospitals at Nakon Sritammarat and Trang. The government has a hospital at Singora and another at Bhuket. Beyond that most of the government doctors are working in health centres, sometimes without facilities for in-patients, seldom with more than one or two beds for the serious cases. In April, 1937, it was announced that Lopburi was to be a military centre and that a large hospital was to be erected there. The king donated *baht* 100,000 toward the buildings.

The hospital programme for Siam still lags, although such an outstanding Siamese doctor as Dr. Boon Itt has carefully plotted a programme whereby new hospitals, which could adequately provide service for a community, would cost only about *baht* 20,000. Two such hospitals a year would soon do much to help the whole nation.

In 1937, there was but one well-trained Siamese dentist in Siam. He was in Bangkok. Part of his time was given to the teaching of dentistry. Presumably there will be other Siamese dentists, for dentistry is a virgin field. A European with a toothache travels from a hundred to five hundred miles to get to the nearest capable dentist. Sometimes a toothache must be endured for months before an opportunity is found for the long trip. Those who cannot afford to travel either endure bad teeth or go to the poorly trained and none too clean Chinese or Japanese dentists. There is no lack of unqualified dentists. The crudest is the Chinese miracle man who works with a tack puller arrangement on the streets in the evening. His pile of old ivory on the mat before him indicates his business success. A step up from this is the Chinese or Japanese who has spent a few months in a dental office in Malaya, China, or Japan. Some of these workers have considerable skill, but none of them are well equipped. The new medical laws, which require the registering of doctors, require the dentists to register also. If all unqualified dentists are forced out of practice by the strict new laws, there will hardly be a dozen dentists in all of Siam. At the present time, few Siamese seem inclined to study dentistry. At any time when the government employs dentists as it now does doctors, there will be no lack of persons interested in dentistry. Private practice for either with anything like adequate compensation is impossible except in a few centres.

Siam has both Senior and Junior Red Cross societies. The Junior Red Cross is a school affair intended to train the children in the knowledge of first aid and cleanliness, and to inculcate a spirit of helpfulness. The Senior Red Cross is a well organized association with the king as its patron, its council consisting of twenty of the leading citizens, and its representatives on the League of Red Cross Societies. There is a Relief Division and a Pharmaceutical Division.

Two medical magazines are sent out monthly to government doctors. One is the *Medical News* which contains popular articles, and deals with everything from "What to do for Poison Gas in Time of War" to "Why don't you Sleep?" Schoolboys in the higher grades have admitted that they read it sometimes. It doubtless has an instructive influence. A monthly medical journal, intended to keep them informed on the latest medical practices, is supplied to the government doctors.

Now that the various spectacular diseases are gradually yielding to the programme of the Department of Public Health—diseases such as smallpox, plague, and cholera—there are other problems that should engage the attention of all interested in solving Siam's health problems. Besides malaria, which is very widespread and very destructive of life as well as of energy and vitality, and besides hookworm, which is equally common and almost equally debilitating, the most important and pressing problem for Siam today from the medical standpoint is that of maternity care and infant welfare.

Some beginnings have been made, but they have hardly touched the fringe of the problem. Vital statistics are not available from all parts of Siam, and even existing statistics are subject to inaccuracy because of the great difficulty in getting them. Competent estimates place infant mortality at between 30 and 50 per cent for the first year of life. In a country that is still underpopulated this loss of potential citizens is a serious matter. Maternal deaths are very common, although for them even fewer means of guessing at a percentage are available.

It is beyond the realm of possibility that there should be qualified doctors enough to care for all of Siam's mothers in this or even the next generation.

In some larger centres graduate nurses with supplementary training in midwifery are connected with the government health stations. In most cases these nurses assist the government doctors during the day, except when they are called out on delivery cases. Thus they are in contact with communicable diseases on the very days when they must also assist at deliveries. This has obvious disadvantages.

One other condition has militated against the success of this plan. In the Siamese tradition young women stay at home until they marry. Often parents are unwilling to allow their daughters to accept positions away from home. Where they have occasionally done so the problem of living quarters for young nurses has been difficult to solve. There are no Y.W.C.A.'s or similar associations in which they can live. Private homes and private quarters have not provided them with adequate protection against temptations that their educations have as yet ill-fitted them to meet.

Probably one of the best solutions of the problem has been worked out by Miss Johanne C. Christensen at the Maternity Home in Bangkok. Coming out originally under private auspices more than twenty-five years ago, Miss Christensen was so appalled at the high maternal and infant death rate that she went to England to secure training in midwifery to supplement her nurses training. Under the auspices of the American Presbyterian Mission she then started a thorough training course for midwives in Bangkok. She is convinced that a short course tacked on to nurses training is not enough, and offers a two-year course with an additional year of internship for a diploma in midwifery. Her plan is to train girls from distant villages with the belief that many of them will return to their villages later. The success of similar work in England and on the continent, and also in the southern mountains of the United States, as well as the success of Miss Christensen's own work so far, suggests that a plan of this sort is the most feasible for Siam.

Siam's health outlook is more encouraging than it has been for many years. Now that representatives from all over the country sit in the People's Assembly and have an opportunity to present the needs of their constituents to the government, and now that municipalities are springing up all over the country through which the people may express their needs and have the opportunity of developing solutions to their health problems, it may be expected that progress will be more rapid. The spiritual values of a healthy race are far different from those of a sickly race. Religion becomes more robust and less supine when the followers of religion are a strong and healthy people.

CHAPTER VII

TRENDS IN METHODS OF COMMUNICATION

MODERN methods of travel have been developed in Siam since the opening of the twentieth century, although tentative beginnings were made earlier. Railroad construction was begun about 1891-92. Several years passed before the steel road went far beyond the vicinity of Bangkok. When it did finally stretch from end to end of the country it found a people who had a very crude idea of time. Some of them could not realize that a train scheduled to leave at 8 a.m. would really leave at 8 a.m. People strolled into the station hours after the train had gone. Finally, when they realized that trains did leave on time, they began to camp out all night at the little stations in order to be sure to catch the train the next morning. Watches were scarce. People felt time by the passage of the sun and by their appetites. Modern methods of travel gave the nation a more exact sense of time than it had before. People learned how to keep an appointment at a set time. They learned how to go from one place to another as agreed upon.

For years the trains could not be run at night for fear of elephants and buffalo that might wander on to the tracks and so cause accidents. Furthermore it was not unusual to find people sleeping along the road-bed, using the steel rail for a pillow. In one generation the Siamese have been trained to a new tempo of life.

Travel was formerly accomplished on foot, by elephant, by bullock cart, or by boat. Bangkok was long known as the Venice of the Orient because of its extensive canal system. The canals are still in use although the majority of traffic is now on land.

Travel in interior Siam, north of Bangkok, used to be by boat up the Chao Phya River. Weeks of hard travel were necessary to cover the 400 miles to Chiengmai. The return trip could be made in a few days of swift floating down the river.

Even in 1938 the elephant is still used for travel in the more remote districts of Siam where roads have not penetrated.

In about the year 1870 the first stage of a trip from Bangkok to Bhuket was made by going along the coast from Bangkok to Singora on a paddle-wheel boat, then by small boats through a narrow stream to Haad Yie. From Haad Yie elephants were employed to the Siamese border at Sadow, where carriages were taken to Alor Star over a good road. From Alor Star the trip was completed to Bhuket by ship.

The trip to Bhuket is usually made by the bi-weekly express to Kantang and then overnight by ship to Bhuket. The trip now takes two days.

The railroad system is under government control, and has been a splendid source of income. There are no competing railroads. Motor roads that did compete with the railroad were allowed to fall into disrepair, while new roads were built to feed the railroad with passengers and freight. Thus the road from Nakon Sritammarat to Trang was at one time an excellent road. A missionary lady rode across the peninsula along 90 miles of this highway in a Chinese rickshaw. After the railroad was built the bridges were not repaired and the road was soon impassable. In 1937, a bicycle club attempted to make the same trip. They crossed the peninsula in two days and had no difficulty tracing the old road, but the trip was very strenuous.

The Siamese railroad system is one of the best in the orient and adequately takes care of the needs of the country. James M. Andrews has expressed the opinion that no more railroads are needed in modern Siam. However, there is an old plan that is being revived to link up the Siamese and the Indo-Chinese railroads.

In the year 1921-22 the Siamese railroad was joined to the Malayan railroad line, and an international express service was begun. The following year the line north of Bangkok was completed to Chiengmai and this service was linked with the line south of Bangkok. The thirty-sixth anniversary of the railroad was celebrated in 1932-33. As it stands, it taps every important part of Siam either with its main line or with feeder lines.

Prosperity depends upon communications. Vegetables and rice cannot be sold unless they are taken to market. In 1931-32 the total income of the railroad was *baht* 10,755,874. Of this amount only

TRENDS IN METHODS OF COMMUNICATION 139

baht 4,823,495 represented passenger fares. The rest was for freight. This indicates not only that the railroad was doing a good business, but that thousands of individuals were able to do business that they could not have done without the railroad. When freight moves there is trade and people prosper.

Freight shipments are being improved. Previously, fruits and vegetables spoiled when shipped because of the slowness of freight and the lack of refrigerator cars. Four hot days in a steaming freight car on the road to Bangkok ruined almost any vegetable or fruit shipment. In 1937, the railroad experimented with a few refrigerator cars on the northern line and discovered that people were willing to pay for their use. The experiment was declared successful and the service is to be enlarged. Freight service was accelerated in 1937. A fast bi-weekly freight service was begun to accelerate the delivery of important shipments. The same year it was announced that a large ferro-concrete godown was to be built at Bangkok to be rented to rice shippers. Rates are still high; not so much when compared to other countries, although they are higher than those of Malaya, as when considered in the light of the price of produce and the national economy generally. As communications and facilities are improved commerce and trade rise to higher levels.

The greatest need in 1938 is for more and better motor roads. The need is recognized by the government, which has laid out a roads programme which will eventually provide Siam with a network of good roads. Unfortunately it has been announced that the programme will be decelerated because of the lack of funds. However, roads are being built more than ever before. The absolute monarchy left few roads, and what there were connected with nothing. This was a deliberate sacrifice of the needs of the country at large to the accepted plan of avoiding competition with the railroad. Thus Bangkok had roads within its environs but no roads to any neighbouring towns. Only within the last four years has a road been cut through to Don Muang, the airport, in order to speed up air travel. South of Bangkok the first important road is from Petchaburi to Rajaburi. The next road is from Chumpon across the peninsula to a point near Renong. Farther south a road runs from Rawnpiboon to Nakon Sritammarat. Continuing south to Patalung a 45 mile road stretches from Patalung to Trang which is a road centre. There is a road from Trang to Kantang, from Trang to Lampey, from Trang to Yantakhao and on to Yongstar, from Trang to Sri Khao, and from Trang to Huey Yot. The Huey Yot road is now completed almost to Krabee and is expected to be opened in 1938. This leaves a short section between Krabee and Pangga without a road, although one is planned. At Pangga the roads lead on to Bhuket, all over Bhuket island, and up the coast to Takuapa. There are more roads around Trang and Bhuket than in any other part of Siam. South of Patalung there is a road from Kuan Niang to Satul. Farther south at Haad Yie there is a road to Singora and another road to the Siamese border at Sadow which links up with the splendid Malayan road system. On the eastern coast there are roads linking Pattani, Yala, and Bangnara.

North of Bangkok there are no important roads until Prae is reached, and here there is a road through to Nan. Farther north at Lampang there is a road to Chiengrai. Chiengmai has more roads than any other northern section reaching out to the towns and villages on all sides.

It may be seen that the roads of Siam are in isolated sections which are linked up by the railroad. Modern Siam is realizing that the prosperity of the railroad may not mean the prosperity of the country. The country needs to be opened up. There are still 100,000 children who cannot get to school because of poor communications. There is a vast productive hinterland that has no markets because of poor communications. Thus the docks of Bangkok are frequently covered with boatloads of produce imported from China while areas of Siam which could provide most of Bangkok's needs are so completely separated from it by poor communications that they are unable to do so. Fruit from the south and vegetables from the north could supply a large share of the city's needs if it were possible to transport such goods economically.

As the roads come, wheeled vehicles come with them. Outside of Bangkok there are few privately owned motor cars. There are many bicycles, however, ramshackle buses, and bicycle taxis. The three-wheel bicycle taxi is replacing the rickshaw in many places and is even competing with motor traffic in some country districts. The usual three-wheel taxi consists of a bicycle with a tandem stand which has a wicker chair perched smartly on top for two passengers. The vehicle has been variously improved to look like anything from a boy's automobile scooter to a trotting horse with cart behind to an enormous wooden shoe on wheels. At first these vehicles were to be found in the market centres. More recently they have been looming up, day or night, at almost any point along the highway. The average taxi-peddler earns about one or two *baht* per day.

The highway traffic is made up mostly of cars for hire. One may feel secure in waving a hand at any car along the road. Almost all carry passengers. The average bus is a "Ford" or "Chevrolet", with a home-made square body seated bluntly on top of the chassis. The usual load is, theoretically, ten or twelve passengers. The actual load may be any number up to twenty, or as many as can pile in on top. A new type of midget bus appeared in 1937, which seats six or eight passengers and carries little baggage or freight.

Traffic is not heavy in the sense that there is a stream of cars all day long. There are seldom more than fifteen or twenty cars a day passing over the average road. Some roads are more busy and some less.

In spite of the fact that one can travel to most places in Siam by train and motor car the connections are so poor that travel is still slow and tiresome. The international express from Penang to Bangkok makes very good speed, but the business man within Siam who must make frequent local trips wastes days of his time each month waiting. Thus in many places there is one train in and one train out per day. An hour's business to be transacted in such a town requires two days, or parts of two days travel.

Motor road appropriations are larger than before, although not large enough to link up the kingdom, even with narrow gravel roads, in less than fifteen years. When the various roads are linked up, commerce and trade will be facilitated and accelerated. In 1933-34 the appropriation for highways was *baht* 1.1 million. In 1936-37 the appropriation was raised to *baht* 4.5 millions. For 1937-38 the appropriation was about *baht* 6 millions. The trend is to stress highway construction.

Other means of communication are being steadily improved. The telephone is widely used in Bangkok, and in 1937 a new and improved system was installed. Outside of Bangkok the telephone is almost unknown. The telegraph is universal, however, and one may send telegrams from almost any town to every part of the world. In March, 1937, a new radio telephone connection was completed with Japan. Siam was already linked to Europe with such a service.

The usual mail services are common in Siam. Air mail has made a beginning within the country but is not used as much as the international air mail service.

As communications are improved, prosperity becomes more widespread. Above all, new ways of thinking and living and behaving are brought to the common people. The world becomes smaller. There is less isolation in reality and in thought. The old quiet village life is disturbed by the horn of the motor car.

CHAPER VIII

TRENDS IN CHARACTER, CRIME, AND FAMILY LIFE

1. SIAMESE CHARACTER

A WORD that indicates an important part of the Siamese character is the word "snuk". In its simplest aspects it means "fun-loving" or "pleasure-loving". The word also means a "deep interest in something, momentarily, to the exclusion of all else." The Siamese are a pleasure-loving people, as is shown by their ready laughter. The people they like are those who can make them laugh and feel happy. Siamese have remarked that they respect those who make them afraid and like those who make them laugh. They enjoy a show, a dance, a game, a trip to some near or distant point. To travel is definitely "snuk". To attend a fair is "snuk". To see a play is "snuk". The idea of "snuk" carries even into religion. A group of Siamese attended a Christian Church service for the first time. They remarked, after leaving the church, that the service was not "snuk" and that they would not come again. When they were asked if Buddhism was "snuk", they said that it was. Their religion not only provided a method of worship, but also a system for satisfying the social needs of the group. The temple is the focal point of the community, the centre around which revolve the religious rites, the picnics, the plays, and the other amusements of the people. The religious year has days for boat racing, sports, games, trips to holy places, shadow shows, and festive parades. So even religion becomes "snuk".

This word carries over into hobbies and avocational interests. A young law student who never seemed to tire of his books explained his devotion to study by remarking that he found them very "snuk". At the moment he was interested in law to the exclusion of all else. A middle-aged government official took up photography. He equipped a modern darkroom, bought expensive cameras, stocked a library of photographic lore, bought a large supply of chemicals, and produced endless prints. He made still pictures in size from miniatures to huge enlargements. He bought a movie camera with a full assortment of lenses and took pictures of everything he could think of. He explained that it was "snuk". He was experiencing a deep pleasure. The fever passed after a year or so and he retained but a few remnants of his hobby.

The word "snuk" is heard constantly. It is used descriptively and as an ejaculation. An exciting play at football or tennis will bring forth exclamations of "snuk cang"—what fun! To say that a person is "khon snuk" (khon means "person") is considered complimentary. The Siamese like people who smile, are pleasant, have excellent manners, and diffuse an atmosphere of well-being and cheerfulness. When the new constitutional form of government was being discussed in the market coffee shops the commonest defence for the new form of government was that it would make everyone happy, allow everyone to be at peace, and to have "snuk".

Le May says:

> It would seem that, in the development of their natural attributes, the Siamese, that is the bulk of the people who are peasants, are at the present time somewhat at the stage which Northern Europe had reached in the Middle Ages. The country has not been settled long enough for any great development in education to have taken place, but the people, being of a free and independent turn of mind, have a lively sense of humour, somewhat broad, of a Chaucerian kind, and their thoughts are mostly tinged with religion, or at any rate with fears of the natural and supernatural phenomena all around them. . . . The peasants are a hardy loveable race, rooted to the soil they till. It is remarkable how all the oppression and all the tyranny of the past centuries have left them still free and uncomplaining. I have been often among them, sat with them at their village councils, and marvelled at their independence of thought and bearing, their patience, and their responsive, sidelong glances at any glimpse of humour. Trust them as a friend, as an equal, and they will open their hearts.[1]

Le May tells the story of a family that lived at Lopburi. The husband was about forty-five years old and the wife slightly over twenty. She desired a younger lover and easily found one. She usually met him in the open front of the shop in which she and her husband lived. Her father-in-law caught the lovers one night while they were asleep and took her bracelet as proof. She awoke at once and realized what had happened, sent her lover away, and went to awaken her husband. She told him that it was too hot to

[1] Reginald le May, *Siamese Tales Old and New* (London: Noel Douglas, 1930) p. 128.

sleep inside and asked him to sleep with her in the open shop. He consented and was soon asleep again. Then she awoke him with cries that she had just had her bracelet stolen. The couple returned to the house for the rest of the night. In the morning the father-in-law came to tell his story and show the bracelet. The husband denied the story for he had been in the shop with her himself when she cried out that her bracelet was stolen. There is guileful humour in this tale. Phya Manunet Banhan explains that the moral, to a Siamese, is not to dismiss the opinions of others lightly. Le May says that it is the subtleties and manoeuvres by which the wife outwitted the husband that gives the chief delight to the Siamese mind, rather than the salacious side of the story.[1]

At an extemporaneous singing party a young man sang that he had come to the girl's front gate and, lover-like, pleaded for admission. The girl did not want his attentions and sang in reply: "I heard the voice of a man mingled with the voices of dogs, and do not know which to respond to." The village home is surrounded by a fence, and dogs are kept which bark at any stranger. Humour and insult are conveyed by the reply. Subtleness and wit are the essence of Siamese humour.[2]

The Siamese language lends itself easily to the pun and play on words. Three or four words may be pronounced alike except for a distinguishing tonal swing or accent. Thus a "su'a" may be a tiger, a coat, or a mat. "Ya" may be grandmother, grass, or medicine. It is easy to say confusing and ridiculous things with such a language.

Another aspect of Siamese character is indicated by the word "phu'ng". It means to depend on someone or something. The idea of dependence is similar to the old Italian one of having a patron for one's art or work. It fits a feudal state where the people look to their lord for protection and in return serve and help him. Thus wealthy and important persons often had an enormous entourage of poor relatives, children of friends, servants and the families of servants, slaves and the families of slaves, all dependent upon them. The larger this group the more important the patron. *Vice versa,* persons attached to such a patron felt themselves to be enhanced by his importance. In Bangkok, a Nai Hli Culin, a gold-

[1] *Ibid.*, p. 43.
[2] *Ibid.*, p. 161.

smith, was such a clever artisan that he succeeded in winning the patronage of a prince of the royal family. When the prince died he was fortunate to have the king as his patron. He had someone to "phu'ng".

What feudalism was to Europe, slavery was to Siam. The desire to "phu'ng" someone developed out of slavery. Le May describes it as follows:

> In his *History of Siam* Wood says that slavery was unknown in the days of Ram Kamheng, the first Thai king, and his successors at Sukhothai in the 13th century, but was a feature of the social system during the whole period of the Ayudhya dynasty from 1350 to 1767. It was apparently always a form of debt slavery, and lasted in one form or another down to modern times; indeed, until the year 1905, when King Chulalongkorn finally abolished it. No doubt the masters were able, in the main, to use their slaves as they pleased in the old days, and were acknowledged indeed, as lord of life over them; but that the slaves were not entirely ignored is shown by the fact that in 1637 a law of slavery was passed, containing, among others, provisions for the punishment of masters who killed or injured their slaves, and also setting forth various means by which slaves could regain their liberty. The chief method, as a rule, as the story relates, was by being bought out or redeemed by someone else; but sometimes, if the slaves found a good master, they were very content to remain in the household, as they gained considerable advantages by doing so, such as protection and free food in return for their services. Knowing the Siamese passably, I have little doubt that a great many of the slaves became such by selling and attaching themselves and their families to the households of important men. . . . It gave them prestige to be called so-and-so's man.[1]

This is a strand of character that will die out of Siamese life as individualism is stressed. When the first elections were held for representatives to the People's Assembly a certain man was elected by the people who had and hoped to continue to "phu'ng" him. They shone in his reflected glory.

A number of country friends descended upon the writer one day and confided in him that they had known him for a number of years and felt that he was worthy of their confidence. They had decided to come and "phu'ng". They meant to come and live near him and look to him for employment, guidance, and protection. In return they would serve him as he directed. Had the agreement been made the writer would have been much out of pocket. He could have expected little in the way of service, since it is always

[1] *Ibid.*, p. 141.

considered legitimate to evade as much work as possible. His importance would have been enhanced, but at considerable expense in time, money, and nervous energy; the last because he would have been expected to be the Solomon of the community, settle disputes, arrange marriages, educate children, rebuke and teach. Even in 1937 the desire to live in the shade of feudal patronage is still alive in Siam. The trend is away from it, however.

Another aspect of Siamese character is lassitude or lethargy. Whatever of this spirit cannot be traced to such diseases as hookworm can probably be blamed on the climate and on the ease with which one can secure enough to eat. Siam is underpopulated. It is a land of plenty where no one needs to starve. It is so warm that clothing, except for style and appearance, is of no great importance. No one could freeze to death. Not unnaturally, jobs involving manual labour go begging in many country districts. A peasant will work for a limited length of time, but, when he has money in his pocket, he prefers to sleep, gamble, and enjoy life in his own way. The idea of working hard every day simply to add to his wealth seems absurd. It is exasperating to the employer who has work to be done and needs people to do it. In Bangkok and other large centres where the modern spirit of bustle and energy has appeared, and where, incidentally, there is a large infusion of Chinese blood, this is no longer true. The era of lassitude will probably end with the spread of modern competitive business methods. But at present even those who work regularly do not overdo it. The mass of civil officials seem to have an incredible amount of leisure in which to enjoy life. Not all have, of course—for some civil officials work long hours—but many do. They reach the office at nine, or as much after as they dare, having sat for some time in the coffee shop for a convivial cup and the morning gossip. They leave at noon, or as soon before as they dare, for lunch. At one, or a little after, they are back at work, and at three they are off for a game of tennis, or an afternoon cup of coffee. A railway station at which two trains a day stopped, one going north, one coming south, had a staff of five—station master, baggage agent, telegrapher, ticket collector, and head coolie, who divided among them the inconsiderable work that one man would do in such a station in the United States. To make the work lighter, senders and receivers of freight were personally responsible for getting it on and off trains, and personal luggage could be checked only a half-hour before train time and only if registered, thus relieving the station of all but the lightest responsibility.

This spirit of lassitude is expressed in another way in the word "choei", which means indifferent or cool. The word is seldom applied in a derogatory manner unless used by a foreigner who is trying to break down lassitude and indifference. Siamese regard it as complimentary, and the attitude it expresses as a virtue. It means the ability to take life as it comes without excitement. He who meets the crises of life with cool mien is "choei". A certain girl, who held a prominent position and who, when caught in adultery and theft and stood to lose both good name and position, met the situation with a coolness that was most astonishing, was described by Siamese as undeniably "choei". The term implies coolness of attitude toward work, responsibility, or trouble. A girl who was asked which of three men she wished to marry and who shrugged her shoulders and took the one selected by her parents was considered admirably "choei". Lassitude and indifference may be sweated out of the Siamese character by modern methods of work and ways of living, but remnants of calmness and coolness of character may remain as a virtue.

Jealousy is manifest in an unwillingness to allow others to get ahead. In a group of people in which one person pushes ahead of the group the tendency of the group is to drag him back to the common level. He may succeed because of ability or because he has enough friends to help him over his difficulties. This characteristic, which is a constant factor in all Siamese life, has been described by Siamese friends as a product of the harem. In a household where there were several wives, each wife with one or more children, all were on guard lest one should get ahead and win too high a position, get more than her share of the gifts, and receive the lion's portion of the inheritance.

A family of very ordinary class, by a stroke of good luck, secured a prominent position. Their home had been of the usual village variety. They left it to move into a modern house with electricity. For a year or two they felt that they were walking on slippery paths. They never knew when something was going to happen to discredit them. Friends warned them that some of their old neighbours were not happy to see them prosper beyond the rest of the village.

Efforts were made to force them back into the village pattern. This characteristic may be modified in a monogamous nation where more democratic and individual expression is permitted, but for the present it explains much of the slow progress made in Siam as compared to that in Japan or India, or the Philippines.

One of the most serious handicaps to progress is the Siamese characteristic of "kan kreng cai", or diffidence. It means a respect for one's superior tinged with fear. Under the absolute monarchy the people were socially ranked in such a way that each rank respected and feared the superior while oppressing the inferior. The word and person of a superior were not questioned. Orders were carried out by inferiors even when the orders were unwise. The result was the destruction of initiative and independent thinking. Foreigners had great difficulty in learning the Siamese language because teachers, paid by the pupil, would not presume to correct their employer's mistakes. If a superior asked for advice, his inferiors tried to find out what he thought or wanted and told him that. Such a characteristic is not conducive to progress. It has been weeded out of the educated and will disappear gradually as the modern spirit of independence and democracy spreads through the villages. It is still dramatically seen in the school system in the relation of pupil to teacher. If the pupil approaches the teacher's desk he must drop to one knee until his head is below the level of the teacher's head before he may address the teacher. This technique is carried all the way through the secondary grades.

The Siamese are one of the most polite of races. Manners are taught from childhood. Words of respect to adults and superiors are drilled into children from the time they begin to speak. Mothers are forever instructing children to put their hands together in order to salute their elders with proper respect. When children are older they are taught how to receive guests by bringing a drink, a cigarette, or some betel nut to chew. Even the crudest homes understand the act of hospitality. The poorest peasant will provide a welcome to unknown guests. There is a spirit of willingness to share what they have, a genuine friendliness, that is at the root of Siamese hospitality. The larger the population centre the more elaborate and sophisticated the manners become. Manners are gradually changing in expression but not in content.

In 1930-31 a booklet was published entitled *Rabiap Phu Di*. It sold for fifteen coppers. By a liberal translation the title was "The Customs of the Well-Mannered." "Phu Di" does not actually mean well-mannered, but refers to that class of society which is at the top, the cultured group who should know good social usage. The booklet deals with such subjects as how to introduce strangers, how to visit friends, how to stay at a friend's house, how to carry on a conversation, what not to talk about, how to act at a dinner party, what to do when someone sends you a gift, how to borrow things, and how to return them.

When a Siamese wishes to make one feel happy his manners are so fine without being servile, so gracious, so elegant, so easy, that one feels like a prince. Like all polite people they understand equally well the best ways in which to insult exquisitely those whom they do not like.

The Siamese are a friendly people. The writer has travelled in all parts of Siam and has yet to meet an unfriendly Siamese. If they are treated as friends and equals they lose all awkwardness and shyness and show a natural friendly spirit. They will ask your name, inquire for your health, age, work, salary, family and children, and anything else that comes to mind. These questions are intended to show their friendly interest in you. Foreigners sometimes mistake these questions for a morbid interest in personal affairs that do not concern the questioner and resent it. If the unsophisticated Siamese does not ask personal questions, it simply means that he is not interested in you and does not care to know you further. How can a friendship be struck up between people who do not know each other's affairs? The educated Siamese understands the European attitude and respects it of course. But the friendly questioning of the simpler people probably came down with the race from China. Chinese good manners require that one ask a stranger's family name, given name, age, health, situation of family and relatives. If one refuses to tell about himself he may be regarded as a suspicious character. Honest people, so they reason, have nothing to hide.

When out walking or travelling one is constantly being aided by friendly Siamese who go out of their way to be helpful. It takes no mental effort to recall instances of receiving portage in boats, or being entertained in homes never seen before, of being dug out of the mud, when the car was stalled, by a group of laughing mud-plastered peasants, of being led along jungle paths for long distances by people who were willing to go out of their way to be friendly and who expected no tip. When met in a friendly way there is no more friendly, courteous person than the Siamese. When the writer expressed a desire to see the king's troupe of dancers, he was overwhelmed to receive a ready invitation from a princess of the royal family to go to her father's palace on a certain evening and see the best dancers in the land. Not only that, but in addition she explained in detail each movement and its significance.

In describing the characteristics of the Siamese people it is not intended to imply that the Siamese have an exclusive claim to any of them. Certain characteristics have been selected for description because they represent the development of important aspects of the national life. Some of these are being changed by the type of life that is developing under the constitutional monarchy. Thus the friendly spirit of the Siamese might be lost in a calculating, competitive world where people scarcely know their neighbours. Unwillingness to allow a neighbour to exceed the common pattern may be lost in a monogamous, individualistic, educated state. Excessive respect, "kan kreng cai," may vanish in a democratic economy.

The Siamese ethic is that of the oriental. They teach and to some degree observe the common precepts of refraining from stealing, killing, lying, and deceiving. Theoretically they are not allowed to take life. Some pious folk will not even slap a mosquito. Cobras are chased into the jungle rather than killed. The pious are more than offset by those moderns who go game hunting. The bag of jungle fowl or the number of deer shot form good conversational material at the club. The Buddhist precept against intoxicants is not observed by many. A merry party, a wedding, a festive day, is hardly considered to have been properly celebrated unless there has been a large amount of beer, wine, and "whi-sa-key" consumed. The beer hall has become a regular part of most large towns.

2. CRIME

Crime is not so great a problem as in more sophisticated countries. There are robberies and murders, but the newspapers are not smothered with such things.

In April, 1937, rubber coupons were forged. When the rubber restrictions went into effect a coupon was issued to allocate amounts of rubber to producers and buyers. Certain individuals decided to sell more rubber or buy more rubber, or simply to deal in the sale of coupons to people who had an excess of rubber on hand, and so forged coupons. People in very prominent positions were implicated.

Kidnapping became popular for a time during the month of December, 1934. The kidnapping wave centred around Rajburi. Large ransoms were demanded. A Chinese rice-miller was held for a price of *baht* 10,000. The ransom for a Chinese merchant was set at *baht* 5,000. Even a Siamese monk was kidnapped and *baht* 200 asked for him. Shops that usually closed at 10 p.m. began to close at dusk. A village of forty families moved out of the area.

Near the same district a Chinese was shot and robbed. A procession of people who had been showing honour to a miniature copy of the constitution was held up by a gang on the highway and robbed of much personal property. One man who objected was shot dead. The police were stirred to activity. The local crime situation was soon solved by eliminating the unlawful individuals. Their pictures, taken after they had been shot and killed, appeared in the newspapers. Peace and quiet returned to that part of the country. From this it may be seen that Siam has its crime waves just like any civilized country.

The Siamese police are efficient in dealing with crime. They seem to be able to locate and return much stolen property, and to bring bandits to justice. In person the police do not appear very terrible. One little hundred-pound police lieutenant of gentle mien has gone on several desperate sallies and, when attacked by the men he has gone to arrest, has coolly and neatly "gotten his man" with his Colt revolver. His mild manners are no criterion of his ability to settle a crime question.

The police have their dignity and ask to be respected. In April, 1934, Phya Pradibaddha was charged with insulting an officer on duty. The Chao Khun's race horse took fright at passing traffic, and jumped into the canal at the side of the road. The Chao Khun came by, saw his horse in the water, and made some derogatory remarks to the officer in charge of traffic. The policeman considered himself insulted and made the affair a court case. This incident is indicative of modern times. Since the 1932 revolution the military and the police have felt more important.

In April, 1937, the bicycle taxi men held an indignation meeting and asserted that the police were treating them roughly. The incident led the writer to recall unpleasant traffic experiences in Siam, America, France, and England. Siam is catching up with the rest of the world in this department, too. The police have even acquired appropriate language for use on traffic offenders. An editorial appeared recently asking for more educated, considerate, and gentlemanly police.[1]

Train robbery has been attempted several times, not always with success. There were heavy losses in registered mail on the trains until the matter became a public scandal. One incident occurred in December, 1933, when *baht* 300,000 was taken. The police were able to get most of the money back and bring some of the robbers to justice.

In March, 1937, the police had advance information that a bandit raid was planned against a certain house. There were to be ten bandits, so a detail of nine police waited in the house. The story, as written by an English-speaking Siamese, reads:

> On being challenged by the police as to their identity, the desperadoes answered with gunfire, but were immediately retaliated by the caretakers of the place. A hot battle ensued, accompanied by the rattling of the duelling gun-fire. Not long afterwards, the bandits, realizing the impermeability of the passage and the state of hopelessness which they were in, retreated, leaving two of their comrades dead and one seriously wounded on the battle ground.[2]

A murder that could happen only in Siam occurred in May, 1934. Two men were pupils of a certain teacher who claimed to be a wizard. Both of the pupils had received charms from the wizard which were guaranteed to resist steel and gunfire. One of the men told the other to shoot him to prove the infallibility of the charms. Believing utterly that the charms were effective the shot was fired. The judge said that the murderer had believed in something that could not be and sentenced him to twenty years in prison.[3]

Siam is free from the "racket" which terrorizes America. There

---

[1] *Nation*, May 6th, 1937.
[2] *Siam Chronicle*, March 13th, 1937.
[3] *Bangkok Times*, May 3rd, 1934.

is no baker's racket, nor laundry racket, nor builder's racket, nor any other racket. Organized crime has not yet gotten a start.

The average citizen may live his life knowing that he is as safe in Siam as in any other part of the world, perhaps more secure. The country people, however, usually carry knives when out walking and the city people have turned to small arms for personal protection. A surprising number of people possess guns.

A crime commission examined the prisoners in 53 prisons to find out why crimes were committed. Many of the prisoners claimed they had done no wrong. A total of 7,399 cases gave answers as follows:

Cause of crime	Number of cases	Per cent
Poverty	1,819	24.58
Evil intent	920	12.43
Taking evil advice	769	10.39
Strayed into evil ways	766	10.35
Yielded to anger	759	10.26
Wanted to do it	692	9.35
Drunk	637	8.61
Evil nature	392	5.30
Self-protection	190	2.57
Love	128	1.73
No work	124	1.68
Gambling	42	.57
Miscellaneous [1]	161	2.18

Most of the crimes were the result of poverty. The cure for such is economic security. The second largest percentage represented crimes committed by people who lacked education. Gambling was the least important cause of crime. However, one district officer said to the writer in 1937 that as gambling permits grew easier to obtain in his area, crimes traceable to gambling had increased.

Siamese like to gamble as much as people of other races, or more so. People gamble on cock-fights, bull-fights, horse races, and cards. Formal gambling is contrary to law except on Sundays and holidays, or with a special permit. The lottery has become popular and there are three annual state lotteries. A first prize, won by a fourteen-year-old girl in the Nang Fah lottery, was for *baht* 60,000. Following are the details of a lottery in behalf of the Red Cross. Half-a-million tickets were printed, 63 were destroyed as imperfect

---

[1] From a departmental government report loaned by H.S.H. Prince Sakol Varavarn.

and 291 were unaccounted for in the provinces. Cash received amounted to *baht* 499,646, which earned interest to the sum of *baht* 1,321. The total expenses were *baht* 70,868. Of this sum *baht* 4,000 was spent for printing, *baht* 50,014 for government tax, *baht* 201 for advertising, *baht* 174 for stamps, *baht* 101 for travel, *baht* 955 for equipment, *baht* 570 for refreshments, and *baht* 14,853 for ticket sellers. The prize winners were paid *baht* 223,250, donations to hospitals amounted to *baht* 90,000, and there was a balance for the Red Cross of *baht* 116,849. In percentages the expenses were 14.16 per cent, prize money 44.56 per cent, and charity 41.28 per cent. Everyone had a good time.

The extent of crime for an average year, 1935-36, was: murder, 1,333 cases; gang robbery, 1,053 cases; hold-up, 304 cases; incendiarism, 143 cases. And this was for all of Siam. It is easy to see that Siam does not have a serious crime problem.

The treatment of prisoners has been revised to meet modern standards. A generation ago the prisons did not expect to prepare the prisoners for a new and better life, and treated them badly. The present plan is to educate prisoners in a trade, to improve their health, and to inculcate a better social attitude. Basket weaving, chair and table making, hat making, and other useful trades are taught. The products are sold in prison stores, and some of them are excellent.

Dr. J. A. Beradelli, an Italian prison expert who has had thirty years of experience in Italy and Somaliland, said that the Siamese prisoners were well disciplined and industrious. For the most part they sleep on the floor. Their food is rice and a little sauce or soup. Their families are allowed to provide mats for sleeping and better food, if desired. He approved of the practice of using them for out-door labour, which serves as an effective cure for delinquency. Prisoners make roads, cut wood, roll tennis courts at government clubs, and do other similar tasks while wearing leg irons and the typical blue prison clothes. They are generally a cheerful lot. He reported favourably on the honesty of the prisoners. He left *baht* 100 in his coat, hanging in a place where prisoners were working. It remained untouched although it could easily have been taken and hidden.[1]

[1] *Siam Chronicle*, June 23rd, 1937.

The ex-prisoner is not held in distrust as in many countries. Siamese usually come out of prison to resume their former ways of life. One man went to prison for two years in the town where he had lived for ten years. When he came out he easily resumed his former life pattern without sense of strain. He is regarded as a good citizen. As he explained himself: "I was poor. I had no food, so I joined a gang who were going to rob a wealthy farmer. After all, what could I do?"

3. WOMAN'S PLACE IN SOCIETY

While there is a precept in Buddhism prohibiting improper relations between one man and the wife of another, there is no law prohibiting polygamy. The trend is toward monogamy, partly because the cost of polygamy makes it possible for only the comparatively well-to-do, and partly because, according to the new marriage laws, only one wife may be registered, and only she and her children may inherit unless specific provision is made for lesser wives and their children in the will. According, then, to the new law, feminine members of the household other than the wife have no legal standing. There is, however, no such thing as illegitimate children, for when a man takes an unmarried girl she is under his protection.

Young men frequently say that their idea of bliss is to have a number of wives and as many love affairs as possible. It is taken for granted that young men will have a certain amount of sexual liberty. At a wedding a friend of the groom mentioned in his toast to the couple that the groom was well known for his love affairs. He concluded his remarks with the statement that this was customary.

The marriage contract is usually maintained. One of the newspapers announced:

> One divorce to 244 marriages in Siam. Isn't it a world record? Siam perhaps holds the distinction of being the country with the lowest divorce rate in the world.[1]

Marriages are not broken casually. This may be because it is still possible for a man to add another woman to his household if he tires of his old wife. The statistics quoted above, however, give a somewhat untrue picture. While the number of divorces is not large, there are a great many separations where no divorce is

---

[1] *Siam Chronicle*, April 20th, 1937.

secured. For instance, a young couple fell very much in love. They were married without the consent of the groom's parents, who were very much opposed to the girl, since she was of lower social class than themselves. After a child was born to the couple the parents of the young man arranged a betrothal between him and a young woman of their choice. The groom, still in love with his bride but subservient to his family, finally left her and married the woman that his parents had selected for him. There was no divorce. On the other hand it is certainly true that Siam has a wealth of fine old couples who have spent their lives toiling and working together. They are living demonstrations of the finest sort of married life.

In January, 1934, a Marriage Bill came before the People's Assembly for discussion and decision.[1] The final decision was in the direction of monogamy, since the registration of but one wife was allowed.

Siam's first law on marriage was promulgated by King Chulalongkorn in 1898, in order to meet the needs of two Europeans who wanted to be married in Siam. The law said that marriage according to Siamese law and custom was a contract between man and wife to which the ordinary principles which attach to other contracts are applicable. That law did not apply when both of the contracting parties were Siamese. One or both had to be of foreign nationality.

King Vajiravudh strongly favoured monogamy. He gave the marriage ceremonial and ritual more importance. He also drafted an Act providing for the registration of all existing and future marriages. No one was to be allowed to register a marriage if he had already registered a previous one. Children of an unregistered marriage were to be considered illegitimate. The draft was pigeon-holed, since custom and Church favoured the old easy ways. In 1931, an amendment to the law was made under which no future marriage was to be considered legal unless registered. It was never enforced. The country slowly turned toward monogamy as the best marriage practice. In March, 1935, the People's Assembly voted to accept Book V of the Civil and Commercial Code which contained marriage regulations. On October 1st, 1935, all marriages in Siam had to be registered to be legal. Only one wife may be registered by a man unless his former wife has died or has been legally divorced. King Prajadhipok set a good example by having but one wife.

[1] Appendix.

According to long established custom, a husband, if his wife had lovers, could divorce her, but if a husband took new wives or concubines, the wife could do nothing. A man might have many wives obtained in various ways. His parents might select a wife for him, he might choose a wife for himself, he might obtain a wife by showing pity to some woman in distress, the king might give him a wife as a reward for services, and he might also have slave or servant wives. A wealthy man might have a very large household. The new law recognizes the man as head of the family, responsible for its welfare, but makes no provision for lordship over the wife. Formerly when there was a divorce the man took two parts and the woman one part of the property. Now they share equally. A woman can now divorce her husband if he breaks the marriage vows to such an extent that it is impossible for the marriage to continue.

The new marriage law was discussed in the newspapers and explained in public lectures. The better educated people understood the law, and immediately registered their marriages. Some women took the opportunity of divorcing husbands who had made marriage unendurable. But for most people the law was just something written in a book. When they saw that if they neglected to register their marriage they neither went to prison nor were fined, they lost interest. From October 1st, 1935, to November, 1936, only fifteen marriages were registered in a district that had a population of 58,400 people, and that a district in Bangkok, which is always better informed and more advanced than the provinces. The larger percentage of marriages were not registered.[1]

Such apathy disturbed many writers and lecturers who renewed their efforts at education for the sake of public knowledge. No figures are available for marriages registered in 1937, but, if one may judge from the large numbers of people coming in from the villages to register marriages, it may be concluded that there is today a better general understanding of the new marriage status, and a greater willingness to comply with the law.

It should not be taken for granted that women have had a minor role in either family or national life. The women are very important and have ways of making themselves felt. How many foreigners, trying to open an ice plant, an electricity plant, or a tin

[1] *Nation,* April 10th, 1937.

mine, have had to arrange local financial details with some elderly Siamese woman. Siamese women are important in family finance. They have long been large land owners.

Miss Civili Sinhanetra in an interview with a correspondent of *The New York Sun*, published in that paper February 8th, 1939, summarized the position of women in Siam as she, an educated Siamese woman, sees it. She was the first woman to take up nursing from her home town, Chiengmai. She graduated in nursing from the Peking Union Medical College in Peking, China, and then returned to Siam to teach in the Nurses Training School of McCormick Hospital. She is now in the United States completing her work for the degree of Master of Arts in Public Health Nursing at the University of Michigan from which she took her A.B. degree in June, 1938. She says:

"Women are equal with men in Siam in everything except social life. Long before the constitutional government came in six years ago, we had the right to vote for the village chiefs. Now, under the new government, women have all legal and civil rights. They can even be in the legislature. And there are several who are. But socially, ah . . . that is a different matter . . . A girl can't go out with a man in Siam alone unless she is engaged to him. Either he must come to the girl's home to see her, or else they must go out in groups with a chaperone."

Miss Sinhanetra urges all Siamese women to have a profession. She believes that there is room for them, especially in the nursing profession, and, further, that Siam offers them every opportunity to secure a professional education. She says:

"The Royal mother of our boy King is a trained nurse. She was one of the pioneers. She had her training over in this country (United States). . . . We need more public health nurses in Siam. Malaria is our big problem right now."

A very modern move is the glorification of the Siamese girl in the "beauty contest". The first contest took place about 1934 when almost every large town held a beauty prize contest. Representatives of the various towns were sent to Bangkok for the selection of Miss Siam. Some of the towns have repeated the contest annually. In 1937, Miss Siam went to Japan with a group of Siamese tourists. She was presented with Japanese gowns and was much photographed. The beauty contest has raised some girls from obscurity and given them social importance. Miss Chiengmai, Miss Singora, or Miss Petchaburi is often an important guest at any large town function or celebration. Fame and tragedy have come to the beauty winners. Miss Nakon Sritammarat was shot to death by the man she was to marry. He had been married before, but had concealed the fact from her and from her family. He was extremely jealous of the attentions showered upon her and kept pressing for an early marriage, which suited neither the girl nor her parents. The girl's mother had consulted a priest who had selected an auspicious day some five months later than the date on which the young man wished to be married. On a Sunday morning in the little roadside shop of the parents the four—father, mother, girl, and fiancé—sat discussing the matter. The girl sat with her head in her hands. She had a severe headache. Her fiancé pressed her again and again to set an early wedding day. Somewhat impatiently she replied: "I am ready to be married at any time my parents say. It is not a matter for me to decide." He stepped behind her and shot her through the head.

A woman writing in 1932 on the place of women in modern Siam says that women are now politicians, lawyers, doctors, nurses, and school teachers. Ten years before there were few women teachers in Siam, but in 1932 they were already found everywhere. Women compete for scholarships to study abroad. One girl succeeded in winning a medical scholarship to America. They enter into athletic contests. They swim and play tennis. Several women have sought election to the People's Assembly. Women write books and report for the newspapers. They manage shows and work as hostesses in beer halls. The same writer claims that in less than five years women have quietly assumed a prominent place in the life of the nation. Women are proving that they have ability not inferior to that of the men.

She says that in the royal family women are now allowed to marry commoners. In the past they had little opportunity to marry. Now, when marrying commoners, they must give up their position as royalty, but at least they may marry as they please.

The writer of the article explained that where there is progress in good there is also progress in evil. In gambling, lying, and drinking alcohol, women are the equals of men. Women have learned to dance and entertain in the beer halls. Her explanation is that as countries become more civilized they develop this sort of life. Progress cannot be in politics, education, and work alone. There must be a parallel advancement in play and pleasure. If this is so, then the dance hall girls are not doing an undesirable work. Women in the entertainment business have real value, she claims. Men make the money and women help them spend it. Men need money to give to women, who may then dress up prettily and entertain them. Then the men may work harder and make more money.[1]

The above writer conveys the idea that women are rapidly developing a new way of life to suit the modern world. The point of view expressed by her cannot be said to be representative. The writer, who has a definite interest in the entertainment business, seems to be trying to rationalize a situation that has been causing a great deal of concern in the Ministry of Public Instruction. School-boys in droves have been patronizing the beer halls in spite of the efforts of the authorities to prevent it. Some responsible Siamese have been quoted by the newspapers as saying that this situation was the most serious moral problem that the nation faced at the moment. The problem of the paid entertainer and of the prostitute is being reconsidered in the light of the recommendations of the League of Nations Commission and the resolutions of the Bandoeng Conference. The registered houses of prostitution have decreased in number in the last ten years. H.S.H. Prince Sakol Varavarn was Siam's representative to the League of Nations Conference on this problem. In a speech before the Rotary Club he said:

> Siam, in common with other countries in the Far East which participated in the recent League of Nations Conference at Bandoeng, Java, will soon be instituting the necessary measures with a view to carrying out the resolutions passed by the conference. The Bandoeng Conference, the first of its kind held in the Far East, was the crowning result of several years of study and investigations conducted by a League Commission on the subject of the traffic in women and children in the Far East, and the methods of effectively combatting the traffic and thereby promoting social security and welfare. . . .
> It must be stated, however, that conditions in Siam with regard to the problem of traffic in women and children is not yet as serious as it is in many other countries, especially when we consider the fact that we still lack any sort of vigilance work or rescue homes. We understand that when the Siamese delegation modestly, but accurately, admitted that organized private

[1] *Duang Pratip,* April 2nd, 1932.

societies carrying on rescue and welfare activities were practically nonexistent in Siam, the delegates were a trifle uneasy as to the conditions prevailing in this country. A good many of these delegates visited Bangkok after this conference and they were highly impressed by the situation—the absolute order, the absence of serious crimes, and the generally clean and satisfactory state of affairs.[1]

A questionnaire was given to the delegate from each nation to fill out. One question was: "Has the trend of traffic in women and children for immoral purposes to or from or through the territory under consideration undergone any change?" Siam answered that there was no marked change.

A second question was: "Has the volume of such traffic in women and children for immoral purposes increased or decreased since 1931?" Siam's answer was that it had decreased.

A third question was: "Can you give any reasons for the changes indicated in the replies to the above questions?" Siam answered:

> The numbers of Chinese brothels and prostitutes have become considerably smaller. This circumstance has been partly due to the economic depression, and partly to the stricter control of immigration. As an example of the latter, three cases of offences against the Traffic in Women and Girls Act, 1928-29, involving four traffickers and nine victims have been discovered since last April. The offenders in the last case were sentenced to three years imprisonment.

A fourth question was: "Can you give, with regard to recent changes in traffic in women and children for immoral purposes, any other information of general interest not covered by the above question?" Siam answered:

> In past years the majority of those who frequented brothels were Chinese from Hainan whose women seldom migrated with their men. The number of Hainanese female immigrants who have become more domestic in their habits has increased. This is believed to have an indirect effect on the traffic.

In a later question it was asked if there were women officials who might share in the work for women. Siam's representative explained:

> The system of compulsory education for both sexes and the improvement of the status of women who now have the right to vote, and the opportunity of governmental or commercial employment, are important contributions

[1] *Siam Chronicle*, March 13th, 1937.

toward any improvement of basic conditions. The ground is thus prepared for more specialized welfare work in which women especially can play a more important role. A certain number of women are already in the police force, but for this aspect of welfare work special training and experience are essential.

Siam's report then showed that the number of Siamese brothels, from 1929 to 1936, remained about the same, although the number of women had gone down from 138 to 97. During the same period Chinese brothels decreased from 137 to 63, and the women from 646 to 326 in number. After that information the following note is given:

> It should be noted that out of the total of seventy provinces in the whole Kingdom of Siam there are only four, including the capital city of Bangkok, in which tolerated or licensed brothels exist. In each of the three interior provinces, however, the number of prostitutes are only to be numbered by tens. The Committee above referred to have already submitted an ad interim report recommending gradual abolition.[1]

In March, 1937, a case of selling a girl for immoral purposes dramatized the traffic, and gave direction to public opinion. The mother of the girl involved had been convicted of manufacturing counterfeit coins. She served a sentence of eight months, and when she returned home found that her fifteen-year-old daughter was missing. An older sister had been left in charge. She explained to the mother that the girl had taken a job in a Chinese house and was well and happy. The mother doubted the truth of this, and, fearing the worst, went to the police. The police discovered that the girl had been sold by her elder sister to a Cantonese man. He resold her to a house of prostitution. When the girl told her story she said that her elder sister had told her that her mother was in prison, needed money, and wanted her to get work at once. The girl was willing to help. She went with her elder sister to a woman who in turn led them to the Cantonese man. The man took them to a trafficker in women. A contract was drawn up and *baht* 80 was paid. The buyer and the brothel keeper then took her to have her registered as a prostitute. She thought she was being registered as a servant. When she was led to her future home she realized, too late, what she had agreed

---

[1] *League of Nations Bulletin,* July 1st, 1936, loaned by H.S.H. Prince Sakol Varavarn, delegate to Bandoeng Conference.

to do. She was compelled to carry out her part of the contract. She estimated that in a month she had earned more than *baht* 200. At Chinese New Year, in three days, she received over a hundred men at one *baht* per head. The brothel keeper took 25 per cent and allowed her to keep the rest. She had no freedom, however, and was a veritable slave.[1]

This incident started the police on a search for other similar cases. For several months the newspapers made constant mention of the campaign against the selling of women and children. Girls who had been sold into prostitution and who were rescued were mentioned in the papers. People who had lost track of young girls related to them flocked to see the girls to learn if they were relatives. In April, 1937, it was reported that some Chinese involved in the traffic were to be deported. Appropriately enough the *Siam Chronicle* for March 14th, 1937, devoted several pages to the passing of the Yoshiwara in Japan, and urged Siam to follow Japan's example.

The problem of prostitution is much wider than the problem of licensed houses, in fact it is as wide as the market towns of the country with their Chinese hotels. Clandestine prostitution in the form of unlicensed street-walkers is to be found everywhere. Most unregistered prostitutes seek their trade on the streets, through the beer halls, or in the Chinese hotels, literally none of which are free of them. A few remain in one locality permanently or for long stretches of time. Others move back and forth within Siam, and even travel across the international frontiers occasionally, especially the southern frontier. Among them are Siamese, Chinese, and Malays.

One notorious Cantonese prostitute crosses the border frequently without experiencing the slightest difficulty from officials on either side. Her passport lists her as a saleswoman. She carries packages of fruit, dolls, and mechanical toys with her, ostensibly the articles which she offers for sale. When she comes to the border she smilingly distributes these to officials for their children. The gifts are too insignificant to be called bribes, but they do help to establish friendly relations with officials and oil her constant shuttling between Siam and Malaya.

---

[1] *Nation*, March 15th, 1937.

The number of Siamese girls involved in clandestine prostitution is unknown. It is probably large. In one average market town, Haad Yie, a doctor and several merchants who live there estimate the number for their town to be approximately one hundred. They estimate further that each girl spends *baht* two a day for powder, perfume, clothing, and other personal effects. The total spent by the prostitutes for luxury goods alone would thus be about *baht* 6,000 a month, a very considerable trade for a small town and a not unimportant factor in the whole problem.

Some of the girls enter the business voluntarily. More, however, come into it unwillingly or by indirection. Not infrequently a procurer will persuade a girl to elope with him by making her many fine promises. He will live with her quite openly as her husband for some time and then will sell her to an agent or will rent her services himself. If the latter, the chances are that he will attempt to secure at least three or four girls for whom he acts as agent, and whose earnings support him. Other girls have been seduced and abandoned. If they cannot or will not return to their homes, they usually become prostitutes since they have no means of support.

The case of Mae Dang is typical. She was a school-girl of about fifteen, rather dull. Going back and forth to school she had to pass through the market district. She was approached one day by an elderly man, whom she knew, on behalf of a business man who had become enamoured of her. The old man acted as go-between during the entire affair. Something of the sort is usually the case. The principal makes frequent presents to the go-between such as articles of clothing, fruit, perfume, or other similar gifts. Nai Dom, the business man, already had a wife. He had no intention of marrying Mae Dang. After several months of exchanging love letters through the go-between, Nai Dom finally persuaded her to run away to him. Six months later he tired of her and drove her out. She had one child by him. After a few months she was taken up by another merchant. She passed from him to a third and shortly after that was on the street.

Occasionally prostitutes marry and attain to a respectable position in the community. For instance, a Chinese girl who had been sold into prostitution during a famine in China, was eventually traced by relatives to Siam. The family arranged a marriage for her with a young man of wealth and some position. While the marriage was not celebrated in the home of either party to it, it was most carefully and thoughtfully arranged in the home of a friend. After the ceremony the bride was cordially received in her husband's home, and was allowed to go to her own home. Since she had had no part in choosing her unfortunate profession, no stigma attached to her after marriage.

No country in the world has solved the problem of prostitution. But the situation can be improved by taking thought. The government hopes to better conditions in Siam by co-operating in the plans for social advancement as laid down by the League of Nations Conference.

4. FAMILY LIFE

There have been many articles in the Siamese newspapers during the last few years dealing with ways for improving family life. There are articles discussing the place of women in the home and her importance to the success of her husband. Others deal with the care and feeding of children, religion in the home, and similar subjects. Family life is considered to be in a state of transition due to the changing form of the modern world. Writers are springing up on every hand to point out guide posts and suggest paths through the wilderness.

Siamese family life varies according to its location, the business of husband or wife, and the social standing of the family. A typical country village stands out as distinctly as an island in the sea. It is surrounded by rice fields which are dry in the hot season and ankle-deep with water during the rice season. The approach to the village is across a checker-board of rice fields. From ten to thirty or forty houses are clustered together under the shelter of palm trees. Each householder fences off his compound from his neighbours with bamboo or some sort of hedge, perhaps of cactus, or barbed wire. The hub of the village is the temple, the grounds of which form a social and religious centre for the people. The average house stands in the middle of a small compound, raised about five feet from the ground on posts. There are many advantages to building so: the house is out of water during flood, the family animals may be kept under the house, and at night the ladder may be drawn up, thus making entrance slightly more difficult than otherwise for thieves. The steps, a shaky bamboo ladder, lead to a verandah. Opening off the verandah, but about five inches higher, are two or three rooms, according to the size of the family. The house is made of wood or bamboo, with attap for the roof. The buffalo, cow, the pigs, and the chickens are kept under the house. There, too, is the weaving frame on which the women make cloth for family needs, although it must be added that the frame is more and more falling into disuse as cheap Japanese textiles come into the markets. There may be one or two pariah dogs which warn the family of the approach of strangers.

The peasant eats two or three meals a day. The family sits on the verandah in a circle, with a large pot of rice at one side and a number of small dishes of curry, fish, and vegetables in the centre. Each person fills his dish with rice, adds a bit from each small dish for taste, and eats with his fingers. Fruits are usually eaten between meals rather than with the meal.

The whole family sleeps in the same room until the children are about thirteen, when they sleep apart. Rush mats are used for beds. Pillows are stuffed hard with kapok and seem very uncomfortable to anyone not used to them.

During the rice planting and rice harvest everyone works in the fields. They make the work sound like pleasure. There is laughing and talking and joking as they work through the fields. The harvest, which is stored in a granary behind the house, forms the staple food for the year.

For entertainment the village people have the various religious festivals and pilgrimages, which feature boat races, tug-of-war, and other feats of strength and skill. There are out-door theatres, and the shadow show which tells the story of the Ramayana.

Early in the morning a Siamese village is made colourful by the yellow robes of the Buddhist priests who appear silently with their begging bowls to receive gifts of food. A pious family does not eat from the rice pot until this gift has been made.

In the rubber growing districts village life is broken up. Houses are scattered through rubber estates so that owners may be convenient to their work, for rubber, unlike rice, requires daily attention.

The town home of a salaried worker is very different from the home of a peasant. The average house is small, two-storeyed, with wooden walls and a tiled roof. The lower floor is of cement.

There is a large room or verandah for receiving guests. It is equipped with a set of antlers for hats, a table, a few straight chairs, about twenty framed pictures of friends, a rack for canes, and a raised platform covered with a rug and pillows for those who prefer to lounge and chat there. Many Siamese find chairs uncomfortable, although they can sit on a mat or squat on their haunches for hours. The room behind has a well for drinking and bathing purposes. Behind that room is the kitchen, separated from the house by a covered passage. Upstairs are two bedrooms and a large hall which may be used for intimate guests. The hall has a few pictures of friends, a few spittoons, and a raised platform covered with a rug and pillows for lounging. The floors are well polished. The equipment is not expensive unless the family is well-to-do, but it is comfortable.

A certain wealthy home in Bangkok was sharply divided to suit two cultures. One side was decorated after the French pattern: it had French tapestries, French chairs and tables, and many copies of famous paintings. The library was full of English and French books. The radio and phonograph stood ready for use. The other part of the house was decorated with old ivory tusks, Siamese porcelains, niello and silver work, Chinese and Japanese prints, and other objects of art. The floors were beautifully polished, and no one wearing shoes was allowed to walk upon them. The library was well equipped with fine Siamese books. It was, needless to say, an upper-class cultured home.

A Japanese reporter visited Siam for two months and then wrote his impressions for the *Japan Times*. He portrayed only the poorer side of Siamese life. He said that people went around without upper garments, and lived in very poor homes. His articles aroused considerable indignation in Siam. But there are many Siamese who work in the fields without an upper garment. And there are many more who enjoy sitting in the cool of the evening clad only in Chinese pants. However, modern Siamese in the towns are fully clothed. Their dress is hardly distinguishable from that of the foreigner. The traditional Siamese mode of dress is fast disappearing in the city, especially now that civil officials are required to wear trousers, coat, shirt, and tie at their work.

A drastic change in the social order, to match the gradual abandoning of the national dress, is the cessation of the granting of titles. Since the establishment of the constitutional government no titles have been granted. In the future all men will be called "Nai" or mister.

Previously it was easy to tell an official's place in the world by his title. That is no longer possible. The abandonment of titles indicates the abandonment of an idea that was formerly fundamental to national life, probably originating in the feeling which still animates fathers and mothers all over Siam when they call their new born "red rat". The term was originally used to deceive evil spirits into believing that the child was not human, but animal, and so beneath their interest. The king was so exalted and high that his name could not be mentioned. But more, his name was not mentioned in order that he might not be exposed to danger from harmful spirits. By using a title the king could be referred to without letting the spirits know that the king was meant and also without detracting from his dignity. This same principle carried over to those whom the king placed in important positions. Titles were given them according to their rank to show them honour. The titles were always used in making reference to them. Even today people are seldom addressed by name or pronoun. Whenever possible they are addressed by title instead.

The idea of class distinctions is unacceptable to modern Siam. The feeling is that all men are equal, or at least should have equal opportunity. In order to express the equality of all men no more titles are granted, since titles perpetuate a class distinction. And titles are no longer considered necessary as a round-about reference used to circumvent evil spirits.

For the first time in the history of Siam a titled civil official asked, in July, 1933, to be allowed to relinquish his title and assume his own name. He is Luang Sundara Asvaraj, whose original name was Nai Chamras Soravisutr.

Under the old system a man might change names or titles four or five times in a lifetime as higher titles were accorded him. He might start as Nai Lek, and then become Khun Pradist, Luang Borirak, Phra Dhun, and perhaps at last Phya Suratstani. This made social life very complicated. One could easily lose track of old friends. The social trend is toward a more democratic basis. Whether the final result of this will be good or bad remains to be seen. Generally titles were given as a reward for years of government service. They represented the rank attained. Lower officials seldom rose above the rank of Khun. District officers were usually Luang, or occasionally Phra. Chief judges were Phra or sometimes Phya. Governors were Phyas. The titles were a definite part of the compensation received for government service, and were highly coveted. They formed one of the chief magnets that drew the most talented youths of the country into government employment. They were the reason that such service was considered more desirable even when less well paid than a commercial career. Now that titles are no longer given the glamour of the government service is less. Many bright young men who fifteen years ago would have refused anything but a government position are now going into lucrative commercial or professional pursuits.

CHAPTER IX

TRENDS IN RECREATIONS, ARTS, AND CRAFTS

1. RECREATION

TAKRAW is one of the oldest sports played by Siamese, and it is as popular as ever. The game is played with a hollow ball made of plaited rattan which is about the size of an indoor baseball. The players stand in a circle, barefooted, and with lower garments tucked up out of the way. The ball is put into play by tossing it to someone across the circle. The ball must not touch the ground and must not be caught with the hands. It may be kept in motion by the foot, knee, shoulder, elbow, or head. Skilful players frequently allow the ball to fall behind them before kicking it back over their heads with a quick motion of the heel or flat of the foot. Most small towns have several circles of players kicking the ball in the cool of the evening. Some players become very expert and keep the ball bouncing in the air from foot to knee to shoulder to head and back to foot again before kicking it on. One player of note went on a vaudeville tour with an act in which he kept six or eight balls in the air simultaneously. Takraw is everyman's game. It is generally non-competitive.

Boxing is a sport both ancient and modern in form. The western type of boxing with large soft gloves has won great popularity, but it is not as popular with the country people as the old style of Siamese boxing. In Siamese boxing there is no such thing as hitting below the belt. No hits, kicks, knee punches, or elbow jabs are barred. One may even butt his opponent unconscious. The boxer's hands are bound with twine that winds on up around the wrists halfway to the elbow and makes a terrible weapon of the flaying arms. The old roundhouse swing with its wide arc is good form. Western boxing has brought in straight hitting and jabbing. At the start of a match the boxers go through a few dance steps to loosen their muscles. Then each performs a brief ceremony of salute to his teacher, real or imaginary. The opponents come in fighting and kicking. A favourite method of attack is to drop to the hands and deliver a kick at the back of the opponent's head. Trial kicks at the face are made to get the distance. A knee to the groin is very effective. A dramatic finish may be accomplished by seizing the opponent's head and jerking it down while drawing the knee up smartly against his face. The sport is brutal and has resulted in many deaths.

Western boxing methods and rules are used in the many boys' schools where the sport is encouraged. Siam has a boxing champion who meets the Malayan or Philippine boxers upon occasion.

Soccer football has become very popular in Siam. The centuries-old Siamese game of takraw was a natural preparatory school for it. The Siamese are quick footed and easily learn a fine control of the ball. They generally play in bare feet. The present educational programme encourages adequate playing fields for schools. Games between the bigger schools are first page news. The "sporting spirit" has not been developed to the point where the losing side accepts defeat gracefully. Young Siamese are aware of this and deplore it. Some of them refuse to play in competitive games because they are afraid that they will take the contests too seriously and come out of them with grudges. Bad feeling engendered at games between schools sometimes reaches serious proportions. In November, 1937, there was a stabbing after a football game at a large Bangkok school. Football generally gives good value in improved physical condition and in increased endurance and co-operation, and young Siam will probably learn some day of the value of the game for the game's sake.

Tennis is a game that is played only by people who can afford to join tennis clubs. There are no public courts. It was popularized by the British, who form sports clubs wherever they go. The best players for many years were British. Tennis courts began to appear in all the provincial towns at the clubs of civil officials. Siam has produced no great players, but many excellent ones. It is an all-year game and provides recreation for thousands of people daily.

Badminton, which is so exceedingly popular in Malaya, is becoming more important in Siam. It is cheap, requires little space, so that it can be played in anyone's front yard, and it can be played even after a rainfall. It is ideal for the average Siamese. The

Malayan players have become very expert, so much so that in 1937 when an English champion came out to demonstrate how the game should be played, he was beaten by almost every local champion that faced him. In May, 1937, a group of players went from Siam to Hongkong and other points in China for a series of matches.

The golf champion of Siam is a Siamese. He also won the Malayan trophy in 1937. There are no public courses, so, as in tennis, play is limited to club members. The Siamese tennis doubles champions went to Singapore in the same year and showed themselves capable of playing excellent tennis.

Newspapers reported field days for the Army, Navy, University, and for various large schools. Pictures of pole-vaulting, jumping, putting the shot, and racing were featured.

A national stadium is being built in Bangkok. Progress is slow because grants of money for the project are difficult to find. Siam hopes to develop athletes who may compete in the Olympics with representatives from other nations.

A coxswain in the inter-university boat race at Cambridge in 1937 was a Siamese. Strangely enough Siam's sports hero won his fame abroad in a sport never seen in Siam. Prince Bira, a young Siamese living in England, has made himself famous by winning numerous important automobile races. There is no automobile racing in Siam, but Prince Bira's exploits are front-page news, eagerly read by all classes, and there is talk of glorifying the young racer by raising a statue to him.

The government is emphasizing sports in the educational programme because of a firm belief that sports are instructive, that games can teach desirable character traits, and that the boy who has learned his character lessons in games will be useful in politics and business. The government has established a new Department of Physical Education of the Ministry of Public Instruction. Luang Subhajalasaya of that department explains the values of sports and physical education for Siamese as follows:

> In ancient times every grown up man of the Thai race was a warrior who took up arms and laid down his life for the safety and independence of the nation. The art of physical culture and training and the science of fighting were imparted to every youth along with instructions in the three R's. . . . A country or a nation, to be independent or progressive, needs not only brains (mental and moral education) but also a good physique (the advancement of national health and physical culture). In its own way, and in line

with the changing times, the Thai nation has always maintained its healthy physique and efficiency; and today, with new life implanted in the nation by the establishment of a democratic form of government, Siam has become fully cognizant of the importance of physical culture in her progressive march to modern statehood. With renewed energy, modern Siam is utilizing up-to-date standards and methods of physical culture and athletic activities with a view to achieving the best possible benefit for the nation. . . . Siam has been one of the few oriental countries which has been able to absorb and adapt Western methods and educational institutions without conflicting with her own ancient civilization and culture.[1]

The trend is to regard sports and physical education as of definite value to the national spirit and character.

In the villages cock-fights take up many an idle hour. Men carry their prize cocks around under their arms. The claws of the cocks are sharpened and trimmed to make them more effective as weapons. Frequently the larger towns have a cock-ring. The excited shouts of the crowds and the crowing of the cocks can be heard from a distance. Almost everyone lays at least a small wager.

The noise at a cock-fight is but a whisper compared to that at a bull-fight. Bull-fighting is a southern sport centering around Trang, Patalung, Singora, and Nakon Sritammarat. The fight is not between men and bulls, but actually between bulls. The crowd is protected from the bulls by a light bamboo fence which would not hinder the flight of a scared boy, but seems adequate to keep the bulls in bounds. Occasionally a bull does dash out, but he is polite and uses the gate and goes prancing up the road in defeat. The bulls are led on to the field by four men, two to a bull, who hold ropes run through a snout-ring. As the men draw closer to each other the bulls are brought face to face. They frequently shy away but are brought back again. With much snorting and pawing the shove-of-war begins. Skull to skull they shove and snort until one is forced back in defeat. And that is all. Occasionally a bull is thrown to its side and left with all feet waving in the air. Now and then there is an inter-city match. At an important match thousands of *baht* are won and lost. The poorest peasant can produce some money to bet on his favourite.

Many wealthy Siamese have followed the British pattern and race horses. Horse racing in Siam has no value beyond the

---

[1] Luang Subhajalasaya, "Physical Education in Siam," *Siam Today*, January, 1937, p. 47.

pleasure it gives the spectators, for horses are not bred in Siam. Race horses are imported from Australia.

Cards and other gambling games are permitted by the government on Sundays and holidays. The banker pays a tax for the privilege of conducting a gambling game, collects ten *stangs* each time the cards are dealt, and leaves the actual game to chance. There is very little cheating because the profit is plainly charged out in advance and is not taken on a percentage basis. Cards are seldom played except for gambling purposes.

The pastime of rhyme-making and singing is a rural enjoyment that has not yet vanished. H.H. Prince Bidyalankarana discussed the subject at some length before the Siam Society. It is a recreation enjoyed by rural rhymsters at the time of the harvest and at other periods of the year when the people are not too busily engaged with the cultivation of the land. Rhymes are extemporaneously composed to suit the occasion and in response to raillery. The rhymes are usually sung by two people or two groups of people (male and female) in opposition. Each side attempts to defeat the other. Amorous advances are made, grave mock charges stated and defended. There is often vulgarity on the part of the men and rudeness on the part of the women. Prince Bidya has described the pastime so well that it needs no further comment.[1] This is a form of recreation that will hardly find place in modern Siam.

Siam's most popular modern amusement is the movies. Both silent films and talkies are enjoyed, regardless of whether the spectators understand English or not. The finest theatre is the Chalerm Krung in Bangkok. It is of the most modern type of construction with indirect lighting, air conditioning, and beautiful decorations. Other Bangkok theatres are inferior to it in physical equipment. The small-town theatres are barn-like buildings with tin walls and roofs.

A Siamese company has been established for the production and filming of Siamese plays, using Siamese characters. It should prove a success if one may judge from the unusual crowds that turn out to see even the most unambitious productions in the native language.

Movie heroes are made members of the community life. The drivers of cars have accepted the ten-gallon hat, wild-west shirt, and

---

[1] H. H. Prince Bidyalankarana, "The Pastime of Rhyme-Making and Singing in Rural Siam," *Journal of the Siam Society*, XX (October, 1926), p. 101.

neck-cloth as standard riding equipment on some of the southern bus lines. Across the top of the windshield flutters a line of famous faces. Many Siamese young men yearn to go to Hollywood, and fail to understand why any American would miss the opportunity. A heroic figure named "Towmick" featured in daily stories recounted by one employee. This fabulous character could fight bandits, save helpless women, and escape from impossible situations. He had a horse that was almost human. A little sleuthing revealed that this was Tom Mix.

The pictures on the screen became so real to the audience in one movie that when a wild motor car came dashing down a mountain straight into the laps of the audience, those in the front seats yelled and dodged to save their lives. The movies are helping to form Siamese character as shown by the candid admission of a certain bandit who said that he got some of his best ideas from the shows he saw. Standards of living shown in the movies, patterns of behaviour that are acted out, and styles of clothing that are shown, are all observed and often are copied.

The radio has gained a place for itself in the life of the people. Almost every provincial town has a few sets where people gather in the evenings to listen to music and news. Many of the shops keep a radio turned on to attract customers. Radio is in the hands of the government which controls the subject matter sent out. Commercial firms have no hours on the air. Broadcasting is theoretically done for the edification and amusement of the people. If more families owned radio sets the government would have in its hands a splendid tool for propaganda and instruction.

In April, 1937, it was reported that a new and powerful radio station was to be erected at Phra Khanong. The station was to have an output of one hundred kilowatt. It was hoped that the new station would make it possible for people to use cheap crystal sets all over Siam. At present there are about 30,000 sets of all types in the country.

2. ARTS AND CRAFTS

Turning to the artistic side of life, one may observe that most Siamese art has been religious. Architecture, painting, usually frescoing, and image-making have all been developed in connection with Buddhism. Until recently no particular effort has been expended on private dwellings. The temple, however, has commanded the best that the community offered. While ordinary houses were built by the family from bamboo or wood taken from the forest, the temple was of brick. Sometimes, as at Nakon Sritammarat, it had rows of lofty pillars slanting into the roof and all perfectly aligned. While houses had attap or leaf roofs, the temple had a graceful, multiple, convex roof of glazed tiles, sometimes in several colours. The walls were frescoed with scenes from the religious epics. Literature, dance, and music have been partially religious and partially secular. Siamese art has not been creative. It has been moulded by foreign influences which came from India by way of Cambodia. Siam and China have been in close contact for ages, but Chinese art has not affected Siam as much as the Indian. Perhaps that is because the Chinese who came to live with the Siamese were not artists, but peasants, soldiers, and traders, while the Indian immigrants were more often than not Buddhist missionaries. The Thai inherited the culture represented at Angkor Wat, in Cambodia.

Borobudur in Java and Angkor Wat in Cambodia are expressions of Indian artistic feeling as it finds a new existence through the genius of other Eastern peoples. At Pimai in Siam there is a ruin suggestive of Angkor.

H. G. Quaritch Wales made an expedition into south Siam to search for the routes by which Indian culture spread over Siam. He traced possible routes overland at various points along the Siamese coast. From his observations he suggests the importance of a kingdom called "Pan-Pan", located somewhere in what is now Siam, which was a diffusing point for Indian culture to Java, Cambodia, and more distant points. While the earliest traders to these countries went by sea through the Straits of Malacca to Indo-China, perhaps as far back as the third century before the Christian era, others went by the slower land route and set up cultural centres along their eastward way. Their traces may be found yet in various parts of south Siam, as is pointed out by Wales.[1]

The resulting artistic products found in Siam are well worth examining. There are not many ancient ruins that have survived

[1] H. G. Quaritch Wales, "Ancient Empires," *Asia*, March, 1936, p. 192.

until today, or, if there are, they are buried in jungles waiting to be dug by future archaeologists. The patterns introduced by the Indian travellers still survive in modified forms. In the Grand Palace there are three halls of audience that are really gorgeous. Dusit Maha Prasad, one of the finest products of modern Siamese architecture, was erected for the reception of foreign envoys. The Amarindr Vinichai Hall, and the Baisal Daksin are rich examples of the Siamese style.

Wat Phra Keo, the Chapel of the Emerald Buddha, is usually considered the most interesting of Bangkok's temples. Its foundation was laid in 1785, and, unlike many other temples, it has been kept in fairly good repair.

Wat Phra Chetupon, popularly known as Wat Po from the ancient temple on that site named Wat Potharam, is one of the largest temples in Siam. The central chapel is surrounded by galleries of sitting Buddhas and small chapels containing other images of Buddha. A colossal reclining Buddha is of particular interest.

Wat Arun, or Wat Chaeng (the old name), is strikingly different from the other temples in that it is a gigantic tower decorated with broken bits of pottery of ancient design. On a sunny day it outshines all other temples.

Glazed tiles form an important part of the colour effect of Siamese temples. One of the most modern in construction is Wat Benchama Bophit. Italian marble and Chinese glazed tiles were used. It combines many Buddhist ideas from other lands. There are two pavilions in the Javanese style, a white alabaster Buddha of the Burmese, and a bronze Buddha made after the figure of the finest image ever cast in Siam, Phra Jinaraj of Pitsanuloke.

Other famous temples are at Nakon Sritammarat, Nakon Patom, and Chiengmai. There is no need to describe the Siamese temples in detail because they have been so often and so well described already. They are rich in colour and stand out from the other buildings as birds of paradise from sparrows. Their lines and grace remind one of dancers.

With the temples one naturally associates the unnumbered multitude of images, mostly of the Buddha. There are certain figures that have gained world-wide fame for their beauty and value. Thus the Emerald Buddha, now at Wat Phra Keo, situated within the walls of the Grand Palace, has had its romantic story frequently told. One of the more recent accounts of it was written by Camille Notton in 1932. The figure is famous not only for its beauty and intrinsic value but because it has gone through wars, fires, and inundations and emerged safely. This image, originally carved in northern India from a large block of green jade, was sent to Ceylon and then on to Ayudhia in Siam. It was carried off to Chiengmai and Chiengrai, and finally brought to Bangkok where it now is. Wherever it has gone it has been the inspiration of countless images.

Another famous Buddha, said to be the most beautiful large image ever cast in Siam, is the one located at Pitsanuloke which is named Phra Jinaraj. There is a legend that says that an angel assisted in the casting.

The making of Buddhist images has been traced back to the inspiration of travelling Greeks who taught the art of casting many centuries ago to the Indians of that day. Oriental races have varied the figure to suit their own idea of beauty. During the last 150 years, the modern period of image making, there has been but little variation from the figures of former days. The tendency is to blend the features of former figures and types. Figures of the Buddha are still being made, but not on a grand scale. Nor is there improvement artistically. There are still some artists who are able, if given the time and the funds, to produce very beautiful images. The art has not died.

The Siamese have developed painting along intricate and curious lines. Their canvases have been the inside walls of the temple buildings. The paintings tell legends, such as the Ramayana. A bird's-eye perspective is used which enables the artist to lay out whole towns on which to place the story of kings, country, people, angels, or the story of Buddha. The composition is confusing and one must know what is portrayed to appreciate it. It is conventionalized and highly decorative.

Wood-carving, metal working, and inlaying on both wood and metal are well developed arts. Wood-carving is seen on temple doors, columns, windows, and on roof decorations. Bookcases and chairs are well done. The metal work that has won fame is called "niello". The design is hammered out and a black metallic compound in the form of a powder is placed in the depressions. The article is heated until the powder fuses. Then the surface is filed down so that the design is flush with the silver or gold of the base. This work is used for trays, boxes, bowls, spoons, knives, buttons, and other articles. For a time the chief centre of production was Nakon Sritammarat. Then the Arts and Crafts School of Bangkok took an interest in the work and developed many beautiful pieces. At the French exposition in 1937, Siamese "niello" ware won high praise.

A minor art that is dying out is the drawing and cutting of shadow-show pictures which are used in the Ramayana play. There are still a few artists left in south Siam who can turn out of cowhide a fine screen of Rama and Sita, Hanuman, monkeys, and giants. The figures are lacy, delicately cut, and very curious. But the demand for them is small.

Siamese jewelry is of great artistic merit and is in demand by both Siamese and Europeans. The Siamese have always liked solid gold jewelry, not only for its beauty, but also for its practicality as an easy form in which to bank extra funds. The most beautiful workmanship is found in the regalia for ceremonial use, such as swords, maces, bowls, and crowns of tapering form. Thin plates of virgin gold are beaten into patterns and encrusted with precious stones. Old bracelets and pins have a beauty that appeals even to moderns. In 1938, an intricately worked bracelet in ancient pattern was shown some Chicago appraisers who were greatly impressed with the artistic quality of the workmanship.

Pottery and weaving have been of importance. Weaving is still a home industry in many parts of the country, but good Siamese pottery is no longer made. Weaving is losing its artistic value because the rich clothes that were used formerly are no longer required. In its place has come modern western style clothing.

Theatre and music show definite progress under the enthusiastic leadership of Luang Vichitr, who has written a number of songs and plays to suit the times. He combines his experience in the French theatre with the Siamese dramatic instinct.

The National Dance and Music School was created by the Department of Fine Arts in 1934. The actors and actresses of the royal palace were placed under the direction of this Department in 1935. It uses about 300 actors and actresses, and about 150 musicians. At present they are regularly producing the Lakorn,

Khone, and Revue. The Khone is classical drama, the Lakorn is classical dancing with some comics added, the Revue is a modern version of Siamese acting.

One of the more recent successes is *Phra Chao Krung Dhon*, a play written by Luang Vichitr. The writer attended the play and was impressed with the presentation. A feeling of new energy infused the old patterns and measures.

CHAPTER X

RELIGIOUS TRENDS

1. TRADITIONAL HINAYANA BUDDHISM IN OLDER SIAM

BUDDHISM is the traditional religion of Siam. Specifically it is Hinayana Buddhism which came to Siam by way of Ceylon, and so is often called Southern Buddhism. Its language vehicle is Pali rather than the Sanscrit, which is used in Mahayana or the Northern Buddhism of Tibet, China, and Japan.

It would seem to be a simple matter to read the historical literature of the religion noting its teaching; and to combine these recorded ideals with the practice of them past and present in order to show religious trends in modern Siam. Analysis is not so simple as that. Religion is far from being a collection of ideals noted down in a book. It is in addition to such principles a technique of living, a matter of thinking, of behaviour, of practice. As such it is not a few clear-cut teachings, but a great anomalous, amorphous mass of custom, attitudes, traditions, and day by day actions.

It has been the writer's pleasure to engage in and listen to countless discussions on religion. In such, an apologist usually compares the high ideals of his religion, as recorded in his sacred book, with the actual life practices of the followers of the religion he would disparage. Invariably the side measured by practice fails to show up well, and the apologist feels that he has won his case. He recognizes the fact that the religion of his opponent in the argument consists of what the followers of it actually are and do, but fails to remember that he is measuring his own religion with another rule altogether, that is by those beautifully inscribed ideals which are likely to be so much finer than the actions based upon them. In order to make a fair comparison, the actual life patterns of both religions must be laid out side by side.

So, in order to discover the trends in modern Siamese religion, it is necessary to compare as far as possible the traditional religious pattern, and pattern here means the combination of thought and action which constitutes the rounded whole, with the modern religious pattern. The traditional religious pattern was formulated around three main streams of thought which might be termed Buddhism, Brahmanism, and Spiritism.

Buddhism was a reform movement in Hinduism. It offered a technique of escape from the misery of life. It had two fundamental conceptions. One of these was a belief in transmigration by which all divine, human, or animal life kept passing through recurring cycles of regeneration. The other was a fundamental confidence in the virtue of the human act for good. The technical name applied to this latter idea is "karma", which means in simple language that every good or evil deed has a consequent result in the present or in the future life. Thus a Siamese peasant will explain illness or calamity in his family by saying: "Do good and receive good. Do evil and receive evil." An elderly Siamese woman who had never had any children explained this—to her—most unfortunate circumstance by saying that she must have committed some heinous sin in a previous existence.

Buddha felt that life was evil and that the wise man must escape from it. There is a difference of opinion as to whether Gautama was embittered with all of life and wished to end the very reality of existence itself, or whether he was merely dissatisfied with the misery of life as lived on earth and was seeking and teaching a technique of living which would dissipate that misery and guarantee a happy life on earth. Perhaps both ideas are embraced by his teaching, one as an immediate aim and the other as the ultimate goal of religion. Deliverance from the evil of existence is attained, according to his teaching, by suppressing every act that entails a consequence. This method of suppression is peculiarly Buddhist. Transmigration and karma may be considered Brahman, or Indian, ideas rather than essentially Buddhist.

The conservative Siamese conception of the universe is found in a work entitled *Thrai Phum* (three places). The three places are earth, heaven, and hell. There are sixty books in the set compiled by royal command. Space is occupied by an infinite number of cosmic groups. Each one contains a world with heavens and hells. The inhabitants as well as the places are constantly being destroyed and being brought to life again because of the imperfections found in perfect formless Brahman angels. Desire manifests itself, and tangible dwelling places, food, and material things are provided. The groups, each of which is called a Chakrawan, surround a great central mountain named Phra Meru. There are eight belts of ocean divided from each other by seven mountain ranges with an eighth ring called the crystal wall of the world. In the outermost belt of ocean are four groups of islands. The southern group is the world of man. The others are peopled by square-headed, half-round faced people. On Mount Meru are six lower heavens where those who have practiced virtue and charity may hope to be born as angels to lead an existence attended by every sensual pleasure for hundreds of millions of years. Above the lower heavens are nine stages where the Brahma angels dwell. These are without sex organs and intestines, and have only the senses of sight and hearing. They dwell in beatitude for twenty-six million *kalpas* before their merit is exhausted. Above these are the four highest heavens where formless angels exist for periods almost infinite, in the expectation of Nirvana after their next earthly life.

A hundred miles beneath the earth is the uppermost of the 5,120 hells in which most horrible sufferings are dealt out to those whose demerit in the world has exceeded their merit. The whole system rests in a vast sea in which huge fish which cause earthquakes play. This sea is supported by the wind.[1]

A Siamese servant, who was asked by his master if he expected to go to Nirvana, answered that he hoped not. He preferred one of the lower heavens where the joys were sensual. Failing that, he wanted to be reborn into this world in a higher station and with more worldly benefits. He hoped, of course, to escape the hells and to avoid being born a lower animal. This very human story gives a quick insight into the practical religious man's mind. What he hoped to get from his religious exercises was the good life, as he imagined it, fulfilled in this world.

The precepts of the Buddha as commonly taught are the three fundamental principles, the four noble truths, the eight-fold path, and the moral code.

The three fundamental principles are:
1. The impermanence of everything.
2. The inherent sorrow in everything.
3. The non-reality of a separate self.

[1] W. A. Graham, *Siam* (Chicago: F. C. Browne & Co., 1913), II, 483-484.

These three principles make clear the doctrine that all existence is illusion with no substantial reality underlying change. This is always becoming. The human being is an elemental aggregate which at death dissolves, leaving no ego. Man's cardinal sin is the desire to live. Karma is all that continues, linking the "I" of the next. The usual illustration for this difficult concept is that of the fire which passes from a stick to a bundle of straw, to a barn, to a village, to a forest. The fire of the stick and of the forest is the same, and not the same, and is continuous.

The four noble truths are:
1. All life is suffering.
2. Life is the result of desire.
3. Cessation of desire ends life and suffering.
4. Cessation of desire is attained by following the eight-fold path.

The eight-fold path is known as the middle way between extremes of living. It is:
1. Right belief, clear apprehension and acceptance of the four noble truths.
2. Right aspiration, sentiments of compassion and brotherhood.
3. Right speech, correct recitation of Buddha's teaching and avoidance of sins of speech.
4. Right actions, keeping the moral law and avoiding the sins of the body.
5. Right livelihood, not gaining money by harmful means.
6. Right effort, mental effort to progress in knowledge.
7. Right mindfulness, alertness of mind for teaching.
8. Right contemplation, serene calmness due to meditation.

There are five moral precepts intended for everyone:
1. Do not destroy life.
2. Do not defraud.
3. Do not commit adultery.
4. Do not deceive.
5. Do not take intoxicants.

Three more are added to the list for nuns:
6. Do not eat solid food after noon.
7. Do not dance, sing, or attend plays.
8. Do not use ornaments, perfumes, or oils.

Two more are added for novices:
9. Do not sleep on a high bed.
10. Do not accept gold or silver.

The monk observes these ten precepts and about two hundred more arranged according to importance.

As to eschatology, there is the expectation of another Buddha to come whose name is Ariya Mettaya, or Phra Sri An. The legend which prophesies this epiphany says that millions of *kalpas* ago a white crow laid five eggs. Earthquake, thunder, and storm scattered them. Each was taken and cared for by a foster mother, and each eventually was hatched. They became Kakoosuntak, Konahmanah, Kasappa, Kotama, and Ariya Mettaya. These beings were reborn into the world above as water lilies, or lotus. Among themselves they agreed that the lotus which budded first should be born on earth as a Buddha, who would bring blessing to man and animal. Kakoosuntak's lotus budded first. He became and remained a Buddha for 5,000 years. His appearance was as gold. At the end of the period he entered Nirvana. After him came Konahmanah, who was as a jewel, and who continued on earth for 3,000 years, after which he too entered Nirvana. Then came Kasappa who was as white as milk. He existed as a Buddha for 2,000 years before entering Nirvana. After this the lotus of Ariya Mettaya budded, but Kotama traded lilies with him and so came to earth before him. It is admitted that Kotama's natural life was but 80 years. According to the legend he then entered upon the second of the three stages of Nirvana. Kotama was a preparatory manifestation. He was negative in that he offered negative virtues and warned against positive vices. After 5,000 years Ariya Mettaya will be born to take his place. He is to combine all the powers and virtues of his brothers and to reign for 84,000 years. All who have had clean hearts will be reborn at that time and will enter Nirvana with him. After an indefinite period the cycles of the ages will begin again with the five brothers.

The coming of Ariya Mettaya will be preceded by a period of great wickedness, accompanied by a gradual decrease in the length of human life, until marriages will take place at five years of age and old age will come at ten. Family relations will be disregarded, human begins will cohabit like goats, chickens, or dogs. Human life will be held in such light esteem that men will hunt and kill each other as they now do wild beasts. When Ariya Mettaya appears they will abandon this state of lawlessness and will come forth from their hiding places, embrace each other, and agree to forsake evil ways. A new reign of righteousness will begin, and human life will increase to 100 years, and then to 1,000, and finally to 100,000. Physical blessings will be showered down in abundance. Nirvana will be opened with the true key of right knowledge. Perfect bliss will come to all.[1]

The Siamese, or Thai, probably received Buddhism as early as the Chinese. In the first century before the Christian era, Buddhism entered China through Yunnan, crossing Thai territory on the way. Local warfare resulted, because the Thai suspected Buddhist missionaries of being spies. In the first century of the Christian era, the Thai king, Khun Luang Mau, is reported to have declared himself a Buddhist. His conversion may have resulted from a mission sent out by the Chinese emperor, Ming Ti. The Mahayana Buddhism, which he embraced, did not deeply infect the people, however, for it was soon smothered by the Hinayana Buddhism that came up later from the south.

Reginald Le May says that Buddhism, according to hallowed tradition, was originally brought to north Siam at Lamphun, where it was propagated by Princess Cham Thewi of Lavo, or Lopburi. This event occurred during the seventh century. The type of Buddhism imported at this time was Mon or Peguan. In the fourteenth and fifteenth centuries priestly intercourse with Ceylon had definitely begun. Many Buddhist temples were built by the Burmese as early as the sixteenth century, when they held the land for a time.[2]

Le May tells of an abbot, Phra Uthumpon Bupha Maha Sawami, who was originally a Mon priest at Martaban. About 1331 he went to Ceylon and entered the priesthood. He returned to his home with a thorough education in Buddhism. His fame as a scholar of the Tripitaka in its Singhalese form spread rapidly. Two Siamese monks of Sukhodaya, Phra Anomata Sri and Phra Sumana, who had studied at Ayudhya, went to Martaban for advanced work with Phra Uthumpon. They returned to Sukhodaya and taught a group of young men so successfully that after ten years a large number

[1] Howard Campbell, "Ariya Mettaya, The Buddhist Messiah," *The Siam Outlook*, April, 1930.
[2] Reginald Le May, *An Asian Arcady* (Cambridge: W. Heffer & Sons, Ltd., 1926), p. 180.

were thorough Buddhist scholars. The ruler at Chiengmai invited them to teach there. A group of ten were sent and the new doctrine spread rapidly. Eventually the whole Siamese nation became imbued with Buddhist ideas, practiced the same ceremonies, and supported the monkhood.

Sir John Bowring wrote:

> Neither the customs of the people, nor the character of the government has changed materially in the centuries since the time of King Rama Kamheng, until the days of King Maha Mongkut. Descriptions of A.D. 1250, 1650, or 1850, scarcely differ in any respect as to custom, usage, and fundamental attitude of mind. Diego De Coute's descriptions of A.D. 1600 as to festivities would serve as well as in those centuries ago.[1]

This fact simplifies the work of drawing a picture of Buddhism as it was practiced. One may feel sure that important changes have come only with the modern invasion of European civilization.

Turning to Buddhism as it has been and is still practiced to some extent, one finds that it is protean. It has been adapted to suit the lives of all kinds of people. Buddhism for the householder has meant an occasional visit to the temple, feeding the monks, observing the five prohibitions as to deceiving, stealing, adultery, killing, and taking intoxicants, and once in the lifetime to become a monk for a few days.

The Order, however, was the only legitimate way of escape for the sincere full-hearted Buddhist who spends his time in meditation and inaction. Buddhism admits of no sacrament, no rite, no magic formula, no belief, no organization or sacred institution that can confer escape from misery. Theoretically there is nothing outside of oneself that can be of assistance. There is no saviour or helper. Each man must work out his own salvation. The Buddhist Order offered a detailed technique by which this might be done. Women, who were a lesser breed without the Law, were at a disadvantage in that they could not join the Order, although an order of nuns is permitted. However, women have always been the chief supporters of the temples. The laymen and especially the laywomen have provided generously for the service of the community of monks.

Theoretically Buddhism is without a god, in the ordinary sense

[1] John Bowring, *The Kingdom and People of Siam* (London: John W. Parker & Son, 1857), I, 101.

of the word. When Buddha attained to Nirvana he passed out of reach of this world of misery. He is not a creator nor a saviour. Thus the cult of respecting images, relics, and footprints of Buddha is merely the result of the high respect shown to a great human leader who has broken a new trail through to the promised land. When the intellectual Buddhist went through the rites before the image he was expressing a wish that his karma might be acceptable and that he might escape misery and attain happiness. Actually to many of the common people Kotama Buddha was a god to whom they addressed their petitions and before whom they did obeisance. The intellectual and rational Buddhist was an infinitesimal minority.

Until about a decade ago most men at some time in their lives spent a few days or a few months in a monastery to acquire merit which would insure a happy future.

There is no dearth of temples. Siam has more temples for its population than the United States has churches. It has been estimated that there is a temple, not counting ruined temples, for every 500 people. Those sections of the country thickly inhabited by Chinese and Malays have made less provision for Buddhist temples.

The widespread religious practice of the people past and present is shown in no way better than by the prevalence of votive tablets. These small stamped images are not Brahmanistic in origin, but are distinctly Buddhist, and are found at nearly every Buddhist site. The subjects of these tablets are generally the four great objectives of Buddhist pilgrims in India, namely: Kapilavastu, where Buddha was born; Buddhagaya, where he became omniscient; the Deer Park near Benares, where he preached the law for the first time; and Kusinagara, where he attained Nirvana. The stupa marks the site of Kusinagara. The wheel of the law, or a wheel supported by two deer, symbolizes Benares. The evergreen fig tree represents Buddhagaya. The emblem for Kapilavastu is uncertain. A tree, a wheel, and a stupa remind the pilgrim of the objects of veneration. The pictures usually represent the site the pilgrim has visited.

From far back in Buddhist history it was considered an act of merit to make an image of Buddha. Poor people could not afford the outlay for a large image and so the idea of an inexpensive pressed image was born. Moulds were made of copper, and the tablets were turned out by the hundreds for the poor people who wanted to venerate Buddha. The verse which appears on many of these reads:

> The conditions which arise from a cause,
> Of these the Tathagata has stated the cause,
> Also the way of suppressing these same:
> This is the teaching of the great ascetic.

This formula is printed on the tablet in Pali, Sanscrit, Cambodian, or occasionally some other language. According to tradition this stanza was used by Buddha to convert two disciples to the new way of life as taught by himself. The verse, since it had convinced two such notables, was much venerated. It was believed to have unusual power as a means of conversion to the faith.

In Siam, the miracle of Sravasti, the miracle by which Buddha made an immense number of converts, is one of the commonest subjects of votive tablets. Thus the tablets were used not only as an expression of veneration by the faithful, but also as vehicles of religious propaganda among the unconverted.

If all other evidence of the religion be swept away, and some archaeologist were to study only these remains of a once great religion, he would soon be convinced that they attested the one time existence of an all-powerful religion, holding sway over a great part of the regions that we call the Far East. They would reveal to him the representation of the founder, interpreted according to the artistic perceptions of the different countries in which, and epochs at which, this cult was followed. They would show to him the principle deities that by degrees invaded and contributed a pantheon to a doctrine originally atheistic. And also the brief inscription would make known to him, embalmed in a single sentence of striking laconism, the quintessence of the very religion itself.[1]

The votive tablets are an example of what the common people did with the lofty, intellectual teaching of Buddha. They accepted the heart of his message. They venerated his way of life and honoured him. They added a pantheon of gods. They blended the purity of Buddhism with their own ways of living and thinking and produced something quite different from anything that its founder intended. Buddhism, which began as a reform movement out of Hinduism returned eventually to the family roof where it was permeated with Brahman ceremonies.

[1] G. Goedes, "Siamese Votive Tablets," *Journal of Siam Society*, XXI, 1927.

2. BRAHMANISM IN SIAMESE BUDDHISM

A Buddhist in good and regular standing thus indulged in many Brahman practices, such as those described below.

The Indian Brahman from birth is involved in a whirl of religious ceremonial such as naming, weaning, first footsteps, first speech, adoption of clothing, ear boring, and hair cutting. The ceremonial of marriage seems to end his troubles for a time only to involve him again in putting his children through their religious paces. He is at last swallowed up in that last ceremonial of cremation. This ceremonialism spread, and different nations accented certain ritual. Thus the Burmese and Laos pay great heed to the naming and ear boring, while neglecting the rest. The Mohammedan Malays in south Siam, in spite of the fact that such things are anathema, perform the ritual for the first footsteps, and have also gotten the Islamic rites of circumcision mixed up with the Brahman topknot cutting to an amazing degree. The Siamese consider the naming, topknot cutting, and cremation of prime importance. The rite of marriage is desirable but not necessary, and the rest are of no account.[1]

There was no competition between Buddhist monks and Brahman priests. In fact, they shared many religious ceremonies.

Brahman influence is not recent in Siam. One Siamese historian claims that as early as the days of Khun Yee Mao, in 779 B.C., seven Brahmans were engaged in Thai government service. Certainly the Brahmans were responsible for the exaltation of the process of government. The monarch was transformed into a sacred being with high sounding titles, and was surrounded with numerous taboos. The Brahmans taught that all land, possessions, and people belonged to the king. The king was absolute. Brahmans were acceptable because their doctrine gave dignity and power to the rulers. Brahman development is shown in its full flower in H. G. Quaritch Wales' book entitled *State Ceremonies*. It is not necessary to describe here in detail the ceremonies so ably described there.

Aside from the state ceremonies peculiar to the king, such as coronation and royal marriage, there were other ceremonies practiced by prince and commoner alike, such as the topknot cutting ceremony, marriage ceremony, new year's festival, oath of allegiance to the crown, ceremonies connected with the elephant cult, swing ceremony, and ploughing ceremony.

The topknot cutting ceremony of Prince Chulalongkorn was a very grand affair. It has been described in detail by Mrs. Anna Leonowens in her book *An English Governess at the Court of Siam*.

[1] W. A. Graham, *Siam* (Chicago: F. G. Browne & Company, 1913), II, 516.

King Mongkut had explored the annals and records of Siam and Cambodia. The ceremony became a mammoth play or set of tableaux with a cast of several thousand people in which the customs and history of the country were set forth. The ceremony marks the passage from childhood to adulthood and takes place usually when a boy is thirteen and a girl eleven years of age. The conch shell plays an important part in the ceremony just as it does in most Brahman rites. Fabulous sums were formerly paid for perfect shells which opened to the right and not to the left. A bounty of 60,000 rix-dollars per annum was formerly paid the British government for the privilege of fishing for them. Demand has failed with the waning of the importance of the various ceremonies in this modern age, and the fishing is now free. So has Brahmanism declined.

Until recently it was the custom to shave a child's head from babyhood with the exception of a little tuft of hair, which was never cut until the topknot cutting ceremony. The head was held in great reverence and was not supposed to be touched except by worthy persons. For this reason Siamese still show respect for the head of another by crouching low enough to bring their own heads at least level as they pass one another. For the same reason, about the middle of the last century, a prince who had a deep interest in printing was unable to inspect the first press ever set up in Bangkok because it was located under a house where people were living. There was danger that if he entered the first floor, someone on the second might pass over his head. While time has modified this excessive reverence for the head, the feeling regarding it is far from being completely dissipated. According to Hindu legend there is a microscopic hole under the tuft of hair through which the human spirit finds an entrance at birth and an exit at death. Thus the ceremony, uncovering as it did this hole for the first time, was made more solemn by a sense of danger.

Both Buddhist monks and Brahman priests shared in the ceremony. The Brahmans appealed to Dewa and Siva, they cried to Vishnu, to the four-armed Brahma, and to Indra. The Buddhist monks chanted about the sorrow and transiency of life. During the ceremony the spirit of the child was captured in a cloth and for three nights he slept with this clutched to his breast. If nothing terrible happened during the three days his future was assured.

The ceremony is still practiced, though not so elaborately or faithfully as it used to be. Neither boys nor girls wear the topknot any more except in an occasional back-country town, or perhaps in some unusually devout family. Only twenty years ago it was still common. Mothers arranged it neatly on the forefront of each little bald pate. Sometimes they decorated it with a tiny wreath of flowers, sometimes with gold or jeweled ornaments. But even so embellished it was not becoming. And this is probably a factor in its disappearance as much as the decline of interest in the ceremonies. Little girls now wear black straight bobs, which are, let us add, very becoming, and boys the same sort of haircut used elsewhere in the world for them. Occasionally a topknot is started a year before the ceremony, if it is to take place.

At these rites the book of the soothsayer was much in evidence. It is, even today, the handbook of the common people as well as of the soothsayer. It is considered to be so powerful that some people fear it too much to keep it in the house. The writer has known some who kept it hanging on a nail, outside the window. The choice of a mate, the auspicious moment for marriage, the right time to perform certain acts may be decided correctly from the information found on its pages.

A couple who were planning marriage consulted the sorcerer's book to be sure they were well-matched. If a man was born in the year of the tiger and the woman was born in the year of the rabbit the marriage would be unfortunate, for the tiger could eat the rabbit. If they were well suited to each other, the auspicious time for marriage was sought in the same book.

The Sonkran festival marked the beginning of the new year in April. Indra was supposed to have descended to earth a few days previously. The Brahmans observed his coming and so could prophesy what sort of year was to be expected. If he carried arms it meant trouble; if he carried fire it meant drought; a water-pot implied rains. After the Brahmans announced the sort of year that was to be expected the people came out and poured water over everything and everybody to help the rains to come. The day was turned into a water throwing contest. Old and young ran about laughing and shouting and wetting each other. As recently as 1937 Bangkok foreigners riding along in motor cars were astonished to have water thrown at them. They were bewildered, since they did not happen to be aware that the throwing of water encouraged the rains to come.

The oath of allegiance to the crown has always been an important ceremony. If anyone harboured a rebellious thought he was supposed to swell up and die after drinking the cup of fealty. Failure to attend the ceremony was regarded as treason. If anyone had difficulty in drinking, or choked, it was regarded as reason enough to suspect his sincerity.

The white elephant was one of the seven characteristics of the universal monarch. There came to be a cult of the elephant. White, or, more properly, albino elephants were highly coveted and were *per se* the property of the king. A king's favour with heaven could be measured by the number of albino elephants captured during his reign. No king was believed to have made an auspicious beginning until at least one had been taken and presented to him. Wars have been fought for possession of one. The Siamese and the Burmese practiced the same cult. When one country or the other had many white elephants, the country without made war in order to capture such evidences of supremacy. The elephants were regarded as royal and were given titles.

A swing ceremony was used to express gratitude for the harvest. It was held in January. A nobleman played the role of Indra. This ceremony is still very popular. The swing seat is about fifteen feet from the ground and is six feet long and a foot wide. On the west side of the swing a pole is erected with a bag of money hanging from it. Indra in the person of the noble arrives from a temple. He is seated in a hut by the swing between two Brahmans. As he crosses a foot across his knee the men begin to swing. A team of four swingers swing until one can catch the bag of money with his teeth. They are allowed only one try. There are usually several teams competing.

The ploughing ceremony, another ceremony that is still popular, is held in May at the beginning of the rainy season. This is one of the oldest ceremonies in existence. It was used in China for thousands of years as a technique for guaranteeing good crops. Three bamboos are placed in a line east and west. The corners of the field are marked off with screens to keep evil spirits out. In one corner is a shed containing figures of Ganesh, Siva, and Laksmi. From the altar a white cord passes out of the shed and links up the corners. This cord is charged with power to keep evil spirits away. The charge is introduced by the all-night prayers of the Brahmans. Oxen are yoked and the master of ceremonies makes light furrows. As he goes along he hitches his lower garment, the panung, which seems in danger of slipping off. The people watch this garment with much interest because they know that if it drags too low there will be drought, if it rides too high there will be floods, and if it is just right then rains will be adequate. Two old women appear with seed rice which the plougher scatters on the ground. The onlookers rush out and scramble for the seed, which is supposed to give fertility. It is an ancient version of fertilizer. Various grains are presented on a tray to the oxen. The grain of which they eat the most will yield the poorest crop for that year.

These ceremonies were the practical technique of former generations of Siamese for guaranteeing good crops, happiness, and success.

3. SPIRITISM IN SIAMESE BUDDHISM

Before the Thai ever heard of Buddhism or Brahmanism they had a religion by which they adapted themselves to this inexplicable and sometimes hostile world.

> In spite of the vast numbers of temples built, the innumerable images of the Lord Buddha fashioned and venerated, the endless pilgrimages to the more famous shrines, the countless store of money spent on gold leaf and incense, and the armies of priests that have been ordained, the Laos people remain at heart what they have been from time immemorial—animists.[1]

Le May was writing of the north which he knew so well. To a lesser degree the same thing might have been said of the south.

They seemed to feel that while it is good and right to live a life of virtue and to lay up merit for the future, the dangers and evils of the present life must be met. The world to them was full of evil spirits who helped or hindered. Spirits were ghosts of the dead, or the astral bodies of the living. They existed on their own account in this world, or they belonged to other worlds.

The birth of a spirit has been described as follows:

> When a Laos villager dies, his family washes the body with water, and dresses it in a panung and a new coat, which latter is put on inside out with the buttons facing inward. This is because the dead man has become a "phi"

[1] Reginald Le May, *An Asian Arcady* (Cambridge: W. Heffer & Sons, Ltd., 1926), p. 135.

and spirits always wear their clothes inside out. The wrists were tied together, and flowers and candles were placed in the hands. The body is laid in the centre of the room and a string is fastened to either wall running across the centre of the body at a height of six inches, supporting the cloth that covers the body. A small basket of wicker frame is made and hung across the doorway to keep the evil "phi" out. Sometimes this basket is never taken down. The body remains alone for one night. The next day the coffin is made and four priests are called to chant over the dead. The body is nailed up in the coffin. Cremation takes place after six months or longer.[1]

There are a number of spirits included in the category of ghosts of the dead. The term "phi lawk" is applied to those spirits that haunt old houses or ruins. They love to frighten people by sitting on the end of the bed and pulling their toes. There is a story told of such a spirit pulling a doubting foreign government official out of bed by the ankles even though he had taken the precaution of locking all doors and windows.

The "phi am" is a spirit that sits on the chest and liver of a person on a journey. The one afflicted can do nothing but groan and utter inarticulate sounds. The English Channel would probably seem to the Siamese to have a superabundance of the "phi am".

The "phi pret" is a giant about twenty-five feet high, the ghost of an evil doer. Its mouth is as small as the eye of a needle and so it is always hungry. It makes a noise like a whistle. Little red spots on the arms and legs are not the result of some mosquitoes' activity during the night: they are tiny holes through which the "phi pret" has been getting as much of a meal as his small mouth allows.

The "phi tai hong" are the ghosts of those who have died sudden or violent deaths. They are very malevolent.

Sorcerers are interested in "phi prai" or "phi put". The sorcerer goes by night to the spot haunted, and by incantations calls the spirit to appear. He then places a torch under the chin of the spirit, which to the untutored eye is a corpse, whose fat is melted and allowed to drip into a waiting vessel. This fat is mixed with sweet smelling oils. This is a powerful charm which may be used to drive men mad or to attract the love of women.[2] In one instance known to the writer a grave was guarded by relatives with shot-guns

[1] *Ibid.*, p. 120.
[2] A. J. Irwin, "Siamese Ghost Lore Demonology," *Journal of Siam Society*, 1904-1910.

for three nights after a funeral to prevent a sorcerer from practicing his art upon the corpse buried in it.

Then there are spirits that exist of themselves and are not the ghosts of the dead. There is the "phi ruen", who is the guardian spirit of the house. Every home has one. It may often be heard grumbling to itself. There is a guardian of the land named "prapum chao ti".

A third class of spirits dwell in other worlds and so concern the people very little.

In a previous chapter it has been shown that Siamese medical ideas came from India. The body consists of the four elements of wind, water, fire, and earth. Since spirits have control over the elements of the world they may control the elements of the body too. A spirit may cause a disproportion of some bodily element and bring on sickness. When this happens, the thing to do is to exorcise the spirits and expel them by incantation and the sprinkling of holy water.

In obstetrics there is danger that a woman's future life will be ruined if the water element, which is believed to have increased in her body, is allowed to lose its correct proportion. It is further believed that an evil spirit will hold her body in that state of disproportion if nothing is done about it. At the time of childbirth the only aid given is pressure on the uterus. After the birth is completed the mother lies in front of a fire—and this in a tropical country—in order to dry out the water and so defeat the spirit. Smoke from the fire escapes through the cracks in the room, which is darkened. After the first baby, thirty days of such treatment is recommended; after the second baby, fifteen days; after the third, ten days; after all other births five days is adequate. As modern medicine moves forward step by step this cruel practice is abandoned of course.

Dr. Henry R. O'Brien, formerly of Chiengmai, tells of one of his cases in which the birth was incomplete. The doctor removed the placenta just before the woman died. To his surprise the family was grateful beyond measure for his help in delivering them from a danger which he had not apprehended at all. The spirit of a woman dying in childbirth is fearsome. If she dies with the placenta within her she is twice dreadful. The most terrible spirit of all is that of a woman dying with child unborn. The family hardly regarded the death because they were grateful to have been saved from a malevolent spirit that would almost certainly have returned to trouble relatives and friends. In what would probably have been a futile effort to escape the spirit, they would have had to lower her body through a hole torn in the floor, take it out of the compound through a hole torn in the fence, presumably to confuse the spirit so that it could not find its way back, and then dispose of the body by burial instead of cremation.[1]

The belief that people who die violent deaths become malevolent spirits led formerly to a horrible type of human sacrifice. Jeremias Van Vliet wrote the following:

> The kings counted their subjects so little that if palaces, towers, or resting places had to be built for them, under each post that was put into the ground a pregnant woman was thrown, and the more near this woman was to her time the better. For this reason there was often great misery at Ayudhia. Although this description seems to be fabulous these executions have taken place.
>
> The people, who are very superstitious, believe that these women, after dying, turn into horrible monsters or devils, who defend not only the post beneath which they are thrown, but the whole house also. The King usually ordered slaves to catch, without regard, all the women in a pregnant state. No women were taken from the houses unless none could be found in the streets. These women were brought to the Queen who treated them as though they were of high birth. When the time was ready they were thrown into the pit with the stomach turned upwards, and the post was driven through.[2]

Van Vliet also tells a story about Ayudhia in 1936 when the gates, seventeen in number, were renewed. The king ordered two pregnant women to be thrown under each post, requiring sixty-eight women for seventeen gates. It happened that on each of two succeeding days five women were caught, and as they were led within the palace grounds they immediately gave birth. This caused great dejection in the court for it was believed to be a miracle. All the women were spared except four, who were used at a gate nearby.

Mrs. Anna Leonowens also tells a story of human sacrifice. In 1865, the king and the French consul had a grave misunderstanding so that the French threatened war. The king became frantic and called in his ministers who advised a new fort and gate. Six men

[1] Henry O'Brien, "The Evil Pees," *Siam Outlook*, April, 1929.
[2] Jeremias Van Vliet, "Brief History of Siam," *Journal of Siam Society*, 1904-1910.

were seized at night. In the centre of the gateway a deep ditch was dug, and over it an enormous beam was suspended with two cords. The victims were fed an elaborate banquet and then led to their fatal post of honour. The king and all the court made obeisance and the king begged them to guard the gate with devotion. The cords were cut, the ponderous engine crushed the heads of the men, and some ragamuffins were metempsychosed into guardian angels.[1]

The spirit cult was used to protect property and to ward off danger. Fortunately human sacrifice has ceased.

The fear of spirits and the concomitant fear of witches or persons who harbour spirits have not disappeared, however. Famine set in one year during the last century. The missionaries at Chiengmai were accused of angering the spirits, who in turn withheld the rains. The matter was so serious that the case was taken to Bangkok. The American consular representative was called upon to consider the matter. He sent an official report to the Siamese government to the effect that after examining the case he had discovered that the famine condition had begun the year before the missionaries entered the country, and that the famine was not local, but extended through all the northern provinces. He added, however, that he would strictly enjoin the missionaries to be careful in the future not to cause famines.

Because of the fear of spirits and witches, wealthy families have been victimized and driven away like cattle, their homes have been burned and their property scattered thither and yon. The crimes of which they were accused were such as the serious and common one of eating people's livers and of being in league with evil spirits. This type of belief is much more common in the north than in the south.

If one is sick, or if disaster comes, it is common practice to promise valuable gifts to the spirits. Herds of elephants, a hundred buffaloes, or fine houses may be promised. When recovery is complete, paper elephants, buffaloes, or houses are made and given. Sometimes the gifts are burned. Sometimes they are placed on a river and allowed to float away. The spirits are honoured with imitations.

Talismen, amulets, and tattooing are part of the spirit cult. Monks bless charms which are expected to guard off evils. The power of the charm lies in the fact that it enjoins a certain spirit to

---

[1] Anna Leonowens, *An English Governess at the Siamese Court* (Boston: James H. Osgood & Co., 1873), pp. 218-220.

guard the wearer. It is the rare child in Siam even today who does not wear one of these amulets.

One of the most complete descriptions of a branch of the spirit cult in actual practice is given by Francis H. Giles, in his detailed report of elephant hunting.[1] The elephant has always been important to the life of the people in the north. It has been used for war and for transportation as well as for work. Elephants are not bred in captivity but are hunted. A round-up of elephants is approached in a reverential manner. There is a ceremony at the gathering of the men for the hunt. Reverence is shown to the lasso rope. Permission is asked of the spirits to enter the jungle. There is much ceremony in camp procedure. There is a special elephant language. There are rites when the herd is located, more rites after it is captured and trained, and final rites when home is reached. The hunters form a guild and are graded according to task. Success in catching elephants is the basis of promotion. Fifteen elephants must be captured before one can become a "mahout". The elephants themselves are graded as to Brahman, Kahatrya, Vaisya, and Sudra caste. The men who participate lose their identities and are called by the names of their own elephants. They separate themselves from ordinary ways of living, try to be pure in thought and act. The women left at home must be chaste. They may not powder nor paint. On no account must they cut their hair. There is no visiting back and forth while the men are away. If the wife is unfaithful during the hunt, her husband will probably lose his life.

From the start of the hunt to the finish there is one article of clothing that never leaves the hunter's body. That is a cloth which is tied around his waist. When the hunt is over it is removed and burned. From that moment the hunter again uses his native tongue which he had abandoned in favour of a special spirit language during the hunt.

The religious life of the Siamese has not been a simple one, nor has it been particularly logical. The theoretical or book religion seldom coincides with practice in any religion.

The foregoing pages are not meant to imply that any one person held to and practiced everything mentioned, for that would be

[1] Francis H. Giles, "Adversaria of Elephant Hunting," *Journal of the Siam Society*, XXIII, December, 1929.

ridiculous. The meaning intended is that certain practices have been evident in the religious stream of the Siamese way of life until adjustment was made to other ways of living in modern times. Religion is an expression of life and life is not logical or consistent. In Siam, three converging streams of thought have been forced to run through the same channel at the same time. They have been jumbled together and whirled and mixed until each is a part of the other. The stream has carried a burden of sediment collected from points higher up. At a certain point in the stream, when Western influence began to be felt, some elements of the stream's burden began to settle out in catch basins.

Many Siamese were Buddhists in good standing, patronized the Brahman ceremonies, and protected themselves from the spirits by approved methods without any sense of inconsistency. To some extent beneath the surface of modern life the stream with its various sediments still runs strongly. The writer knows a very intelligent lawyer, until recently a governor of a province, who had a library on astrology, who always consulted the soothsayers before any important act, who kept a spirit shrine behind his house, and who was a devout Buddhist. Life was like that. His faith in soothsayers, already strong, was confirmed when he consulted them on the proper day for a large outdoor entertainment he planned to give. They set the day and invitations were issued. For days before the fete it rained and for days after, but the day of the fete was perfect.

4. A SUMMARY OF THE OLDER SIAMESE RELIGION

In summarizing the religion of the Siamese previous to modern times it must be asked what their attitude was toward the world in which they lived, what they wanted in life, and finally what means they used to get what they wanted.

First, the world in which they lived was, for some of them, atheistic. In Buddhism there was no god. There was, however, an eternal universe, for even after bliss is attained under Ariya Mettaya the whole process starts over again with the five original brothers who took turns in enlightening the world. There were an infinite number of cosmic groups that were constantly being destroyed and coming to life again because of imperfections in formless Brahman angels. Mount Meru was the centre of the system.

For the mass of people Buddha was a god. The people worshipped and prayed to him as whole-heartedly as any deist or theist to his god. Only a few intellectuals were actually free from the feeling of worship associated only with the supernatural. An American friend, driving a Buick car, was hailed on the road one evening not so long ago and asked to escort a Buddha and some monks to a nearby city. He consented. During the ride he asked the monks if the image had ears and could hear. They assured him that it could and did hear the prayers of the people. He inquired as to the abilities of Buddha. They declared that the Buddha was not indifferent to the needs and prayers of the people who really worshipped him. He was as capable as any other god.

The world about the Siamese was peopled with spirits. Some were the spirits of dead people, some were the astral bodies of the living, some existed on their own account, and some belonged to other worlds. Some spirits were malevolent and some were friendly.

The world of time must be considered also, for there were lucky days and unlucky days. There were good times and bad times. Success in a venture was often due to a careful selection of the proper time. These times varied with the individual. The stars had to be interviewed and understood. And so was the Siamese world constituted.

The second question to be asked in appraising their religion is: What did the people want? Life was simple as far as human desires went. Picture a frail bamboo house, about five feet off the ground on stilts. The roof was made of dried leaves sewn together; the walls of split bamboo woven into place; the floor of slim bamboo strips tied at intervals to cross beams; the water supply was a well or a stream; and the stove a small earthen affair. Under the house there were oxen to help in the ploughing and a few mangy dogs to bark at strangers. The clothing of the people was perhaps one or at most two strips of cloth per person. The food bulk was rice which was home grown. Beside that they ate a little fish, a bit of curry, and various fruits always abundant. Such was a peasant home. Even in modern times such homes abound in country districts. Life was simple and friendly and the wants were few. One needed to have a good crop with not too much or too little rain. The river must be kept below flood point. One needed a good woman to work and bear children. One needed to ward off the spirits that might bring sickness or other trouble. Enemies must be dominated and a way of revenge must be available. Property must be guarded. A good elephant hunt must be assured.

A king's wants were greater, of course. He wanted a peaceful reign in which no treasonable acts occurred. But the common man's wants were simple. Children must be assured a successful adulthood. Sorrow and unhappiness must be subdued. Superhuman helpers were wanted in time of trouble. Some few people yearned after the ultimate goal of bliss, Nirvana, although most common people were satisfied to get to one of the lesser, more boisterous, hearty heavens.

The technique by which the people secured the values they sought was intricate, the product of centuries of adjustment to environment.

For those who tried to live in accordance with the Buddhist ideal of suppressing every act that required a consequence, there was the Order in which they became monks for a day, or for a few months, or for life. The Order offered the honoured and legitimate solution of life for the serious minded. It was also a place where the indolent could loaf and the knave could hide himself.

For the common people Buddhism meant the daily making of merit by support of the monks, by pilgrimages, by ceremonies, and by the offering of flowers, incense, and tapers at the altar. To some, Buddha was god. To some he was a great teacher. The former felt secure in their conviction that in Buddha they had a supreme being to whom they could pray for advice and help. The latter were sustained by the realization of the import of the expression which was daily on every lip: "Do good and receive good, do evil and receive evil." The four noble truths, the eightfold path, and the five moral precepts dominated the religious side of life. They were part of the technique for securing desired values.

But there was more to life than this. One had to choose a mate, one had to get married, and one had to find a lucky day. Here the people turned to the soothsayer and the Brahman. When children came, parents were determined that they should have every advantage, and so amulets were secured and tied on them, and the topknot cutting ceremony was performed in order to guarantee successful adult life.

On the political side of life, religion was important also. The monarch wanted peace, as did the body of the people. The oath of allegiance to the king was invoked to insure a loyal civil service. A traitorous thought made the drinker choke when drinking the cup of allegiance and so revealed his intentions. Preventive measures could then be taken to forestall attempts to destroy the internal peace of the country. In foreign relations the kingdom needed prestige to overawe its enemies, and so the white elephant cult was called into use. Good crops and adequate rainfall were assured by the swing and ploughing ceremonies held according to season. The land was guarded from floods by a ceremony to appease the river spirit.

To protect the living from the dead a spirit cult technique was developed. There were charms to drive men mad, to win the love of women, to protect from danger, to get revenge, to ward off sickness, and to turn bullets or knife blades. There were ways to expel spirits and restore proportion to sick bodies. Sometimes the villagers co-operated to drive out witches who controlled or angered the spirits. There were ways to bargain with spirits by promising hundreds of buffaloes and paying in paper buffaloes. Some smart people were able to use malevolent spirits to protect themselves or their property by manufacturing them on the desired spot, such as at a palace gate or on some valuable location. It was well known that a violent death produced a malevolent spirit. The ordinary business of the day, such as the raising of rice or the hunting of elephants, was organized also with due regard for the power of the spirits.

In modern times these methods, these attitudes of mind, are called superstitions. In former days they represented the best thinking of the people. They were the scientific methods used to establish a family, to get food, to guarantee security, and to win happiness both in this world and the world beyond. They were inextricably woven into the fibre of the thinking of the race. Sometimes certain aspects of Buddhism, Brahmanism, and Spiritism would come to the surface together in some rite such as the topknot cutting. The Siamese way of life had been forming and building up for centuries. It seemed strange to no one to see a Buddhist monk take part in a Brahman ceremony or bless a charm to ward off evil. The actual vital religion which was the expression of the Siamese way of life was no mere Hinayana Buddhism, but Hinayana Buddhism plus the acquired religious baggage of centuries of living. Someone has remarked that the Siamese retained Spiritism to solve their practical daily problems, took on Brahmanism to give themselves dignity, and accepted Buddhism to take care of the future good life.

CHAPTER XI

RELIGIOUS TRENDS (Continued)

1. MODIFYING INFLUENCES

DURING the past century the Siamese religion has had to adjust itself to a changing world. Old values were weighed and judged against new ways of life. A sifting process began in which the essentials of Siamese thought became apparent. In adjusting themselves to modern life, thinking Siamese discarded a great deal of mental baggage which had previously been considered essential to the successful life. Foreign trade and international relations, Christian missions, and an ever-growing body of intelligentsia, were the main factors to bring about a re-thinking of the Siamese way of life. All of these factors developed in importance after the middle of the nineteenth century.

Siam's international trade and the importance of the foreign trader has already been described. The foreigner in teak exporting, in tin mining, in railroad construction, in engineering projects, and in importing a steady stream of the products of a technological world, has made a great impression on Siamese people in every walk of life.

Siam's foreign relations made her abruptly conscious of the size of the world, of the smallness of Siam, of the ruthlessness of foreign powers, and of the potency of an army and a navy. Foreign relations were nothing new. For centuries there had been contact with the Occident as well as with other countries of the Orient. The rise of imperialism in Europe gave to these relations a different and more urgent character, however.

Christian missions spread to every corner of the kingdom, establishing schools, hospitals, leper homes, and churches wherever they went. The impact of Christian missions upon Siamese life cannot be measured in terms of the number of converts. The work of missionaries called for a re-appraisal of many of the fundamental ways of life. The practice of medicine alone was revolutionized. Surgery was an innovation. The old ideas of the content of the human body were questioned. With a new materia medica and a new theory of medicine even the validity of charms and the power of evil spirits was doubted.

Through the schools the missionaries influenced the lives of the young. In a land where the teacher is revered by his pupil the teaching missionary had a unique opportunity to impress his message. Classes in geography, science, history, and ethics opened up totally new worlds. The scientific method of study was encouraged. Ideas incompatible with the new learning fell into disrepute. What could the Siamese think of Mount Meru and the series of heavens and hells after studying the astronomers' heaven? A spirit of scepticism arose among students, who came to question the existence of heavens, hells, and miracles, regardless of whether they were Buddhist or Christian. The value of charms was discounted. The teaching of agriculture called into question the power of the swing and ploughing ceremonies. The conquests of Napoleon made the contributions of the white elephant cult seem unimportant and faintly ridiculous.

Missionaries in churches, in market places, and on street corners preached a message of mercy and the doctrine of helping one another. The idea of a saviour appealed to some. With this teaching, and often directly traceable to it, came prison reform and practical expressions of mercy to such unfortunates as the lepers.

The ever-growing body of intelligentsia, product of the mission schools, the government schools, and schools abroad, sets the pace for the adjustment of Siam's agricultural economy to a technological world. In 1932 the process already in motion was accelerated. In politics, economics, education, and, in fact, every department of life, this intelligentsia has whipped up the energy of the people with a constitution, new plans, and definite projects for advancement.

A study of the dictionary alone would indicate what has been going on in Siam. New words have been coined, old words have been given new content of meaning. Several dictionaries have been printed in which many new words have been recorded. Countless numbers already in use are waiting to enter the lists of new words in the dictionaries to come. Language is a collection of symbols which represent the various aspects of life. People talk about what they are doing, attempt to describe what they are thinking. The medical profession alone has created a new dictionary.

The national religion has changed with the changing times. According to the new Constitution, Buddhism is not compulsory for anyone in Siam with the exception of the king, who is the "Upholder of the Faith", and so must be a Buddhist. Chapter I, Section 4, says: "The King shall profess the Buddhist faith and is the upholder of religion." Chapter II, Section 13, says: "Every person is entirely free to profess any religion or creed and to exercise the form of worship in accordance with his own belief, provided that it is not contrary to the duties of a national, or to public order, or to public morals."

As far as one can observe, Buddhism has as strong a hold on the people as ever, although it is no longer obligatory like Shintoism in Japan, for instance. H.S.H. Prince Varnvaidyakara, in 1933, surveyed Buddhism in Siam and recalled that when he was a child the temples were packed with old people, mostly women. Buddhism is now voluntary, but when he goes to the temple he finds the situation unchanged, and concludes that Buddhism is not losing ground at least. He pointed out that the Siamese give liberally for meritorious works. Siamese in central Siam give 7.5 per cent of their total income. The north have an average gift ratio of 5.7 per cent, the south 6.3 per cent, and the east 4.9 per cent. He was pleased with the average, but expressed doubt as to whether the people who gave and who went to the temples were any better than people of former generations. Referring to the idea, commonly accepted, that Church and State should be distinct, he urges that religion should be an actual part of everyday life in order to be vital. For without religion, he feels, there can be little mercy and justice in the world.

The constant mention of religious rites and ceremonies in newspapers would seem to support his conclusion that Buddhism has maintained its hold on the people. At the end of Buddhist Lent, in 1937, the newspapers had pages of pictures of the faithful taking their presents to the temples. Other pictures showed tens of thousands of people in boats and along the shores of streams during the festal season. The sub-titles suggested that here was evidence that the people retained a deep devotion to Buddhism. The seasonal festivities yield much pleasure and satisfy the fun-loving nature of the Siamese, but in addition they are definitely religious.

Statistically the Buddhist Church shows very little fluctuation from year to year. From 1932 to 1937 about 300 monasteries were added to the previous number, making a total of 17,408 for all of Siam. Figuring that Siam has about 14,500,000 people, that allows approximately one monastery to every 800 people. During the same period the number of priests rose about 15,000 to a total of 150,213. The numbers of novices and sisyas remained almost stable with 75,079 and 135,392 respectively.

Siamese Buddhism seems to have grown to match the normal expansion of the population. In 1929-30 there were 197 Pali schools with 7,846 students. There were also 2,195 theological schools with 38,434 students. In 1933-34 there were 284 Pali schools with 8,954 students, and 2,935 theological schools with 55,547 students. The latest statistics for 1936-37 show that there are 391 Pali schools with 9,551 students, and 4,056 theological schools with 69,357 students. In seven years the number of Pali schools doubled, but the actual student body increased by only one-fifth. The number of theological schools also almost doubled, and the number of students was but a few thousand short of twice the previous number. The figures indicate an active interest in Buddhist theology and a desire on the part of many students to get a scholarly foundation in religion. The most spectacular growth has come since the constitutional form of government was inaugurated. While little outward change in numbers is observable, a quiet inward revolution of thought seems to be proceeding.

2. CONSERVATIVE VERSUS LIBERAL

A Siamese government official who was asked about the religious opinions of his co-workers said that a minority group were conservative in that they believed in the miraculous stories of tradition, heaven and hell. This group also believed in spirits, and were patrons of the soothsayers. The majority group held to the same outward forms of religion as their grandfathers, but actually believed only in the moral and ethical values. Both groups hold as focal to their religion the golden rule that he who does good receives good, and he who does evil receives evil. He pointed out the rather interesting fact that in the town in which he was living both groups had joined together to build a pavilion for a footprint of Buddha, although one group felt no particular reverence for a shrine whose supposed power they no longer accepted. In outward observance, in behaviour, there was little to distinguish them.

Going to Bangkok one day the writer met an old friend and talked with him about his religion. He was a well-educated Siamese. He had completed the secondary school work and had had special advanced courses to prepare him for his work. He was one of fourteen young men who one year took examinations for study in Europe at government expense. He alone was finally dropped from the eligible list. At the time he was very much upset, but when he thought the matter over he was comforted by his religion, traditional in form and thought. Heaven became the place where pure happiness could be found. He said that the truth had come home to him that we build our heaven and hell with our own actions and so determine what manner of happiness or unhappiness we shall have. This was, of course, merely a re-stating of the do-good-to-receive-good principle. He thought it quite probable that there is a future heaven and hell, but that one need not wait for the next world. One may build one's heaven now. His favourite illustration of the depths of religious knowledge possible to men was as follows. The understanding of religion is like the knowledge of a tree which is made up of bark, wood, and heart. Some people are able to understand all, from the heart out, and some only get at the bark. Whatever they get is good if it helps them to be happy. As dinner was served he remarked that when he knowingly did anything wrong he asked forgiveness in advance. This somewhat anomalous belief in the expunging power of such a request did not seem inconsistent with the do-good-to-receive-good principle to him. He then drank six brandies and ate a hearty dinner. Although intoxicated, and perhaps not quite intelligible, he was still the perfect gentlemen as he went off to bed.

The living adherent of a religion is never a mirror of the ideal, but is a shadow of the ideal blanked out in shades of the culture of his day.

While many modern adherents of Buddhism reject the traditional miraculous aspects of the religion, and retain only what they consider the rational elements of the teaching of Kotama, there are still many, even among the intelligentsia, who are very conservative in their point of view. Three examples will suffice to illustrate the types of apologia which they represent. Among them is Luang Vichitr Vadhakarn, a talented writer and Director of the Department of Fine Arts, who wrote a book entitled *Phutanuphap,* in which he attempted to offset the modern tendency to accept the moral and ethical teaching of Buddha without yielding any personal religious loyalty to him.[1] The writer admits that the showing of reverence for both Dharma and Buddha is an old-fashioned idea. However, he says that when one finds himself wandering out of the channel of truth, even if that channel is old, it is wise to turn back into it. In this case the channel of truth is reverence for Buddha as a supernatural being. He explains that there have been three ways of regarding him. Buddha has been honoured as the most precious and unique individual in history, possessing an ability that exceeded that of all mankind, indeed exceeding even that of the angels Indra and Brahm. Buddha has been regarded also as scarcely different from any other man except insofar as he was a finer scholar than others. And third, he has been regarded as an idea rather than an actual person, invented to authenticate a school of thought. Luang Vichitr dismisses the latter point of view. The second point of view is partially commended. The author returns to the first point of view and attempts to prove that Buddha was superior to mankind in that he had the power of working miracles. These miraculous works were threefold. The first works demonstrated his ability to divide the waters or to ride through the heavens on the wind. They thus showed that he controlled the elements of wind, water, earth, and fire. The second class of works proved his miraculous power to move the hearts of men. The third class of miraculous works were his doctrines or teaching, which were so profound as to make it evident that they were the product of a more than human mind. Luang Vichitr says that the latter two classes of miracles are accepted by all Buddhists. He then attempts to show that there are good grounds for accepting the miracles which demonstrate control over the elements also. He says that this sort of miracle was necessary to clearly define the powers of the Buddha as distinct from those of mortal pretenders who might have won the devotion of the people, leading them from the paths of truth

[1] Luang Vichitr Vadhakarn, *Phutanuphap* (2d Ed.; Bangkok: Wiriyanuphap Press, 1931).

by means of simulated miracles, which were actually mere sleight of hand. The people were accustomed to teachers who could do remarkable tricks. Thus the Yogi in India could control the four elements of earth, water, wind, and fire. They could make the earth open at their command, the waters separate, the winds blow strongly enough to carry them, or the fire spring up. The Buddha had to excel all such spurious competitors, who also laid claim to divine revelation, in order to win and hold the devotion of the people; and to force these other clever ones to own him as their leader. The final chapter discusses the possible return of the Buddha to this world. The idea parallels the second coming of Christ. The theory is that the original elements of the Buddha would, in the end of time, reform into the Buddha again. This idea rests on the theory that the entering of Nirvana was threefold. The first step was accomplished when the passions entered Nirvana at enlightenment, the second when the Buddha was eighty years of age and entered Nirvana, and the third is to be accomplished at the final entry of the primary bodily elements of Buddha in the future. Luang Vichitr presents a powerful, capable Buddha to the people, a Buddha to be revered. He suggests that if they are willing to accept the Dharma they should also accept the person of the Buddha.

In 1935, a corroboration of this conservative point of view was given by a Pali scholar of the sixth grade named Nai Pui Saeng Chai.[1] The subject matter of his book described hell, heaven, and the place of mankind in the eternal scheme. The writer claims that if the traditional teaching on these subjects is abandoned, Buddhism cannot stand. He says that the lower class people are restrained from sin by their fear of hell. Middle class people with some education are saved from sin and won to do good by their desire for heaven. The choicest element of mankind is held to the true course by the search for Nirvana. When these three fundamental ideas have their proper place in social thinking, then progress can be guaranteed. The world will be a quiet, peaceful place in which there will be no injustice. The problems of government will be immeasurably simplified. In his book, which received the approval of the Prince Patriarch of the Order in Siam,

[1] Pui Saeng Chai, *Phutaprachaya* (Bangkok: Supa Akson Press, 1935).

there is evidence that even in modern times the common people fear hell and hope to win heaven.

Another very interesting volume, published in 1937, by Phra Mahachot reaffirms ancient practices.[1] It is a book on meditation. It teaches the procedure for mystic control of the heart and other organs of the body; and finally of the elements around one. A master of this technique can control disease by directing the bodily elements. The author claims that his teaching is in perfect accord with Buddhism; and that it has assisted many individuals to a better understanding of the Dharma. The actual subject matter is a collection of centuries of religious lore handed down through the history of the Thai. Some of it was collected from Ubon, some from Nakon Wiengcan, some from Lopburi, some from sources of knowledge of the Ayudhian period and some from Bangkok. The author's purpose in writing it was to help the monks achieve that intuitive enlightenment which comes from meditation, properly directed.

However reactionary the points of view expressed above, changes in practice of one sort and another occur not infrequently. There has been some talk of eliminating obsolete ceremonies which no longer serve the needs of the people. For instance it has been suggested that the ploughing ceremony be discontinued since it is no longer a satisfactory technique for determining the rainfall and the quality of the crop for the new year. Modern agricultural methods, the Weather Bureau, and the Department of Agriculture have replaced the values once believed to be found in the old ceremony. However, to date the ceremony has been continued from season to season because it is an ancient rite which yields satisfaction to the older generation, and because it gives pleasure to the crowds that go to watch.

Sentiment favouring change, wherever it occurs, is moderate. Newspaper discussions recall the sudden innovations made by King Amanullah with disastrous results. The general opinion is that ancient Siamese customs and ceremonies should be changed slowly. Many of the old ceremonies, such as the swing ceremony or the water throwing ceremony, are picturesque customs. They will

[1] Phra Mahachot, *Samata Wipasana Baep Boran*, (Bangkok: Akson Caroen That Press, 1937).

probably continue as such, even if emptied by the years of religious content.

Although there are sharp divisions of opinion both as regards religious ideology and religious practice, Siamese Buddhism is surprisingly free of sectarianism. There are two Buddhist sects, the Maha Nikaya and the Dharmayuttika. The latter was a reform movement started by King Mongkut. Today, almost the only distinguishing mark between the two is a slight variation in the way the robe is worn.

Siam is not like China or Japan, both of which have strong religious sects. There are no great religious movements within the Church strong enough to be divisive, or even to be symbolized by a name expressive of the sentiment of the people. Individuals with varying points of view there certainly are, but no such movement as the Pure Land School of China, headed by the venerable Yin Kuang, with its emphasis on faith as the one vital thing, is to be found in Siam. The view of that school may be there in the persons of certain individuals, but no movement to make them vocal has arisen. The Mi-Tsung School of Mysteries, which is led by T'ai Hsü, and which specializes in the practices and formulae of chanting charms, is found in Tibet, China, and Japan, but not in Siam; although many people will risk their lives on a magic formula. The ascetics in the Chinese Chan or the Japanese Zen, who emphasize the supreme importance of meditation, are not duplicated in any movement of importance in Siam. Here again there are individuals who meditate. There is even an attempt to open a refuge for meditation at Chaiya. But there is no formal movement or sect. The Chinese intelligentsia who cluster around an idealistic-philosophical school called Wei-Sih doubtless find individuals in Siam who sympathize with their movement, but there is no school of thought to represent this position. The ways of Hinayanists are not the ways of Mahayanists. In Siam the intelligentsia have neither departed from Buddhism nor started sectional movements within the fold. The traditional pattern is maintained, at least outwardly.

Leading Buddhists explain the absence of sectarianism in various ways. Strong differences of opinion do exist. They admit, for instance, that many prominent priests do not believe the various miraculous narratives. Yet these priests continue to preach as they have always done because of the high respect they feel for the religion.

It is possible that the explanation is to be found in the national character. Siamese, by nature, are a quiet people. The idea of mass movements against authority seems foreign to their nature. This quietness has been produced by Buddhism, or, as is equally probable, was a national trait which determined the character of Siamese Buddhism. A very noticeable thing about large gatherings of Siamese is their orderliness. An unruly mob of Siamese is difficult to imagine. It is impossible to picture them bursting out upon a playing field to tear up football goalposts, as an American crowd might do. Even the Siamese revolution was neat and orderly. This spirit carries over to their religion. Buddhism is the official religion of the country, although there is religious tolerance. Siamese say that anyone having advanced views at a tangent with traditional Buddhism can think and believe as he pleases within the church. Orthodoxy is more a matter of behaviour than a matter of belief. Even if radically new views should be developed, the traditional outward pattern could probably be retained. The slight apparent division in the Buddhist front seen in the existing two sects, which are hardly distinguishable, is lamented occasionally.

Such changes as are coming in the Church seem to be in the nature of gradual omissions rather than in the introduction of new ceremonies or patterns. During the early days of the constitutional form of government a monk made an innovation in his sermon by saying that in Siam there were now four rather than three refuges. Formerly there was the Buddha, the Scriptures, and the Order. To these have been added the Constitution. Such a departure from the traditional angered many people, even those who loved the constitution.

If one considers the large numbers of Chinese in Siam, one naturally wonders why Chinese influence has not extended to Buddhism and so modified Siamese thought along the various lines referred to before as being prevalent in China. No conclusive answer is possible. It may have been because the Chinese who came to Siam were of the peasant and merchant class. Few if any Chinese scholars have made Siam their home. Or it may have been because the inferior social position of the Chinese in Siam, where they are regarded as servants, gave to their religious or philosophical views, even if expressed, little influence.

From 1932 to 1937 the Annamites maintained nine monasteries and the Chinese six. The number of priests for both Annamites and Chinese remained between forty and fifty year after year. Chinese Buddhism is at a standstill in Siam. There is no tendency to spread or to win Siamese adherents.

There seemed to be a possibility, at least for a time, that changing political patterns would accelerate the process of gradual adaptation to changing ways of life that has been observable since King Mongkut's time. The government of the Church had always been orderly. It was patterned on the political divisions of the government. There were three large divisions which were subdivided to coincide with the governmental divisions of Cangwat and Amphoe. The Prince Patriarch was the executive head of the Order.

At the time of the revolution in 1932, novices and monks became excited over the idea of a constitution for the temples similar to the civil constitution. One was drawn up which provided for the liberty and freedom of members of the Order. The rulers of temples were to be under a constitution even as the king.

The new political ideas penetrated into the temple grounds in spite of efforts of the leaders to keep the temples places of quiet, cut off from worldly affairs. Novices and young monks were sometimes requested not to leave the temple grounds during the periods of revolutionary activity. The pull was too great, however. The roads of Bangkok were dotted with yellow robes during the exciting days. Some temples forbade discussions of political subjects. There were people who suggested that a democratic form of government was needed in the temples as well as elsewhere. To this some of the head priests agreed. Many more objected. A good deal of feeling was generated. Even the children in school expressed themselves to the extent that the pupils went on a strike in one temple school because they felt that they were unjustly treated.

Articles in newspapers mentioned abuses in temple government as a reason for reform. Writers claimed that there was no uniformity of temple government throughout Siam. Some temples were governed by one man and some by a committee. Some monks ate rice in the evening contrary to rules, some had cock-fights for sport, some smoked opium, some used the drug Indian hemp. The suggestion was made that there be fewer temples with higher standards and that all be governed by the committee system.[1]

Another article suggested that boys who are too young and men who are too old, or are physically infirm, should not be permitted to enter the Order. The practical suggestion was also made that every monk and novice be required to carry a passport. If anyone misbehaved the authorities could easily trace him.[2]

The chief income of the monks is from "kan nimon", or from invitations to render religious service at a wedding or a funeral. The head monk collects and spends the money in most temples. Critical articles were written claiming that the funds were dispensed, too often, for the comfort of the head monk or his relatives rather than for the benefit of the Order. Very little came of all the excitement, although on paper the controversy flourished.

3. THE RISE OF THE LAYMAN

The very fact that such a discussion as outlined above took place indicates a new trend, the rise of the layman. A hundred years ago discussions of this sort would have been thought unseemly. Now many phases of religious practice and thought are being sifted through the minds of interested people not professionally connected with the Church. In answer to some of the criticisms previously mentioned there was published, in 1934-35, a book by Nai Sridharma which defended the established and customary method of carrying on the business of the Order.[3] He said that while authority rests in the High Priest, the power which authenticates this authority rests in the monks themselves. The book admits that the government of a religious body takes on the colouring of the political government to which it is contiguous because both are expressions of the same people. Three words popular in modern secular Siam are lifted into the religious setting and are shown to fit the religious system also. The words are freedom, equality, and brotherhood. The author claims that the Buddhist Order already practices freedom, equality, and brother-

---
[1] *Thai Mai*, June 27th, 1933.
[2] *Ibid.*, January 5th, 1933.
[3] Nai Sridharma, *Kan Pokkhrong Khna Song* (Bangkok: Supa Akson Press, 1934-35).

hood, so that no governmental change within the religious body is necessary.

A second answer to the flow of adverse criticism came from a Buddhist lawyer who interested himself in the question of Church government. He felt that no change was necessary because the government, as revealed by his investigations, was not arbitrary as some of the critics had claimed. On the contrary it was democratic. He said that the usual procedure, whenever there was a question of discipline, building, or extraordinary expenditure, was to call a meeting of the leading monks. Decisions reached by them were seldom overruled by the ecclesiastical powers. He agreed, however, that the education of monks was at a low ebb and needed to be radically improved.

The whole question of the function of the monks in the modern world has been raised by these discussions. It is doubtless true that there are ignorant, incapable, too young or too old, members of the Buddhist Order. Some monks have found ways of becoming wealthy and have provided for families, contrary to the rules of the Order. Some have become involved in activities that are not usually considered religious. But on the whole the questions relative to such abuses as these are of far less importance than the question of the place the monks are to hold in a changing world. They seldom leave the temple to propagate their religion as they did in former days; thus their missionary function has been curtailed. They are not teaching in the homes very much. They are no longer ministers of healing. The religious teaching of the young is more and more in the hands of laymen. And many of the more vigorous books on religious subjects both for young and old are the product of lay pens.

The People's Assembly discussed the Buddhist Order on several occasions during 1937 with the thought of modernizing it in order to improve the teaching disseminated to the people. One representative asked that trained monks be sent out on speaking tours of several months duration through the country districts.[1] Another representative asked whether monks were being permitted to practice medicine of the Siamese variety. The Minister of the Interior answered that they were not. He added that from time immemorial the monk has been the family doctor, but that in the

---

[1] *Nation*, December 19th, 1936.

modern specialized world he has lost his function of healer. In the chapter on education it has been shown that the monk is losing his position as school-teacher as well. He is thus being fashioned by the times, which have sheared him of many of his older functions, into a religious specialist, and as such he must acquire high religious learning or lose the respect of the people.

Not all monks are ignorant, however. There are many well-educated and brilliant men in the organization. But, a highly educated religious body is almost impossible for a nation that is still struggling with the problem of primary education. Monks are expected to study and are given annual examinations. In 1934-35 there were 49,064 monks who took examinations. Of this number 16,928 were successful. Of the 8,176 theological students who took examinations 2,724 passed either the first or second degree. Out of 2,771 Pali students who were examined only 790 passed. In the final ceremonies three monks received the highest or ninth degree in Pali study, and 42 received the sixth degree.

But if enthusiasm for teaching in the homes seems to have declined within the Order, the importance of the layman as a religious teacher has increased. Religion is taught in all the schools. To emphasize the close relation between education and religion the name of the Department of Public Instruction was changed from Suksati-karn, which is literally Department of Education, to Dharma-karn. The deliberate intention of this changed terminology was to emphasize the religious aspect of education. Provincial inspectors of both Cangwat and Amphoe grade are now called Dharma-karn Cangwat and Dharma-karn Amphoe. Religious books are included as part of the regular curriculum in all schools, non-Buddhist as well as Buddhist. They are taught, for the most part, by teachers who are laymen. Regular times are set aside for devotional exercises in which pupils and teachers take part. Many, probably most, schools have images of the Buddha which are used in these exercises. The pupils sometimes bring flowers and do obeisance before the images. Monks are invited to preach at such services. Thus, although the monk is less and less prominent in the educational field, religious and secular, religious teaching of children is widespread.

4. BUDDHISM FOR THE YOUNG

In spite of the widespread teaching of religion in the schools, many writers feel that not enough is being done in this direction. A newspaper article laments that since the World War there has been a tendency away from religion. The younger generation, so the article claims, is growing up without any adequate respect for religion. The blame for this belongs to the parents, who are urged to take their children to the temples. Parents are told to demonstrate the value of religion in their own lives and so make religion attractive to the young. The old way of frightening children by telling them that they will go to hell if they do evil, and trying to stimulate them by promising them that they will go to heaven if they make merit, is strongly condemned. The positive spiritual values of religion should be made clear so that once again religion will be attractive and vital.[1]

Another article from the same paper suggests that the young people tend to be irreligious. Here again blame is laid at the door of parents who fail to instruct their children about Buddha and his teaching. Children from such homes often learn nothing about Buddha until they are grown up. If they do go to the temple they fail to understand the ceremonies. The article concludes with a description of the ideal parents who teach their children the sublime values of religion, and of the ideal son who is clever, whose language is worthy, who is good-hearted, who has the heart of a monk and never loses his temper, who is never jealous and has no enemies. How familiar these words sound.[2]

Concern for the welfare of the Buddhist child goes far beyond newspaper discussion. Prominent people in all walks of life are talking and writing about and for children. Phramaha Khumsaen, in an address to an assembly of teachers at Chiengmai on June 14th, 1933, spoke of the importance of furthering religious knowledge among children. His point of view was social. His thesis was that education produces knowledge, knowledge produces work, work produces wealth, and wealth produces happiness. The root of happiness is knowledge. Wealth was defined broadly, not in terms of money or possessions alone, but as an inner wealth of character, of the spirit. Buddhism, so he said, was a stabilizing

[1] *Nation*, December 10th, 1936.
[2] *Ibid.*, December 31st, 1936.

force in the community. Through it children were taught to reverence parents, teachers, marriage partner, friends, servants, and monks. Obedience, faithfulness, patience, kindness, helpfulness, and other values of community life are the result of such teaching in the young. The life of the community depends on the perpetuation of these values, and these values depend on the life of the community.[1]

King Prajadhipok, in the preface to a widely used textbook of religion, expressed the opinion that the essential of Buddhism for young people was the realization of the principle that what the child becomes depends upon himself and nobody else. He who does good receives good, and he who does evil receives evil, not only in this life but in the existences of the future. This is the mainspring of religion and the basis for morals and character. He also insisted upon the importance of faith. Respect for the Buddha, the Scriptures, and the Order must be inculcated, even though the children do not understand why. Karma and rebirth cannot be demonstrated, but must be accepted on faith. His Majesty says nothing of Heaven, Hell, or Nirvana.[2]

Princess Phun, author of the text, which is widely used in schools and which won the King's prize for the year it was issued, has a few definite practical principles which she puts forward in her book. She suggests that everyone should have an image of Buddha in the home to reverence, not as a god, but as a wise teacher. Everyone should determine to follow Buddha's example and do good.

She then teaches that we should do unto others as we would have others do unto us. The things we dislike other people also dislike. Her teaching parallels the Christian doctrine.

One who thinks more of others than of himself is a true Buddhist. Buddha did not spare himself in order to teach others. The doctrine is written in all of life. At the movies the hero is loved and the villain is hated. This is because the hero is good and the villain is evil. Everyone really likes good and hates evil. She concludes one chapter by paralleling the Christian teaching: that to him who knoweth to do good and doeth it not, to him it is sin.

[1] Phra Rachaniphon Khamnam, *Thit Hok* (Bangkok: Sophon Phiphatanakorn Press, 1932-33).
[2] Princess Phun Phitsmai, *Satsnakhun* (Bangkok: Sophon Phiphatanakorn Press, 1929-30).

She says that since monks have left home, family, and worldly riches in order to carry the teaching of Buddha to everyone, they should be honoured. Young people should read and study religious subjects and should attend the temple. Respect is shown the Buddha by having a good image of him. Respect is shown the scriptures by reading them. Respect is shown the monks by supporting them.

A letter from Princess Phun dated May, 1937, adds the thought that failure in religion is not a failure of the religion, but of those who use it. The essence of religion is to help oneself and others to find happiness in this world.

It is worth noticing that Princess Phun's book says nothing about Heaven, Hell, or Nirvana, nor are miracles described. The emphasis is upon the importance of moral character and good works. The reward of a religious life is happiness in this world.

One more expression of opinion will suffice to show the widespread interest in the re-statement of the essentials of Buddhism for children. Dissatisfaction with the religious teaching given young Siamese was expressed by Phya Sritammarat in conversation with the writer. Phya Sritammarat, who was at one time Lord Lieutenant of Monton Sritammarat, is one of the finest minds in Siam, and is a rationalistic Buddhist as opposed to a traditional Buddhist like Luang Vichitr. In an article for a school magazine he outlined four rules of progress for the young.[1] Children should be given a deep interest in religion; they should be taught to put earnest effort into definite projects; and they should be taught to weigh cause and effect. "Conquer yourself and win," is his concluding advice. He feels that religion is not something static. Religion changes with knowledge and science, but retains its service as an anchor to morals and character. The good life must be sought by each individual for himself. It is not a gift. One's elders and one's religious teachers are purely advisory in capacity.

The general concern for the inculcation of Buddhist principles in the young has expressed itself in another way. An attempt has been made to start religious youth movements, patterned on the Y.M.C.A. and the Y.W.C.A. Phya Metathibodi, a retired government official, who was educated in England, has been very influential in the Buddhist youth movement. As a young man Phya Meta

---

[1] Phya Sritammarat, "Ithibat Si," *Mahawachirawut*, 1936-37.

was a Christian, and, in fact, was the author and translator of many of the hymns in the Christian hymnal. He thus brought to Buddhism, upon his conversion, a thorough knowledge of Christian patterns. Soon after the revolution in 1932, there were three organizations through which the youth movement was expressed. One was the Smakhom Phutthamamaka, another was the Smakhom Yuaphutthasasanik, the third was a more scholarly movement called Smakhom Parien. This last named organization hoped to raise the educational standards of the leading monks and to make all monks more worthy of respect.

Occasional newspaper articles lament the failure of these or any other movement to reach the young people with religion. It is true that they have accomplished little, although the very formulation of such groups shows a possible development. On the writer's desk is a letter from a friend at Chaiya who has founded a Buddhist missionary school called Buddhanigama. He says:

> Buddhist education in Siam is of the old type. But we are trying to have boys lead a perfect life, free from drugs, cigars, betel-nut chewing, etc. . . . the goal is perfect life, here and now in this world today.

The examples given so far in this chapter all serve to show the direction of the main trend underlying the various movements found in modern Siamese Buddhism. Briefly this seems to be an attempt to widen the base of the religion, to make Buddhism a part of the vital, daily life of the people, rather than a matter of observances. Buddhism has been a religion within a religion. There has been the householders religion consisting of rites and ceremonies, and of the five great prohibitions. This much has been for all. Then, within the walls of this simplified area of general acceptance, there has been the philosophical Buddhism of the Order.

Considered in this light the pronouncement of H.S.H. Prince Varnvaidyakara is of great significance. When he deplores the separation of Church and State, when he says that religion should be an actual part of everyday life, he is striking a new note in Buddhist thought. The popularizing of Buddhism has begun. Laymen are pressing to the fore. Laymen are vocal in their criticisms and plans for the church. Laymen are teaching the young in the schools. The schools themselves are vehicles of religious teaching. Youth movements have begun. And possibly more significant than all of these is the agitation for a vernacular canon. The Siamese have never had their Bible in their own language. It has always been in Pali, a language used only by professional monks. Since 1933 there have been many newspaper articles urging that a Siamese translation be made and printed in an inexpensive format so as to be available to all the people. The last report is that the Fine Arts Department has recommended the translation and printing to the Ministry of Public Instruction.

When one considers the far-reaching effect of the Wycliffe Bible, and later the King James' version, on the English people, one is more than a little interested in the vast possibilities for change inherent in vernacular scriptures. What the laity will do with the Bible remains to be seen. It is almost certain, however, to produce change and to further the popularization of the religion, which has already begun.

In 1934 the old Buddhist magazine *Dharmacaksu* was revived. At one time it was the official organ of Siamese Buddhism. It had been a failure for years, and had finally lapsed. It has been brought to life again with the idea of popularizing Buddhism with the people who cannot read Pali but who want to know the teaching of the Buddha and the progress of the Church. Its stress is "back to Buddha" and its teaching is that of pristine Hinayana Buddhism.

A number of books have been published in the last five years which are either translations of books written by foreigners, or are founded on some particular line of thought found in such volumes. Actually they are few in number as compared to books of a similar nature listed in the catalogue of a Chinese book firm. Too few translations into Siamese have been made. Many Siamese realize the lack, and more of them are turning to the production of books.

5. THE ABSENCE OF MISSIONARY ZEAL IN SIAMESE BUDDHISM

As was stated earlier in the chapter, the propagation of the Buddhist religion among non-Buddhists, in fact all missionary activity, has been in a state of pause. So much so that Siamese themselves frequently comment on the static situation in their religion. King Prajadhipok himself once remarked in the introduction to a pamphlet entitled *Phutthamamaka,* published in 1928-29, that Buddhist missionary effort was at a standstill.

There has been in recent years one curious exception to the general rule. An Italian Buddhist monk startled the country, in 1933, with a proposal to lead a mission of monks from Siam to Rome. The mission would have as its objective the conversion of others to Buddhism. The Italian, Phra Lokanat, gave an address at Chulalongkorn University in which he declared that Buddhism would end all wars. He said that he intended to preach Buddhism until wars were forever ended. He suggested that poverty was an aid to righteousness. He preached widely with interpreters both in Bangkok and the provinces. While he spoke on many related subjects the doctrine that impressed most of his average listeners was that they should eat vegetables and no meat. He counted his converts carefully and announced in the press each additional hundred won. By the month of January, 1934, he had sixty-four monks signed up for his pilgrimage. The king granted a sum of money to the project, and limited the number of monks to a hundred. Monks enrolled from all over the country. The pilgrims set out for Burma shortly after, and soon found themselves in difficulty. By April, it was reported that over twenty monks had left the Italian leader and were considering a return to Siam. A letter from Phra Lokanat to Nai Chong Chai Bhakdi, reprinted in the public press, hinted at the difficulty:

> We are all well and happy . . . external jungles are nothing. The worst jungle is the jungle that each one finds in his own heart, the jungle of ignorance. We have seen no tigers. The worst are the internal tigers, the Raga passion which continually crucifies humanity.
>
> I always forget and forgive, because I always overflow with gratitude and appreciation. I have absolutely no enemy in the whole world. To be angry at nothing is the height of foolishness. . . .
>
> I can cure Sugata's baby mind and can change him into a real lion if he always stays with me. So please tell him to stay with me and not to spend all his time playing with my Secretary. I believe that he will become more serious as time goes on and he will eventually become a great man if he stays always with me. . . .
>
> Please tell Nai Chawerlit Apaiwongse that he has given me the highest happiness in taking his solemn vow to refrain from cock-fighting forever.[1]

Siamese monks began to drift back into Siam and at last there

[1] *Bangkok Times,* April 21st, 1934.

were only thirteen who stayed with their leader. The leader felt that these thirteen lion-hearted ones would make religious history. Of the forty or more monks that had returned to Siam not one had given a public explanation of his withdrawal from the mission. In June, the secretary of the pilgrimage wrote back to say that those who left the group had been disciplined for quarreling, fighting, stealing, and slander.[1] Foreign mission work did not progress under Phra Lokanat. The public lost interest. The press ceased to report upon the movements of Phra Lokanat, who subsequently dropped from view, and began to carry instead stories about a prominent Chiengmai monk who had performed a number of well-attested miracles. As far as the writer knows there are no Siamese inspired missionary efforts to other peoples.[2]

6. THE RISE OF RATIONALISM

One aspect of the popularization of Buddhism has been the attempt to rationalize accepted beliefs in the light of modern thought. The general effect among the well-educated has been to produce a group of Buddhist intelligentsia, who, while they do not entirely agree among themselves, are alike in their acceptance of scientific thought. They are alike also in their acceptance of pristine Buddhism, which they consider rational and ethical. They are generally opposed to accretions of the sort which they consider superstitious. There is a minority among these highly literate and highly vocal modern Buddhists who, like Luang Vichitr and Phra Mahachot already referred to, are preaching and teaching a supernatural Buddhism superior to modern scientific thought. The majority, however, are trying to eliminate from Buddhism anything which conflicts with modern scientific knowledge. Among them there are writers who insist that no conflict exists between science and religion, in this case Buddhism. Every religion has had to resort to considerable rationalization in order to reconcile anachronistic religious thinking with the modern world. Buddhism is no exception. The usual solution among the writers referred to is to explain that both science and Buddhism are

[1] *Ibid.*, June 23rd, 1934.
[2] Unless one considers the Siamese temples, two, I believe, in Malaya and one in Ceylon, as missionary effort.

rational and intelligent and that Buddhism supplies what science lacks in ethics and morals.

A new Buddhist catechism, prepared by a European and printed in both Siamese and English in Bangkok, has met with much approval.[1] The preface says: "This catechism has been prepared with the utmost care, and deals only with the original word of the Buddha, as it has been handed down to us in the Sutta-Pittaka of the Pali canon." He expresses thanks to two Siamese who assisted in the production of the book and remarks:

> Both of them expressed the hope that it might be of benefit to the new generation which is at the present time putting too much faith and hope in science and civilization, i.e., in the modern materialism of the West, whilst on the other side is neglecting to cultivate the heart through the true and practical religion of the Buddha.[2]

One departure from the original pattern which he criticizes is the previously unquestioned practice among the monks of living in large temples in the cities. In Buddha's time they lived in the forest. He says that the monks are too much attached to worldly ways. They are fond of society, idle talk, and a comfortable life. He gives as reasons for the change the lack of general education, insufficient knowledge of the Buddha's deep philosophy, and of the comparative science of religion. The order of the monks retains only the form, not the spirit of the movement. As soon as general education and modern science have, as in the West, penetrated the broad masses, then the Eastern nations may take up again the high aim and ideal of a new Buddhist life and culture. The change is to come within Buddhism through a return to the original teaching interpreted in terms of the best scientific thinking.[3]

The views of several well known Siamese Buddhists of the rationalistic school may well be included here. A monk named Phramaha Thong Su'p who had studied Buddhism for over twenty years and attained to the highest or ninth grade, states that Buddha was a man and no god. He also claims that his teaching is not a religion but is a way of living. He does not think of religion as

[1] Bhikkhu Khemo Navayanist, *New Buddhist Catechism* (Bangkok: Krungdebarnagar Press, 1936).
[2] *Ibid.*, p. iv.
[3] *Ibid.*, pp. 94-98.

something theological.[1] He claims that there is nothing in Buddhism that needs revising unless it be the customs and traditions that have grown up around it. Pristine Buddhism suits this age as it has suited all ages. The traditions and customs only need to be revised to suit the times. He feels that there is more real interest in Buddhism now than there has been at any time in the previous ten years.

At the time of the Visakha Buja, the day when the birth, enlightenment, and death of Buddha are celebrated, a representative of the Buddha Dharma Society, Luang Rajtakar Kosala, presented what he considered to be modern Buddhism. He said:

> Buddha, the founder of Buddhism, was a mortal man of brilliant intellect.
> Buddha's teaching is based on one's own actions. If one wishes to obtain happiness, one must act for one's own benefit. No prayer or confession can be relied upon, and no God to help. Buddha is a scientist, his conception of psychology is superb. His theory of life stands the test of modern science. Buddha was a great social reformer, there being no distinction of caste or creed when entering the Order, all being equal. His rules for disciples remain unaltered to the present day, though provision to do so was allowed on the resolution of the members, a proof of his teachings being adaptable to all periods of time.
> His teachings are: first, not to commit sinful actions; second, to do good; and third, to make one's mind pure. These in brief are the main principles of the Buddha's teaching.[2]

Buddha is thus transformed into a scientist, a psychologist, as well as a social reformer.

A slightly different emphasis was given in an article by Dr. Luang Suriyabongs, M.D., who spent three-and-a-half months in the Order and then described what he felt to be the essentials of Buddhism.[3] During his time as a monk he learned a few Pali prayers, but took little interest in the rites and ceremonies, which in his opinion had nothing to do with Buddhism as taught by the Buddha himself. He feels that mankind is deeply involved in materialism. Life is everywhere a struggle for wealth and power. Even science has been abused to satisfy mankind's greed for pleasure, wealth, and power. The poor accuse the rich of exploit-

---
[1] *Siam Chronicle*, May 24th, 1937.
[2] *Nation*, October 3rd, 1936.
[3] Luang Suriyabongs, *The Buddha's Doctrine of Truth* (Bangkok: Krungdebarnagar Press, 1936).

ing them, and the rich are dissatisfied with the poor who want more money and less work. Both are wrong; both suffer alike from materialism. Although science has led to marvellous inventions, and has made life more agreeable, it has failed to develop man's mind to higher ideals and to finer culture. It has failed to make man happier. Man has begun to doubt the value of science. Cultural education is needed. People should have more leisure for self-contemplation and ethical development. To the vast majority, Buddhism has become a cult full of Brahman ceremonies, a venerable tradition. With the education of the people this half-blind belief will be gradually destroyed, but there is great danger that the pious may fall prey to extreme materialism unless steps are taken to enlighten their minds.

The general trend of the religious thinking of the men quoted is "back to Buddha", back to the simplicity of pristine Buddhism, back to ethics as opposed to ceremonies. Miracles, heaven, hell, and nirvana, interest these thinking people less and less. Of course pristine Buddhism, like the first century Christianity of the Oxford Group movement, is a modern interpretation of what twentieth-century followers believe their religion in unpolluted form, to have been. It is probable that in both cases the resulting simplification and emphasis is a rationalization, a not unthoughtful and unintelligent form of wish-fulfillment.

In this connection a series of discussions in the *Nation* running through the month of May, 1933, are relevant. The idea of nirvana as a state which the righteous attain after death is objectionable to many people. Nirvana is defined as the highest good, the highest ethic of Buddhism. The usual definition is that nirvana means the annihilation of the whole being. Material existence is snuffed out like a flame. The explanation offered by the articles in the *Nation* is that Buddha was teaching annihilation of his evil passions and not of himself or anybody else. Complete control of passion and desire was his goal. How can one attain to nirvana while yet alive if nirvana means physical annihilation? Yet Buddha attained nirvana before his death. This would seem to demonstrate that nirvana is something other than physical annihilation; is something attainable during earthly existence. The final paper in the series suggests that knowledge and love are the foundations of Buddhism. Without these one cannot hope to attain to nirvana.

Love is love of family, of nation and of the world. The poor, the lowly, and even the animals can learn and love.

7. NEW RELIGIOUS GOALS

This shift in emphasis is resulting in a shift in goal. Indifference is no longer the virtue it was once considered. H.S.H. Prince Sakol Varavarn discussed the subject "What is Good?" before the Teachers' Association. He sought to discover in his address the highest good for which mankind can strive. He said that mere actions, such as those of losing oneself in a hobby, or even of becoming a priest, are no guarantee that good will result. He considered instinct, experience, and nature as means to the discovery of the ideal goal. His conclusion was that the highest good is one not limited to the benefit of the few, in other words universal. Peace and love between individuals and nations represent to him the ideal goal of mankind in the search for the good life.

The Premier, Phya Bahol Balabayuha, spoke over the radio on this subject, that is, the goal of universal peace.[1] He recalled that both Rome and Ayudhia fell because the citizens of those cities were selfish, lazy, and pleasure-seeking. His ideal for the Siamese is a general knowledge of dharma, which he believes would result in progress for the nation. He says that by following it, citizens become law abiding and hard working, soldiers are inspired to be kind as well as brave, governors become just and generous, judges are led to be impartial and honest, officials to be industrious and sincere, merchants fair and reasonable, princes dignified and gracious, and monks adept at leading the people in paths of righteousness. To him the dharma, the doctrine of Buddha, is the cure-all for the nation's ills.

The characteristics to be avoided and the virtues to be sought in these modern times were detailed by Phya Bahol in an address to the students and faculty of the University of Moral and Political Science on June 6th, 1937. The teaching of the dharma will eradicate the evils and encourage the growth of the virtues. The evils to be avoided in this modern interpretation of the householder's religion are:

[1] *Siam Chronicle*, June 25th, 1937.

1. Greediness
2. Revengefulness
3. Pride
4. Haughtiness
5. Snobbishness
6. Miserliness
7. Stubbornness
8. Jealousy
9. Resentfulness
10. Dishonesty
11. Arrogance
12. Anger
13. Boastfulness
14. Intemperance
15. Selfishness
16. Undue self-assertiveness.

The list of virtues are but half the number:

1. Intelligent generosity
2. Thoughtfulness
3. Uprightness
4. Endurance and contentment
5. Honesty and humility
6. Gratefulness
7. Graciousness
8. Sincerity.

These virtues and vices are not the traditional ones in Buddhist thinking; nor are they, on the other hand, out of accord with customary standards. They are a revised version to suit the times.

8. A SUMMARY OF THE MODERN SIAMESE RELIGION

In attempting to survey the religion of the Siamese in modern times, there are three questions to be asked. What is their attitude toward the world in which they live? What do they want in life? And what means do they use to get what they want?

The old world which centred around Mount Meru has been swallowed up in the astronomers' heaven. Modern Siamese may well feel that the universe is eternal, although cast in a pattern far different from the one imagined by their ancestors. If their minds turn back to a beginningless point they alight not on an everlasting creator but on an everlasting universe which has been the womb of all that is. The present life has great significance, for it is the only one that they can be sure of living. The location of heaven and hell in the astronomers' universe becomes a dubious matter. And nirvana or extinction, what is that? Perhaps all mankind is extinguished at death anyway. So nirvana or victory over self must be sought in the present life.

Desire drives have remained the same. People still want food, home, sex satisfaction, children, security, pleasure, and recognition. But the desires are expressed in a more complicated manner than ever before. There are men out of work, perhaps for the first time in the history of Siam. No Siamese government has ever had to deal with this problem before. There are strong, intelligent young men who wish to have an important place in the political life of the nation. There are people who feel themselves unjustly taxed and who look for some instrument by which to express their dissatisfaction. There are people in debt who wish to make a fresh start, nothing new, one may add. There is a desire on the part of an intelligent minority among the common people to make all men equal, to obliterate class distinction, titles, and that evidence of class distinction, the court language. These desires and many more turned to revolution as a ready solution in 1932.

There is a desire for rule by the peoples' representatives, and a constitution is conceived to guarantee the new party control of the government for at least ten years, while at the same time gradually allowing the masses of people more expression. The people are going into the business of city sanitation, garbage disposal, fire fighting, city water, city roads, and other projects. New desires have called forth new instruments.

The old desire for national security remains and is expressed in terms of a strengthened army and navy. Friendship with all nations is reaffirmed. New political treaties are negotiated. A new military spirit is inculcated in the youth.

There is an express desire to improve the economic status of everyone. A Ministry of Economic Affairs is brought into being, which engages experts and in a modern way attacks the economic problems of the nation. Trade is encouraged by Chambers of Commerce. Dealing in fraudulent products is severely punished. There is a desire to know where the nation stands socially and economically, and so a census is taken. There is a desire for adequate income from tin production, and so Siam becomes a member of the tin agreements. The peasants want capital funds to help them enlarge and improve rice cultivation, and so the co-operative society plan is stressed. Better rice is obtained by improved methods of irrigation and fertilization. There is a desire to put more Siamese into commerce and trade, and so trade and craft schools are brought into being.

The desire to include all nationalities dwelling in Siam in a closer union has had various results. In order that everyone shall be equally well-prepared to meet the new standards of life, Malays and Chinese must be educated to the Siamese way of life. Immigration is decelerated and standards are raised. The Bangkok language and way of doing things is propagated in every remote part of the kingdom.

The desire to have an intelligent and educated nation has resulted in emphasis on primary education as a minimum goal for everyone. There is a desire for trained leaders, and so the university and foreign study are encouraged. It is desired to help youth to help others, and the Junior Red Cross is stressed. It is desired that boys be more manly and capable, and the Boy Scout movement is given added pressure.

The desire for improved health has resulted in improved methods of fighting plague and cholera and other contagious diseases. A modern school for training doctors has been completed. Rats are killed, injections given, and vaccination administered. To eliminate quacks the registration of doctors and dentists is required. To win the masses of the people to modern health programmes medical newspaper propaganda is carried on regularly. The educated desire fewer children, and so birth control information is given. There is desire to supply every part of Siam with at least a minimum of modern medicine, and so the junior doctor scheme is promulgated.

The desire to open up the whole country to trade and modern commerce has resulted in improved communications. The railway was built and a highway scheme has been drawn up by which Siam will be equipped with a network of motor roads. To speed up and improve freight service new and necessary equipment is secured.

There is a desire to abolish prostitution, or at least to control it better. A programme of re-education, rescue, rehabilitation, and refuge is considered. The position of women is unsatisfactory and there is a determination to bring the women up to the standards of the men. Education for all is offered; monogamy is encouraged; and the registration of marriage is required. A means of lowering the crime level is being sought through education, better economic status for the peasant, teaching some practical trade to criminals, and by an efficient police force.

The desire for pleasure and recreation is found in new sports and plays as well as in the old fashioned ones. The old Siamese theatre is transformed to suit the times. There is desire to revitalize the artistic side of the Siamese along such lines as dancing, singing, wood carving, and writing. The Department of Fine Arts is made responsible for this side of life.

And, finally, in the field of religion the goal is the diminution of evil characteristics such as greed, jealousy, revenge, anger, pride, and hate, in order that the people may be generous, loyal, merciful, and loving. It is desired to improve the status of the monk, and so education is planned to give him new dignity. It is desired to educate the youth in ethical and moral matters, and so special literature is prepared for that purpose. Some people retain a Buddhism wrapped up in tradition, custom, and miracle. They hope for heaven, fear hell, think wistfully of nirvana, and appease the spirit world. Some people seek a simple, pure Buddhism, with Buddha as the teacher of the great standards of ethics and morals. And some few, regardless of any religion in particular, study community values and ethics, and use the social and religious sciences to achieve their goal.

To show more sharply the transition from the old way of life to the new the following contrasts are offered. The old had an absolute monarch, but the new a constitutional government. The old required the drinking of the cup of loyalty to the king, but the new, even though retaining the old symbol, has drained the act of all significance and established a democratic ideal. The old way had taboos around the monarch, but the new says that all men are equal. The old way required a special royal language and the use of titles, while the new uses one tongue for all and has abolished the giving of titles. The old way had ploughing and swing ceremonies to assure good crops and proper rainfall, while the new has a department of agriculture, soil studies, seed culture, and a weather bureau. The old way had a white elephant cult to demonstrate warlike prowess; tattooing was used as armour to ward off knife and bullet; and human sacrifice was practiced to a small degree for the manufacture of malignant spirits to guard the palace gates. Now there is an army and navy with tanks and gunboats. The old had roots and herbs as medicines, and hung charms on the body for health, while the new has scientific medicine, inoculation, and vaccination. The old way guaranteed youth a successful adulthood by the topknot ceremony, but the new depends on education and schools. The old way had plural marriage, but the new has birth control. The old way had a temple school which consisted of monk and boy, but the new has a modern school system. In the old the monk was the intelligentsia, but in the new the university graduate and the student from abroad fills the place. The old way required learning by rote, but the new is supplying books and libraries. The old way favoured polygamy, but the new favours monogamy. The old way had spirit controls, lucky days, charms, and benevolent gods, but the new has a reasonable Buddhism which resolves itself into peace and charity; do good and receive good, do evil and receive evil.

Siam, religiously, is allowing the accumulated sediment of ages to settle out of the life stream. The settling has begun at the top, or surface, where the better educated people live. The constitutional form of government has been a settling agent that has speeded up the process and will doubtless see the clearing of the religious stream to greater and greater depths.

The die has been cast. The country can never turn back the pages of history. The people must make the best of a new world, must prove it to see what it offers. It remains to be seen whether the new way of life will yield more or less happiness than the old.

BIBLIOGRAPHY

Akat Dam Koeng, Mom Cao. *Lakhon Haeng Chiwit.* 2d ed. Bangkok: Aksoniti Press.
———. *Wiman Thalai.* Bangkok: Wiriyanuphap Press, 1931-32.
Aksorn, Khun Chen Chin. *History of the Relations Between Siam and China.* Bangkok.
Alabaster, Henry. *The Wheel of the Law.* London: Trubner & Co., 1871.
Anderson, John. *English Intercourse with Siam in 17th Century.* London: Kegan Paul, Trench Trubner & Co., Ltd., 1890.
Andrews, James M. *Siam, Second Economic Survey.* Bangkok: The Bangkok Times Press, Ltd., 1935.
Angier, A. Gorton. *The Far East Revised.* London: Witherby & Co. 1908.
Anudhuvadhi, Phya. *Buddhism in Simple Words.* Bangkok: Daily Mail Press, 1930.
Archer, William J. *The Siamese Laws on Debts.* Bangkok: S. J. Smith's Office, 1885.
Asvabahu. *A Siam Miscellany.* Bangkok: Siam Observer, 1912.
Bacon, George B. *Siam, the Land of the White Elephant.* New York: Scribner, Armstrong & Co., 1873.
Barnett, J. C. *First Annual Exhitition of Agriculture and Commerce.* Bangkok: Bangkok Daily Mail, April 1910.
Bastian, A. *On Some Siamese Inscriptions.* May 12th, 1864.
Besso, Salvatore. *Siam and China.* Translated from Italian by C. Mathews. London: Simpkin, Marshall, Hamilton Kent & Co., Ltd.
Board Letters to the American Presbyterian Mission in Siam. 1847-1884.
Bock, Carl. *Temples and Elephants.* London: Sampson Low, Marston, Searle, & Rivington, 1884.
Book of Brahman Astrologers.
Boriban Buriphant, Luang. *Boran Watu Sthan Nai Syam.* Vol. I. Bangkok: Phra Can Press, 1933-34.
———. *Boran Watu Sthan Nai Syam.* Vol. II. Bangkok: Phra Can Press, 1936-37.
———. *Boran Khadi.* Bangkok: Phra Can Press, 1936-37.
———. *Ngoen Tra Syam.* Bangkok: Aksoniti Press, 1936-37.
Bose, Phanindra Nath. *The Indian Colony of Siam.* Lahore: The Punjab Sanskrit Book Depot, 1927.
Bowring, John. *The Kingdom and People of Siam.* 2 vols. London: John W. Parker & Son, 1857.
Bradley, Cornelius Beach. "Vignettes from Siamese Legend and Life," *University of California Chronicle,* XIII, No. 4.

Bradley, D. B. *Prachum Pongsawadan.* Vol. XXXI. Bangkok: Sophon Phiphatanakan Press, 1925-26.
———. *Nangsu' Samdaeng Cao Khrong Sakon Lok.* 4th ed. Bangkok: American Presbyterian Mission Press, 1895.
———. *Bangkok Calendar.* Bangkok: American Missionary Association, 1859, 1863-66, 1868-1873.
Brief Manual on Buddhism. Bangkok: South Siam Mission, 1918.
Brown, Arthur J. *The Expectation of Siam.* Philadelphia: Presbyterian Board of Publication.
Buddharakhita, Siddhartha. *Religious Intercourse Between Ceylon and Siam in the 18th Century.* Bangkok: American Presbyterian Press, 1914.
Bun Roe, Caroen. *Pramuan Hetkarn Lae Phap Nai Kan Plian Kan Pok Khlong Khana Raston.* Bangkok: Thai Mai Press, 1932-33.
Caddy, Florence. *To Siam and Malaya.* London; Hurst & Blackett, Ltd., 1889.
Campbell, J. G. D. *Siam in the 20th Century.* London: Edward Arnold, 1902.
Candee, Helen Churchill. *New Journeys in Old Asia.* New York: Frederick A. Stokes Co., 1927.
Candler, Edmund. *A Vagabond in Asia.* London: Greening & Co., Ltd., 1900.
Canthana Bupha. *Nivai Khomdam.* Bangkok: Aksoniti Press, 1928-29.
Carpenter, F. G. *From Bangkok to Bombay.* New York: Doubleday, Page & Co., 1926.
Carter, A Cecil. *The Kingdom of Siam.* New York: G. P. Putnam's Sons, 1904.
Case of Kieng Chek (Kham Muon), before the Franco-Siamese Court: The trial and condemnation of Phra Yot. June 1894.
Chai Ru'angsin. *Prawat Sat Chat Thai.* Bangkok: Daily Mail Press, 1935-36.
Chevillard, Similien. *Siam et les Siamois.* Paris: E. Plon Nourrit & Co., 1889.
Child, Jacob T. *The Pearl of Asia.* Chicago: Donohue, Heneberry & Co., 1892.
Choisy, Abbe de. *A Journal du Voyage de Siam.* Paris: 1687.
Chot Phanyo, Phra Maha. *Samata Wipasana Baep Boran.* Bangkok: Akson Caroen That Press, 1936-37.
Chot Phrae Phanthu, (Ya Khop). *Phu Chana Sip Thit.* Bangkok: Syam Phanit Chayakarn & Aksoniti Press, 1934-35.
———. *Ru'ang Rak San San.* Bangkok: Syam Phanit Chayakarn & Aksoniti Press, 1934-35.
———. *Yot Khun Phon.* Bangkok: Supa Akson Press, 1933-34.
Chun Kasikan, Luang, *et al. Prawat Sat Syam.* 3d ed. Bangkok: Sri Heng Press, 1935-36.
Chulalongkorn's Advice to his Sons Going Abroad to Study. Issued at the death of Krom Phra Jantaburi. Bangkok: Sopanapipatanakan, 1885.

BIBLIOGRAPHY

Clifford, Hugh. *Further India.* London, Alston Rivers Ltd., 1905.
Colquhoun, Archibald Ross. *Amongst the Shans.* London: Field & Tuer, 1885.
Commercial Traveler's Guide to the Far East. Department of Commerce series No. 29. Washington: Government Printing Office, 1926.
Commission of Enquiry into Traffic in Women and Children in the East. League of Nations Publications series IV, 8. Geneva: December 10, 1932.
Coomeraswamy, Ananda. *Buddha and the Gospel of Buddhism.* London: George G. Harrap & Co., Ltd., 1928.
Correspondence Concerning the Affairs of Siam. Presented to both Houses of Parliament by command of Her Majesty, August 1894. London: Harrison & Sons, 1894.
Cort, Mary Lovina. *Siam, the Heart of Farther India.* New York: Randolph & Co., 1886.
Cosenza, Mario Emilie. *The Complete Journal of Townsend Harris.* Garden City, New York: Doubleday, Doran & Co., Inc., 1930.
Crawfurd, John. *Journal of an Embassy to the Courts of Siam and Cochin-China.* London: Henry Colburn, 1828.
Credner, Wilhelm. *Siam Das Land Der Thai.* Germany, Stuttgart: J. Engelhorns Nachf, 1935.
Curtis, Lillian Johnson. *The Laos of North Siam.* Philadelphia: The Westminster Press, 1903.
Dalton, William. *Phaulcon the Adventurer.* London: S. O. Beeton, 1862.
Damrong, H. R. H. *Phongsawadan Ru'ang Rao Rop Phama Khrang Krung Sri Ayudhya.* Bangkok: Thai Press, 1920-21.
———. *Phongsawadan Ru'ang Rao Rop Phama Khrang Krung Thonburi Lae Krungdeb.* Bangkok: Thai Press, 1920-21.
———. *Phraracha Wican Nai Phrabat Somdet Phra Cun Com Klao Cao Yu Hua.* 2d ed. Bangkok: Thai Press, 1916-17.
———. *Sadaeng Banyai Phongsawadan Syam.* Bangkok: Prasert Samut Press, 1924-25.
———. *Tamnan Phram Mu'ang Nakorn Sridharmaraj.* Bangkok: Sophon Phiphatanakorn Press, 1930-31.
Davies, R. D. *Siam in the Malay Peninsula.* Singapore: Fraser & Neave Ltd., 1902.
Dodd, William Clifton. "The Relation of Chinese and Siamese," *Journal of the North China Branch of the Royal Asiatic Society,* LI, 1920.
———. *The Tai Race.* Cedar Rapids, Iowa: The Torch Press, 1923.
Doehring, Charles. *Art and Art Industry in Siam.* 2 vols. Bangkok: Asia Publishing House.
Dokmai Sot. *Kam Kao.* Bangkok: Thai Kasem Press, 1935-36.
———. *Khwam Phit Khrang Raek.* 2d ed. Bangkok: Thai Kasem Press, 1935-36.

Douglas, Robert K. *Europe and the Far East 1506-1912*. Revised and corrected with additional chapter 1904-1912 by Joseph H. Longford. Cambridge: University Press, 1913.
Dharmapadarthakatha. Translated by Swami Satya Nanda Puri. Bangkok: Mahamakut Rachawitayalai Press, 1936-37.
Dowson, John. *A Classical Dictionary of Hindu Mythology and Religion, Geography, History and Literature*. 6th ed. London: Kegan Paul, Trench, Trubner & Co., Ltd., 1928.
Dutch Records. 2d series, Vol. 3, No. 103.
European Settlements in the Far East. London: Sampson Low, Marston & Co., Ltd., 1900.
Exhibits of Articles Used in Siam. Philadelphia: J. P. Lippincott & Co., 1876.
Farges, Gen. des. *An Account of the Revolution in Siam*. Amsterdam: 1691.
Feltus, George Haws. *Samuel Reynolds House*. Chicago: Revell & Co., 1924.
Feudge, Mrs. F. R. *Eastern Side: or Mission Life in Siam*. Philadelphia: The Bible and Publication Society, 1871.
Finlayson, George. *The Mission to Siam and Hue in 1821-1822*. London: John Murray, 1826.
Fleeson, Katherine Neville. *Laos Folk Lore of Farther India*. New York: Fleming H. Revell Co., 1899.
Forty, C. H. *Bangkok, Its Life and Sport*. London: H.F. & G. Witherby, 1929.
Fournereau. *Le Siam Ancien*. Paris: Musee Guimet, 1902.
Franck, Harry A. *East of Siam*. New York: The Century Co., 1926.
Frankfurter, O. *Sixteen Tables of Thai Alphabets*. Bangkok: Vajiranana National Library, 1914.
Freeman, John H. *An Oriental Land of the Free*. Philadelphia: The Westminster Press, 1910.
Full and True Relation of the Great and Wonderful Revolution in Siam: being the substance of letters written in October 1688 and February 1689. London: Randall Taylor, 1690.
Gammell, William. *A History of American Baptist Missions*. Boston: Gould & Lincoln, 1851.
Gerini, G. E. *Siam and its Productions, Arts and Manufactures*. Hertford: Stephen Austin & Sons, Ltd., 1912.
——. *Chulakantamangala*. Bangkok: Bangkok Times Office, 1895.
——. *The Hanoi Exhibition: the First International Congress of Far Eastern Studies*. Bound in the same volume is *Siam's Intercourse with China in the 7th to 19th Centuries*. Woking, Surrey: Publishing Department of the Oriental Institute, 1906.
Gervaise, Nicholas. *The Natural and Political History of the Kingdom of Siam*. Translated by Herbert Stanley O'Neill. Bangkok: Siam Observer Press, 1928.
Graham, W. A. *Siam*. 2 vols. London: Alexander Moring Ltd., 1924.
——. *Kelantan*. Glasgow: James MacLehose & Sons, 1908.

BIBLIOGRAPHY

Grierson, G. S. (ed.) "Mon Khmer and Siamese-Chinese Families," *Linguistic Survey of India*. Vol. II. Calcutta: Office of the Superintendent of Government Printing, 1904.
Grindrod, Mrs. *Siam, A Geographical Summary*. London: Edward Stanford, 1895.
Gutzlaff, Charles. *Three Voyages Along the Coast of China in 1831, 1832, 1833*. 2d ed. London: Frederick Westley & A. H. Davis, 1834.
Hallett, Holt S. *A Thousand Miles on an Elephant in the Shan States*. London: William Blackwood & Sons, 1890.
Harris, Walter B. *East For Pleasure*. London: Edward Arnold & Co., 1929.
Hervey, G. Winfred. *The Story of Baptist Missions*. St. Louis: Chancey R. Barnes, 1886.
History of the Siamese Red Cross Society. Book I. Bangkok: Bangkok Times Press Ltd., 1926.
History of Cambodia. Prepared by order of King Mongkut.
History of Siam 1697 to 1708. A bound pamphlet.
History of the Presbytery of Siam from its Organization September 1, 1858 to July 1887. Bangkok: 1887.
Hong Nawanukhro. *Samut Ruptai Phra Phutaruplo*. Bangkok: Daily Mail Press, 1927-28.
Hophrasamut Wachirayan. *Prachum Phongsawadan*. Vol. XXXII. Bangkok: Sophon Phiphatanakorn Press, 1925-26.
Jonquiers, de la. *Le Siam et Les Siamois*. Paris: 1910.
Journal of the Indian Archipelago and Eastern Asia, 1847-1863.
Journal of the Straits Branch of Royal Asiatic Society.
Journal of the Siam Society, 1904-1937.
Kaempfer, Engelbert. *The History of Japan*. 2 vols. Translated from Dutch by J. G. Schouchzer. Glasgow: James MacLehose & Sons, 1730.
Kanlayana Maitri, Phya. *Syam Ku Isaraphap Ton Eng*. Bangkok: Daily Mail Press.
Khana Yuwasan. *Europe Prae Phak*. Bangkok: Yongli Press, 1935-36.
———. *Sura Burut Haeng U-thai Phrathet*. Bangkok: Bamrung Nukunit Press, 1934-35.
———. *Thamyuti Kap Mahanikai*. Bangkok: Yongli Press, 1935-36.
Khema Siri Anuson. *Withi Oprom*. Bangkok: Sophon Phuphatanakorn Press, 1936-37.
Khemo Navayanist, Bhikkhu. *New Buddhist Catechism*. Bangkok: Krungdebarnagar Press, 1936.
———. *Phuta Sasana*. Bangkok: Krungdebarnagar Press, 1934-35.
———. *The Essence of Buddhism*. Bangkok: Krungdebarnagar Press, 1934-35.
Ki Yu Po. *Man*. Bangkok: Yongli Press, 1934-35.
King, D. O. *Travels in Siam and Cambodia*. Read to the Secretary of the Royal Geographical Society of London at Newport, Rhode Island, February 7th, 1859.
Kit Kan Ti Plian Plaeng Khu'n Nai Rabop Kan Pokrong Yang Mai Khong Prathet Syam. Bangkok: Thai Phanit Press, 1935-36.

Kornerup, Ebbe. *Friendly Siam.* London: G. P. Putnam's Sons Ltd., 1929.
La Loubere. *A New Historical Relation of the Kingdom of Siam.* 2 vols. Translated from French by A. P. Gens. London: Theodore Horne, 1693.
Landon, Mary. *Mid Pleasures and Palaces.* London: T. Fisher Unwin, 1907.
Lao Thinapho, Phra Maha. *Athitan Tham 4.* 2d ed. Bangkok: Akson Caroen That Press, 1936-37.
Le May, R. S. *Descriptive Catalogue of the Postage Stamps and Post and Letter Cards of Siam 1883-1919.* Bangkok: Bangkok Daily Mail, 1920.
———. *An Asian Arcady.* Cambridge: W. Heffer & Sons, 1926.
———. *Siamese Tales Old and New.* London: Noel Douglas, 1930.
———. *The Coinage of Siam.* Bangkok: The Bangkok Times Press Ltd., 1932.
Leonowens, Anna. *An English Governess at the Siamese Court.* Boston: James R. Osgood & Co., 1873.
———. *The Romance of Siamese Harem Life.* Philadelphia: Porter & Coates, 1872.
Little, Archibald. *The Far East.* Oxford: Clarendon Press, 1903.
Loti, Pierre. *Siam.* Translated from French by W. B. Haines. Philadelphia: David McKay.
Loubere, de la. *Description du Royaume de Siam.* Paris: 1688.
Low, James. *Marong Mahawangse, or the Keddah Annals.* Bangkok: American Presbyterian Mission Press, 1908.
MacDonald, K. S. *The Brahmanas of the Vedas.* London: The Christian Literature Society for India, 1856.
MacGregor, John. *Through the Buffer State.* London: F. V. White & Co., 1896.
MacNaughton, D. J. *Miscellaneous Publication of the International Tin Research and Development Council, Number 4, Tin and Its Uses.* England: 1935.
Mahawetsandon Chadok. Issued by Krom Tamra Krasuang Thamakan. 4th ed. Bangkok: Bamrung Nukunit Press, 1927-28.
Malcolm, Howard. *Travels in South-Eastern Asia.* 2 vols. 3d ed. Boston: Gould, Kendall & Lincoln, 1839.
The Travels of Marco Polo. New York: Grosset & Dunlap.
McCarthy, James. *Surveying and Exploring in Siam.* London: John Murray, 1900.
McFarland, G. B. (ed.). *Historical Sketch of Protestant Missions in Siam 1828-1928.* Bangkok: The Bangkok Times Press Ltd., 1928.
McGilvary, Daniel. *A Half Century Among the Siamese and the Lao.* New York: Fleming H. Revell & Co., 1912.
Melville, Frederick J. *Siam, Its Posts and Postage Stamps.* London: Offices of the Stamp Collector's Fortnightly, 1906.
Memoir of Mrs. Eliza G. Jones. Philadelphia: American Baptist Publishing Society, 1853.

BIBLIOGRAPHY

Memorandum in the Matter of an Arbitration before Sir Nicholas J. Hannen; claims of the estate of M. A. Cheek against His Siamese Majesty's Government. Bangkok: September 25, 1897.
Metha Thibodi, Phya. *Hlak Thama Haeng Phuta Sasana.* 3d ed. Bangkok: Krungdebarnagar Press, 1936-37.
Milne, Mrs. Leslie. *Shans at Home.* London: John Murray, 1910.
Morgenthaler, H. O. *Matahari.* London: George Allen & Unwin Ltd., 1923.
Mouhot, M. Henri. *Travels in the Central Parts of Indo-China, Cambodia and Laos during 1858-1860.* 2 vols. London: John Murray, 1864.
Mundie, W. H. *Van Vliet's Historical Account of Siam in the 17th Century.* Translated from Dutch by Mr. Mundie. Bangkok: 1904.
Neale, Frederick Arthur. *Narrative of a Residence in Siam.* London: Office of National Illustrated Library, 1852.
Nordon, Hermann. *From Golden Gate to Golden Sun.* London: H. F. & G. Witherby, 1923.
Norman, Henry. *Peoples and Politics of the Far East.* New York: Scribners, 1895.
Official Guide to Eastern Asia. Vol. V. 2d ed. Tokyo: The Department of Railways, 1920.
Orleans, Prince Henri d'. *Around Tonkin and Siam.* Translated by C. B. Pitman. London: Chapman & Hall Ltd., 1894.
Osborn, Sherard. *Quedah.* London: Longman, Brown, Green, Londmans & Roberts, 1857.
Pan Bunyakit, Nai Dap. *Syamrat Plian Plaeng Kan Pok Khrong.* Vol. I. Bangkok: Daily Mail Press, 1932-33.
Pavie, Auguste. *Contes Populaires du Cambodge du Laos.* Paris: Earnest Leroux, 1903.
Penciled Memorandum of the State of Affairs between France and Siam. Bangkok: March 21st, 1893.
Phakdi Nalubetre, Phya. *Phra Phuta Sasana.* 2d ed. Bangkok: Sophon Phiphatanakorn Press, 1935-36.
Phanthu Sena. *Khlang Pariyat.* Bangkok: Songtham Press, 1934-35.
Phatana Nin Watananont. *Phrarat Banyat Thoralek.* Bangkok: Syam Witayakorn Press, 1935-36.
Phanuphanthawongse Woradet, Phya. *Prachum Phongsawadan.* Vol. XXI. Bangkok: Sophon Phiphatanakorn Press, 1921-22.
Phinit Wanakan, Phra. *Ariyasap.* 2d ed. Bangkok: Sophon Phiphatanakorn Press, 1930-31.
Phraracha Pongsswadan Krung Thonburi. Bangkok: Thai Press, 1919-20.
Phraracha Phongsawadan Krung Sri Ayudhya. Vol. I. Bangkok: Aksoniti Press, 1922-23.
Phraracha Phongsawadan Krung Sri Ayudhya. Vol. II. Bangkok: Aksoniti Press, 1927-28.
Phraracha Banyat Calacon Thang Bok. Bangkok: Thai Kasem Press, 1934-35.

Phra Phuta Chinarat. 3d ed. Bangkok: Bamrung Nukunkit Press, 1926-27.
Baep Wai Phra Suat Mon. Bangkok: Phracantr Press, 1929-30.
Phratham Thesana Sipet Kant. Bangkok: Krungdebarnagar Press, 1935-36.
Phuta Sasana. Chaiya: Thamatan Chaiya Press, 1937-38.
Phuta Prawat. Chaiya: Thamatan Chaiya Press, 1936-37.
Pieris, P. E. "An Account of King Kirti Sri's Embassy to Siam in 1750 A.D." *Religious Intercourse between Ceylon and Siam in the 18th Century.* Vol. I. Bangkok: Siam Observer Office, 1908.
Plangkun. *Prachaya Khong Syam Mai.* Bangkok: Krungdebarnagar Press, 1936-37.
Postal Progress in Siam 1885-1925. Bangkok: Bangkok Times Press Ltd., 1925.
Praphan Phai, Luang. *Rabop Kan Thesaban.* Bangkok: Nitisat Press, 1935-36.
Pratt, James Bissett. *The Pilgrimage of Buddhism.* New York: MacMillan & Co., 1928.
Pui Saeng Chai. *Lak Phutasasana.* Bangkok: Cetana Phon Press, 1934-35.
Pui Saeng Chai. *Phuta Prachaya.* 2d ed. Bangkok: Supa Akson Press, 1934-35.
Racho Thai, Mom. *Nirat London.* Bangkok: Aksoniti Press, 1934-35.
Raingan Sthiti Phayakorn Haeng Racha Anacakr Syam. Bangkok: Bamrung Nukunkit Press, 1935-37.
Raingan Kan Su'ksa. Prepared by Krasuang Thamakan. Bangkok: Wat Sang Wet Press, 1934-35.
Rama VI. *Phraphutacao Tratsaru Arai.* Bangkok: Sophon Phiphatanakorn Press.
——. *Lecture on Religious Topics to His Boy Scouts.* Bangkok: 1914.
——. *The Duty of Neutrals.* Bangkok: Siam Observer Press, 1914.
Rat Banthit Sapha. *Lathi Thamniam Tang Tang.* Vol. II. Bangkok: Sophon Phiphatanakorn Press, 1929-30.
Rat Kotca Nubeksa. Bangkok: 1933-34.
Ratyotha, Phya. *Phra Ratana Trai.* 2d ed. Bangkok: Siri Chai Press, 1935-36.
Records of the Relations between Siam and Foreign Countries in the 17th Century. Copied from papers preserved at the India Office. Vol. I, 1607-1632. Bangkok: 1915.
Reid, Eric. *Chequered Leaves from Siam.* Bangkok: Bangkok Times Press, 1915.
Reith, George M. *A Padre in Partibus.* Singapore: The Singapore and Straits Printing Office, 1897.
Relation of the Voyage to Siam by Six Jesuits sent by the French King in 1685. London: T. Robinson and A. Churchal, 1688.
Reports of the Phra Dot Trial before the Special Court. Bangkok: Bangkok Times Office, 1894.

BIBLIOGRAPHY 245

Reports of the Second Exhibition of Agriculture and Commerce, held in Bangkok April, 1911. London: Alexander Moning Ltd., 1911.
Rhys Davids, T. W. *Buddhism.* London: Society for Promoting Christian Knowledge, 1894.
——. *Dialogues of the Buddha.* 2 vols. London: Henry Frowde, 1899.
Roberts, Edmund. *Embassy to the Eastern Courts during 1833-1844.* New York: Harper & Brothers, 1837.
Ross, John Dill. *Sixty Years of Life and Adventure in the Far East.* 2 vols. London: Hutchinson & Co., 1911.
Sakol Varavarn, H.S.H. *Public Health and Medical Service in Siam.* Bangkok: The Bangkok Times Press, Ltd., 1930.
——. *Sakon Thetsaban.* Bangkok: Syam Witayakorn Press, 1935-36.
Salmony, Alfred. *Sculpture in Siam.* London: Earnest Benn Ltd., 1925.
Sararaks, Praison. *History of Burma (Maharajawongse).*
Sasana Khun. 2 vols. Bangkok: Sophonphiphatanakorn Press, 1929-30.
Satya Nanda Puri, Swami. *Khu Mu' Prachaya Wa Duoi Trak.* Bangkok: Pra Cantr Press, 1936-37.
——. *The Origin of Buddhist Thoughts.* Bangkok: Mahamakut Ratwitayalai Press, 1936-37.
——. *Prachaya Fai Bura Phathit.* Bangkok: Mahamakut Ratwitayalai Press, 1937-38.
——. *Prachaya Fai Yokha.* Bangkok: Mahamakut Ratwitayalai Press, 1937-38.
——. *Taka Witaya.* Bangkok Phra Cantr Press, 1934-35.
Saunders, Kenneth J. *Gotama Buddha.* New York: Associated Press, 1920.
Sayre, Francis Bowes. *Siam Treaties with Foreign Powers 1920-1927.* Norwood, Mass.: The Plimpton Press, 1928.
Schouten, Joost. *A Description of the Kingdom of Siam Written in 1636.* Bangkok: Bangkolem Press, 1889.
Second Siamese Embassy to Rome in Reign of King Narai. Bangkok: Siam Panityakan, 1932.
Seidenfaden, Erik. *Guide to Nakon Patome.* 2d ed. Bangkok: The Royal State Railways, 1929.
Siam and Laos. Philadelphia: Presbyterian Board of Publication, 1844.
Siam: a series of pamphlets produced by the Siamese Government, undated, on aviation, aquatic resources and fisheries, co-operative movement, education, forests, irrigation, lac cultivation, public health, resources, and rice industry.
Siam, General and Medical. By the Executive Committee of the 8th Congress of the Far Eastern Association of Tropical Medicine. Bangkok: 1930.
Siam, Nature and Industry. By the Ministry of Commerce and Communication. Bangkok: The Bangkok Times Press Ltd., 1930.
Siam, Natural Features. Bangkok: 1926.
Siam Repository, 1869-1874, 1878-1886. Compiled by Samuel J. Smith. Bangkok: S. J. Smith's Office.

Siam Today, July 1936.
Siam Today, January 1937.
Sinlapakorn. Edited by Nai Ki Yu Po. Bangkok: Phra Cantr Press, 1937-38.
Sin Smathi Panya. Bangkok: Liang Chiang Press, 1937-38.
Siritam. *Kan Phok Khrong Khana Song.* Bangkok: Supa Akson Press, 1934-35.
Smith, Samuel J. *Extracts From Siamese History.* Bangkok: 1880.
Siamese Domestic Institutions, Old and New Laws on Slavery. Translated by Samuel J. Smith. Bangkok: S. J. Smith's Office, 1880.
Smith, Samuel J. *History of Siam in the Reign of Phra Narai 1657-1682.* Bangkok: S. J. Smith's Office, 1880.
——. *Brief Sketches of Siam from 1833-1909.* Bangkok: Bangkolem Press, 1909.
Smith, Hugh McCormick. *A Review of Aquatic Resources and Fisheries of Siam.* Bangkok: Bangkok Times Press Ltd., 1925.
Smyth, H. Warington. *Five Years in Siam.* 2 vols. London: John Murray, 1898.
Sommerville, Maxwell. *Siam on the Meinam.* Philadelphia: J. P. Lippincott Co., 1897.
Spear, Robert E. *Report of Deputation.* New York: Board of Foreign Missions of the Presbyterian Church in the U.S.A., 1916.
Sri Burapha. *Songkhram Chivit.* Bangkok: Hang Samut Press, 1932-33.
Sri Su. *Ruam Ru'ang Krungdeb.* Bangkok: Po Thong Press, 1935-36.
Statistical Year Book of the Kingdom of Siam, 1931-1933. Number 17.
Strong, William E. *The Story of the American Board.* Boston: The Pilgrim Press, 1910.
Suriyabongs, Luang. *The Buddha's Doctrine of Truth.* Bangkok: Krungdebarnagar Press, 1936.
Swettenham, Franck. *British Malaya.* London: John Lane, 1907.
Syam Rat Patiwat. Vol. I. Bangkok: Liang Chiang Press, 1931-32.
Syam Rat Patiwat. Vol. II. Bangkok: Supa Akson Press, 1936-37.
Tachard, Pere. *Voyage de Siam.* Paris: Chez Pierre Nortier, 1688.
Thai Khasem. Edited by Nai Phan Laksanasut. Bangkok: Aksoniti Press, 1925-1933.
Thalaeng Kan Ru'ang Phrabat Somdet Phra Poramintr Maha Prachathipok Phrapokklao Caoyuhua Song Sla Rachasombat. 2 vols. Bangkok: Phracantr Press, 1935-36.
Thalaeng Kan Satharanasuk. Bangkok: Aksoniti Press, 1937.
Tham Caksu. Edited by Phra Phimonseni. Bangkok: Song Tham Press, 1935-1938.
The Directory for Bangkok and Siam. Bangkok: The Bangkok Times Press Ltd., 1931-1937.
Thomson, P. A. *Two Months Tour in Siam.* Singapore: 1866.
——. *Lotus Land.* London: T. Werner Laurie, 1906.

BIBLIOGRAPHY 247

Thomson, J. *The Straits of Malacca, Indo-China and China.* New York: Harper & Bros., 1875.
Tomlin, J. *Missionary Journals and Letters.* London: James Nisbet & Co., 1844.
Treaty Between the United Kingdom and Siam, signed at Bangkok March 10th, 1909. London: Harrison & Sons, 1909.
Turpin M. *History of the Kingdom of Siam.* Translated from French by B. O. Cartwright. Bangkok: American Mission Press, 1908.
Unofficial Mission of John Morgan to Siam in 1821.
Varnvaidyakara Varavarn, Mom Cao. *Aphiprai Ru'ang Rata Thamanun.* Bangkok: Bamsung Nukunkit Press.
——. *Khu Mu' Rabop Mai.* Bangkok: Syam Phanichakan Press, 1934-35.
Vichitr, Tamakhun, Phra Kru. *Thit Hok.* Bangkok: Sophon Phiphatanakorn Press, 1934-35.
Vichitr Vadhakarn, Luang. *Kan Mu'ang Kan Pok Khrong Khong Krung Syam.* Bangkok: Thai Mai Press, 1932-33.
——. *Khana Kan Mu'ang.* Bangkok: Thai Mai Press, 1932-33.
——. *Khwam Fan.* Bangkok: Supa Phak Wiphat Press, 1929-30.
——. *Lati Yoki.* Bangkok: Syam Banakit Press, 1933-34.
——. *Ngan Khong Krom Sinlapakorn.* Bangkok: Phra Cantr Press, 1935-36.
——. *Phutanuphap.* Bangkok: Wiriyanuphap Press, 1930-31.
Vincent, Frank. *The Land of the White Elephant.* New York: Harper & Bros., 1881.
Well, A., Chenin, E. *Contes et Recits Du XIX Siecle.* Librairie Larousse.
Wheatcroft, Rachel. *Siam and Cambodia in Pen and Pastel.* London: Constable & Co., Ltd., 1928.
Whitney, Casper. *Jungle Trails and Jungle People.* London: T. Werner Laurie, 1905.
Wales, H. G. Quaritch. *Siamese State Ceremonies.* London: Stephen Austin & Sons, Ltd., 1931.
——. *Ancient Siamese Government and Administration.* London: Stephen Austin & Sons, Ltd., 1934.
Wood, W.A.R. *A History of Siam.* London: T. Fisher Unwin, Ltd., 1926.
Wood, W. M. *Fankwei.* New York: Harper & Bros., 1859.
Wright, Arnold. *Twentieth Century Impressions of Siam.* London: Lloyd's Greater Britain Publishing Co., Ltd., 1908.
Young, Earnest. *From Russia to Siam.* London: Max Goschen Ltd., 1914.
——. *The Kingdom of the Yellow Robe.* Westminster: Archibald Constable & Co., 1900.
Zimmerman, Carle C. *Siam Rural Economic Survey 1930-31.* Bangkok: The Bangkok Times Press Ltd., 1931.

APPENDIXES

APPENDIX I

A. SYSTEM OF TRANSLITERATION

The system offered by Mom Cao Varnvaidyakara Varavarn in the *Journal of the Siam Society*, XXVIII, Part 1, July 1935, was generally followed. However, it was not faithfully followed because many Siamese have chosen to write their names or the titles of their books according to some other system; or the newspapers have popularized their names in some other form.

The vowels are pronounced as Italian vowels except that:

ae equals the sound of ea in the English "bear";
o, equals the sound of aw in the English "dawn";
oe equals the sound of eu in the French "peuple";
u' is a more open sound than the German "ü".

The consonants are English consonants except that:

Initial k, p, and t are unaspirated as in French;
Final k, p, and t are unexplosive and unaspirated;
kh equals k aspirated;
ph equals p aspirated, not the English ph;
th equals t aspirated, not the English th;
c is the hardened form of ch as cz in "Czechoslovak";
ch is always as the English "church";
ng is as in the English "singer", never as in "linger."

B. BUDDHIST CALENDAR

The Siamese year begins April 1st, and coincides, month by month, with the Christian year. Thus the Buddhist year 2480 equals April to December 1937 plus January to March 1938. To represent this fact the year 2480 is written, according to the Christian calendar, 1937-38.

APPENDIX II

A. THE DECREE PROROGUING THE PEOPLE'S ASSEMBLY

Whereas the present Assembly is temporarily composed of nominated members till the time when the people shall be given an opportunity to elect their own representatives, and

Whereas, being so composed, the Assembly should not consider changes in vital economic policies, on which the national welfare depends from time immemorial, and

Whereas many members of the Assembly have expressed a strong desire to make such changes and have attempted to bring them about by using undue pressure upon the Assembly, and

Whereas such conduct shows clearly that the present Assembly cannot properly carry on its public functions and is a menace to the safety of the State and welfare of the People,

His Majesty the King declares that an emergency exists, and; in order to prevent a disaster that threatens the country and the people issues the following Royal Decree:

1. The present session of the Assembly of the People's Representatives is hereby prorogued and no further session shall be called until the formation of a new Assembly after the election of the Representatives of the People, in accordance with the provision of the constitution.

2. The present State Council is hereby dissolved and a new Council is created composed of a President and not more than twenty other State Councillors. The President of the present State Council shall be the President of the new Council; State Councillors in charge of the Ministries shall be ex-officio members of the new Council; the other members shall be appointed by His Majesty upon the recommendation of the President.

3. Until the new Assembly is called into session after the election and a State Council is appointed, the new Council hereby created shall exercise all the powers conferred by the Constitution on the State Council.

4. Until the new Assembly is called into session after the election, His Majesty shall exercise legislative power by and with the advice and consent of the Council.

5. All provisions of the Constitution inconsistent with this decree are hereby suspended until a new Assembly is called into session after the election, and a State Council is appointed. In all other respects the Constitution remains in full force.

Given April 1st, 1933.

SIGNED BY FOURTEEN MEMBERS OF THE STATE COUNCIL.

B. GOVERNMENT COMMUNIQUE REGARDING THE PROROGUING OF THE PEOPLE'S ASSEMBLY

The Government desires the people to understand the serious reasons that made it necessary to prorogue the present National Assembly, to form a new State Council and to suspend temporarily certain provisions of the Constitution.

The present State Council is divided into two groups holding divergent and irreconcilable views. The minority desires to establish a new economic policy in Siam of a communistic nature. The majority deems such policy contrary to all the traditions of the Siamese people and certain to bring disaster to the people and menace the security of the State.

It is not to be expected that a State Council composed of twenty members will agree in all matters, but it is fundamental to orderly and efficient government that the body charged with executive power should agree on essential policies. The situation now existing would not be tolerated in any country whatever its form of government.

The present National Assembly contains only appointed members. Under the Constitution it exercises legislative powers until the new Assembly is created after an election. An Assembly so chosen and exercising power only for a temporary period should not attempt to establish an entirely new and subversive policy. While the Assembly has not passed any acts of this nature, it is clear that a considerable number of the members desire to do so, and are in sympathy with the extremist group in the State Council.

These fundamental divisions in the legislative and executive bodies are a serious menace to the stability of the State. They create delay and friction within the government and in the public mind fear and uncertainty for the future. This situation cannot be permitted to continue. The safety of the community is the supreme law of any state, and that law has compelled the Government to prorogue the Assembly and to create a new State Council. The Government desires to emphasize the fact that it has suspended only a few provisions of the Constitution and those only for the time being.

April 1st, 1933

C. ACT CONCERNING COMMUNISM

Whereas any attempt to establish communism in Siam would bring disaster to the people and would menace the security of the State,

It is hereby enacted by and with the advice and consent of the State Council, as follows:

Section 1. This Act shall be called the "Act Concerning Communism."

Section 2. It shall come into force on and from the date of its publication in the Government Gazette.

Section 3. In this Act

(1) "Communism" means the economic system or theory, which rests upon the total or partial abolition of the right of private property, actual ownership being ascribed to the community as a whole or to the State.

(2) "Communistic doctrine" means any doctrine which implies the advocation of nationalization of land, or nationalization of industry, or nationalization of capital, or nationalization of labour.

Section 4. Whoever by words or writing or printed documents or by any means whatever advocates communism or any communistic doctrine shall be punished with imprisonment not exceeding ten years and fine not exceeding five thousand ticals.

Section 5. Whoever is the chief, manager or any official of any association secret or otherwise, the purpose of which is to advocate communism or any communistic doctrine, shall be punished with imprisonment not exceeding ten years and fine not exceeding five thousand ticals.

Any member of such association shall be punished with imprisonment not exceeding five years and fine not exceeding one thousand ticals.

April 2nd, 1933

D. GOVERNMENT COMMUNIQUE ON THE POLITICAL PRISONER, January, 1934

Some people understand wrongly that the prisoners and those under detention in connection with the recent rising have been badly treated, differently from political prisoners in other civilized countries. Some newspapers have printed news to the effect, but it is news without an atom of truth. The officials in charge of those under detention for the rising abide by the following rules:

1. The use of fetters.—(a) Fetters are never placed on those under detention before judgment is given. (b) All prisoners on whom sentence has been passed have to wear fetters, in accordance with the regular prison rules.

2. The mosquito.—Everyone is permitted to have a mosquito net over him when lying down.

3. Lying on a cement floor.—Mats are supplied; and permission is given to the family to send blankets and bed sheets.

4. Walking with bare feet on concrete.—Permission is given to wear boots or shoes; but anyone who does not have them cannot wear them.

5. Heavy work.—At the present time no one is put to heavy work.

6. Reading.—Permission to read has been given, but the authorities must examine the reading matter beforehand. If the printed matter is not considered proper, permission is refused.

7. Food.—This is the same as for ordinary prisoners and ordinary persons under detention (not more than 12 *stangs*). A person under detention whose case has not yet been decided is allowed to get his own food.

8. Visits.—Weekly visits are allowed in the case of those whose cases have not yet been decided. Once sentence is passed, only one visit every four weeks is allowed; but on condition of good behaviour, that is gradually increased to once a week again.

E. FINAL REUNION OF THE ROYAL FAMILY

There was a big gathering of members of the Siamese Royal Family in Sumatra on the occasion of the brief visit of Their Majesties the King and Queen to Belawan and Medan, prior to their embarkation for Europe last Saturday.

Field Marshal His Royal Highness the Prince of Nagor Svarga arrived at Belawan by the Melchior Treub on the 9th of January and was accompanied by the Princess of Nagor Svarga (a full younger sister of Prince Thavara); Their Royal Highnesses Princess Nibhā Nabhatala of Uthong (sister of the late Prince Yugala of Lopburi); Princess Dibyaratna (Aunt of the Prince of Nagor Svarga and a daughter of King Mongkut); Princess Hemavati (a daughter of King Chulalongkorn); Princess Siriratnapushpongs, Princess Suddhavongsvichitra, Princess Bisishht-sobsmai, Princess Churairatnasiriman, Princess Chandrakāntmani, (daughters of the Prince of Nagor Svarga); Their Highnesses Princess Induratnā, and Prince Sukhuma (daughter and son of Prince Nagor Svarga). Also included in the party was Her Serene Highness Princess Guntharos, a daughter of the late Prince Rabi.

Arriving on the Kiran on January 17th were Their Royal Highnesses Prince and Princess Svasti. In Penang they have been staying at the residence of Mr. Khoo Sian Ewe.

On the 19th instant His Royal Highness the Prince of Kambaeng Bejra arrived by the Cremer.

On the morning of the 20th His Royal Highness Prince Damrong with Their Serene Highnesses Princess Poon Pismai, Princess Pilai Lekha, Princess Baddhanayu, and His Royal Highness Prince Vudhijai of Sinha and his daughter (a granddaughter of Prince Damrong on her mother's side), arrived by the Kedah. By this steamer there also travelled Phya Manopakorn, Lady Rama Raghob and Phya Bisal Sukhumvid to meet Chao Phya Rama Raghob due to arrive from Europe the following day, after a long sojourn in England. The latter party went to Brastagi.

Their Majesties arrived at Belawan about nine o'clock on the morning of the 18th instant aboard the Valaya of the Siam Steam Navigation Co., Ltd's fleet. . . .

The meeting of the Sovereign and his brother the Prince of Nagor Svarga was a moving scene. The King had not seen the Prince since the latter's departure from the homeland in 1932, and warmly embraced him and his other relatives.

Bangkok Times, January 27th, 1934

F. A TYPICAL CONFESSION OF FRAUD

I, Sombati Lekjuoongs, Proprietor of Naraphon Store, having my place of business at Pratoomai, Phra Sumang Road, do publicly make this statement:

That I have been manufacturing a brand of hair tonic known as "Snow Hair Tonic", indicating that it was trade marked under this name and was manufactured by "The White Bat Mfg. Co., Chicago, U.S.A." The name of the company being fictitious, and that I have sold this article to shopkeepers and dealers in Bangkok.

I freely confess that shopkeepers and customers have been deceived by the false marking into believing that the article was made in America although it was actually manufactured by me in Bangkok, and I now freely admit that it was inferior to hair tonics offered in the market which are actually made in America and imported into Siam.

My entire stock of Snow Hair Tonic bearing the false trade mark and a fictitious name of an American manufacturer with a Chicago address has been confiscated by the police, together with the equipment used for the production of the lotion. I shall suffer a heavy loss through the confiscation and destruction of this supply of falsely marked lotion, but realize that otherwise I am subject to prosecution under the law for deceitful and fraudulent use of such a label.

This notice will inform all shopkeepers and customers who have purchased Snow Hair Tonic indicating that it was produced by the White Bat Mfg. Co. of Chicago, U.S.A., that the article should be returned at once and the purchase price will be refunded by me because it is illegal to sell this lotion as marked.

I hereby publicly acknowledge and apologize for this venture into false production and labelling of this lotion, and faithfully promise to make no further attempt to deceive the public by offering goods marked in this manner to indicate that they are made in America, when they are not imported from America. I make this public statement by publishing it in Bangkok newspapers at my own expense.

(*Signed*) Nai Sombati Lekjuoongs

Daily Mail, June, 1933

G. A DISCUSSION OF THE SIAMESE FAMILY

The question that took up so much time (of the Assembly of Representatives) was the report of the Commission appointed to consider the draft of Book V of the Commercial and Civil Code dealing with the family. The point raised was whether a man should be empowered to register only one wife or several wives. Perhaps certain facts pertaining to this point may be of interest. Originally the Department for Legislative Redaction submitted the draft of this law to the Assembly of the first period, when it was referred to the Commission dealing with draft laws. The Commission agreed first to hear the views of the members of the Assembly on this important point, whether a man ought to have only one or several wives. On or about the 5th of October last, Colonel Phya Bahol, the Premier in the former Government, submitted his opinion to the Commission that the point as to the number of wives a man should have was a most' vital one, which would bring forth an important climax similar to a world split, and therefore it should not be settled then, but should be left to the Assembly of the second period to decide, because then there would be members elected by the people present to give their final decision.

The anxiety of the Commission may be gathered from the following endorsement prepared by it:

The Commission considering the draft of Book V of the Civil and Commercial Code consulted with one another on the point as to whether a man should be empowered to have one or several wives. This question dealt with the custom and position of the family and hence because of its vital nature in the drafting of this book of the law it should not be allowed to pass without due consideration being given it.

This question had been brought up on several occasions, commencing in the Sixth Reign, and even when the drafting of this Book was taken up opinions differed. It was then thought at that time first to leave things as of yore. Later, in the present Reign at the time when an amendment was being drafted to the law of husband and wife, the Supreme Council, which was charged by the King to discuss this draft, debated this point at great length. But the two opinions remained, and ultimately it was decided to allow polygamy to exist. However, a limitation was arrived at, making it lawful for one major wife to be registered, and providing that the minor wives should receive no share of the Sin Somros. That was an alteration that showed an inclination towards the one wife policy. The Act was of a temporary nature, and the point as to the number of wives that a man might have was not at all ended then.

The time had now arrived to promulgate Book V of the Civil and Commercial Code, which would directly control this point. Once a principle was laid down and accepted, it would be hard to revise later, being different from the issue of an amendment Act as formerly. That being so it was reasonable to finally decide the point as to whether a man should be allowed to have many wives according to the old law, or that he should be limited to only one wife similar to the laws of other countries.

This Commission felt it a difficult matter to decide, but the point was thoroughly considered and it was decided to adopt the direction requiring a man to have only one wife based on the following:

(1) Polygamy originally existed generally in countries in the East, not being confined to Siam alone; but those of our neighbours that had occasion to enact new laws on the subject were the Japanese and Chinese, who altered this custom by allowing a man to have only one wife, the same as in other civilized countries. In Turkey the law is based on custom and the Moslem religion which allows polygamy; but even there a law was promulgated only allowing monogamy to be practiced, the custom being adopted from the Swiss civil laws.

Therefore if we wish to remain stationary, we may decide to make no revision on this point. Still it would be hard to find the laws of any other country which provide for polygamy.

Please compare the civil laws of Japan, Section 766; of China, Section 985; of France, Section 147; of Switzerland, Section 101; of Germany, Section 1309.

(2) As a matter of fact according to the old law a man is allowed to practice polygamy; but as is generally understood the number of those practicing monogamy is not less by any manner and there are some who even think that the majority of our people have only one wife. Because polygamy costs more it is hard for the ordinary people to practice it. With the change in the general circumstances, coupled with the progressive strides of education, the practice of polygamy is not in keeping with the times and should be reasonably changed.

(3) Such a change in the law, providing for a man to have only one wife, should improve the position of the family to a level similar to that in other countries. Apart from that the honour of the woman is thereby lifted up, and thus conforms to the principle of equality which allows the woman a voting power in the election of Tambon and Changvad representatives. In some countries where monogamy is practiced the woman is still not allowed to enjoy equal rights to that extent.

(4) According to the provisions in Book V of this draft many changes have been affected in the old law; but still it retains the features of an Amendment to the Act of Husband and Wife. But a definite revision should be made confining registration to one wife without need for separating the major from the lesser wives.

Such a change will better maintain relationships in the family, and misunderstandings between husband and wife will decrease thereby. At the same time the common property of the husband and wife will not be scattered while disputes accruing from such will decrease in a marked manner. It is a saving or an economy in itself and even the children will not have to consider whether they are those of the major or lesser wives. Such causes bring about a lack of co-operation in the family.

(5) The change to be effected is to be compulsory solely as a matter of civil right. For the future for the enforcement of the law those men and women who are now husbands and wives will be left alone without any change being effected in their case; the present system is to be allowed to die a natural death. That being so there is no question of hardship in any manner. As for later generations, they may readily adhere to this new principle. Moreover the change to be effected by this law will not affect the regulations for the administration of the seven muangs of R.S. 120 in any manner, because such are special laws for localities (in Pattani, Yala, Naradhivas, and Satul) which are populated by those who adhere to the Moslem religion, in regard to the law of husband and wife. For such cases there will be exemption clauses in this Book V of the Civil Code.

(6) As to there being cause for anxiety in the fact that, if only one wife may be registered, illegitimate children will increase in number, this point has been considered and should not be a cause for any anxiety. Provision is made in this law compelling children born by women not registered as lawful wives of men to be recognized as legitimate and they also are to enjoy

equal rights with those of the children born during the course of marriage. This measure it is which provides for the protection of illegitimate children.

(7) According to the old law the living together as husband and wife does not necessitate a registration and the wide meaning is adopted that man and wife may be so recognized when they live together as such or when a child is born between them. However, according to the draft of this new law the registration is held to be highly important in that even a man and woman living together as husband and wife and having children between them *if the marriage is not registered, they are not considered to be husband and wife according to the new law.* The result therefore is that if the man refuses to register the woman, the woman cannot be considered to be his legal wife, and *the woman may not ask for the man to be forced to register her as his wife.* The forcing of registration necessarily brings about a great change in the method of living as man and wife according to the old law. Another thing; the lessening of the position of the lesser wife to still a lower level will also help to prevent women becoming lesser wives of a man as formerly. When such is the position of things *although the draft law allows the registration of many lesser wives very few cases will be registered as such.* Because of this it is clearly shown that the revision of the law providing for a man to have only one wife should give good results.

Because of these causes this Commission therefore decided for the revision of the draft to read: A man shall be allowed to register only one wife the same as under the laws of other countries; but as this matter is an important measure of policy, it has therefore to be submitted to the Assembly for its decision first. Once the Assembly has given a final ruling the Commission will proceed further.

Bangkok Times, January 19th, 1934

H. KING PRAJADHIPOK'S ABDICATION ANNOUNCEMENT

Noel, Cranleigh, England.

When Phya Bahol with his party seized the powers of government by the use of arms on the 24th of June, B.E. 2475, they sent a letter inviting me to become their King under the constitution. I accepted the invitation because I understood that they would establish a government similar to that of other democratic nations, so that the citizenry would have the right to express their opinions on government, and so the people as a whole would be benefitted. I had already had great interest in that form of government and had planned to make a definite change to it in a quiet and orderly way. When unsettled conditions arose and when those who were leaders claimed that their intentions were to establish democratic rule, I saw that our hopes were identical. I accordingly felt that it was proper for me to fall in with their plans for the progress and peace of the nation. I did my best to maintain peace in the country but my best efforts were without avail because the new Government did not actually establish equality and freedom for all in matters of politics. They were unwilling to listen to the opinions of the people. In Section two of the Constitution actual power to carry on the Government is given to the People's Party who originated the movement and is not given to the representatives elected by the people. The temporary constitution shows that those not approved by the Government could not become members of the Assembly. The permanent constitution was an improvement. According to my request the people were allowed to elect one-half of the membership of the Assembly without interference. I was willing to allow both elective and appointive membership because I hoped to be able to appoint men experienced in government work without regard to their party affiliations. I expected those appointed to assist the elected membership with advice on matters of government. When the time came to appoint the members I had no voice in their selection at all. The Government selected only those who were members of their own party and without regard to their experience or ability. Furthermore, some members planned to change the economic policy of the country in a drastic manner. There thus grew up a division of opinion until the Assembly had to be prorogued for fear of violence. Several sections of the Constitution had to be made temporarily inactive. This was done by advice of the Government then in power. Later on Phya Bahol with his party again used the army to seize the powers of government. From that time there was little hope for favourable progress.

Because the People's Party did not give full democracy to the nation, the people had no opportunity to express opinion before important decisions were made. There was another rebellion of an independent party and much life was lost, Siamese killing Siamese.

When I pleaded that the Constitution be revised along true democratic lines so that it might be acceptable to all of the people, the Government and its party was unwilling. I begged that the people be given a voice in important decisions that directly affected them. I had no favourable reply. Even the Assembly was not allowed to judicially consider my requests to the Government in behalf of the people. They were forced to come to a final decision in a single session without going into detail on any point. Furthermore, the Government set up a law to punish those who were suspected of having plans against the Government. They were treated in a manner contrary to the commonest principles of justice in a secret court, without aid of attorney, and so with no chance to fight. This is a method I never used even in an Absolute Monarchy. I begged the Government to change this law and it refused.

I feel that the Government and its party uses methods contrary to the principles of a free people and common justice. I am unwilling to allow anyone or any party to carry on such a government in my name.

I am happy to turn over my power of rule to the people as a whole. I am not willing to give it over to any person or to any group to use in an absolute manner without heeding the voice of the people.

Now I see that my intention to allow everyone a voice in the government is without fulfillment. I feel that there is no longer any way to assist the people in my official capacity. I feel that it is necessary for me to resign my office as King dating from this present time. I wish to give over all of my kingly privileges but I desire to retain all of those privileges which were mine before becoming King.

I do not care to name anyone as my successor although it is my privilege according to law.

Furthermore, I do not care to have anyone rise up in rebellion in Siam against the Government in my behalf. If anyone names me as their instigator in rebellion kindly understand that I have no share in it and am not pleased.

I am exceedingly sorry that I am unable to serve my people and country according to my plans and hopes which I received from my royal ancestors. There remains only a sincere prayer that Siam will prosper and that the people will have peace and happiness.

PRAJADHIPOK

March 2nd, 1935

APPENDIX III

A. NATIONAL ECONOMIC POLICY OF LUANG PRADIST MANUDHARM

[*The presentation to the government in March, 1933, of a National Economic Policy which had been drafted by Luang Pradist Manudharm resulted in the initiation of a series of important events of far-reaching political significance: the proroguing of the People's Assembly on April 1st, 1933; a trip abroad for Luang Pradist, which lasted from April 12th until September 29th, 1933; the second revolution of June 20th, 1933; and the official whitewashing of Luang Pradist from the charge of being a communist, by a commission appointed by the government on March 21st, 1934. The Policy and the following Acts were never officially promulgated, and together with the Minutes concerned with the Policy, which are all included in Appendix III, were never made public in Siam, nor were the newspapers allowed to print or discuss any portion of them. The ban established then continues in effect at the time of this printing in 1939.—Trans.*]

Why do you officials with salaries and pensions oppose the granting of salaries and pensions to the people?

[*This question appeared at the top of each page of the Policy.—Trans.*]

PREAMBLE

POINTS TO BE KEPT IN MIND DURING THE READING OF THIS POLICY

Division of the economic system into co-operative associations

In seeking a means to promote the welfare of our people I have taken into consideration not only their present mode of existence but also those peculiar traits which characterize them as a nation. I have come to the conclusion that, for the advancement of their well-being, only one course is feasible: namely, the government must undertake to administer a national economic policy by which the economic system will be sub-divided into diversified co-operative associations.

My conclusion is not the result of my adherence to any particular social philosophy. I have borrowed elements of value from various systems whenever I found in them something appropriate to Siam. These ideas I have organized into a co-ordinated policy.

APPENDIX III

It is well to remember, however, that there are certain to be many divergent theories concerning the best means for promoting the economic welfare of a people; and that the advocates of these various theories are unable to come to any agreement. For this state of things Professor Deschamps of the University of Paris has offered three possible explanations: *Reasons for bias*

(1) Not everyone is well-informed on the various economic theories. There are, for instance, people who have never studied or never actually read the literature of the various systems, and who are, therefore, incapable of forming an opinion about them. *Involuntary ignorance*

(2) Some, through choice, continue to remain ignorant of the actual facts. For example, a certain type of person overhears street-corner accusations made against a certain social theory that it incites people to kill each other, to confiscate the property of the rich and distribute it equally among the poor, and to make women common property. He credulously accepts this market talk and is firmly convinced of the truth of these vicious allegations. And he does not investigate further to determine whether the philosophy in question actually has incited people to kill, to confiscate the property of the rich and distribute it among the poor, or to make women common property. *Voluntary ignorance*

(3) Some fear the loss of special privilege. To illustrate: a certain class of people recognizes the benefits inherent in some of the social philosophies, but declines to acknowledge them. Such people oppose the adoption of anything inimical to the special privileges which they enjoy. Thus they oppose the adoption of socialism, which places the government in control of industry for the benefit of the people at large. As capitalists they find socialism unacceptable inasmuch as it may entail the expropriation of their investment in industry. Again, there are people antagonistic to the government for private reasons. They may realize that a certain policy is excellent. But let the government adopt it, and they avow some other policy for no better reason than that they have stubbornly pitted themselves against everything that the government may attempt. Such people are social parasites who think only in terms of selfish advantage and are not concerned for the welfare of the general public. *Special privilege*

It is my observation that for Siam still another explanation exists, to wit "pride and prejudice". On occasion I have read articles by Siam's intelligentsia pointing out alleged dangers supposedly immanent in certain social *Pride and prejudice* theories. I have asked the writers whether they were conversant with authoritative discussions pro and con of the theories in question or whether they had based their remarks simply on rumour. As a general rule I have found that they have been influenced by rumour. I have suggested to them that it might be well to study the disquisitions of impartial persons. When they have done so, they have seen that their own expositions were inaccurate. But in order to maintain their reputation as scholars, in other words because of "pride and prejudice", they have continued to affirm their former position, even after they have acknowledged to me that they were in error. They do this, of course, because of false pride. And they are as much social parasites as those selfish individuals whose only concern is personal gain.

Impartiality

Therefore, the reader of this exposition of mine is requested to approach it impartially. He is asked to avoid the pitfalls defined above and to try to judge fairly whether or not the programme which I have drafted would be of benefit to the people, in accordance with the former proclamation of this government. If any who read are puzzled or in doubt about some point, they are invited to consult me. If you hear objections to the plan, I should like to ask you to be so kind as to inquire of the objector whether his reasons are his own or are criticisms that he has heard on some street corner. Ask him what reliable literature he has read or seen on the subject. And kindly report the whole matter to me as well.

The reading of this exposition does not require a university degree. One not so equipped can, with application, uninfluenced by gossip, determine the facts far better than he who has a degree but has made no attempt to search out the truth.

Part I

THE ORIGINAL PROCLAMATION OF THE PEOPLE'S PARTY

Third clause

On June 24th, 1932, the People's Party announced its programme to the general public in a six-point platform. The clause which deals with the economic system of the nation reads:

> The new government promises to promote the economic welfare of its citizens by providing remunerative employment for everyone and by promulgating a national economic policy designed to end poverty.

APPENDIX III

The ideal so stated has been planted deep in the hearts of our people everywhere. It will be emblazoned upon the history of this revolution. I, therefore, emphasize its importance again and again. For I am convinced that, if the government succeeds in promulgating a suitable economic policy, it will most assuredly be possible to provide remunerative employment for everyone and to terminate poverty. Such an accomplishment, great as it is, is not outside the realm of possibility. *Not beyond the ability of the government*

My one paramount aim and purpose in furthering the revolution was to promote the welfare of our people. Essentially my concern was not to replace a single monarch with a multiplicity of monarchs, which constitutes the external semblance of a democracy. I was resolved above all else to do just this one thing: "to advance the welfare of our people." And I hold that the Constitution comprises the key which is to unlock the door of opportunity to them so that they may have a share in determining the course of government along the lines of their felt needs. Now that the door, which has been shut against them so long, has at last swung open, it is the responsibility of this government to lead them triumphantly through it to a land of happiness and prosperity. We must not lead the people regressively into some backwater.

It is, therefore, the duty of this government, which accepted the six-point platform of the People's Party, to implement the policies of that Party.

Part II

INSTABILITY OF THE PRESENT ECONOMIC SYSTEM

Humane people cannot but be moved with compassion and pity for their fellowmen when they see the condition of the masses of peasant farmers or the poverty-stricken poor of the capital. Sympathy springs up unbidden at the sight of their inadequate food, clothing, and shelter, the bare necessities which are all they have in life. Even when they have food for today, tomorrow and the days after tomorrow are unpredictable. The future is at best precarious. When one considers the uncertainties of life, the way in which we are all subject to old age and disease, one may well ask whether these who, while they are still well and strong are so poor and needy, will in such eventualities have even food to eat. *The poverty of the people*

SIAM IN TRANSITION

The rich, middle-class, and poor may all know want

The uncertainties of existence are not confined to the poor alone. The people of the middle and wealthy classes are each and every one of them subject to the same uncertainties. Consider well whether the fortune which you have been able to amass can be made secure not only for your lifetime, but for that of your children, grandchildren, and great-grandchildren.* There are many examples of families of wealth who in a generation became poor. The inheritance left a son melts away and is gone, and the once rich heir becomes poor. Such examples serve to show the impermanence of wealth, which cannot guarantee the continuance of a mode of life. Again, can you know certainly that your bodily members will remain strong throughout your life? If you become ill or infirm so that you can no longer work, you will have to use the money which you have saved to the last penny. And when that has happened, where will you get food to eat during your illness and infirmity? Have you ever thought seriously of what your feelings would be if such a thing were to happen to you?

Part III

SOCIAL INSURANCE

The government should guarantee the security of every citizen

Such is the instability of the economic order that scholars have thought that the only solution lay in having the government undertake to insure the well-being of its citizens. That is to say, all persons who are citizens by birth are to be insured by the government so that from birth to death, regardless of whether they are children, are ill or crippled, or incapacitated for work, they will have food, clothing, and shelter, in other words, the necessities of life. When the government can give such guarantees, every citizen will sleep in peace, for he will know that he need no longer be apprehensive that in illness or infirmity or old age he will be in want. He need no longer fear that his children, if he has any, will be in need when he is dead and gone. For the government is the insurer. And the insurance which it gives is far more valuable than the accumulation of wealth, since wealth is subject to the unpredictable contingencies already mentioned.

Private companies cannot so undertake

It is beyond the scope of privately operated companies to issue such insurance as this. Or if they do so people must pay a heavy premium for the protection. And where can people secure money enough to pay for it? No, only through "government" can it be done. Because a government does not have to collect premiums directly from its citizens. A government can work out some method other than the insurance premium one. Thus it can increase the productive power of the people and then collect an indirect tax which amounts to so little per day that the people will scarcely feel it.

In some foreign countries the beginning of national prosperity is held to date from the initiation of a plan for social security. To establish a programme of social insurance in our country it will be necessary for the government to proinulgate a Social Security Act which makes it the duty of the government to distribute money to all of the people in sufficient quantities so that they may exchange it for the necessities of life such as food, clothing, and shelter, according to their individual status. (See the Social Security Act.)

<small>Social Security Act</small>

The plan to issue monthly wages to all of the people is peculiarly well adapted to the special character of the Siamese people. It is well known that all Siamese want to work for the government and that they like to receive regular salary. And yet some government officials travel around campaigning against this programme because they are unwilling to have all of the people work for the government. And they do this while at the same time they themselves are government employees receiving salary!

<small>Siamese like to be government employees</small>

If the government is to distribute wages to the people, where is it to get the money? Before we discuss this subject, let me remind you that money cannot be eaten. Money is only something to be exchanged for the necessities of life such as food, clothing, and shelter. The distribution of money is equivalent to the distribution of food, clothing, shelter, etc. Kindly remember why you accumulate money. You accumulate it in order to exchange it for the necessities of life. Thus if we call money a token or a measure we make no mistake. The distribution of wages is equivalent to the distribution of tokens which the people may exchange for the necessities of life, according to their needs. The ultimate which the people will receive is these necessities of life, namely food, clothing, shelter, etc.

<small>Money is used in exchange</small>

The government does not need to expropriate the property of the wealthy in order to secure money with which to distribute wages to the people. The government can provide the necessities of life by establishing co-operative societies which will exchange material things for the wages the government will pay the people, by a method of com-

<small>Government need not expropriate property of the wealthy</small>

pensation or balance. Thus if a citizen receives *baht* twenty monthly, and if the necessities of life for him amount to *baht* twenty, the money which the government pays him returns again to the government. The amount of money which will remain in the hands of the people will be that amount which is in excess of their living expenses. Only this sum will have to be provided by the government out of capital funds, according to the custom of the rest of the world, in gold or silver or their equivalent. If it is not desirable to issue large amounts of currency which must be guaranteed by gold or silver reserves, the government can establish a trustworthy national bank for the deposit of the people's money. Then the depositors may use cheques or the above described method of compensation to draw their money. In this way the currency issued for circulation need not be a great sum.

<small>Government administers the economic system</small>

Since the government is to establish social security by paying salaries to all citizens, it is obviously necessary for the government to establish co-operative societies which will produce the necessities of life and will act as the distributing agencies for those necessities. If the government does not establish societies to produce and distribute the necessities of life, or if it does not control such production and distribution, how then can it insure the security of the people? Where then can the government find the money to pay wages to the people?

The administration of our economic system depends on:

1. Land, which includes the wealth in, on, and under the land.
2. Labour.
3. Capital.

<small>The people lack land and capital</small>

Our first question is: Do the people have land and capital enough? We shall see that 99% of the people lack sufficient land and capital for the maintenance of life at a proper level under the present system of private enterprise. The people have man-power, true, but how can they use their man-power when they lack land and capital?

<small>Land, labour, and capital of the nation</small>

If we survey the land, labour, and capital of the nation, we shall see that in Siam there are five hundred thousand square kilometers (over 320 million *rai*) of land. The land is potentially rich with trees and other vegetation. Under the land there is great mineral wealth. As for labour: there are over eleven million people. And as for capital: although there is not a great deal, Siam is not an undeveloped country. The natural resources and the excellent reputation of the nation are assets which can be used to

APPENDIX III

attract foreign capital according to some plan to be proposed by the Treasury, without unduly inconveniencing the people.

Part IV

LABOUR WASTE AND SOCIAL PARASITES

It is a pity that because of the existing economic system this rich land of ours is not more fully developed. As a direct result of the system of private enterprise much manpower is wasted, labour efficiency is lowered, there is a lack of tools and machinery needed to increase production, and there are social parasites whose labour value is negative, as will be shown in the following:

CHAPTER 1

Labour is Wasted by Not Being Fully Employed

It is apparent that the peasants, who form the majority of the population of Siam, till the fields, on the average, not more than six months out of the year (inclusive of ploughing, sowing, harvesting, etc). Thus six months of their time is wasted. If there is a way to utilize this wasted six months in productive activity the prosperity of the people will be increased. I am glad to be informed by those interested in economics that this is possible. But how can private enterprise accomplish this? The answer is, of course, that it cannot. As I see it, the only way to avoid this waste of time is for the government to draw up a national economic plan so that the people can use their extra six months productively.

40% of labour is wasted

CHAPTER 2

Labour is Wasted Because of Unsatisfactory Economic Administration

Even the effort employed in the six months of actual labour is inefficiently used because each one works for himself, thus each farmer works only his own individual plot. Accordingly much more effort is required than would be necessary if people co-operated. Each peasant raises his own cattle, does his own ploughing, sowing, and harvesting (except for those occasions when certain groups voluntarily employ a system of communal harvesting), and secures his own food. If the peasants were to co-operate they could decrease the amount of labour expended. Thus in the

SIAM IN TRANSITION

Labour is wasted because each works for himself
raising of a cow, a peasant under the system of private enterprise has to care for it himself. But if peasants co-operate, they can throw their cattle into a herd and have one person look after the whole herd. Thus, in one particular, the amount of work would be decreased. Household work, such as the preparation of food, could be lessened by a club system. A shop could be established to provide the day's food for all the people in a community. In this way only one or two cooks would be needed. Thus we see that in the preparation of food, in the raising of cattle, and in other similar activities, the co-operative method would decrease the labour expenditure. The labour thus saved could be employed in economic enterprises which are still needed. If we permit the present individualistic system to continue there is no hope of harnessing the full productive power of the people.

CHAPTER 3

Labour is Wasted Because Machinery is Not Used

Labour wasted because of primitive methods
Everyone knows that our present method of agriculture (ploughing, sowing, and harvesting) employs the strength of men and cattle. This method was necessary in primitive times, before machinery was invented. However, mechanical experts could invent machinery which would meet the requirements of this country. This is possible because of the development of science. The only obstacle would be the lack of interest on the part of the experts. A fundamental economic principle is that machinery multiplies the efficiency of labour. Thus in the matter of ploughing, which was tested out recently, it was clearly seen that the mechanical plough, which uses one or two men, can plough many thousands of *rai* of land in one season. Siamese are

Machinery a boon
slight in body, not as strong as Chinese and foreigners. If we depend upon man-power in our various enterprises we can never compete with Chinese and foreigners. If we use machinery we can compete successfully. But at present are all of the peasants able to get machinery? Do the farmers have sufficient money to buy it? True enough, there are a few people who have enough capital to buy machinery without the aid of the government. In this connection be sure to observe the fact that machinery is both a blessing and a curse. Thus in foreign countries more and more people are unemployed. Is not this because machinery has displaced labourers? As machinery becomes prevalent, more and more people are thrown out of work, naturally.

APPENDIX III

A mill which customarily employed a thousand weavers at hand looms requires only a hundred weavers after machinery is installed. Thus nine hundred people are thrown out of work to enter the ranks of the unemployed. But we cannot blame the machinery, for machinery is a boon which lessens the labour of mankind. The unemployment situation has been created by the competitive methods of private enterprise. It is customary for factories which need only a hundred employees to release the nine hundred unneeded workers. The owner of the factory is under no obligation to support people he does not need in his work. And where will the nine hundred find employment? If all factories and all agriculturists used machinery, there would be a great multitude of unemployed and accordingly huge economic loss. But if the government were to administer the whole economic system the results from the employment of machinery would be good.

Machinery a curse

Machinery under government control is only a blessing

Thus if the mill which released nine hundred employees because efficient machinery was installed was under government control, the extra nine hundred people would be re-employed immediately in a new project such as a sugar mill, silk factory, road construction, or the clearing of jungle for fresh planting. But supposing the country expands its factories and agricultural projects to the limit so that no more labour is needed. The working hours could then be decreased unilaterally. Thus, if people were working eight hours a day, their working time could be cut gradually to 7-6-5-4-3-2-1 hours a day without reducing salaries. In this way only good would come from the use of machinery which would lessen the burden on man. As long as there is private ownership the decrease in working hours carries with it a corresponding decrease in wages. It is an economic law that as unemployment increases wages decrease; and that the hardship entailed in this process then falls upon the working people; and that, therefore, machinery ruins the citizens. The only solution then is not to use machinery, say some. But if machinery is not used we will lag farther and farther behind other nations.

When the government administers the whole economic system by establishing co-operative societies, aside from solving the labour question it makes it easier to secure capital because the government treasury department can work out an acceptable plan for securing it. For instance, the government can collect indirect taxes from the people in small daily sums which the people will scarcely feel, but which, in a year, will amount to a great deal. Thus an

Easier to find capital than machinery

270 SIAM IN TRANSITION

Indirect taxes

indirect tax which collects one *stang* a day from every person totals in a year, from eleven million people, about forty million *baht*. Aside from this the government can base its borrowing upon its good name and the national resources, which is a better guarantee than private industry can offer. The government may agree with foreign nations to buy machinery at cheap prices in huge quantities, to be paid for in instalments. Other countries have already used this system to good advantage.

CHAPTER 4

Labour is Wasted Because of Social Parasites

Social parasites retard prosperity

In Siam some people are born social parasites, dependent upon other people for support. They do not engage in any economic enterprise even though they are well able to work. They depend upon others for food, clothing, and shelter. At best they do only a little work. This situation may be seen both in Bangkok and in the provincial centres where great numbers of people are living on the largesse of the middle and the wealthy classes. Aside from being non-producers they force the price of things higher by their very existence. Thus if a hundred people can raise a ton of rice apiece there are a hundred tons produced. But another fifty people who are non-producers help eat the rice. If these fifty helped the hundred raise rice there would be an extra fifty tons of rice. If they are allowed to live as at present, they will become slothful people indeed. By permitting private enterprise to continue and by permitting non-productive people to depend on others for support, we force the economic prosperity of the nation down rather than up. There is no method better than government control of the economic system, because the government can require all people to work and can make social parasites become producers for the good of the nation.

PART V

METHOD BY WHICH THE GOVERNMENT SECURES
LAND, LABOUR AND CAPITAL

An important principle to remember is that the government must use legal methods and in addition must depend upon the co-operation of both the poor and the rich to accomplish its aim. The government must not destroy the wealthy class.

CHAPTER I

Securing the Land

At present all land under cultivation is controlled by individuals; all other lands are jungle or undeveloped lands which are not yet cleared. Cultivated land yields a profit hardly equal to running expenses and taxes, or running expenses and interest, as the case may be. This is because 99% of the farmers are in debt and have either mortgaged their land, or given it as security to their creditors. Their creditors, on the other hand, can collect neither the full interest nor the principle. The landowners at Rangsit, for instance, are unable to collect the full rent from those to whom they have leased their lands, and actually pay out more in taxes than they receive. Thus both poor and rich are losing money. Landowners everywhere would be glad to sell, even if they had to lose a part of their principle. Creditors, who have made loans to the farmers, would like to recover their principle. They do not want to continue to hold the land as security, for if the mortgages were to be foreclosed and the land sold at public auction, little could be realized since the market value of the land is at present so low. This state of affairs is the direct result of the government's present policy which permits competitive private enterprise to operate as it will. Taking all these factors into consideration it becomes clear that, if the government were to offer to buy the land at a fair price, the farmers, the landowners, and the creditors would be delighted. For the business of owning or of holding land for security has proved to be a liability rather than an asset. The method to be used in purchasing the land which I am about to suggest is far different from the communistic one of expropriation.

At present landowners receive inadequate returns

Purchasing land

Where Shall the Government Get Money to Buy the Land?

At present the government does not have in its possession sufficient reserve funds to purchase the land, but the government could issue bonds to the landowners to the amount of the value of their land. The per cent of interest on the bonds would be determined by the government in accordance with the rates of interest prevailing on the day of purchase, not to exceed the maximum legal rate of fifteen per cent. Suppose a piece of land is evaluated at *baht* one thousand: the owner will receive a bond from the government for *baht* one thousand. Suppose that the prevailing

Purchase with bonds

rate of interest on the day the bond is issued is seven per cent: the owner will receive *baht* seventy per year on it. This interest, assured as it is by the government, would be more dependable and certain than hypothetical profits to be derived from the land. Instead of holding a document showing how much land he owns, the individual concerned would hold a bond showing how much money the government owed him.

Kind of Land to be Purchased

<small>Land not to be purchased</small>

The type of land which the government would wish to buy back would include all productive areas such as fields and gardens. There would be no need to buy residential sections unless the owners wished to exchange their property for government bonds. When the amount of land used for residences is compared to the amount used in agriculture, it is evident at once that the amount needed for residences is so small a part of the total arable land that it will not in any way interfere with a programme of economic advancement and expansion. So the residential sections may well be allowed to remain in *status quo*.

When the aforementioned arable land has reverted to the possession of the government, the government can determine how it is to be sub-divided and used in various economic projects. Further, the government can indicate in detail what kind of machinery and how much is to be used. It can plan a complete system of irrigation. Under the present policy each landowner works out a system of irrigation as best he can. When the government controls the land a better co-ordinated and cheaper system can be created. Fewer pipes and drains will be necessary. In the same way ploughing and cultivating can be planned as units. The scattered individualistic methods used at present waste time and effort. Technical methods for enriching the land can be worked out by the government, too, and the ancient formulae of the peasants discarded. The present method which relies upon the constant teaching of the peasants by agricultural experts is too slow. But if the government takes charge a great deal can be accomplished immediately, for peasants who are government employees will have to obey their superiors.

Love of Land

<small>Love self or love race</small>

Among scholars who advocate economic systems based on private enterprise, it is axiomatic that love of land vanishes simultaneously with the transfer of ownership from individuals to government. This idea is actively inculcated into the citizens of those nations which fear that successful communal enterprise will spell the overthrow of the present system of government. It is also asserted that the consequence of loss of ownership is, after loss of love for the land, a cessation of interest in land improvement. Now those who so asseverate seem to do so with their eyes shut. The process of causing the people to regard their land as a part of themselves, in the language of philosophy, finds its basis in the principle of *egoism,* the ethical theory that self-interest or self-development is the end of moral action. It is, therefore, the exact opposite of nationalism which rests on the principle of *altruism* (regard for and devotion to the interests of others). We hear a great deal from some people about nationalism, or love of race. Is it not obvious that love of self and love of personal possessions is diametrically opposed to this declared love of race? Personally I doubt the sincerity of people who claim to embrace the theory of nationalism, but who travel about advocating what amounts to egoism. At heart do they truly love their race? That is the question.

I have already pointed out that, in order to maintain the status of the family, the government should not attempt to purchase the homes of the people. This provision disposes of the question of attachment for land, allowing as it does for quite enough ownership of land to satisfy any need for an object of affection. But in this connection, consider for a moment the situation in Bangkok where many people rent the land on which they live, rent a house, or rent a room in some tenement. They obviously have no land to love. And if we accept the maxim that love of race finds its source in love of land, must we believe that these people in Bangkok are devoid of love of race? I hardly think so. As a matter of fact some of our great landowners under any economic plan are concerned primarily for their own holdings. Let the reader look about him carefully to see whether he can determine which class, landowners or non-landowners, loves race the more. I say there is no observable difference between them. The ownership of land is irrelevant to the question of nationalism, or love of race.

In regard to the charge that non-landowners will not improve the land under their care, the contention is ridiculous. When the government buys all the land it is equivalent to saying that all of the citizens are landowners, because they have become shareholders in the great corporation which is the government. As a matter of fact a corporation usually improves its property more zealously than the individual owner does. We have in Siam government employees who are expert agriculturists and whose duty it is to direct the development of the land. When the land reverts to the government these experts with their special education, skill, and ability will supervise all such development. In my opinion it is idle criticism of our staff of agricultural experts to say that the land will not be developed actively once private ownership ceases.

On the contrary, as I see it, the exact opposite will occur, the land will be improved with irrigation, better grades of seed will be used for planting, the correct fertilizers will be employed. Our agricultural experts will have the widest opportunity for the full use of their knowledge. They will not be hampered and limited as they are now by the unwillingness of the people, who shut their eyes and ears to everything new, to adopt the methods which the experts advocate.

People who wish to engage in agriculture, but who have no agricultural land to turn over to the government, will be permitted to volunteer for that branch of the government service. If the department is overcrowded, they will, of course, have to volunteer for some other branch. They will be guaranteed food, clothing, and shelter, in any case. Their poverty will certainly be no greater than it is at present. On the contrary, the likelihood is that, when the government administers the economic system itself, they will be considerably more prosperous.

Or again, returning to our discussion of the question of nationalism and the ownership of land, consider for a moment the origin of most of the government employees of today. In the beginning almost all of them came from families which were engaged in agriculture. They left their fields and their lands when they accepted government service in Bangkok or one of the provincial towns. Can we say that people who left their land to serve their nation love their race less than those who stayed on the land to raise rice? If that were the case they should never have left their fields at all; but I do not believe that it is.

Beware of deception

Insofar as I have studied the argument of people who contend for the private ownership of land, I have found their basic premise to have been derived from a belief in the principle of private enterprise. They add other reasons, of course, to strengthen their point, reasons designed to appeal to the selfish and acquisitive nature of man, and thus comparable to indirect bribery. As for those government officials who become palsied at the idea of the people leaving their fields and flocking to work in industrial centres, they seem to be afraid that, if the people live together in populated centres, they will discover the inefficiency of these officials. Or perhaps they are overcome with the fear that they will be unable to guarantee the economic welfare of the people and as a result of the ensuing debacle will lose their own choice positions. All such fears contribute to the retardation of prosperity. For the people of these various categories make it their business to convince others, who are easily won by specious arguments since they have never studied the question or the validity of the reasoning, and these too in their turn join the procession.

CHAPTER 2

Finding Employment

It is the nature of the Siamese people to like to work for the government, that is to desire to exchange their services for a regular government salary. This characteristic is obvious to everyone. And yet the very persons who argue against government administration of the nation's industries are for the most part officials. They seem blind to the fact that they themselves are government employees at the very time that they are opposing the granting of this status to other people who presumably share their desire to work for the government. The reader is asked to beware of their arguments. Embarrass them with this simple question: "Are you in government employ? If so, why do you oppose the granting of the same status to others?" Some officials oppose the granting of the same status to the people

Since, then, it is the nature of the Siamese people, as has been said, to prefer government service, there will be no difficulty in enlisting the entire nation as government employees. But this does not mean that such employees will merely sit at desks keeping books and giving orders. All economic projects under government control will be called government service. The people as government employees

The government will next decree that all persons between the ages of eighteen and fifty-five are to be employed in various projects according to their education, strength, and abilities. Beyond the age of fifty-five they will be eligible for pensions for the rest of their lives. Before the age of eighteen they will be expected to attend school and do such light work as they are able. All employees will be entitled to receive salaries from the government or the co-operative Work according to strength and ability societies. These salaries will necessarily vary according to education, strength, and abilities; in order that all employees may be encouraged to develop and use their abilities to the utmost. But however that may be, the minimum salary will be adequate for the purchase of the necessities of life such as food, clothing, shelter, etc.

Question: Will the government compel all people to become government employees?

Exceptional citizens need not enter government employ

Answer: It will not be necessary for the government to compel everyone to become a government employee. There will probably be exceptions made for well-to-do people and others who object to entering government employ, preferring to earn an independent living; provided, of course, they can prove their ability to so do even in sickness and old age as well as to assure their children of proper education and support. Everyone else must enter government service, because such service is equivalent to accumulating reserve funds for the eventualities of sickness and old age.

Question: When the government administers the whole economic system, how can people engage in private enterprise?

Independent professions

Answer: The administration of the economic system is to be constituted in such a way that individuals can successfully engage in certain types of private enterprise, as, for instance, the independent professions of author, doctor, lawyer, special teacher, etc. When any person wishes to engage in such private professions as these, he will be able to secure permission to do so. Again, in the case of factories already operating under private ownership, permission will be granted to continue to do so, if the owners do not wish to enter government service. If they do prefer to enter government service, they can exchange their properties for interest-bearing bonds issued by the government, the interest from which will yield them a living. Or again, persons engaged in certain types of trade and agriculture may be granted permission to engage in private enterprise when it has been shown that they can support themselves satisfactorily.

Results from this plan

No unfortunate results are to be anticipated from having the majority of the people become government employees. On the contrary the results may be expected to be excellent: the potentialities of the people for productive labour will be fully and efficiently employed. After deducting regular holidays the people as a whole will be provided with work for the entire year. The fact that at present the farmers are idle six months of every year need worry us no longer

APPENDIX III

for they will all have full-time employment. The government will provide extra work for the period that is wasted under the present system. Thus, when the field work is done, there will be work of other kinds such as gardening, road building, etc., as the national economic plan indicates. In addition, when all of the people are in government employ, the government can require them to study the arts and crafts in their spare time, or can drill them as soldiers, thus lessening the time they must normally spend as conscripts in the army.

CHAPTER 3
The Raising of Capital

The government will need two kinds of capital for administering the economic system:

1. Capital to be invested in machinery and manufactured products which the government cannot as yet produce.
2. Capital for the payment of wages.

This second kind of capital will be used in workmen's compensation, and will be constantly in circulation. Thus those who receive wages will use their wages to buy food, clothing, and shelter from the government. If the amount of money required is estimated correctly, debits and credits will balance very closely. The amount of credit balance in favour of government employees will have to be provided in cash by the government. But as I have already said, if the government were to establish a national bank, government employees would bring their money to the bank for deposit. That is, the people would become the creditors of the government to the amount deposited. There would be no need for them to carry their money on their persons where it might very easily be lost. *[Circulation of money]*

Question: How does the government propose to raise the two kinds of capital required?

Answer: Siamese scholars who lean toward the social philosophy of communism advocate the expropriation of the wealth of the people to provide the necessary capital. Personally I am opposed to the expropriation of property, believing, as I do, that the government can secure the needed capital in other ways, such as:

(1) Through the collection of such taxes as inheritance taxes, income taxes, or indirect taxes which take only an infinitesimal sum per day from each citizen. In a year, however, these small sums amount to a great deal. Thus a tax which draws one *stang* a day from each of eleven million people produces in a year the huge sum of *baht* *[Indirect taxation]*

forty million. The salt tax is a case in point. The government buys salt from the salt farmers at the current price, and then sells it to the people at a slightly higher price. Other indirect taxes are the sugar tax, tobacco tax, match tax, etc.

Lotteries

(2) Through lotteries. Although lotteries are a form of gambling, I feel that they have no moral implications. It is true that purchasers of tickets must depend upon luck, but the amount risked is too small to be important.

Borrowing money

(3) Borrowing within the country. Internal loans can in all probability be raised by co-operating with the wealthy class. Such loans may be in the form of notes for the amount involved or bonds secured by specific government-owned factories. For instance, if the government were building a sugar mill to the value of *baht* one million, the government could issue bonds to that amount, which would yield the buyers interest, as specified, from the profits of the company. Or it may be possible to float loans abroad; although money derived from such loans should be used only for the purchase of machinery and other manufactured products which cannot be produced here, and should not be spent within Siam.

(4) Or, if the government cannot float loans abroad, it may be able to arrange to buy machinery abroad on the instalment plan, as other nations have been able to do.

Securing credit

Siam should purchase such foreign products from the companies of friendly nations such as England and France, unless, of course, they are unwilling to sell on the instalment plan, or unless their prices are too high. Or perhaps the government could finance the erection of branches of foreign companies here in Siam for the manufacturing of the required products, holding the physical plant and profits as security against the loans to the companies. Some such methods as these can certainly be employed, since it is well known that the markets of the world are flooded with modern machinery, which the companies manufacturing it are anxious to sell even if they must sell on credit.

Part VI

BALANCING THE GOVERNMENT'S BUDGET

When we speak of government administration of the entire economic system, which entails regular monthly wages for all citizens, the questions which naturally arise in the mind of the reader are: whether the budget can be balanced; whether the government will be forced into bankruptcy; and whether the value of the currency will be depreciated by inflation.

CHAPTER 1
Balancing the Budget within the Nation

I have already said that the wages of the people are to be debited for the amounts spent on the necessities of life purchased from the government. That means that the government will have to provide these necessities in abundance, in order that the people in turn may purchase them from the government. If month by month and year by year the people save their money, they save it in order to spend it in the future for things which they still must buy from the government. So the balance of the financial system of the country is assured. It would also be possible, though undesirable, to fix the prices of goods offered for sale. Instead, however, the government should provide more things which the people will want to buy. The system of compensation

The needs of mankind differ. The more man prospers, and the more extensive his contacts with others of his kind, the more he feels that he must possess. Professor Charles Gide teaches that to say a people have advanced is merely to say that their wants have multiplied. (The Teaching of the Science of Economics: Vol. I, page 49.) Thus primitive people need little more than a cloth to protect parts of the body. As they become more civilized they desire clothes that cover the entire body. So, as the Siamese people prosper, their needs will multiply. In the matter of clothing they will demand more and better materials, such as silks. They will want better homes and more and finer personal effects. In the matter of communications, they will want automobiles, and roads on which they can travel long distances even to foreign countries. They will want better opportunities for recreation, theatres, and sports especially. When the government supplies all of these things, the wages paid the people will return to the government as considerations for them, and will re-establish the internal balance of the financial system. The needs of man

Manufacturing the necessities of life

CHAPTER 2
The Balance of Foreign Trade

The government will inevitably have to contract debts abroad to finance purchases of machinery and other manufactured products which cannot be produced here. Where, Surplus production

280   SIAM IN TRANSITION

then, is the money to come from to repay such debts? In the first place every effort should be made to increase the production of native products so that there will be a surplus, beyond what is required for internal consumption, which can be exported for sale abroad. Money derived from this source can be applied on the debts. In this category are rice, teak, ore, and other similar products.

<small>Unnecessary imports</small>

Even under the present system of private enterprise Siam has a foreign trade of about *baht* 134 millions. This trade is in products produced in quantities which exceed the needs of internal consumption. But Siam imports many things besides machinery. For instance we import food,

<small>Only necessities to be imported</small>

sugar, cloth, etc. If the government were to produce all articles now imported which could be manufactured here—and that would mean a very large share of present importations—the money derived from our foreign trade of *baht* 134 millions could be applied on purchases of machinery which we cannot yet produce. Whenever this is possible we shall see how rapidly the nation can progress. Another advantage from government control of foreign trade will be that the potentialities of the people for productive labour, at present only partially employed, can be used by the government to increase the volume of such exports. The nation will then be able to import even more of those goods such as machinery which it requires. And so progress will be secured without incurring an adverse balance in our foreign trade.

PART VI: Continued

THE ADMINISTRATION MUST NOT REDUCE MANKIND
TO THE LEVEL OF ANIMALS

Readers with a preconceived antipathy for this policy may conclude immediately that, when the government controls the whole economic system, the people will be reduced to the level of animals: i.e., women will become common property; family life will be destroyed; interest in progress will cease, etc. This type of criticism is ill-grounded.

<small>Government employees shall be similar to government officials</small>

It is true that I have said that all the people are to become government employees with the same privileges and perquisites which officials now enjoy; salaries in exchange for their labour, and pensions for their old age. I have taken care that none of the provisions of this plan shall reduce man to the level of the beasts. I want man to be more of a man than he is at present, harassed by the worries and anxieties implicit in the competitive system of private enterprise. I reverence the family. I do not make women common property. I honour very deeply the ties of kinship which exist between grandfathers and grandmothers, fathers and mothers, and their descendants. The marriage laws will not be repealed. The people are to continue to have their own homes, the only difference being that the homes will be better homes. I believe that the people will strive to advance the wheels of progress as the government officials do today. If it were true that the mere fact of employment by the government destroyed initiative, why would present day government officials strive with all their might for the sake of national progress as they do? *Family life*

There are some who declare that the enactment of this policy will mean the end of scientific research. This certainly is adverse criticism in an exaggerated form. Scientists will be encouraged to continue their programmes of research by rewards offered by the government. Their inventions will continue to be purchased by the government as they are today. So please do not go around saying that after this policy is in force there will be nothing left for man to do except to live in a hole and eat his rice out of the frying pan. If you will ask critics who make remarks of this sort what books they have been reading to get such ideas as these, and will then let me know, I shall consider it an act of kindness. *Scientific research*

Part VII

THE ESTABLISHMENT OF CO-OPERATIVE SOCIETIES

In the administration of the whole economic system it is obviously impossible for the central government to oversee and direct every individual project. Siam is a great nation with a population of more than eleven millions of people. It thus will be necessary to subdivide the administration of the economic system into units or co-operative societies. *Central government cannot oversee all details*

Each co-operative society will accept members who will be entitled to receive monthly wages according to the established wage scale, in return for which they will be expected to work for the society to the best of their ability. If they are incapacitated by illness, old age, or physical disfigurement, they will be entitled to pensions. *Society members to receive salaries*

The co-operative societies will administer the units of the national economic plan. Thus the agricultural societies will be responsible for farming and gardening, cattle raising, etc. They will also be expected to undertake certain other definite projects such as the building of roads, erection of houses and other buildings needed by the society, etc. Besides their regular salaries, members of the co-operative societies will be entitled to bonuses from the profits of the societies. The societies to be set up under this plan are thus very different from the present co-operative societies for membership in which the ownership of land is a prerequisite. The farmers who rent their fields, and they are in the majority, cannot secure membership in them.

<small>Bonuses</small>

The number of members to be received by any one society and the boundaries of its activities will be determined by the nature of the society itself. Thus an industrial association will probably have as members only persons engaged in a certain trade. The size of the society will be determined by the size of the trade. The size of an agricultural society will probably be determined largely by the boundaries of the land to be worked, and the number of people needed to work it scientifically.

<small>Co-operative effort</small>

The members of the co-operative societies will be expected to unite to accomplish their share of the sum total of economic endeavour, as follows:

1. The government will supply land and capital. The members of the society will supply the labour and assume responsibility for production.

2. The members of the societies are to assume responsibility for the merchandising and distribution of the products which they produce, under the guidance and direction of the central government.

3. The societies are to assume the responsibility of providing food and drink to their members. That is the society will undertake to sell food, drink, wearing apparel, and other necessities to its members, but will not be responsible for preparing such food as is sold. Its responsibility will cease with the distribution of uncooked food to its members such as rice, raw meat, etc., which the members will be expected to prepare for themselves according to their own tastes. But if the members so desire, a society may arrange to prepare all food which is to be sold to its members.

4. The societies will be responsible for the erection of homes for the members under the supervision of the government. Each member-family shall have its own home, built according to the society's plans, and designed to safeguard health, to provide adequate protection from danger, and to make for ease in administration.

APPENDIX III

When the people have been organized into co-operative societies, it will be easy to initiate the municipal form of administration and to arrange for an effective public health service. For instance, a society will wish to secure a doctor, who will draw up health regulations. Group education will be facilitated by the fact that the members live close together. After the day's work is over the society can, if it wishes, require its members to study in order to improve their knowledge. The subject matter of such study may be books, lectures, or moving pictures. The suppression of thieves and robbers will also be facilitated. The military can co-operate with the societies for the training of the citizenry before they reach the conscription age; or may train reserves who are outside the ordinary provisions of the conscription requirements. Military training would thus be facilitated, as would possible later conscription.

<small>Municipalities, public health, education, military service</small>

Part VIII

WHAT LINES OF ECONOMIC ENDEAVOUR SHALL THE GOVERNMENT UNDERTAKE

The fundamental aim of the government should be the administration of all kinds of agricultural and industrial enterprises with a view to rendering this country entirely independent of all foreign nations. This should be done to protect the country from dangers arising from trade restrictions of various sorts. When we are entirely self-sufficient, trade restrictions and embargoes will not unduly disturb us. Adam Smith, who has many devoted if erring followers, taught that the work of the world should be divided up among the nations, each nation becoming a specialist in one thing. An agricultural nation, according to his philosophy, should engage only in agriculture and never in industry. This theory would be excellent in a world where nations were absolutely honorable in their treatment of each other, and did not erect trade barriers or artificially lower prices. But at present this is hardly the case. We should rather proceed along lines laid down by the German economist, List, who taught that Germany must make herself completely self-sufficient: to be specific, must develop a complete system of agriculture, industry, and crafts so that, in the event of international conflict, Germany would be in a position to ensure her own prosperity and advancement. By following this policy closely, the German government was able to attain remarkable results, especially

<small>Safeguarding the country against trade restrictions</small>

<small>Opinions of a German economist</small>

in such undertakings as the railroads. And at the present time Germany is firmly convinced that her welfare depends upon the successful administration of the economic system by the government. That is why Hitler has been given the key position in that government. He is a strong believer in the theory that the government should exercise complete control of the economic system. In England the head of the government is MacDonald, and in France Daladier. What theory of government these men hold is well known. They are both believers, at least to some extent, in the system of co-operation between government and citizens in the field of economics, and in social assurance.

Hitler, MacDonald, Daladier

PART IX

THE SOLUTION OF THE CAPITAL AND LABOUR QUESTION

If Siam continues to allow private ownership of manufacturing plants, the advocates of the system should know that it inevitably entails industrial conflict. Siamese who have studied in Europe are well aware of the fact that the industrial situation there with its quarrels and hatreds between employer and employee has often resulted in lockouts on the one side, or strikes on the other, because of disagreement over wages, or hours of work, or vacations, or insurance. And further that the cause of this discord was the system of private ownership. Even though Siam is a small nation with few industrial plants, we have seen the beginnings of these problems. For example, there was the case of the tramcar men. The more a nation prospers, the more factories there are. And when industry is fully developed here you will see how extensive will be the discord even in Siam. But when the government administers the entire economic system it will not matter whether the people are labourers or other kinds of government employees. For whichever they are they will be equitably rewarded for their services on a basis of achievement. In a very real sense the government will be the representative of the people, which is the same thing as saying that the people themselves will own everything in the nation. When the profits of their joint enterprise are greatly multiplied, labourers and other government employees will share this prosperity equally. The government will have no reason to reserve the larger share of the profits for any special class, for there will be no special class. How different this is from the system of private enterprise in which the owners of industrial plants attempt to retain the bulk of

Private ownership creates discord

Competition for profits in private enterprise

APPENDIX III

the profits for themselves and in so doing often oppress the workers whose labours produce the profits.

It is true that there are some who claim that, when the government administers the economic system, there will be nothing but deficits. They attempt to prove their point by citing prejudicial examples from other countries. Thus in a certain country where the organization of labour was faulty, the workers did not produce their full quota. The deficit caused by this situation could not possibly be attributed to government control of the economic system. Even in privately operated industry the same sort of deficit would result from a lack of organization, or from faulty organization of labour. Essentially the cure is not to be found either in government or in private control, but in efficient management of the factories and adequate supervision of the labourers. A further point in favour of government administration of the entire economic system is that the government is assured of profits by the fact that it can utilize what are now only latent abilities for work; can conserve the expenditure of labour; and can multiply its efficiency by employing proper machinery. That being the case, how can government control result in a deficit?

Profits from government control

Part X
NATIONAL ECONOMIC PLAN

In order that the administration of the economic system should be both well-regulated and beneficial the government ought to promulgate a national economic plan. The promulgation of such a plan presupposes the preparation of careful estimates and the close examination of such elements as those mentioned below, on which any economic plan must rest.

1. It will be necessary to investigate carefully and prepare estimates of the necessities of life required by the average citizen of a civilized nation in order to assure him a happy and prosperous existence. Estimates should not be so low as to leave the people in a state of poverty. Thus in the case of food the estimates should give the approximate quantities needed, for a specified period, of rice, meat, salt, vegetables, fruit, sugar, etc., for an average citizen who is accustomed to living well. In the same way with regard to clothing: the estimates should specify how much in the way of wearing apparel the average citizen will require, inclusive of cotton cloth and silk for clothing, hats, shoes, suits, stockings, etc. In the matter of housing, every family

The example of civilized nations

should be provided with a separate home, which is neither a hut nor a shack, but a proper residence such as a substantial brick building, in which an ordinary citizen can live comfortably. We must endeavour to change from the jungle type of home, which is still the accepted type in the remoter parts of Africa, to well-constructed buildings comparable to homes found in civilized countries.

Plans for a complete system of transportation should include details of the future construction of railroad lines and motor roads, which will serve to facilitate the inter-relations of the people. Every co-operative society centre and every district in the kingdom should be linked together by a co-ordinated system. Canals and docks should be projected to improve communications by water. Airlines should also be extended over the whole kingdom. Each individual family or each co-operative society should be provided with vehicles, such as automobiles, so that the *pro rata* distribution of vehicles amongst the Siamese shall be comparable to that among the people of civilized nations.

2. When these various estimates and investigations have been completed, further estimates will be necessary to determine how much land, labour, and capital will be necessary to produce them. Thus in the cultivation of sufficient rice to feed eleven million people, let us suppose that 2931 millions of kilogrammes are necessary. Let us suppose further that the growing of this amount of rice will require 15 million *rai* of land, and definite amounts of labour varying according to whether men and animals are used, or men and machines. Thus if one man can plough ½ *rai* per day by using animals, the ploughing will require 30 million units of labour, on the basis that a unit equals a day's work for an average man. But if two men, using a mechanical plough, plough forty *rai* per day, the number of work days required will be only 750,000. The efficiency of a single labourer is thus greatly increased.

Suppose then, that for the harrowing and sowing without machinery 15 million units of labour are required. If machinery is used that amount is reduced to 750,000 days. (Estimated roughly from the above example.)

Harvesting by man power normally requires 30 million units of labour. If the fields can be levelled and drained so that harvesting machines can be employed, this figure will be cut to 750,000 days.

Transportation of the harvest into barns, which ordinarily requires 15 million labour units, will require only 750,000 if machinery is used.

To sum up, the expenditure of labour counted by units or days required for the task of raising the amount of rice mentioned above would be:

a. 90 million labour units, if the work was to be done by labourers working with animals.

b. 32,250,000 labour units, if machinery was to be used in ploughing, harrowing, sowing, and transporting, but not in harvesting.

c. 3 million labour units, if machinery was to be used in every department of the work. But in this case the amount of capital needed would be greatly increased because machinery and oil would have to be purchased. If the ploughing of 15 million *rai* of land requires 5,000 mechanical ploughs at *baht* 3,000 per plough, the amount of the initial investment would be 15 million *baht,* which the government would have to pay in instalments. Additional capital would be needed for the purchase of oil, unless, of course, it was to be invested in drilling oil wells and building refineries here in Siam. Or possibly some other crude fuel could be found.

3. When all the estimates as discussed above have been prepared, it will be necessary to make further estimates of the land, labour, and capital now available to the government either potentially or actually as a basis for the proposed economic system.

First, our country has over 320 million *rai* of land, of which 18 million is already under cultivation. Questions which naturally arise in this connection are: Is the remainder suitable for crops? Is it suitable for orchards? Could some of it be used profitably for national forests? What mineral resources are there available?

Second, the amount of available labour will have to be carefully estimated. Thus in our population of eleven million persons, suppose that five millions are under or over the age limit. This leaves six millions who can work eight hours a day, 280 days a year, 85 days being set aside for holidays. A total of 1,680 million days of work is possible. In preparing the estimates it will, of course, be desirable to divide the potential labour supply into such classifications as those of unskilled labourer, skilled labourer, intellectual worker such as engineer, doctor, teacher, supervisor, and government official, and to give the approximate number available in each classification.

Third, the amount of capital available will have to be estimated so that the government can know its potential strength in this particular. Questions to be decided in this connection are: How much can be borrowed from the wealthy? And how much can be collected in indirect taxes without making such taxes unduly oppressive?

When all these estimates have been completed, we will be in a position to know how much land, labour, and capital are available; how much additional capital will have to be secured; how much undeveloped land can be utilized; and how best to divide the economic system in co-operative societies. Finally, from all this data an estimate can be made of the time required to lift the economic level of the people to a higher plane on which their welfare and prosperity will be assured. The amount of progress toward this goal possible in a single year can then be determined.

Inaugurate it a section at a time

Finally we can decide in what section of the country to inaugurate the national economic plan, and also what particular economic project is to be the initial one. And so starting in this comparatively modest manner we can gradually extend the plan until it embraces the entire country. If in any particular project all available assets are not carefully estimated, it is difficult to achieve the goal, hence the importance of preparing the various data required in a meticulously accurate manner.

Training skilled workers

When the carefully prepared surveys reveal the fact that Siam still lacks certain essential types of skilled labour, we can take steps to supply that lack. It is obvious that we do lack certain classes of specialists. Perhaps at first we will have to hire foreigners to do the necessary work while we are training some of our own people to do it by establishing special training schools.

PART XI

SUCCESSFUL REALIZATION OF THE SIX-POINT PLATFORM

The administration of the economic system of the country by the government through co-operative societies will provide a means for the realization of the other aims embodied in the original platform of the People's Party in a manner far superior to anything possible under the present system of private enterprise.

CHAPTER I

Independence

a. *Independence in the courts.* There is no need to discuss here the body of legislation proposed by the government because at the time of this writing the formulation of these laws is almost completed.

b. *Independence in the field of economics.* When the government assumes all responsibility for the production of the necessities of life such as food, drink, etc., and regulates the fluctuation of prices so that it is no longer possible for individuals to raise and lower them at will, we will have attained some measure of economic independence. We will no longer be persecuted and oppressed by others in the field of economics. But just so long as the system of private enterprise is allowed to continue, just that long will we be unable to get out from under the yoke that lies so heavily upon us.

c. *Independence in politics.* When at last our nation is well furnished with the necessities of life, food, drink, etc., we will then have the weapons necessary to protect ourselves; and can turn our attention to other such important matters as education. We can select and train better teachers. We can give the people more adequate instruction in matters pertaining to health, using for the accomplishment of these aims the same methods employed in administering the economic system. For this type of administration will make it possible to advance along many new lines.

And what foreign nation will care to oppose such a worthy programme of orderly progress as this? At present there is an almost universal fear of foreign intervention, and this fear is a deterrent to all forward looking endeavour. But when we show that we are concerned only to set our own house to rights in accordance with the rights and privileges that are the prerogative of any free nation; when we keep our treaty agreements scrupulously; when we do not discriminate against citizens of foreign nations resident in Siam; when we continue to trade with such nations, buying from them manufactured articles like machinery which we cannot produce ourselves; what nation will care to attempt to tyrannize over us? However, if we are so paralyzed by the fear of illegal foreign intervention, even when we know we are acting within our rights, I suppose we will have to remain supine, attempting nothing new. But, when we recently effected a change in the form of government, did we not at first fear foreign intervention? And our fears proved to be groundless. The nations whom we had feared proved well-intentioned enough. They were members of the League of Nations, like ourselves. And although the League today has many critics who say that it has proved ineffective, the fact remains that it has been able to adjudicate some international disagreements in a manner never before known. Take for example the case of the English oil company and the Persian government. Persia is a country with an area and population not unlike our own. Its state of advancement approximates ours. Why was it then that when the Persian government revoked the leases previously granted to the English company that England did not step in and use force to settle the issue in their favour? I believe that it was because they were honourable enough to bring the case to the court of the League of Nations rather than to resort to a display of arms. When our purpose is not to discriminate against or oppress foreign nationals, but rather to advance the progress of our own nation, what reason is there to believe that foreign countries will try to interfere with us?

CHAPTER 2

Internal Order

I gave a lecture at the Teacher's Association in B.E. 2471 (A.D. 1928) in which I showed that crimes are committed for two reasons:
1. Either because the nature of the criminal predisposes him to crime,
2. Or because economic pressure drives otherwise honest citizens to theft, burglary, armed robbery, etc. Now when the government guarantees the prosperity of its citizens by undertaking to provide them with adequate food, clothing, and shelter, this second type of crime will largely disappear, leaving only such crimes as arise out of the nature of the criminal. The cure for such will have to be found in training and education. Here, too, the economic security of educators and teachers should render their training and teaching more efficacious than before.

CHAPTER 3

Economics

The People's Party announced that the government would undertake to guarantee the economic welfare of the people by providing remunerative employment for everyone, promulgating a national economic plan designed to terminate poverty. This ideal can now be realized and need not any longer be a source of dissatisfaction. At present there is a great deal of misunderstanding concerning it, because the government has not as yet attempted to do anything about it. But this is only because we have failed to advance in accordance with my plan. When my plan has been adopted —whereby the government administers the entire economic system—there will inevitably be remunerative employment for everyone because all of the people will become government employees. And even if they are children, are sick, are crippled, are old, they will receive salary. There will be no more poverty and want because the lowest wage paid by the government will be sufficient to provide food, clothing, and shelter, in accordance with the needs of the people.

CHAPTER 4

Equality of Rights

The plan will bring about the equality of all the people, not a paper equality but actual equality of opportunity by which all can become employees of the government. Regardless of whether they serve in administrative work or as labourers on some economic project, they have equality in their mutual freedom from poverty. Not equality, of course, in the sense that if one person possesses *baht* one hundred when the plan goes into operation, his *baht* one hundred will be expropriated and divided equally among a hundred people. Some of Siam's intelligentsia who advocate the social philosophy of communism believe that we should attempt something of that sort. But personally I hate this communism of Siam's intelligentsia, and have no intention of advocating the expropriation and redistribution of wealth.

CHAPTER 5

Liberty

Persons who examine this policy superficially will claim that, when all the people are employees of a government which administers the entire economic system, there will be less personal freedom than there is now. And it is true, that there will be less freedom of a sort, but the loss in personal liberty will be more than compensated for by the general increase in the happiness and prosperity of the people as a whole, as guaranteed by the third point in the platform of the People's Party. The government will not interfere with personal liberty in any other way. The people will continue to enjoy freedom of speech, of person, of home, of wealth, of education, and of assembly. When the people are secure within the framework of this economic system, they will at last know true physical well-being. Do you think that they will prefer personal liberty secured at the cost of starvation? It seems hardly possible. Under the present system they are certainly not free from the necessity to work. With the exception of those social parasites who derive their sustenance from the labours of others, all the people of this country work, and work hard for a living. Complete personal liberty is not possible under any social system. Such liberty is always limited by the good of society. That is why the programme of the People's Party said specifically that personal liberty was to be defined in terms which did not interfere with the principle of equality set forth in point four of the platform, as previously stated.

CHAPTER 6

Education

The plan provides that the people are to receive the most complete education possible. When a new era of prosperity has come as a result of the new order, the people of this nation will be able to devote themselves to the pursuit of education in a manner not possible while their chief concern had to be for the conservation of their wealth. Even citizens who are between the ages of twenty and fifty-five, adults in other words, can be required under the new order to continue their education. And one of the provisions of this plan is that all employees of the government should be required to study. Anything of the sort would be impossible under the present system of private enterprise.

Conclusion

When the administration of the economic system by the government shall have brought about the final consummation of the aims set forth by the People's Party in their six-point platform, that state of prosperity and felicity which is the laudable desire of every heart and which, in classical language, is called *Sriaraya*[1] will have dawned. Shall we, who have opened the door of opportunity to the people, now hem and haw and fumble and hesitate to lead them on to the place where they can gather the fruits of the tree of life?[2] There at last they will be able to feast on its fruits

[1] Utopia.
[2] Thon Kanlaphaphru'ksa, in Pali Kalpa-vriksha, or one of the five trees found in Swarga or the lower heaven to which mortals may attain.

of happiness and prosperity in fulfillment of the Buddhist prophecy to be found in the story of the religion of Araya Mettaya.[1] According to this prophecy every act of devotion on the part of faithful followers of religion brings that golden age a little nearer. It is a common saying among the people that an oath made in court and honourably kept, in other words true witnessing, brings us closer to the age of Araya Mettaya. Religious ceremonies properly observed and in fact all acts of honesty and integrity likewise bring nearer the dawn of that era. In this plan we have a system by which we can press forward to this golden age. And yet there are some people who hesitate, who draw back so violently that one would suppose they contemplated a return to the age of unenlightenment of 2,475 years ago when Buddha had not yet come.

---

[1] The last Buddha and the one next to come.

B. FIRST DRAFT—SOCIAL INSURANCE ACT

(Assurance Sociale)

By the King's Most Excellent Majesty,

Section 1.—This Act shall be called "The Social Insurance Act of B.E. 2475." [A.D. 1932—*Trans.*]

Section 2.—It shall come into force from the day of publication in the Government Gazette.

Part I

SALARIES AND PENSIONS FOR CITIZENS

Section 3.—From the day that the National Economic Plan is promulgated every Siamese citizen resident in Siam shall be entitled to receive regular income from the government or from one of the co-operative societies in an amount to be determined by law according to the following graduated schedule: [1]

1. Persons less than one year of age, per month .. .. — *Baht*
2. Persons from one to five years of age, per month .. .. — *Baht*
3. Persons from six to ten years of age, per month .. .. — *Baht*
4. Persons from eleven to fifteen years of age, per month .. — *Baht*
5. Persons from sixteen to eighteen years of age, per month .. — *Baht*
6. Persons from eighteen to fifty-five years of age, per month — *Baht*
7. Persons more than fifty-five years of age, per month .. — *Baht*

Section 4.—Citizens with special education, abilities, or powers shall receive higher salaries commensurate with their education, abilities, or powers, and with the type of work to be done, in accordance with the following schedule:[2]

Grade	*Baht*
1	80
2	90
3	100
4	110
5	120
6	130
7	140
8	150
9	160

[1] The minimum schedule shall be adequate for food, clothing, shelter, etc.

[2] This schedule is to replace the recently enacted law by which salaries of officials are determined.

APPENDIX III

Grade (continued)	Baht (continued)
10	170
11	180
12	190
13	200
14	220
15	240
16	260
17	280
18	300
19	320
20	350
21	400
22	450
23	500
24	550
25	600
26	650
27	700
28	800
29	900
30	1,000

Section 5.—In addition to stated salaries, officials and other employees of the government shall be eligible for bonuses from any profits derived from their work, in amounts to be determined by the government or co-operative societies.[3]

Section 6.—Officials and other employees receiving salaries above the minimum schedule shall,[4] upon retirement, receive pensions proportionately higher than those in the minimum schedule established in Section 3.

Section 7.—Salaries, bonuses, and pensions shall be increased when the government and the co-operative societies prosper.[5]

Part II

EMPLOYMENT

Section 8.—All citizens from eighteen to fifty-five years of age shall enter government service, and shall be classified according to education, ability, strength, sex, and age as follows:

[3] Such bonuses are in line with a policy of allowing workers a share in the profits derived from their labours, and are called in France "Participation au benefice."

[4] Salaries of officials and other employees naturally vary according to education and ability. Those who have been receiving higher salaries should also receive higher pensions.

[5] This increase is obviously appropriate. When it becomes apparent that the administration of the economic system by the government has resulted in increased prosperity, salaries, bonuses, and pensions can be increased. Thus a twenty-five per cent increase will mean that a salary of baht 80 becomes baht 100, and a salary of baht 400 becomes baht 500.

1. *Education.*—Educated persons shall be eligible for employment in occupations for which their education has prepared them. If any particular occupation becomes overcrowded, competitive examinations shall be established. Successful candidates in these examinations shall be entitled to available positions in the occupations for which they have applied.

2. *Special abilities.*—Persons with special abilities shall be eligible to the same treatment as that designated in paragraph one for educated persons.

3. *Strength.*—Persons lacking special education or abilities, or those who have been unsuccessful in competitive examinations, shall enter occupations suited to their strength and abilities.

4. *Sex.*—Light work such as that of caretaker, clerk, teacher, children's nurse, or purveyor of food and drink, shall generally be allotted to women except in special cases where it is necessary to employ men. But this provision shall not be construed to interfere with the right of women to compete for other positions for which their education and special abilities have prepared them.

5. *Age.*—Older persons shall have lighter work than younger persons. [By definition "older" means "over fifty" and "younger" means "between twenty-one and thirty-five."—*Trans.*]

Section 9.—Persons between the ages of eleven and eighteen and above the age of fifty-five shall not be required to work except under unusual circumstances as, for instance, when a shortage of labour precipitates an economic emergency. In the event of such an occurrence persons in this group may be conscripted for work commensurable with their strength, but they shall under no circumstances be overworked. Thus, if a shortage of labour arises during the harvest, or if insect pests threaten crops, persons of this group may be drafted temporarily.[6]

Section 10.—Persons in the following categories, whether within the working age limits or not, are exempt from work, and are entitled, with their minor children, to receive salaries as usual:

1. Pregnant women.[7]
2. People in ill health.[7]
3. Cripples.[8]
4. University students and other students of advanced standing who have successfully passed competitive examinations for entrance into the university or other schools of advanced standing.
5. Persons who have been in government service long enough to be entitled to pensions.

[6] Some countries have laws which provide for the compulsory enlistment of citizens in the fight on insects and pests. In our own country occasions may arise in which the available machinery is not adequate to take care of the harvest, and the grain is in danger of being left standing in the fields. On such occasions it might be necessary to enlist the assistance of this category of people insofar as they are able to help.

[7] According to the Social Insurance Act this class of persons shall receive pensions.

[8] This provision is included in order that only skilled and able-bodied persons shall be employed in the crafts and trades.

Section 11.—Persons in the following categories are exempt from government service and are not entitled to salaries for their children as long as they are not employed by the government:[9]

1. Persons who can show proof that they are in the possession of adequate capital or assured income to support themselves.

2. Persons who engage in private professions and who can show proof that their professions yield adequate income for themselves and their dependents, such as: doctors, lawyers, artisans, authors; and in addition persons who have government permits to engage in trade, manufacturing, and certain kinds of agriculture.

PART III

METHOD OF PAYING SALARIES

Section 12.—The government or one of the co-operative societies shall issue salaries to the people in one of the following ways:

1. Salaries shall be issued in the form of cash in the amounts which the recipients are entitled to receive according to the salary schedule.

2. Salaries shall be issued as cheques against the national bank in the amounts to which the recipients are entitled according to the salary schedule after deductions (French: *compensation*) of the sums owed the government or co-operative societies for food, clothing, shelter, and the other necessities of life have been made. The balance, if any, may be deposited with the national bank, or may be used for the purchase of government bonds or co-operative society stocks, or may be withdrawn and spent as the individual concerned desires.

PART IV

FOREIGN GOVERNMENT EMPLOYEES

Section 13.—The government may employ foreign specialists, who shall enjoy those rights and privileges specified in their contracts.

PART V

BEHAVIOUR OF GOVERNMENT EMPLOYEES

Section 14.—All government employees, whether in positions of authority or common labourers, shall be required to work to the limits of their strength and capacity. Indolent persons shall be punished by having their salaries cut, or the hours of their employment increased, or in some other manner to be decided upon as the occasion demands.

Published on the . . . . .B.E. . . . .
being the . . . . . year of the present reign.

---

[9] This exception is made in order that the well-to-do, and others who do not wish to enter government employ, may have an opportunity of making a living in their own way, if they are able to do so.

C. FIRST DRAFT—ECONOMIC ADMINISTRATION ACT

B.E. . . . .

By the King's Most Excellent Majesty,

Section 1.—This act shall be called "The Economic Administration Act of B.E. . . . . . ."

Section 2.—It shall come into force from the day of its publication in the Government Gazette.

Section 3.—From the day that the National Economic Policy is adopted, the government shall be empowered to administer the economic system, to wit all enterprise agricultural or industrial, inclusive of all forms of transportation and distribution, but exclusive of such concessions as the government has previously leased to private companies and individuals. Such lessees shall retain the right of private enterprise; for example, in the cases listed below:

1. Tin mines, timber companies, and public utilities for which the government has previously issued leases or licenses.[1]
2. Privately owned factories, previously established, which shall be permitted to continue to operate under licenses to be issued by the government.
3. Establishments of foreign merchants from countries with which Siam has special treaty arrangements.[2]
4. Other enterprises commercial, industrial, or agricultural for which private companies or individuals have received specific permits[3] or licenses; when it has been demonstrated in a manner satisfactory to the government that these independent businesses are capable of affording an adequate livelihood, and do not violate other acts of the government which relate to the National Economic Policy.

Part I
PURCHASE OF LAND [4]

Section 4.—The government shall be empowered to buy all lands except those required for private dwellings and those which have been granted or leased to citizens for use in private enterprises.

[1] This provision is included in order not to summarily undermine the means of livelihood of private individuals.
[2] This provision is included in order not to be unduly oppressive to the business enterprises of foreigners.
[3] In order to allow persons who are not desirous of becoming government employees a means of livelihood.
[4] The condemnation of land already exists in the case of railroads, motor roads, etc., which constitute public benefits. In this law we construe the administration of the economic order by the government to constitute a like public benefit; inasmuch as the failure of the government to so undertake will be inimical to the best interests of its citizens.

APPENDIX III

All unoccupied or undeveloped areas for which there exists at present neither claimants nor deeds shall cease to be available except through leases issued by the government.

Section 5.—The value of the land shall be determined by a committee of three persons, one of whom shall be appointed by the landowner, one by the government, and the third, who shall have the deciding vote, by the two others conjointly. The price of the land shall in no case exceed its assessed value as of June 24th, 1932.

Section 6.—Payment for the land shall be made to the owner, according to the amount so determined, either in cash or in bonds. In the event that payment is made in bonds, the rate of interest to be paid on such notes shall be at the prevailing bank rate on the day of sale; but shall in no case exceed fifteen per cent, the maximum legal rate.

The holder of such a note shall in addition have the right to receive a dividend from the profits of the co-operative society which derives its income from his land, in amounts to be determined by the government.

Part II

CAPITAL FUNDS AND CREDIT

Section 7.—The government shall establish a capital fund and credit from the following sources:

1. Inheritance taxes.[5]
2. Income taxes.
3. Indirect taxes on tobacco,[6] matches,[6] salt,[7] etc.
4. Registration fees to be collected in return for personal licenses issued to

---

[5] The collection of inheritance taxes is not inspired by jealousy of the rich. It is justified by the fact that the rich have accumulated their fortunes through the combined efforts of many people from whose labours profits have accrued to them either directly or indirectly. The collection of inheritance taxes should be made proportionate to the size of the estate, very large estates paying a super-tax, and smaller estates paying less. Such a distinction is desirable in order that inheritance taxes shall not be unduly oppressive to any of the propertied class.

[6] A tax on tobacco and matches enabled France to pay off her 1870 indemnity to Germany expeditiously, with the result that the standing and value of the franc rose. Now suppose that in our own country one million people smoke, and suppose that we collect a one *stang* tax per day per person—a tax so light as to be hardly felt—we should increase our yearly income by three million *baht*. But the establishment of the monopoly, which would be a prerequisite for the collection of such a tax, would involve some adjustment of our treaties with other countries. It might be simpler, therefore, to collect a tax on shops selling tobacco and on factories preparing it for sale, being careful not to cripple the trade in the home-grown product, which must meet competition from imported tobaccos.

[7] It should be possible to collect an indirect tax on salt by some such measure as having the government purchase the salt from the salt farmers at a stipulated price for re-sale either direct or through a dealer who is guaranteed a monopoly. Suppose that by so doing the government collects one-tenth of one *stang* per day from each citizen; the yearly total would exceed three million *baht*.

gamblers who wish to continue to play.⁸ They shall be required to pay the fee in instalments on a scale graded according to the type of gambling in which they desire to indulge. It shall be illegal to register and license persons who have not yet learned to gamble at the time that this Act is promulgated.

In addition to the fee for a license, a permit to play shall be required in each instance in which there is to be gambling.

5. Bond issues floated within the country, which well-to-do people would purchase.⁹ The government would secure such bonds either with its factories or specie reserves.

6. Lotteries.¹⁰

7. Loans from the national bank.¹¹

8. Loans from foreign nations.

9. Credit from foreign companies willing to sell their products to us on the instalment plan.

---

⁸ The most persistent efforts to prevent people who are accustomed to gambling from so doing are doomed to be futile, inasmuch as such persons will, if necessary, contrive some means of playing in secret. That being the case, effort should be concentrated on developing some system whereby the next generation will be prevented from learning to play. Experienced gamblers should be allowed to continue to play, but should be required to register in much the same way as opium smokers are required to do at present. The fee for such registration could be collected in instalments of, say, one *baht* each; in a year four such instalments. Suppose that there are one million gamblers in this country, in a year the amount which they would pay for fees would amount to approximately four million *baht*. An additional tax could be collected for permits to be issued on each occasion when there was to be gambling. In every Tambol there are, on an average, at least two games a day. There are 5,000 Tambols in Siam. Thus there would be 10,000 permits issued daily. If a permit costs five *baht*, the daily income from this source would be 50,000 *baht*. The yearly total would be about 18,000,000 *baht*. The hours in which gambling is to be permitted should be revised in order not to interfere with the working day. The original schedule permitted gambling from noon to 2 a.m., but this is not practicable. Rightly the time in which gambling is to be permitted should be limited to the hours between 16 and 22 o'clock. [4 p.m. to 10 p.m.—*Trans.*] Outside of this time gambling should be prohibited to prevent waste of time and energy.

⁹ The intent of this provision is to conserve the resources of the wealthy and not to destroy the propertied class.

¹⁰ Although a lottery is a form of gambling, since it depends upon luck, the gambler risks little. If there were thirty lotteries a year with tickets issued in each to the amount of one million *baht*, the share reserved for the government would amount to many millions. Some thin-skinned Siamese are afraid that, if we establish state lotteries, we shall be accused of encouraging our citizens to gamble. But let us examine the French system of national credit. When France needed capital to rebuild cities destroyed in the World War, she floated loans secured by proceeds to be derived from lotteries. In England horse racing is very popular, and gambling on the horses yields a large income to the government by way of tax. We have no desire here in Siam to go to such extremes. We wish only to hold state lotteries in which people risk a little with the hope of receiving much.

¹¹ The national bank should be of substantial assistance to the government because money in the provincial treasuries, largely taxes derived from duties and royalties, would be put into circulation through it. The residue of salaries deposited by government employees in the branch banks would likewise pass into circulation. In addition there are other ways by which the government could borrow from the national bank.

Part III

NATIONAL BANK

Section 8.—The government shall establish a national bank, the original capital to be supplied from government reserves and money loaned by private citizens. The national bank shall transact business in the same manner as any other bank. It shall have the authority to issue bank notes, and for this purpose the Currency Department of the Ministry of Finance shall be transferred to it. The various provincial treasuries shall become branches of the national bank.

Section 9.—It shall be the duty of the national bank, according to its resources, to lend the government money as need arises.

Part IV

NATIONAL ECONOMIC POLICY [12]

Section 10.—A council shall be created with authority to draw up a national economic policy by which all productive activity shall be divided into several major departments as follows: agriculture, industry, distribution (transportation, commerce, and communication) and the building trades (to build houses for all the people of this nation). These large fields of endeavour shall be further sub-divided into diversified co-operative societies.

Section 11.—The National Economic Policy shall establish objectives defining what it is estimated can be accomplished by the government year by year; and shall provide for weekly bulletins designed to keep the citizens informed of progress.

Section 12.—After the National Economic Policy has come into force, if need arises for revision either because the government cannot secure adequate capital or labour, or because the government has an over-supply of capital and labour, the National Economic Council shall be empowered to convene and to make such revision as is necessary. Such revisions shall consequently be published to the people at large.

Section 13.—Whenever the National Economic Policy is to be introduced into any particular section of the country it shall come into effect clause by clause with adequate explanation of its implications to land, capital, and the duties of government officials, skilled labourers, common labourers, and experts.

Part V

RIGHTS AND PRIVILEGES OF CITIZENS

Section 14.—Every citizen shall be entitled to retain his right to all personal property which he has accumulated.

[12] Furthermore our system of government will have to be adjusted to co-ordinate with the National Economic Policy.

Section 15.—Inventors of articles having commercial value shall be entitled to patents on such articles (French: Brevet d'Invention). The inventor may secure a license to manufacture his own invention, may sell it to the government, or may manufacture it in partnership with the government.

Published on the . . . .

D. MINUTES OF A MEETING OF A COMMITTEE TO CONSIDER A NATIONAL ECONOMIC POLICY AT PARUSKAVAN PALACE

MARCH 12TH, 1933

MEMBERS ATTENDING

Luang Gahakarm Bodi [Secretary of the People's Assembly]
Luang Dej Sahakorn [Member of People's Assembly]
Luang Dejātiwongs Vararatana [Member of People's Assembly]
Phya Song Suradej [Member of the State Council]
Nai Thavi Bunyaketu [Member of People's Assembly]
Nai Nab Baholyodhin [Member of State Council]
Luang Pradist Manudharm [Member of State Council]
Nai Prayoon Pamon Montri [Member of State Council]
Phya Manopakorn Nitithada [President of the State Council]
Phya Rajawangsan [Minister of Defence and member of State Council]
Nai Vilas Osathanond [Member of People's Assembly]
Phya Srivisar Vacha [Minister of Foreign Affairs and member of State Council]
H.S.H. Prince Sakol Varavarn [Adviser to Ministry of Interior]
Luang Arthasarn Prasiddhi [Member of People's Assembly]

Luang Pradist Manudharm: Luang Pradist opened the meeting with the following statement: Before we take up the discussion here, let me say that the original revolutionary party held a special meeting in which this policy was considered. It was then forwarded to the State Council for its consideration. The State Council appointed this committee to make a recommendation regarding the proposed policy. It is possible that the discussion here tonight may become heated. But since strong language is excusable when it is spontaneous it will be so considered here. The topic for discussion is related to the original six-point platform of the People's Party, and in particular to point three of that platform, which has three sub-headings dealing with the promotion of the economic welfare of the people: i.e. (1) that we shall not allow the people to want; (2) shall provide remunerative employment for everyone; (3) and shall establish a national economic policy to guarantee that the people shall not want. Thus we must raise the general standard of living and provide such employment for everyone as we ourselves enjoy. A detailed plan for the accomplishment of these aims is now before you in this booklet. We cannot hope to accomplish everything overnight but we can do our best. It is possible that the statistical information included in this booklet is not absolutely accurate, but it has been included to provide a temporary standard of comparison.

Let me say that this plan is not COMMUNISTIC! It is a combination of capitalism and socialism. Communists reading it would find much to criticize. For instance, they would object to our providing for the continuance of a propertied class. I have already remarked that the figures are included merely for comparison. Our duty here is to decide whether or not this policy should be adopted. When it has been accepted by the government, experts can be called in to work out accurate and detailed statistics.

Nai Thavi Bunyaketu: In considering the first draft of this economic policy, I wish to second the remarks of Luang Pradist so that we may have a definite basis for discussion. If we read the draft superficially, or are prejudiced by our adherence to some other economic theory, we may conclude immediately that this policy is communistic or socialistic. But, if we examine in detail the actual methods which are suggested in the plan before us, we will see, first of all, that it does not expropriate property, that is deprive the people of their wealth in order to divide it up into equal shares for redistribution. It does not make women common property. It does not command or compel all of the people to work in co-operative associations. It does not reduce them to slavery through conscription. How, then, can anyone conclude that the methods of this policy are communistic or socialistic?

The purpose of the government, as defined in this plan, is to provide social insurance for all people of all classes through their co-operative efforts under the direction of co-operative societies. However, it is not necessary that all of the people become employees of such societies, as would be the case if the system of private enterprise was summarily discontinued. Those who have ability and wealth enough to make an independent living may continue to do so, in fact should do so. Only those who need the help of the government will be assisted: the poor, the unemployed, the homeless, and the unfortunate. We do not intend to interfere with the activities of the well-to-do class, as has been the case in some other countries. But if the poor receive no help from the government, who is to help them? And if they are not helped the result will be disaster: for the moral excellence of our people will be lowered, and sedition will rear its ugly head in this nation.

There is no slightest danger that the societies will not be able to secure sufficient workers, inasmuch as the number of the unemployed is at present very large. If we can guarantee such persons prosperity, do you think they will not want it? Who is there that does not desire wealth? Who is there that prefers to starve?

Now as to the question of procedure—to state the matter simply: co-operative societies are in no way different from the stores, companies, and corporations which we already have. Why then should the government which has built a railroad, established electricity plants, organized water companies, and gone into the business of distilling spirits, be unwilling to permit the establishment of co-operative societies? For in addition to helping the needy peasants, such societies develop the country and increase the prosperity of the nation. Such are the fruits yielded by co-operative societies.

In brief, the method of procedure outlined in this policy is: the government will buy the fields from the owners, making payment with bonds which will yield equitable interest. The reason for wanting such a large tract of land in one great continuous stretch is to facilitate the administration, and the cultivation, such as the ploughing, harrowing, and irrigating. When the co-operative societies have acquired all the land that they need for their purposes, they will then advertise for workers, or, as Luang Pradist calls them, government employees, who are to be drawn from those classes of persons in need of government aid, who have no way of making a satisfactory living, in other words, the depressed classes. People of means and others who do not wish to work for the societies may continue to earn their living as they please, if they are able to do so. They will not be forced to work for the societies.

I fail to see that it is a crime to compel the hungry to be fed, to compel the homeless to be sheltered, to compel the unfortunate to become prosperous. Let us remember that Phya Ratsda (Sim Bee) used his authority to compel the people under his jurisdiction in his southern province to prosper, with such excellent results that they still recall him with gratitude.

Furthermore, for a co-operative society to accept members is the same as if that society hired people to work for a monthly or yearly salary. And in addition to their salary they are entitled to a share in the profits of the society as well. This arrangement is similar to that of the organization of any large company or corporation.

The salary scale of the co-operative societies may well be established in some such way as the following: determine the working strength and ability of an individual who is weak, indolent, and stupid, in order to see how long it takes him to do a typical piece of work for the society, and from this minimum establish a basic wage. Care should be taken to ensure the fact that such a person receives an income from his labours adequate for the support of life, namely for the purchase of food, clothing, etc. When the minimum wage has been established, we need waste no time supervising the work of such people. Good workers, on the other hand, will be able to complete their tasks quickly; and will have an advantage in that they can employ their leisure time in recreation or in doing extra work for the society, in order to supplement their basic income. In this way good workers will be encouraged to do their best. The products of the workers will belong to the society and the society will market them. All money in excess of wages will be divided into several classifications: a portion will be reserved for hard times, a portion will be used to improve the social life of the members, and a portion will be divided as bonuses among the workers.

There will be no need to use much actual currency in the payment of monthly and yearly wages if careful thought is given to the subject. Wages may be balanced by a method of compensation and circulation according to which the society will require its members to buy from the society's store at reasonable prices. This policy cannot be anything but a success. And its success will bring happiness and economic prosperity to the poor peasants of Siam.

Phya Rajawangsan: In so far as I have read the booklet setting forth this policy it seems to describe an ideal to which I subscribe. But the working out of that ideal is another matter, and much attention will have to be paid to details. The working principle of both the old government and the new, although never so called, is actually socialistic. As it should be, because our capitalists are for the most part foreigners. So I do not disagree with the principle involved. But it is my opinion that we still lack a practical means for implementing this ideal.

Luang Pradist Manudharm: My policy includes points selected from many economic theories, which I have co-ordinated and adapted to fit the needs of Siam. One of my basic principles is borrowed from the solidarists, not the communists. It holds that all men are debtors and creditors to each other; and, thus, people are poor because society makes them so. For example, weavers who use hand looms cannot compete with power looms and as a result are deprived of their livelihood. Conversely, people now rich are so not because of their own efforts alone. For example, a certain individual in Bangkok owns a valuable piece of land on which are fine buildings. Originally his land was of little value, but the increasing density of the population around it raised land values and as a result his land increased in value through no effort on his own part. By the very nature of things people are inter-dependent. Accordingly we ought to co-operate in a united effort to ward off possible misfortune and to advance the economic welfare of the people.

H.S.H. Prince Sakol Varavarn: Of course there are very few great landowners in Siam.

Luang Pradist Manudharm: We may compare our Siamese people to children. The government will have to urge them forward by means of authority applied directly or indirectly to get them to co-operate in any kind of economic endeavour. If we continue to go along in the old paths, our revolutionary change of government will have accomplished nothing of value because we will not have attained our most important objective, which was to correct the grievances of the people. The plan which we are to use should rest on the best scientific knowledge of our day, on a well co-ordinated policy, and on a definite method of procedure. Socialism is a scientific system. I agree with Prince Varnvaidyakarn that the present change in government is no mere *coup d'etat*, but is indeed a *revolution* in the economic system; it is not merely a change politically from one king to many.

Phya Rajawangsan: Luang Pradist's policy seems to embody no single economic theory so I should like to know what principle he holds as fundamental?

Luang Pradist Manudharm: I hold no single principle as basic. I have borrowed from many sources.

Phya Rajawangsan: It will probably take too much time to discuss socialism as a whole. But let us divide the subject and speak of state-socialism as compared to communism. I personally would advocate the economic philosophy of Charles Gide, that is, a system of co-operative associations.

Phya Song Suradej: I should like to hear the opinions of a number of people, particularly that of Phya Manopakorn.

Phya Manopakorn Nitithada: I will reserve my remarks until later.

Luang Pradist Manudharm: There are many details such as those concerned with the national bank which we will want to discuss. But before we get to them we ought to accept the policy in principle. My policy follows the socialist pattern with an admixture of liberalism.

H.S.H. Prince Sakol Varavarn: According to this outline it would appear as though the author has based his thesis upon the economic theory known as *Surplus-Value*. That is, the hypothesis that the farmer himself is not the beneficiary of the bulk of the profits derived from his land. Personally I do not believe that this applies in Siam. As for saying that the Siamese people are poor: Dr. Zimmerman concluded from his survey that the Siamese are twice as well off as the Indians or the Chinese. *Surplus-Value* in the northern districts usually remains in the hands of the people themselves.

Luang Pradist Manudharm: My land theory was not derived from the *Surplus-Value* theory of Karl Marx, but from the known fact that there is a great waste of Siamese labour every year. The problem is how best to employ this labour to the utmost. And we may as well say that it is better to live like savages (Primitive) as to say that the Indians and Chinese are worse off than we are. And perhaps that is not such a bad thing after all. If we can turn back time and persuade people to want nothing more than a bit of cloth to cover part of the body as savages do. At present we are a good deal better off than any jungle people. Of course if we return to savagery, we will not have to do very much work. But the question is: are the people generally willing to go back to savagery? Nowadays people the world over have reciprocal relations. What we ought to do is not to compare our state of advance to that of people less fortunate than ourselves but rather to that of the people of a civilized nation in order to see how far we still lag behind. And then we ought to make every effort to equal them.

H.S.H. Prince Sakol Varavarn: I am interested in the subject of the surplus time of workers in the various occupations. Even though it is true that they have some six months of leisure at present, is it not a good thing to allow them plenty of rest and recreation?

Luang Pradist Manudharm: If we are going to discuss the things that contribute to individual happiness, then the less we make people work the better they will like it. And we may as well let them all return to the jungle where they will have nothing at all to do. But if we are concerned here with the development of the nation then excess leisure time is undesirable because it will eventually result in the progressive invasion of our national economic system by outsiders.

H.S.H. Prince Sakol Varavarn: You do not admit then that leisure time is desirable?

Luang Pradist Manudharm: No, I do not admit that it is. Because with so much time wasted we cannot hope to come abreast of foreign nations.

H.S.H. Prince Sakol Varavarn: I should like to suggest a compromise scheme which allows for co-operation with capitalists.

Luang Pradist Manudharm: The principles of my economic policy do not interfere with capitalism, which will continue to exist within the framework of the new system. We must have capital and we shall have to depend upon the wealthy here and abroad to supply it.

H.S.H. Prince Sakol Varavarn: The outline which we have been reading here does not seem to contain enough material to form a basis for judgment. You ought to explain your policy step by step.

Luang Pradist Manudharm: This is merely a rough outline submitted to you in order that you may approve the policy in principle. When it has been approved, we will have to call in experts to work out the details.

H.S.H. Prince Sakol Varavarn: I personally am well satisfied with the findings of Dr. Zimmerman. I should think we could go along as he suggests, step by step, undertaking one thing at a time.

Luang Pradist Manudharm: I did not grow up in the city like you Bangkokians and I know from long residence in the country what the farmers have had to endure in the way of hardships and poverty. Many of my friends in the provinces are very poor. Dr. Zimmerman has never lived the life of a poor peasant in Siam. How can anyone who has not lived in it hope to appreciate such poverty. Wherever a survey is to be made local officials primp and powder and give receptions. Even Bangkok government officials who go out into the provinces fail to grasp the true situation since they continue to live comfortably, and need never endure the hardships which are the lot of the peasants.

H.S.H. Prince Sakol Varavarn: Whether a way of life appears primitive to the liver or not depends upon what he has been used to. If he has always lived in a certain manner without ever knowing anything different, he does not realize that any hardship is involved in his mode of life. So, regardless of whether our people are to be considered primitive or not, I attach the greatest importance to respect for their legal rights and privileges.

Luang Pradist Manudharm: In this policy we do respect the rights and privileges of the people. For instance, we do not interfere with the right of ownership of private dwellings, except in exceptional cases. The reason for wishing to nationalize the land is that one great tract will be easier to administer and to cultivate with machinery in a scientific manner. Anything of this sort would be difficult to accomplish as long as the land remains split up into tiny sections as now.

H.S.H. Prince Sakol Varavarn: We all know, of course, that the fields are at present divided up into small sections. At Supanburi, for instance, nobody is quite sure where his land begins and ends because it has never been surveyed. The important question is, though, how the nationalization of the land is to be accomplished.

Luang Pradist Manudharm: Questions of detail should be left for later discussion. As things are now it is obvious of course that the land is divided up into small sections. If they were all to be united under one central system of control, scientific methods could be employed which would produce better results. How can this be accomplished? Luang Dej Sahakorn was asked this very question before the change in government took place. He recommended the expropriation of property. Now personally I prefer a more moderate method by which the land will be purchased with bonds.

If any of you wish to discuss any of the principles involved now is the time to do so. Let us reserve discussions of detail until later.

H.S.H. Prince Sakol Varavarn: I approve of the principle of nationalizing land and labour for agricultural purposes.

Phya Srivisar Vacha: I do not agree that principles are important and details unimportant. We must examine the details. Every phase of the problem is vitally important.

H.S.H. Prince Sakol Varavarn: Referring again to the principle which I mentioned a moment ago, I think no one will disagree with it. In nationalizing the land we can rest upon the old idea that all of the land of Siam belongs to the crown.

Luang Pradist Manudharm: That is an important point because it makes clear the fact that in a sense the land already belongs to the government.

H.S.H. Prince Sakol Varavarn: The proposal about the land should be considered separately.

Phya Manopakorn Nitithada: This proposal concerns only agricultural lands does it not?

Luang Pradist Manudharm: That is only one part of it.

Phya Manopakorn Nitithada: In that case of just what does this proposal actually consist?

Luang Pradist Manudharm: There will continue to be both government and private enterprise. The government will not undertake to administer everything. Thus in certain lines of work such as tin mining, concessions will be granted as heretofore to private industry. And there is no need to fear that the owners of the land will not be satisfied. A law condemning land for sale will be invoked only when, as now, the government needs land which the owners refuse to sell or which they hold for an exorbitant price.

H.S.H. Prince Sakol Varavarn: I agree that we should nationalize the land outside the cities for agricultural purposes. I also feel that we should nationalize all of the land in the cities for industrial and residential purposes. We should draw up a plan by which the areas reserved for industry and those reserved for agriculture are clearly defined. I agree that it is wasteful to have the land divided into small sections. We should bring these sections together into an ordered system of land control.

Luang Dej Sahakorn: The most important question is, what method is to be used for bringing these small holdings together into a unified system. I agree in principle with the idea of so doing. This principle is vitally important. But we must examine very closely every clause of the suggested plan to see how we can best approach this ideal. This plan goes so far as to involve the government in the business of buying and selling. What repercussions if any will there be abroad? As you know, our trade is now largely in the hands of foreigners.

Luang Pradist Manudharm: Foreign nations are very well pleased with the fact that we do not engage in trade to any great extent. I agree with you there. But, if we do enter into trade, how can they object?

H.S.H. Prince Sakol Varavarn: At first we shall have to continue to share our trade with foreign nations, but later we shall gradually be able to encompass our objective. Progress toward our goal, in effect the government in business, can be accomplished either by having the government assume control of certain businesses or by having it purchase shares as it has done in the case of electricity companies.

Phya Srivisar Vacha: When the government is in control how does it then intend to proceed?

Luang Dej Sahakorn: Our plan is to proceed cautiously a step at a time.

Luang Pradist Manudharm: Quite right. That is the way we shall have to proceed. We will attempt to open diplomatic conversations with the foreign nations concerned. If no progress can be made in this way other methods will have to be employed.

Phya Manopakorn Nitithada: What is your opinion Luang Gahakarm Bodi?

Luang Gahakarm Bodi: In economic affairs we ought to follow the advice of Luang Pradist. If we do not, the middle man will continue to reap all of the profits as he does at present. So far as I can see there is no other way to get around this.

Phya Rajawangsan: There are many ways to cut out the middleman. Co-operative stores would do that.

Luang Pradist Manudharm: Co-operative stores are all right in other countries but the system would not work here. Where would the peasants get money to buy from these stores? Even now they are over their heads in debt to the Chinese.

Phya Rajawangsan: As you please. I believe that we could work out the co-operative store plan, but let us leave it for the moment.

Luang Gahakarm Bodi: What we really ought to do is to follow Luang Pradist's advice and set up a complete system of co-operative associations.

Phya Manopakorn Nitithada: What is your opinion Nai Vilas?

Nai Vilas Osathanond: I have given careful consideration to the various methods that have been used in the development of agricultural lands and I endorse the method suggested by Luang Pradist.

Phya Manopakorn Nitithada: What is your opinion Nai Nab?

Nai Nab Baholyodhin: I am in favour of Luang Pradist's policy, but think we should revise the salary schedule.

Luang Pradist Manudharm: The salary schedule is only an approximation. When the policy has been accepted it can be revised and corrected.

Phya Manopakorn Nitithada: What do you have to say on the subject Luang Dejā?

Luang Dejātiwongs Vararatana: I have very little knowledge of general economic problems, but I am familiar with the economic problems in the field of communications, for example those relating to the railroad system. The government invested two hundred million *baht* in its construction. If the government had allowed private competition and had not retained control of the traffic lines, the railroad would have gone bankrupt, like those in England, with the result that it would now be as dead as the English companies which have had to operate bus lines to meet competition from motor transport companies organized to compete with the railroad. The economic plan which is before us is an exactly parallel case. Therefore it seems to me that we ought to undertake to administer the whole economic system. Accordingly I concur in the opinions advanced by Luang Pradist.

Phya Srivisar Vacha: The government is the sole owner of the railroad of which Luang Dejā speaks: the railroad is comparatively easy to control. The case is not parallel to our present question.

Phya Manopakorn Nitithada: What is your opinion Luang Dej?

Luang Dej Sahakorn: My opinion will be conditioned on the way in which the details of procedure are to be worked out.

Phya Srivisar Vacha: I agree, and I want to ask Luang Pradist what his plans are in this connection?

Luang Pradist Manudharm: My basic plan is to nationalize land, labour, and capital and to go to work.

Phya Srivisar Vacha: If we approve of this policy in principle, then, we will have committed ourselves to approval of all of the details of procedure involved as well. Flatly, I will not agree to anything of this sort. What we really ought to do is to proceed more cautiously a step at a time. As I see it this policy is pure socialism.

H.S.H. Prince Sakol Varavarn: I have studied the plan in detail and I am very much in favour of Luang Pradist's ideas. But I do not agree that doctors should be allowed to enter private practice. I would like to see all doctors in government employ.

Phya Srivisar Vacha: Well, well. There we get into unimportant details again. I thought we were supposed to stick to general principles.

Luang Dejātiwongs Vararatana: But I think that the medical work is very important because it is equivalent to a kind of life insurance. There must be doctors in the workshops to look after the workers. And we are planning to give them social insurance as well which will guarantee them a means of livelihood and furnish them with clothes and find employment for their children as they grow up to replace their aging parents. The workers will be contented when they receive such all-around care. As I see it this is what Luang Pradist's plan amounts to.

Phya Manopakorn Nitithada: Is not Luang Pradist's plan actually equivalent to the nationalization of land, labour, and capital; consequent upon the accomplishment of which the government will, by securing additional capital, undertake to administer the whole economic system? Is not that substantially what we are being asked to announce?

Nai Nab Baholyodhin: If we announce anything we ought to publish the whole draft of the policy, but I think we ought to revise the salary scale first.

Luang Pradist Manudharm: If we were to publish only such a brief statement as Phya Manopakorn has made, the people would not know the details and so would misunderstand, with the inevitable result that there would be widespread and groundless adverse criticism.

Luang Dej Sahakorn: What method is to be used to accomplish the nationalization of the land?

Luang Pradist Manudharm: As you well know the nationalization of the land in other countries has been accomplished either by direct or indirect legislation. Thus in some cases the land tax has been greatly increased as a measure directed against people who have refused to co-operate voluntarily; but generally, we understand, the people have been willing to sell to the government.

Phya Manopakorn Nitithada: Then the heart of the matter is this, is it not? You plan to bring about the nationalization of the land either by forced sale, or by voluntary sale, or by involuntary sale accomplished through indirect legislation. The government would then secure needed capital through increasing indirect taxes. Is there anything beyond that?

Nai Vilas Osathanond: The detailed methods to be used for raising capital are set forth in the policy.

Nai Thavi Bunyaketu: I have already read to you the detailed ways to be used in securing capital as listed in this policy; there were five or six of them.

Phya Manopakorn Nitithada: What exceptions on behalf of private industry are to be made in those fields of activity which the government does not propose to administer itself?

Luang Pradist Manudharm: In the policy, which has already been distributed to you, a number of exceptions are mentioned.

Phya Manopakorn Nitithada: Does your plan include a provision concerning the granting of salaries?

Luang Pradist Manudharm: That is the ultimate step. As a matter of fact when the policy is fully operative, currency will become merely a token. Our responsibility is to guarantee the social security of the people.

Phya Manopakorn Nitithada: What do you think Phya Song?

Phya Song Suradej: It seems to me that it would take fifty to a hundred years to carry this plan out fully. Would it not be better to agree not to promulgate it? and just go ahead and do as much as we can? To put the matter plainly, the government would have to spend fabulous sums of money merely to acquire the land, and twenty to thirty years from now the government would still not have been able to buy it all. Now as for the nationalization of labour, again we lack sufficient funds to pay the salaries required. So, our only hope would be that, when we had acquired all of the land, we could dominate the people by force, as we now dominate the Chinese, who have to do whatever we happen to want them to. Now Phya Prasert Songgram says that there is still much undeveloped land, and that there are also many unemployed. Perhaps we could help these poor people out by settling them on this land. But even such a comparatively simple plan as this could not be carried out very effectively. That being the case, my opinion is that we should certainly not promulgate this policy.

Luang Pradist Manudharm: To date the *fait accompli* of the change of government has not resulted in any evidence of our intention to better the economic status of the people. They are asking what we intend to do. In particular the Nationalist Party is waiting to find out. Secrecy foments suspicion and sometimes causes unfortunate results. Thus H. M. King Prajadhipok drew up a constitution for the people and sent it to Phya Srivisar, but made no public announcement. As a result there was a revolution to effect a change in the government. If we publish this economic policy suspicions will be allayed. Therefore, I believe that we ought to publish the complete policy inclusive of the methods to be used and the steps to be taken. And then that we ought to issue weekly bulletins to show what progress is being made.

Phya Song Suradej: I earnestly request you not to publish it. Rather, let us just go ahead and do whatever we can.

H.S.H. Prince Sakol Varavarn: Are you ashamed of it, or what is the matter? Are you afraid to have it published? Personally I have long believed that publicity is an excellent thing in matters of this sort.

Phya Song Suradej: I feel that in this case publicity will prove unfortunate. For example, the publication of just the single clause dealing with the nationalization of the land will cause a panic.

Luang Pradist Manudharm: That would be true if our announcement were as brief as that. But if we were to publish a complete explanation of our purpose, and of our proposed method of procedure, step by step, I believe that the people would understand. Misunderstanding would arise only if we failed to prepare effective publicity.

Phya Song Suradej: How much understanding do eleven million people have?

H.S.H. Prince Sakol Varavarn: A publicity scheme has already been drawn up designed to acquaint the people by degrees with the principles involved in the policy, and so to circumvent possible misunderstandings. Then if we put the plan into operation a step at a time the people will come to understand it automatically. Furthermore, we will not need to be afraid of the reaction abroad because, if we are united among ourselves, I fail to see that there is any cause for alarm. And even if some of the older people do become panicky, it will not matter greatly.

Phya Song Suradej: I think that we should publish only as much as we can really accomplish in the next five or ten years, because the people are very apprehensive.

Luang Pradist Manudharm: The publication of a national economic policy is tantamount to implanting a nationalistic spirit which would result in a tremendous surge forward in the progress of the race.

Phya Song Suradej: But why is it not better to announce only those things that we can hope to accomplish in the next five or ten years? Because according to this policy it will take another two or three hundred years to work out the details. Look at the old government. It ruled for a hundred and fifty years without any economic policy. And I fail to see that the absence of a policy was in any way detrimental. I reiterate, we ought to publish only so much as we can hope to accomplish.

Phya Manopakorn Nitithada: And I assert confidently that in my lifetime this policy cannot be made completely operative.

H.S.H. Prince Sakol Varavarn: Chao Khun, you are too sure of yourself. At this very time the economic systems of European countries are becoming more and more liberal with the result that unrest is almost universal. Socialism will come increasingly to the fore.

Luang Pradist Manudharm: Prince Sakol is right. There are prophets to say that class war may break out any time that the economic situation changes for the worse and poverty becomes rampant. We should take steps at the outset to protect ourselves from such an eventuality. If we do not publish this policy *in toto* and if the Nationalist Party does decide to advocate a socialistic platform, we shall have lost out to them completely. But by making our plan public now, we shall obviate possible misunderstandings.

Phya Song Suradej: Well, then, suppose that we agree to publish the policy tentatively over the name of an individual such as Luang Pradist, and that we do not commit the government officially? How would that be?

Luang Pradist Manudharm: That would be even better. The people will then understand exactly how things are. Everywhere I go they come to me and complain that we are accomplishing nothing. I shall be glad to accept full responsibility for this announcement. And if they curse me, let them curse me.

Nai Vilas Osathanond: We should ask for some money for publicity.

Luang Pradist Manudharm: I already have money for publicity.

Phya Song Suradej: Good.

H.S.H. Prince Sakol Varavarn: We cannot publish the whole thing in its present form because people will not understand it at all.

Luang Pradist Manudharm: It will have to be revised and simplified, of course.

Phya Manopakorn Nitithada: As I understand it, the majority of this committee approves the economic policy of Luang Pradist, and my own opinion, therefore, is at variance with that of the majority. Now that leaves me in a very unfortunate position for two reasons: first, because I am not a student of economics as are most of you, and second, because, if this policy is promulgated, in my official capacity I shall have to accept full responsibility for the principles and methods of a system of which I do not personally approve. But I am a man of very strong convictions. On a number of occasions we in the government have felt sure that a certain course was the correct one, only to be proved wrong by subsequent events. In this present instance, I firmly believe that we cannot possibly hope to carry this plan through to a successful conclusion. Why? Because we lack experts, we lack reserve funds, we lack the confidence of the people at large. For I am convinced that this policy is unacceptable to the people. If, then, we publish it at a time when they do not have much confidence in us, the results will be disastrous. We must take public opinion into consideration, even gossip. We have just had a change in government. The people are still undecided as to just what they think about it. I have been accused by some people of being overly fearful of foreign intervention. And my point of view being what it is, I cannot entirely deny this. Other people claim that I am trying to arrogate all authority to myself, with the consequence that gossip says that I am in favour of a return to the absolute monachy. Please understand that my motives in coming here are sympathetic. But if I believe that the course decided upon here leads to ruin, I shall have to oppose it. And if it is carried over my head I shall have no recourse but to resign. But if we agree to announce merely that we are going to enlarge the credit facilities of the co-operative societies of the sort that are now serving the farmers, or that we are going to enlarge the co-operative society stores, I am willing to agree to that much. But if we publish the whole policy most people will not be able to grasp the implications of it at all. Even a small rumour can start a panic. We are in a position where both the French and the British can bring pressure to bear upon us. If they wish to take advantage of us, in the event of such an emergency, Phya Song will assure you, we will not be in a position to resist them. As I see it then, if this policy is published, the inevitable failure of the people to understand it will result in their wholehearted opposition. I cannot even hazard a guess as to how many hundreds of years it will be before such a policy as this one would be practicable. Perhaps the people of the millenium of the age of Ariya Mettaya (Phra Sriarya) can do something like this.

H.S.H. Prince Sakol Varavarn: I should like to call your attention to the fact that right now the capitalists are so poor that they would like to sell their land.

Phya Srivisar Vacha: That is only an opinion.

Luang Pradist Manudharm: That is not only an opinion. It is the truth.

Nai Thavi Bunyaketu: I was talking to a big landowner just the other day and he said that he would be glad to sell for just half-price.

Phya Manopakorn Nitithada: The possibility of the publication of this economic policy is already causing comment. Now listen for a moment to one of the things that is being said by people outside. They are saying that Luang Pradist is the actual power behind the present government and that Nai Sanguan and Nai Sim are his Moggallāna and Sāriputta [two Brahmins, early converts of Gautama Buddha and his inseparable and staunch friends and companions, who became known as his left and right hand disciples—*Trans.*], and that there is no dividing them.

Luang Pradist Manudharm: As a matter of fact Sanguan and Sim are really your disciples. [In the sense that they had been his pupils—*Trans.*] If you will look in the registry of the Law School you will find that Sanguan graduated in B.E. 2469. And at that time I was not even teaching in the university. You were professor of the laws of inheritance.

Phya Manopakorn Nitithada: By rights, of course, they ought to have remained my disciples rather than yours.

Nai Vilas Osathanond: Only members of the party are aware of the fact that these two men are disciples of Luang Pradist. Outsiders do not have any idea that they are his personal agents. Or if they do, it is because insiders, who are intestinal parasites, have been spreading the idea. But actually there is nothing really wrong with these two except that people who hate them have been spreading gossip about them.

Phya Song Suradej: What constitutes the scheme that you said you were willing to have published, Phya Mano?

Phya Manopakorn Nitithada: Well, I would suggest that we enlarge the co-operative societies, extend credit, build silos, and decrease indebtedness. I would appoint Luang Dej and Prince Sakol to work out the details.

Luang Pradist Manudharm: What is the consensus of opinion of this committee in regard to the publication of my policy?

Phya Rajawangsan: I suggest that we plan to publish the entire policy, but that we do it a clause at a time, and in the meanwhile educate the people step by step so as not to alarm them.

Phya Song Suradej: I should like to see the committee agree to allow Luang Pradist to publish the policy over his own name. If the government decides to approve it, there can be an official announcement later. But in the event that the government does not approve of it and decides to substitute a policy of its own, Luang Pradist will not object will he?

Phya Manopakorn Nitithada: My previous statement was an expression of my own opinion. I do not know whether the government will agree with me or not. Members of the government who are now here are Phya Srivisar, Phya Song, Nai Nab, Luang Pradist, Nai Prayoon, Phya Rajawangsan, and myself.

Luang Pradist Manudharm: Actually, of course, your opinion constitutes the opinion of the government.

Phya Rajawangsan: This meeting is not a meeting of the state councillors, is it?

Luang Pradist Manudharm: No, but most of us are state councillors.

Phya Manopakorn Nitithada: The consensus of opinion of this committee favours a trial of Luang Pradist's policy. Apparently I am the only one who dissents, or are there others?

Phya Srivisar Vacha: I have already said that if the committee accepts the policy in its entirety I will dissent, but if we divide it into sections and recommend selected portions of it, I will be agreeable.

Luang Pradist Manudharm: We are an official committee here and we shall have to reach some sort of a decision. Under the circumstances what would you have us do, Phya Manopakorn?

Phya Song Suradej: Let Phya Mano make a statement for the minutes.

Phya Manopakorn Nitithada: At this juncture I believe that all we should attempt to do is to enlarge the credit societies which are already in existence, etc.

Luang Pradist Manudharm: Will Luang Dej Sahakorn be so kind as to take Phya Mano's statement for Luang Arthasarn as he is familiar with the subject?

Luang Dejātiwongs Vararatana: If we were to do that it would simply mean that the present government would be following in the footsteps of the previous government, would it not?

Luang Pradist Manudharm: I interpret Phya Mano's opinion to mean that he believes that the government should move ahead as opportunity offers much as the previous government did. But, that he recommends some slight changes of procedure. Is that right?

Phya Manopakorn Nitithada: Yes, that is correct. That is the way I think we should proceed.

It was agreed that Luang Dej Sahakorn should give Luang Arthasarn Prasiddhi, Phya Mano's recommendations as follows:

1. Expand the credit facilities of the co-operative societies to provide the peasant-farmers with additional working capital while, at the same time, helping them to decrease their indebtedness.
2. Expand the co-operative stores so that the peasant-farmers can buy food and clothing at the lowest possible prices.
3. Build grain elevators in strategic places to store rice bought from the peasant-farmers for subsequent transshipment to Bangkok.
4. Build rice mills to prepare the rice produced by the co-operative societies for sale abroad.
5. Initiate a settlement scheme to locate peasant-farmers, who own no land, on the undeveloped areas belonging to the government.

The granaries, the business of transportation, and the rice mills, shall be organized as government-owned corporations.

Luang Pradist Manudharm: What is the will of the committee? One faction will not accept this policy; they are in favour of a programme of liberalism and opportunism such as we have had previously, with additions of course. The other faction approves the policy *in toto*. Phya Mano has culled certain sections from the policy which meet his approval, but he is not willing to advocate the adoption of any complete system. Thus the rice mills which he has proposed that the government establish might be operated either under a system of liberalism or socialism.

Phya Song Suradej: We came here today not to reach an agreement but to express our opinions.

The committee agreed to submit its minutes to the revolutionary party and to forward to the state council both a majority and a minority report:

1. THE MINORITY OPINION (Phya Manopakorn Nitithada, et al): we recommend that the government follow the economic programme of the previous government, incorporating into it certain specific changes whenever they can be effected; and that the government not promulgate any particular economic plan.

2. THE MAJORITY OPINION (Luang Pradist Manudharm, et al): we recommend that the government adopt a definite system of economic procedure; and that, in particular, it promulgate the national economic policy of Luang Pradist Manudharm; that when a system has been adopted, a national economic council be established to prepare estimates and a programme of procedure; and that consequent expansion be limited only by the financial position of the government.

It was further agreed that, since the committee could not reach a unanimous decision, Luang Pradist Manudharm should be permitted to publish his economic policy over his own name in an attempt to win public approval for it, provided that the government agreed with the opinion of Phya Manopakorn Nitithada. He (Luang Pradist) was instructed to be careful not to confuse the people by creating the impression that the government was publishing the aforementioned economic policy; and he was also to make it clear that he was not speaking for the state council.

(signed) LUANG ARTHASARN PRASIDDHI
Secretary

E. REPORT OF THE COMMISSION ON THE ALLEGED COMMUNISM OF LUANG PRADIST MANUDHARM

1. The Commission elected Momchao Varnvaidya Chairman and Phya Nala Rajsuvachana Secretary General.

2. According to the Resolution of the Assembly the terms of reference are whether Luang Pradist Manudharm, Member of the 2d Category and State Councillor, who was accused of being a communist at the time when Phya Mano, the then Premier, closed the Assembly, is really to be so stigmatized.

3. Inasmuch as the said accusation was a general political accusation and not a judicial indictment and the point at issue is whether Luang Pradist is a Communist and not whether his Preliminary Draft of an Economic Scheme was communistic, the Commission resolved that the points to be considered are: what are the peculiar features of communism and what are Luang Pradist's political views in regard to those features? The decision could then be taken as to whether Luang Pradist is a communist or not.

4. The Commission requested the Two Experts, Sir Robert Holland and Monsieur R. Guyon, to draw up a joint memorandum defining the peculiar features of communism by taking into account the programmes of various Communist Parties such as those of the Communist International, the British Communist Party and the French Communist Party as well.

5. When such Programmes had been procured, the Two Experts drew up a joint Memorandum defining the peculiar features of communism, upon which they were in agreement, by adopting the following criterion: anything which appears solely and exclusively in the Communist Programmes, and is not in the Programmes of the other political parties, is an unquestionable element of Communism. Subsidiary and separate Notes were also submitted by the experts in regard to the points on which they failed to reach agreement.

6. The Commission gave Luang Pradist the opportunity to make observations on the Joint Memorandum. As a result of Luang Pradist's observations the Experts made certain modifications in the Memorandum.

7. When the peculiar features of communism had thus been agreed upon the Commission asked Luang Pradist to state his political views in regard to each feature.

8. Luang Pradist stated his views on each feature as follows:

9. *Political*

(I) To establish a Government by soviets (Councils of the workmen, peasants, and soldiers).

Luang Pradist: I entertain no idea of setting up a Government by soviets because I am in favour of a constitutional regime, as evidenced by the part I have played in setting up the Constitution of the Kingdom of Siam and also by the part I have taken in the promulgation of the Electoral Law, which is a proof of my faith in the constitutional and parliamentary form of government.

Sir Robert: Do you intend to bring about fundamental changes in the present Electoral Law?

Luang Pradist: I intend to maintain the fundamental principles of the law. I only contemplate such modifications as replacing election in two stages by direct election by the people and any such modifications will be made through constitutional channels. In any case, I entertain no idea of establishing a Government by soviets.

10. Financial

(1) To nationalize by confiscation private Banks and to transfer to the State all gold reserve, securities, deposits, etc., found therein.

Luang Pradist: I entertain no idea of nationalizing by confiscation private Banks or transferring to the State all gold reserve, securities, deposits, etc., found therein, because I am in favour of private ownership.

(II) (2) To cancel and repudiate the debts to foreign and home capitalists.

Luang Pradist: Much less do I entertain any idea of cancelling and repudiating the debts to foreign and home capitalists because I am desirous of firmly preserving the friendly relations with foreign countries. When I drew up the statement of Policy for the Mano Government I inserted a passage to that effect. In any case I have no wish to repudiate debts either at home or abroad.

12. Social

(1) To overthrow forcibly the whole of the existing traditional social order, as the only means of realizing communist aims.

Luang Pradist: The words: "The whole of the existing traditional social order," I take to refer to such matters as family law, etc.

Sir Robert: They refer to matters concerning the family, the form of government, class divisions and the whole fabric of society. The point is whether the changes contemplated are to be made constitutionally or whether they are to be brought about forcibly so as to make a clean sweep of the existing order, only in the latter case would it be a part of communism.

Luang Pradist: I entertain no idea whatever of starting as a clean sheet. In matters of government, I am in favour of a constitutional form of government as I have stated above. In matters pertaining to the family, when I was at the Department of Legislative Redaction, I took part in the drafting of the Civil Code relating to this matter and my views are in the direction of maintaining the Siamese traditions in this respect. In other matters too, I intend to preserve those customs which are suitable to the time, and any changes I may contemplate will be brought about in a constitutional way. I see no use of making a clean sweep of things. With regard to class warfare,

I have endeavoured to point out to various people how improper it was, because it would only lead to bloodshed.

13. (2) Under the dictatorship of the proletariat, to wage perpetual war against the forces and traditions of the old society and against any upshoots of new bourgoisie that may appear.

Luang Pradist: I utterly dislike dictatorship in any form, not only the dictatorship of the proletariat but also the dictatorship of any class whatsoever.

14. (3) To abolish inheritance.

Luang Pradist: I entertain no idea of abolishing inheritance. M. Guyon is well aware that I was in favour of incorporating provisions regarding inheritance in the Civil Code when it was being drafted.

15. Economic

(1) To confiscate without indemnity all large private (capitalist) undertakings such as factories, works, mines, electric power stations, railways, transport, communications, large landed estates, machinery, etc.

Luang Pradist: I entertain no such ideas at all for the same reasons as already stated above in regard to financial matters. I repeat that I am in favour of private ownership.

16. (2) To transfer landed estates so confiscated to peasants.

(3) To forbid afterwards any sale and purchase of land so transferred.

(4) To confiscate big house property and remove workers and poor people to rich or bourgeois dwellings and residences.

(5) To relieve peasants who are poor of their burden of debt by the annulment of all mortgages.

Luang Pradist: The same with items (2), (3), (4), and (5), for they are all consequences of (1).

17. (6) To unite the local soviet republic to all other soviet republics in a world union in order to realize the economic unity of the toilers in a single world socialist economic system.

Luang Pradist: I entertain no such ideas at all. I do not at all contemplate to set up a government by soviets or to have Siam join the Soviet Union.

18. The points on which the experts fail to agree concern religion, the family, and labour, in regard to which they have submitted subsidiary and separate Notes.

19. The commission gave Luang Pradist the opportunity to state his views on these matters as well.

Luang Pradist: I have already stated my views on the family. As for religion, I think that religion is necessary, that everyone should be allowed to adopt the religion he likes. Everyone should have a religion: as long as he has a religion it is sufficient. I have no intention whatever of doing away with religion.

20. With regard to labour, Sir Robert thinks that the communist policy can be formulated as follows: to apply uncompromisingly to the idle bourgeois the principle "who does not work shall not eat" and generally on the basis of a

predetermined plan, to utilize all labour power as well as all material resources, in order that through the abolition of private ownership and competitive production, work may eventually become, not merely a means of livelihood, but a necessity of life.

Monsieur Guyon, however, considers that the fact that work will become a necessity of life, will be a consequence of the abolition of private ownership and private property. Compulsory labour of the kind that is contained in the communist programmes is also to be found in the programmes of other parties, such as the Nazi Party, while a plan is only a means and not an end.

The Commission gave Luang Pradist the opportunity to state his views on this matter also.

Luang Pradist: The situation in Siam is the reverse of that which obtains in Western countries. In Siam it is the bourgeois who works and the peasants who are unoccupied for the greater part of the time, which tends to make them idle and spend their unoccupied time in undesirable ways, such as indulging in intoxicating drinks, in dacoities, etc., which we should reform. There are also a great number of unemployed in Bangkok. These people should have an occupation to prevent them from criminal ways. They can choose the occupation they like, they will not be compelled to take this or that occupation but they should be required to have an occupation. This is for social safety, and the measures I contemplate are on the lines of the Social Work of the League of Nations. I am only aiming at providing occupation and work for the people. What I have in mind is to make the people keep their own poultry and grow their own vegetables as it has been done at Bhuket, but any such measures will of course have to be taken in the form of a law, which will have to be passed by the Assembly in a constitutional way. What I am contemplating is to bring out a law requiring people to have an occupation and to develop professional training.

21. The Chairman put the following question to Luang Pradist: Does the assurance you gave to the late Government that you would not have recourse to any new system of compulsory purchase of land or compulsory labour as the means of economic development, still hold good for the present Government?

Luang Pradist: It still holds good for the present Government. The requirement that everyone should have a profession which I contemplate, will be on the lines of the Social Work of the League of Nations, with the object only of finding work for the people and ensuring that everyone should have a profession, without having any intention whatever of following the Communist or Nazi system.

22. *The Chairman*: Are the essential ideas which you have set forth before the Commission just the ideas which you now entertain or are they also the ideas which you have entertained heretofore?

Luang Pradist: They are the essential ideas I have entertained heretofore.

23. *The Chairman*: Are you a Member of the Communist International, or are you connected with it in any way?

Luang Pradist: No, I am not a Member of the Communist International, nor am I connected with it in any way.

24. The Chairman asked Sir Robert and Monsieur Guyon whether Luang Pradist had stated his views on every distinctive feature of communism, as defined in the Joint Memorandum.

Sir Robert and Monsieur Guyon replied in the affirmative.

25. The Chairman asked Phya Sri Sangkara and Phya Nalaraj whether they had any further questions to put to Luang Pradist. Phya Sri Sangkara and Phya Nalaraj replied that they were satisfied, they had no further questions to put.

26. The Chairman asked the Commission to vote on the following question: From the above investigation, are you of the opinion that Luang Pradist is clear of the stigma of communism that was imputed to him at the time of the Mano Government?

The Commission resolved unanimously that Luang Pradist is clear of any such stigma.

February, 1934

CHAIRMAN VARNVAIDYAKARA VARAVARN
PHYA SRI SANGKARA
PHYA NALA RAJSUVACHANA

INDEX

Air mail 142
Airports 8, 139
Architecture 178
Army 54-57
Arts and Crafts 176-181

Bangkok Daily Mail 32, 34, 36, 63, 74, 115, 117, 119
Bangkok Times 10, 15, 23, 24, 58, 109, 125, 153, 225, 226
Boy Scout Movement 7, 104, 105
Brahmanism 191-195, 205
   top-knot cutting 191-193
Buddhism 6, 47, 182-190, 202, 203, 204, 208, 209, 212, 214, 215, 217, 218, 222, 226, 227, 230
   "back to Buddha" 229
   corruption of the Order 216-217
   examination of the Monks 219
   for the young 220-224
   new Catechism 227
   Siamese Buddhism 195-201

Calendar reform 7
Capital funds, loss of 64-68
Chamber of Commerce *see* "Trade"
Character, trends in 143-151
Charms 204
Censorship 20, 49
Chinese, the 1, 47, 66, 86-95
   Chamber of Commerce 90
   customs 87
   immigration 91
   influence in religion 215
   money-lenders 89
   newspapers 90
   schools 92-93
   remittances 67
Christianity 5, 47, 206, 207
   missions 5, 206, 207
Cinema 175, 176
Citizenship
   privileges and duties of 27-29
Climate 3
Commerce *see* "Trade"
Communications 137-142
   air travel 139
   canals 137
   railways 7, 78, 137, 138, 139, 141
   roads 139, 140, 141
   telephone 141, 142
Communism 48
Conscription 56
Constitution 17, 18, 28
Cotton growing 78
Crime 151, 156
   causes of 154
   treatment of prisoners 155

Dentistry 134
Division of country into
   Montons, Cangwats, etc., 44, 45
Divorce 156
Drama 181

Economics 61-81
   Chinese remittances 67
   loss of capital funds 64-68
   Ministry of Economic Affairs Programme 61-64
   new policy 61-64

Education 7, 85, 96-113
  extra curricular activities 104-106
  libraries and literature 112-113
  primary and secondary 98-104
  religious influences 106-109
  students abroad 111-112
  universities 109-111
Elephant hunting 200
Epidemics 126, 127
European nations
  early relations with 5, 6, 7
Extraterritoriality 7

Family budgets 79-81
Family life 166-170
Finances 81
Fishing 76, 86
Foreign Treaties 60

Gambling 7, 154, 175
Government, local
  system of 45-46
  duties of 46
Great Britain
  Siam's relations with 58
  trade 59
  treaty with 60

Hospitals 133-136

International affairs 57-60
  relations with Western Powers 58
  Siamese as excellent politicians 58

Japan
  radio phone connections 142
  Siam's relations with 58, 59, 60
  trade 5, 59
  treaty with 60

King Ananda 44
  coronation 44
  regency 44
King Chulalongkorn, 7, 58
King Prajadhipok 7, 8, 9, 10, 11, 16, 17, 18, 19, 20, 21, 33, 45, 48, 50, 221
  abdication announcement 257
  abdication of 39-43
  proclamations 15, 21
  reply to ultimatum 10
King Vajiravudh 7, 18, 19, 20, 48

Language 2, 4, 82, 83
Luang Pradist Manudharm 13, 14, 17, 22, 23, 24-25, 29, 30, 33, 35, 60, 61
  alleged Communism of 319
  economic policy 29, 30, 34, 35, 48, 61, 260
Leprosy 129, 130
Liberty of People 46
Libraries and Literature 112-113
Lotteries 154, 155

Marriage 156, 157, 158
  registration of 157, 158
  Marriage Bill 157
Malay, the 5, 47, 83-86
Medical trends 114-136
  epidemics 126, 127
  impeding difficulties 120
  "junior" doctors 128
  magazines 135
  medical beginnings 114-117
  medical schools 117-120
  midwifery 136
  propaganda 125
  surgery 116
  vaccination and inoculation 7, 116
Military 54-57
  budget 54, 55
  formation of the Yuvajon 57
  influence in Government 56
Mohammedanism 47, 84

Nation 54, 57, 79, 94, 99, 111, 153, 158, 164, 218, 220, 228
National savings 7
Navy 54, 55
Newspapers 20, 48, 49
  closure of 49
Nobility, decline of 50-54

INDEX

Opium 7

People's Party 9, 11, 13, 14, 16, 17, 22, 24, 32, 61
  announcement 11-12
People's Assembly 13, 14, 16, 17, 24, 29, 30, 35, 44, 45, 53, 136, 157
  discussion of Buddhist Order 218
  election to 14, 16
  military members 56
  system of election 35, 36
"Phu'ng" 145, 146
Police 152, 153
Political Parties 50
Posts 7
Press Act 48
Prince Nagor Svarga, H.R.H. 9, 13, 16, 303
Public Health 131-133

Radio broadcasting 13, 20, 50, 57, 176
  radio phone 142
Railways 7, 78, 137, 138, 141
Rationalism, rise of 226-230
Recreation 171-176
Red Cross Society 105, 134
Religion 182-235
  Christian missions 8, 47, 206, 207
  evils to be avoided 231
  new religious goals 230-231
  old Siamese religion 201-205
  rise of the layman 217-219
  summary of modern Siamese religions 231-235
Revenue 69
Revolution
  causes of 18-24, 27
  leaders of 24-27
  of June, 1932, 9-18
  of June, 1933, 31-36
  results of 27-29
Rice growing 74
  export 74, 75, 79
  Chinese middlemen 79
Roads 139, 140, 141

Rockefeller Institute 118
Royalist Rebellion 36-39
Rubber planting 72, 167

Schools 85, 96-109
  attendance 99, 100, 101
  cost of 103, 104
  extra-curricular activities 104-106
  foreign teachers 102
  government 97
  health work 104
  local 97
  municipal 98
  number of 100
  private 97
  religious teaching 103
Siamese Buddhism 195-201
  lack of missionary zeal 224-226
Siam Chronicle 50, 110, 126, 153, 155, 156, 162, 228, 230
Siamese modern religion
  summary of 231-235
Silk-worm culture 78
Spiritism in Siamese Buddhism 195-201
  fear of spirits 199
Sports 105, 171-176
State Council 16, 17, 18, 24, 29, 30, 31, 44, 45
  military members 56
Students 21
  students abroad 111-112
Sugar industry 78
"Snuk" 143

Taboos 51
  concerning Royalty 51, 52
Talismen 199
Tattooing 199
Taxation 7, 17, 20, 91, 94, 95
  of immigrants 91
Teak industry 73, 74
Telephone 141, 142
Theatre 180
Tin Mining 70, 71
Titles, 169
Tobacco 77

Trade 59, 68-70, 77-81, 206
    Chinese influence 68, 77
    Imports and Exports 70
    Siamese Chamber of Commerce 68

Universities 109-111

Vital Statistics 135
Vocational Training 101-102

Waterways and canals 3
Wit and humour 144, 145
Women's places in society 156-166
    traffic in women 161-164